PRAISE FOR— *I Found My Niche*

"If you ever have participated in getting legislation passed, you will enjoy this book. If you have managed a professional or trade association, or have wondered what these organizations do, you will enjoy it. Are you a student interested in lobbying, or wanting to work for an association? If so, you will gain from reading it. And, what if you're a regular citizen? Yes, you too will find it informative."

— FROM THE FOREWORD BY BIRCH BAYH,
FORMER U.S. SENATOR

"No legislative effort in the history of the American Bar Association brought more favorable attention to Congress, the media, and the public than its work on the 25th Amendment. Serving in the shadow of others, Lowell Beck played a seminal role in this accomplishment. He then helped lead the ABA during its defining years of rapid growth and advancement. This life story of one of America's unsung heroes is captivating and inspiring."

— JOHN D. FEERICK,
PROFESSOR AND FORMER DEAN OF FORDHAM UNIVERSITY LAW SCHOOL
AND FORMER PRESIDENT OF THE NEW YORK CITY BAR ASSOCIATION.

"In 1945, GEICO was a founding member of the National Association of Independent Insurers, which became the nation's largest property and casualty insurance trade association. This vividly stated book by Lowell Beck tells his personal story of leading the NAII from 1980 to 1996, and why its member companies, including GEICO, consider it so valuable to them. A successful association leader must be spokesperson, lobbyist, manager, and many things to many people. Lowell Beck was all of these, and tells how his work with the NAII, to him, was a labor of love."

— TONY NICELY,
GEICO CHAIRMAN AND CHIEF EXECUTIVE OFFICER

"The highest satisfaction for a broadcast professional comes from creating programming that will enrich audiences. Meeting Lowell Beck, and learning about his career story and personal friendship with thought-provoking 'friends,' helped me experience that satisfaction as general manager for Chicago station WYCC-TV. After retirement from association management, Lowell, with our production staff, created First From Chicago, a television series of 50 'one of a kind' half-hour shows. As host, he gleaned life lessons from famous people who participated because of their respect for him. Readers of this book will see how there can be meaningful life in retirement."

— CAROLE B. CARTWRIGHT,
FORMER GENERAL MANAGER OF WYCC-TV PUBLIC TELEVISION
AND AWARD-WINNING TELEVISION PRODUCER

I FOUND MY NICHE

A Lifetime Journey of Lobbying

and Association Leadership

A memoir by
LOWELL R. BECK

the Peppertree Press
Sarasota, Florida

For information regarding permission,
call 941-922-2662 or contact us at our website:
www.peppertreepublishing.com or write to:
the Peppertree Press, LLC.
Attention: Publisher
1269 First Street, Suite 7
Sarasota, Florida 34236

ISBN: 978-1-61493-386-1

Library of Congress Number: 2015916094

Printed March 2016

FOR MYRNA

My life partner who shares these memories
of our adventures together

FOREWORD

If you ever have participated in getting legislation passed (or defeated), you will enjoy this book. If you have managed a professional or trade association, or have wondered what these organizations do, you will enjoy it. Are you a student interested in lobbying and how to influence legislation, or wanting to work for an association? If so, you will gain from reading it. And what if you're a regular citizen? Yes, you too will find it informative.

Lowell Beck and I first met and became good friends in early 1960, when we had a crisis in Presidential succession if the President could not fulfill his duties. The U.S. Constitution had no provision for an Acting President if one was needed, and this omission had caused problems throughout history. As U.S. Senator, I sponsored the Twenty-Fifth Amendment to rectify this dilemma; and Lowell, through his Washington office position with the American Bar Association, helped marshal support for it from the legal profession and the public. The Amendment was adopted, but not before hard work by all of us pushing for it. Working hard is the key to public policy success, and Lowell was one who always worked as hard as he could. He set an example for others to follow.

This memoir, *I Found My Niche*, is unique. I'm unaware of another book quite like it. Lowell tells his personal stories of how he helped obtain the adoption of the Amendment and many other significant public policies, with the respect of Democrats and Republicans alike on Capitol Hill. If, for example, you are benefiting from an airbag in your car, he is one you can thank for his tireless efforts to secure them.

He was a top association leader, and tells his personal stories of managing them, often during times of grave national difficulty. You will feel like you're there when he talks about his work at the American Bar Association during Watergate, his major role in creating the "citizens lobby" Common Cause, and his guidance of the property and casualty insurance industry through the commercial liability crisis when insurance was virtually unavailable for many sectors.

I wished to write this Foreword because I know the author well; and know that his personal stories will intrigue and interest you. Because *I Found My Niche* is a memoir, it contains some personal, family-oriented stories. They will help you understand the author as a person, as well as a professional leader. So, sit back and take some time to read it. You'll be glad you did.

Birch Bayh,
United States Senator
(1963–1981)

CONTENTS

FOREWORD v

PREFACE 1

PROLOGUE 5

CHAPTER 1: 7
    Growing Up

CHAPTER 2: 28
    My First Job, American Bar Association in Chicago

CHAPTER 3: 36
    My Second ABA Job, Washington, D.C.

CHAPTER 4: 56
    The National Political Environment

CHAPTER 5: 74
    Our New Washington Life

CHAPTER 6: 80
    Adoption of the Twenty-Fifth Amendment to the Constitution

CHAPTER 7: 106
    The Legal Services Program of the Office of Economic Opportunity

CHAPTER 8: 120
    The Bail Reform Act of 1966

CHAPTER 9: 128
    We're Back in Illinois with the ABA

CHAPTER 10: 147
    The Urban Coalition Action Council

CHAPTER 11: 166
    The Planning of Common Cause

CHAPTER 12: 188
    The First Year of Common Cause

CHAPTER 13: 216
    Return to the ABA in Chicago

CHAPTER 14: 266
    Final Days at the ABA

CHAPTER 15: 280
    The National Association of Independent Insurers

    RETIREMENT 336

    EPILOGUE 345

    BIBLIOGRAPHY 355

    ACKNOWLEDGEMENTS 357

    INDEX 359

PREFACE

If you find a lifetime career that suits your liking very well, you're fortunate. I was one of the fortunate ones. This is a portrayal of that fulfilling career of lobbying and creating and managing nationally prominent institutions, ranging from the American Bar Association, the National Urban Coalition and Common Cause, to the nation's largest association of property and casualty insurance companies, the National Association of Independent Insurers (now Property Casualty Insurers Association of America).

At the urging of our children, Rich, Jonathan and Lori, I undertook this project for my grandsons, Chris, Stephen, Spencer, Matthew, Liam and Ryan and their children. Years from now, they might be interested in knowing what their grandfather did for a living, and hopefully would have a greater understanding of his perspective on the inner workings of the political system. It was to be a relatively simple personal narration of my personal role in the political arena and the remarkable people whose paths I was privileged to cross.

As I wrote about my own specific activities, it became more than a personal narration. It's impossible to write meaningfully about one's role in political issues, and as an association leader, without giving glimpses into the life and history of the times. Americans had good reason for pessimism in the '60s, '70s and '80s. The Soviet Union was threatening the world with its nuclear power, a president was assassinated, there were riots over civil rights, our cities were burning, and the Vietnam War was killing tens of thousands of Americans and Vietnamese. Inflation and interest rates were at their highest levels, reaching 13.5 percent and 21.5 percent, respectively. A President and Vice President were forced to resign because of their alleged criminal activities and certain impeachment. They were not times of ease and calm.

This is not a textbook with descriptions of the various branches of government, and how they function. Others have written excellent books on that subject, and they are well suited for students and persons specifically interested in the structure and internal workings of government. This instead is a personal journey, with all of the frustration and enjoyment and fulfillment of participating in the arena, not as a politician, but as an advocate. Lobbying, or in other words, advocating a position before governmental bodies, is a Constitutional First Amendment right to petition government. While some have abused that right and have cast a blemish over the entire profession, most lobbyists have nothing to be ashamed of. I never, not once, felt I was engaged in something "dirty" or unseemly. Seasoned lobbyists might find these stories elementary. They might also find them enjoyable as they compare them with their own experiences.

This personal narrative also provides detailed insights into the staff leadership of large, prominent national professional and trade lobbying organizations. Managing the staff and operations of a membership organization like the American Bar Association, which engages in a broad range of activities from lobbying to continuing education, is different than managing businesses to achieve healthy financial bottom lines. Managers and leaders of associations, large and small, might find these stories helpful as they too compare them with their own activities.

Students of political science and association management might enjoy the stories as instructive if they should decide to enter the worlds of lobbying and/or associations as their life work.

The political process of formulating and enacting laws affects all of us, and yet only a few people know anything about the actual experiences of engaging in it. I hope that my personal stories will take the general reader inside that world in an enjoyable way. It should be noted that my time in the legislative arena was from 1961 until 1996. Those were the years I know best and have written about. Bipartisanship wasn't the dirty word it seems to have become with many legislators today. Basic principles of lobbying applied, such as enlisting people "back home" to support your issue, and getting influential bipartisan sponsorship on Capitol Hill. Today, however, while most basic lobbying principles still apply, sharp ideological divisions in the country that are reflected in Congress, and ever changing technology are among the changes that are influencing the political environment.

As I began to write, I was pleasantly surprised at how much detail, dating to my first job at the American Bar Association in 1959, came back to me, sometimes vividly. But time takes its toll, and without a lot of assistance and research I could not have completed this project. To refresh my memory, I used personal notes, books on specific events (some recounting my own role in those events), personal conversations, newspaper and magazine articles, and the Internet. I'm constantly amazed at how "Googling" to jog one's memory provides more helpful information than I ever could have imagined. And, to be as accurate as possible, some of my colleagues from each chapter's time frame have reviewed and verified the facts as well as they could.

This narrative, written over a six-year period from 2009 to 2015, has taken on special meaning since my friend John Feerick, former dean of the Fordham University Law School, wrote to me about it. He challenged my statement that this personal account might not be scholarly or profound enough for eventual publication and use by those interested in political science or association leadership. He advised me to "develop some context of the significance of the matters you worked on, not simply at the time, but how the foundations they established have played out to the present day." He further wrote, "But, there was a time they were not in place, and you found yourself being part of the groups that did the creating in a very special way. There is a profundity to it all as deep, if not deeper, than the scholarly narratives and stories. Your stories involve the building of a civil society, a society that is unparalleled in the history of the world."

This memoir continues to have been written for my family, most notably my grandchildren when they are interested someday, and friends who might have a special interest. However, because of its thorough discussions of legislative results through personal lobbying, and specific stories of professional and trade association management, I hope other readers will enjoy it also.

The memoir is written in the first person about my own work. Consequently, it might seem like I'm writing with a major share of conceit, which memoirs often can convey. But legislative strategy and success (and failure too), and effective institutional leadership cannot be attributed to only one person; and throughout these chapters I try to show that the big picture here is about others with whom I have known and worked to achieve our goals. I have written extensively about so many notable individuals because it has been such a distinct privilege and pleasure to know them, and in many cases, consider them my friends. *Recounting his personal experience with President Franklin Roosevelt, the renowned lawyer and Supreme Court associate justice Robert H. Jackson observed, "The conceit of writing recollections may be forgiven only if the author has accomplished something memorable himself or has witnessed episodes of enduring importance. I invoke the latter excuse."* *

I invoke the latter excuse as well.

Lowell R. Beck
Burr Ridge, Illinois

---

* From *That Man: An Insider's Portrait of Franklin D. Roosevelt; 2003*, Oxford University Press, Robert H. Jackson

PROLOGUE

I CAN'T BELIEVE I'M HERE

It was hard to imagine that I was arriving in Washington, D.C. to live in 1960. I had visited Washington only once before, and was in awe of it then. I was even more in awe of it this time. Just driving by the Lincoln Memorial and White House gave a feeling of exhilaration now that I was in the presence of these glorious landmarks that I had known from pictures and history.

I was here because I had joined the American Bar Association's Chicago headquarters staff in late 1959; and within a short time, had been invited by its Washington Office director, Donald Channell, to join him on the Washington staff. Or should I say, I invited myself, and he accepted.

As a new law graduate, I was serving as the administrative assistant to the ABA's Junior Bar Conference (now Young Lawyers Division) while studying for the Illinois Bar exam; and had become acquainted with Don when he made occasional visits to the headquarters office. Don, who was formerly the chief lobbyist for the Georgia Chamber of Commerce, was relatively new with the ABA, and was its Washington Office's first professional director. Historically, the office did not lobby with a professional lobbyist. It had only one full-time employee, whose two jobs were to answer questions about the ABA and make arrangements for ABA leaders when they were in town to testify. All legislative liaison was by volunteer members. The new ABA leadership wanted a savvy lobbyist who would, working with volunteer members, serve as liaison to Capitol Hill. Don was just the right one for this, coming from the rough and tumble of Georgia politics.

Don would meet with me occasionally when he visited the Chicago headquarters.As we came to know each other, I kiddingly asked him if he could use an extra hand in Washington. His response was surprisingly immediate. He said, yes, he would be looking for another person because the ABA Board of Governors that day had authorized him to hire an assistant. And, yes, he would like me to do it. I replied that I hadn't even been to Washington, had no experience doing legislative work, and that I had just been kidding. Surely he didn't mean it. He said that he easily could teach me the Washington ropes in no time; and because he already had worked with me, he knew I could do the job. I would add a special value, he said, because I knew so many younger lawyers who were active in the ABA, and I particularly knew the ins and outs of the headquarters office.

This was the beginning of my new personal journey in the world of public policy. As a new lawyer, I had thought that, in time, I would return to my hometown of Peoria, Illinois, and practice law there. Instead, as fate would have it, I became a lobbyist in Washington and a national association leader for my entire career. I had found my niche.

CHAPTER ONE

Growing Up

ILLINOIS, 1934–1941

According to my mother, Hazel, my birthday in 1934 was the hottest day on record. While my mom was known occasionally to slightly exaggerate, weather records confirm that summer was the hottest ever recorded in the United States. It wasn't a comfortable time to bring a newborn to a second floor, one bedroom apartment with no air conditioning and few amenities.

This was a very difficult economic time. 1934 was during the heart of the Great Depression, with 25 percent of the population out of work, 19,000 homeless men in New York City alone, and a collapsed stock market. There were no government safety nets such as Social Security or Unemployment benefits.

Dad was one of the fortunate ones. He had a job. He was the bookkeeper with the Faber-Musser slaughter and meatpacking house on Peoria's South Side. It was from this location that he met my mother. She was the office assistant for Dr. Alan Foster, who practiced just a few blocks away, and they began dating when he took injured workers to the doctor's office (injuries were from knives or raging animals).

George and Hazel both were from families dating back to before the Revolutionary War. They grew up on Illinois farms: Dad, 60 miles south of Peoria, near Mt. Pulaski; and Mom, just 15 miles west of Peoria.

Dad was the youngest of four children. An ancestor was a Puritan and one of the original "Braintree Company" followers of the Reverend Thomas Hooker, founder of the Colony of Connecticut; another migrated from the German Rhineland in the late 1600s; and another fought in the Revolutionary War. Because of him, my son, Jonathan, and I are members of Sons of the American Revolution.

According to oral history, my dad's great grandfather, John Turner, knew Abe Lincoln, and they both looked upon the same girl with great admiration.

Turner allegedly told Abe that "nobody as ugly as you was gonna get a girl."

My dad wanted to attend college, but the economic times prevented that. So, after graduating from his small-town high school, he received an accounting competency certificate, and landed the slaughterhouse job to be followed as a Standard Oil regional office accountant.

My mother was the fourth McMeen child of 11 brothers and sisters. She was a descendent of Scottish-Irish immigrants, who had migrated from Scotland to Ireland in the 1600s, and then to America in the early 1700s. Some of these ancestors were involved with the Patriots of the Revolutionary War who declared independence from England. It's said that when Washington was passing by the home of one of her ancestors in Pennsylvania, he received a drink from my fifth great grandmother. This story is from *Flickinger Families in the United States*, a genealogy of the widespread Flickingers that includes the McMeen family:

> *According to the Reverend J. Vernon Rice in 1900, Abigail Hartman Rice was a stout, well-built woman, warm hearted and ever ready to lend a helping hand. It is related, that after the Battle of Brandywine, Washington retreated across the Chester Valley to Yellow Springs, passing by way of the (Zachariah and Abigail) Rice home. Halting with his staff officers, he asked for some water to drink. Mrs. Rice quickly sent one of her daughters to the spring for a pail of water. Mixing into it some sugar, and spice, to make flip, then a common drink, she presented it to Washington, addressing him as, "My Lord." Washington immediately replied, "We have no titles here, we are all brothers; my heart is with my poor men, who lie on the battlefield of Brandywine." This was one of Washington's dark moments, but genius drinks the cup of sorrow to the dregs, and is strengthened thereby.*

I suppose the moral of these ancestral stories is not that my ancestors go back so many generations, but that the Beck side wasn't as polite as the McMeens'. One told Abe that he was ugly and couldn't get a girl. The other addressed Washington as "My Lord," and gave him a drink.

One of my favorite things was to visit the Beck and McMeen farms, and occasionally stay alone with my McMeen grandparents, who lived close to Peoria. At the farm I had a lot of attention because, while there would be 14 McMeen grandchildren, I was the oldest by four years. Being there at hog butchering time or watching my grandmother kill and dress a frying chicken were eye-opening and lifetime experiences.

But everything on the farm wasn't about killing for food to eat. Most of it wasn't. My grandfather loved his bee hives and collecting honey. He would cover his face and head with special netting (veil), put on gloves and a jacket, and tell me to stand back while bees swarmed around him. He showed me how to milk a cow, and it was always fun to watch him squirt milk into the mouths of barn cats who were around at milking time.

Some of my most enjoyable farm memories are from my grandmother's cooking, and particularly her home-made pies with lard from their own hogs' fat, and freshly picked cherries and peaches. The only thing was that the kitchen was very hot in summer because she cooked on a wood-burning stove. She was happy when I was there to bring in wood.

I never tired of the farm, and when I was old enough to help my uncles in the fields in the summer, I did. Today, my wife, Myrna, who grew up on an Illinois farm, and I still enjoy visiting them, and are lucky to have my cousins, Chuck and Vanna Zeigler, Lynnette and Roger Beecher, and Steve and Becki McMeen who continue to farm not far from the old McMeen homestead. To us, the farm is a magical place.

Attending Central Christian Church (Disciples of Christ) was an important part of our family life. Dad was an elder, and both of my parents were active members. Their church friends were their best friends, and consequently their children were my best friends with birthday parties galore.

In 1939, the American economy was beginning to improve slightly, fueled largely by war material orders from Great Britain and France. Even though war was raging in Europe, and Japan was sweeping into China, the United States asserted its neutrality, not wishing to get mixed up in what many believed to be "Europe's War."

By early 1941, the U.S. was technically still at peace, but the subject of the war dominated everything else. American defense factories were humming for allies in Europe, but the country still was not prepared to fight a war.

Dad was then with Standard Oil, but unhappy there. His best friend and first cousin, Sherman Miller, had been an official of the LeTourneau Company, a major maker of earth-moving equipment like Caterpillar. The company was expanding because of war exports, and Sherman moved from Peoria to the northeast Georgia town of Toccoa to be office manager of LeTourneau's new plant there. He encouraged Dad to apply for the Toccoa accountant's position, so in early fall of 1941, we moved to the red hills of Georgia. The United States was at war all over the world by that December.

1941 began an entirely new life for the Becks, particularly for me. Not only did I have a massive adjustment to a rural town in the South with new kids and school, but I also had a two-year-old sister, Carol, who was changing our household order as all two-year olds do.

Note: In 1934 the average yearly income was $1,601;
Gasoline was 10 cents a gallon; bread was 8 cents a loaf;
A new house was $5,972 and a postage stamp was 3 cents;
The first Masters tournament began in Augusta;
The Chicago Blackhawks won the Stanley Cup; and
Bonnie and Clyde were killed in an ambush.

TOCCOA, GEORGIA, 1941–1947

Time in Toccoa was a defining time for me in many ways…war sacrifice, a Midwestern boy in a Deep South small town (virtually like a foreign land to me), and hurdles of a different culture to overcome. This period was filled with experiences that I would not have had "at home" in Illinois. While living there, even at my young age, I wanted to be back in Illinois. But, Toccoa was pleasant for me much of the time, and I am glad that we lived there.

A New Home, New Friends, and World War II

Going into the second grade, I wasn't prepared for what small town Georgia life would be like for a Yankee kid from Illinois. It wasn't fun when I entered school. The kids were still fighting the "War Between the States." I was a foreigner to them. And, I wasn't just a "Yankee," the term used for Northern visitors. I was a "Damned Yankee," one that had moved in to stay awhile. And the red clay dirt. My mom couldn't stand dirt in clothes, much less the clay that wouldn't wash out.

On December 7, the Japanese hit Pearl Harbor. The United States wasn't yet at war, even though Europe was a battlefield with Hitler on the move. But the attack by the Japanese did it, and I remember sitting by the radio with Mom on December 8, listening to President Franklin Roosevelt announce that we were going to war. Mom cried, and immediately called Dad at his office. It was such an earth-shattering event that he came right home.

So, the country was at war, but it didn't mean much to a 7-year-old. I had my own life to be concerned about, with those foreign Southern kids, and being far away from my extended Illinois family. The war didn't seem to worry Dad and Mom or their friends. When, as an adult, I asked Dad why I couldn't remember hearing them show distress about it, he said it was because they never doubted the outcome, regardless of how long it took. They were very concerned, he said, about my uncles who were fighting, the massive devastation and death, and the total upheaval of world order which was producing an uncertain, if not frightening, future. But they tried to keep that worry away from Carol and me.

I do remember rationing. You couldn't buy a new car, travel very far, or buy all kinds of the food you wanted. The one food I disliked the most was the canned salmon (with those little bones) that we seemed to have all the time. I guess that wasn't rationed. Television didn't exist, so we got our visual news from newspaper pictures and at the movie theater. We didn't go to movies often, so we didn't see much about the war; but when we did go, the bombing and street fighting were vivid on the big screen.

Shortly after we moved to Georgia, my parents realized that I had a speech problem, and to a lesser extent, a writing problem. I couldn't pronounce "R's" properly, and I sounded funny. I was constantly erasing because I couldn't connect the letters properly. So, they hired tutors (which, surprisingly, were available in Toccoa) to help with both. The writing assistance worked well. The speech lessons, though, were tortuous, trying to get the sound right with the tutor, and saying it over again for what seemed like endless days. I pronounce my "R's" okay today, but even now have a quasi-Southern-Central Illinois accent.

Another issue was some crooked teeth, and particularly my lower jaw that gave me a pronounced under bite. I had a difficult time chewing, and it didn't look good. There were no orthodontists in Toccoa, and that specialty was new. If one could be found, it was very expensive. My parents found a specialist in Greenville, SC, a day's trip from Toccoa, and they managed to scrape up the money to pay for it. It was a happy day when the rubber bands came off, and my teeth were straight. This was one of those personal sacrifices

11

that parents make for their children.

Most of the kids in my class weren't sure what to think about a new Northern classmate. And, for a while they didn't include me in birthday parties or befriend me at recess. While they seemed to tolerate me, it was more like, "They wouldn't let poor Rudolph play at any reindeer games."

My biggest embarrassment was when the PE teacher had us "try out" for after-school basketball. I was first in line to make a basket. Not seeing others dribble the ball, I just ran to the basket, and it went who knows where. Everybody laughed, and even the teacher said something like, "Oh my, that won't do." I think he encouraged me to come back and try again, but after that I didn't want to risk embarrassment again. Not being coordinated for recess games didn't make a lot of difference because we didn't have organized sports such as little league. And, by the fourth or fifth grade, I was included in after-school baseball (playing right field), and some touch football.

Some of my worst times were with older boys on the playground. They taunted me with things like, "You think you're so smart, being from up there in Illinois. Georgia is the best. Illinois is nothing." That was hard for me to take. After all, no state, certainly not Georgia, raised corn as tall as my grandpas' and uncles' in Illinois. I said that to them, and two of them got me down and twisted my arm until I would say that Georgia raised more corn than Illinois. Talk about humiliation!

After several months, life got better. One of my teachers, Mrs. Addison, was particularly friendly and encouraging. She was popular with teachers and students alike, and luck would have it for me that her son, Allen, was in my class, and we became friends. Other kids liked him, which was a big help for me in gaining friends.

An especially happy time for me was the arrival of a new friend, Johnny McEwen, whose family moved to Toccoa from West Palm Beach, Florida. A stranger from West Palm Beach was just as foreign to the local kids as one from Illinois. We became like brothers, and, while life had gotten better for me before Johnny moved in, it still was great having a friend who wasn't from Toccoa. He and I continue to stay in touch. Continuing to communicate with a close grade school friend gives a feeling of connectedness and stability.

Another boy I remember was always barefoot, was scrawny, and not from a business-professional family. He was a quiet kid and liked by others. One day he invited me to go home with him to play. I did, and had a shock. His house was an old unpainted and weathered shanty on a dirt street. The floors had no rugs, and were old unpainted, unstained, soiled planks. *I couldn't believe that I could see through the separations in the planks to the ground.* Here was a Southern "poor white" family, who, while not segregated from other whites in schools or other public places, did not live much better than blacks. He was embarrassed, and simply couldn't "fit in." I began to realize that there were more kids like him, and after school they would fade away.

Black People and White People

In the 1940s in the South, most white families with any resources at all had "Negro" domestic help. This included us, even with our limited means. Often I would go with Dad to pick up the black lady who would clean our house. I remember vividly her neighborhood, which makes me cringe, even now. All the buildings were unpainted, weathered shacks, and most were without the basic utilities such as running water and electricity. The streets were unpaved, and after a rain, we couldn't drive to her house because of the mud ....she would meet us on the main road. When we did drive to her house, particularly in summer months, the neighborhood people milled around, staring at us, the women holding their babies. Many of them needed work, so it was like they were saying "please hire me," or maybe it was just curiosity to see a white person in their area.

Observing up close the discrimination that was official and sanctioned continues to ring vividly with me. I was too young to think about its implications then, but it was so strikingly different than what I had experienced in Illinois, particularly in the rural towns near our families' farms. There were no black people in rural Central Illinois. And in Peoria, where there were black slums, they were too far removed from us for a grade school student to think about.

I suppose that Dad and Mom carried some prejudice, like other white adults at that time. This changed, though, when we moved back to Illinois, and Dad joined the Bradley University administration. They became friends with a prominent black professor; and Dad befriended Joe Billy McDade, the first black Bradley basketball player. He had been recruited from Michigan, and my parents occasionally had him to dinner since he had no local family. Joe Billy was a winner at everything, and they loved him. The personal experiences with African-Americans at Bradley opened their minds and changed their thinking. Joe Billy became a lawyer, stayed in Peoria, and was appointed federal district judge at a young age.

Before the 1954 *Brown vs. Board of Education* school desegregation decision, many schools in America, and in all of the South, were strictly racially segregated, so I never saw a black kid in school. In Toccoa, while the population was probably half black, we seldom saw black people downtown. All public facilities such as restrooms, drinking fountains, and bus station waiting rooms were marked "white" and "colored." If we did occasionally meet a black person on the sidewalk, he would move to the side for you, even if it meant stepping on to the street.

Think about seeing an actual lynching in a newspaper picture today! I did, and remember it. Who wouldn't remember it? The local Toccoa paper reported a hanging at a public park just a few towns away. It showed a black man hanging by the neck from a tree limb, hands and feet tied, with a crowd including youngsters, watching. My parents were outraged, and I heard them talk about leaving the South as soon as they could after the war.

Dad liked his job, and he and Mom had many friends. But, they were recoiled by the lynching, and had a difficult time living in the political and cultural environment of Governor Eugene Talmadge, the arch-segregationist who ruled Georgia with his own political dynasty.

Make no mistake about it. Discrimination and segregation in the South were debilitating, humiliating, and harsh. Of course, while the Northern culture today considers itself tolerant and anti-discriminatory, life for black people in the North wasn't always pleasant either. I've thought a lot about the comparison of race relations in the North and South today. And, I wonder if there isn't now in the South, after decades of close black-white proximity, an environment where blacks and whites understand each other better and coalesce more closely in everyday life than in the North. The North in many ways continues to be more segregated than the South. Most Northern whites, in contrast to those in the South, have little or no knowledge of black culture or individual black persons, unless they know one or two individual blacks at work or as a neighbor. It's said, for example, that Chicago is the most segregated city in America.

I had some personal experiences involving Southern whites and blacks together that, as I became an adult, helped me understand better the relationships of blacks and whites in the South.

- One of these experiences was my friendship with the Agnew family, who owned a farm just a mile from Toccoa. Ken, the younger son, was my classmate, and invited me to stop by occasionally. The family raised cotton, had dogs and cats that were fun to play with, and, of course, chickens strutting around the property. I felt at home there because of my love for my relatives' Illinois farms. They didn't have tractors, but they had mules for field work, and their primary crop was cotton. When Mr. Agnew asked if I would like to help pick it, I said yes, and was there Saturday morning to begin this new adventure. I was given a big bag, and along with Ken and his older brother, went to the field. There I was introduced to three black men who would be working with us. Being up so close to these people, with a cotton bag in hand, was certainly a new experience for me. I didn't know what to expect, but learned immediately how nice and courteous they were. Ken took a row with one of them, his brother with another, and I with another. My partner, a tall, slender man, showed me how to pick the cotton ball and put it in my bag without bruising it. (This was not an easy job. In sweltering sun, you had to stoop over as you walked down long rows, and wear good gloves to keep the dry bristles from cutting your hands.) He treated me like a good friend, and as we walked along together he would hum songs. As I think back, I recall a deep respect that these black workers and the Agnews seemed to have for each other. The black folks returned to their shanty town shacks at night. They weren't allowed to live as the whites did. But they seemed to function, when together with whites, more as a family than as bosses and workers.

- One of my deepest impressions of the South was when we would visit Mrs. Mary Jarrett White at her huge old house about six miles east of Toccoa. She lived alone, and had lived there all of her life. She sold fresh milk and eggs (I didn't like pasteurized milk). The house was built in 1785 by a Revolutionary War officer and local political leader who was killed by Indians near there. The 10-room house was bought in 1838 by Mrs. White's ancestor, Devereaux Jarrett, who converted it into his home and a public "traveler's rest." It later became the headquarters home for his 14,000-acre plantation. Mrs. White still owned it, and was living there in the 1940s.

Here's why my memories are so strong: Mrs. White took us to the attic to look out of the hole where her ancestors shot at Indians. She described an Indian massacre nearby where several whites were killed before the Civil War, and told us how unsafe this area had been then. But, that wasn't the most vivid memory. As we started to leave early in the evening, we heard singing from behind the house. Several families of black people had gathered outside their shanties in the hollow, and were singing and chanting spirituals. These sounds were the real thing, not rehearsed for a stage, and had warmth, beauty and spirituality that were unforgettable. Mrs. White said that we could stay and listen for a while, but we would have to stand back near the house so as not to disturb or embarrass them. The ancestors of these folk had lived here for many generations. Mrs. White continued to care for them, and give them work with her cows and chickens. She did not treat them like inferior people, but instead, as I'll always remember, treated them like a family and felt that she had obligations to them. My current research shows that the house was sold by the Jarrett family in 1951, four years after we left Georgia. Mrs. White died in 1957. I don't know what happened with the black families. But the house is now known as Traveler's Rest, is open to the public, and is listed on the National Register of Historic Places, as well as being a Georgia Historical Commission Site. One last thing…While the Jarrett family owned the house that they called Jarrett Manor, Mrs. Mary Jarrett White, the last family owner, made history. She was the first woman in Georgia to vote.

Our Church Life and My Baptism

Dad and Mom joined Sherman and Erma Miller and some local people to organize a new Christian Church in Toccoa. The Disciples of Christ, known more commonly as the Christian Church, had been their denomination in Illinois, and was active in the South as well as the Midwest. My folks were not unhappy with the Baptist church where we began attending, but it was more conservative than they preferred. Dad and Sherman Miller provided leadership to organize a congregation that met in a house near the community swimming pool. Since the Disciples practiced immersion for baptizing, my dad said that it was handy to have the pool next door. Established Disciples churches have baptismal tanks located behind the chancel.

The congregation wasn't large, but was congenial, and I liked going to church in this setting. It was where I first spoke from a pulpit, something I would do more regularly as I got older. I don't mean it was much. It simply was reading scripture or saying a prayer. I learned it from my dad, who was an excellent public speaker. As an elder, he would administer the bread and grape juice communion by speaking about its meaning, and saying beautiful prayers. Dad was an excellent, thoughtful speaker who taught Sunday school and gave devotional talks at the company. I was very proud of him.

I was baptized on June 11th, 1944, just after my 10th birthday. And, yes, it was in the pool next door to the church.

My Trips Back to the Illinois Farms

Because of war rationing and Dad's work schedule, we weren't able to travel on vacations. However, my parents decided that, when I was old enough to travel without them, they would let me go to Illinois for several summer weeks.

Mom's brother, Harold, and his wife, Jimmie, wanted me to come and stay with them on the farm.

Occasionally, Mr. R. G. LeTourneau, the owner of the LeTourneau Company, would take a rider on his two-engine plane (no jets them) when he flew from Toccoa to Peoria. Mr. LeTourneau invented the earth-moving equipment that his company built. He would fly into Toccoa, spend a day at the drawing board designing new equipment, and leave. He was called the "Dean of Earthmoving," and 70 percent of that kind of equipment used in WWII were his designs and produced at his factories. He wasn't a good business manager, so he left all Toccoa company management to others.

I couldn't have gone to Illinois if I hadn't had this free ride. I didn't know what to expect when I boarded the plane without my parents. Not only was it my first plane ride, I would be flying with this great man. When I entered the plane, Mr. LeTourneau already was seated at his special desk, with his Texas hat on (he had plants in Longview, Texas, as well as in Peoria, Toccoa, and Mississippi). He might have looked up and smiled, but I don't recall it. All I can remember is taking a seat, and planning to hold on for dear life. I know he didn't say hello. We were the only passengers, and I believe he didn't look up from his work or remove his hat during the entire trip. He didn't seem unfriendly, and obviously had given approval for my tagging along, but he seemed oblivious to my presence. I don't think we said goodbye to each other either. I flew on that plane two other times, but he wasn't along. Each flight was easier for me, as I became an "experienced" flier, and Mr. R. G. wasn't there for me to worry about.

I looked forward to those summers with Uncle Harold and Aunt Jimmie. Harold had work for me, and my primary job was punching wires on his hay baler. He and Uncle Delmar, who joined him in farming when he returned from the war, baled hay and straw of their own and other farmers. It was a major operation, with the John Deere tractor pulling the huge baling machine. Harold stood on the top platform, guiding the hay with a pitchfork. I stood on a board ledge, punching wire through holes in wooden blocks that separated the bales, and another guy tied the wires on the other side. Sometimes the dust and 90 degree heat would get to me, but Uncle Harold always would give me breaks. The really good part was stopping for lunch, and going back to the house for Aunt Jimmie's fried chicken or pot roast.

Two Bygone School Practices

The Georgia public school system either allowed or encouraged two practices that are not allowed today in American public schools. One was school prayer, and the other was corporal punishment. Every morning after we checked in at our homerooms, we went to the auditorium to say the Pledge of Allegiance, sing the Star Spangled Banner *and* Dixie, and pray with a local minister leading us. It wasn't easy for me to sing Dixie at first, but I got used to it, and think it was changed from every day to just a few times a month. The preacher was generally Baptist, and I don't recall ever seeing a Catholic priest or rabbi at the school. This obviously pre-dated the School Prayer Decision.

The second practice was physical punishment. It didn't maim you, but it did hurt and humiliate. In one of my classes, my teacher would hit your outstretched hand with a ruler, or have you sit on a stool facing the corner of the room. There were some boys who seemed to be her regular targets. While I wasn't one of those guys, I did experience both (for whispering). The ruler would sting and was humiliating. It was kind of a badge of honor with some of the other kids, though.

We Move Back to Peoria

Sherman, Erma and their daughter, Ardella, returned to Peoria before us when he was promoted to National Credit Manager of the LeTourneau Company.

Soon after, Dad was offered the internal auditor's position at Bradley University in Peoria. While it wasn't a high-paying job, it helped get us back to the Midwest, and promised a free college education for their kids that my parents considered good income in and of itself.

So, in 1947 Dad and Mom bought a brand new Chevrolet with their life insurance cash value, and we moved back to Illinois. But, guess what! I missed Toccoa and my friends there. So, three years later, when I was in high school, I was able to hitch another ride on Mr. R.G.'s plane and fly back to Toccoa for a few days. Johnny, Allen and others welcomed me like I was a native of Dixie, and I felt right at home. And guess what again. Mr. LeTourneau was on the plane, and said hello to me.

HIGH SCHOOL, COLLEGE AND LAW SCHOOL, 1948 TO 1959

Fortunately, in 1947, I had a year back in Peoria to make friends before starting high school in the next year. Most frightening for any high school student is to enter school without friends already established. I didn't have that to worry about on my first day at Peoria Central High School because two students entering with me, Gordon Selkirk and Ken Walters, had become two of my best friends who would remain best friends for years. And a girlfriend too, who would be stolen from me in high school by another guy, Warren Goelz, who would become a best friend and best man at my wedding.

While I wasn't good at any sport, which generally is the ticket to popularity, I thrived in high school. Wanting to do at least one sport, I began running the quarter mile, but came down with acute appendicitis and was hospitalized after surgery for a few days. That took care of the track experience that year. I was a member of the National Honor Society, sang in the A Cappella Choir, and was active in some civic clubs like the Key Club. I tried the marching band with my dad's old cornet, but after my music went flying all over the field at a half time one cold night, I decided it wasn't for me.

I found my mark primarily in the student council, which then was an acceptable and competitive activity. From my freshman year until graduation, I won every student council election, but had to settle for vice president of the student body after a vigorous campaign for president with six others. I was active in the Illinois Association of Student Councils, and became its president in my senior year.

Although I did some speaking at church, public speaking to large audiences wasn't my strongest suit when I entered high school. A turning point, a true watershed event for me, was in speech class during my freshman year. Each of us had to give a three-minute talk without notes on a platform in front of the class. The teacher, Miss Spickard, sat at the back of the class, tapping a long pointer on her desk. I was first up alphabetically, and literally froze when I faced the class and Miss Spickard with her tapping pointer. I was up all night memorizing, but once on that platform couldn't remember a thing. Not one kid was smiling, though, because they knew it soon would be their turn. I told Miss Spickard that I couldn't do it, that I couldn't remember anything, and would have to sit down. She kept tapping her pointer, and said that I couldn't sit down. She said that if I was prepared, I could do it, and that the class had an hour to go. I would have to stand there for the full hour if I had to, but there would be no sitting down. I gave the talk. Everything actually did come back to me, almost word for word. Miss Spickard began to applaud, and the entire class did too. After that, I could speak almost anywhere, and did. Not that I wouldn't be nervous before talking before large audiences; I would be. But the fear of it was over. I opened all-school assemblies, and gave sermons at our large Disciples of Christ Church on youth Sundays. I had no trouble giving "campaign" talks, and even became an orator of sorts as state high school student council president. (Interestingly, my wife's sister, Carol Browning, when meeting me for the first time, said that she remembered hearing me speak at a state student council meeting when she was a delegate.) Thank you, Miss Spickard.

We had boys' and girls' social clubs that functioned outside of school. I had heard that earlier, Illinois allowed high school fraternities and sororities similar to those in college, with Greek names and rituals. After they were outlawed, Peoria Central students organized social clubs that took their place. Mine, the Toppers, consisted of about 20 guys who were good friends and ran around together. We had athletes, student council members, Honor Society members, and just plain good guys. The girls had theirs as well, and would eat every Friday night at a member's home, where the boys' clubs would arrive. There's a big difference in high school between then and now in 2015. By the time we were seniors, there were some students, but only a limited few, who would have a beer and maybe a cigarette. But that was it. Any form of drug was unheard of.

In addition to my public speaking opportunities in student council activities, my church provided them as well. Two or three times a year I was asked to deliver comments from the pulpit on Sunday mornings, and spoke at youth meetings sponsored by the Peoria Council of Churches. For a couple of years, I toyed with idea of being a minister, however didn't have a "call," or, in other words, an intense inward feeling that it was an occupation that, spiritually, I must pursue.

As a junior, I was asked to serve as a disc jockey and school news reporter on radio station WPEO for students getting ready for school. The program, *Musical Breakfast*, which began at 7:00 each morning, featured music requested by students and events of the day at each of the three Peoria public high schools. I covered events at Peoria Central, and other students spoke for their schools. While such early mornings weren't my cup of tea, this was one of my most enjoyable activities.

Many of my best high school friends, including Ken, Warren, and Gordon, have passed away. I always will have the fondest memories of them and the years of our times together. At this time in our lives, there's something particularly special about a continuing relationship with an old friend who dates back as far as grade and high school, such John McEwen in Georgia, and Jack Wilson, who lives nearby. As author Lois Wyse said, "It's a connection to life and a tie to the past that's key to sanity."

Bradley University, Peoria, 1952 to 1955

At Bradley, I was on its nationally known debate team and student court, and active in Lambda Chi Alpha fraternity and college life in general. This section, however, is more about my dad than me. It's because so much of my life at Bradley was affected by events that my dad, as a university official, faced there.

Dad joined the Bradley staff as internal auditor in 1947, and served for 25 years as controller, treasurer, secretary to the board and vice president. Even without a college degree, he was highly respected for his financial knowledge and fairness in administering the school's finances. In his eulogy at his funeral, the university's president, Dr. Jerry Abegg, praised Dad for "his leadership when it was so vital, and for dealing fairly and honestly with everybody."

Whether in business or the non-profit worlds, there will be challenging situations to deal with. I'm sure, however, that when my dad joined the Bradley staff he had no idea just how challenging the next few years would be.

Bradley's basketball team was one known as a national powerhouse, winning NCAA and NIT tournaments. On July 24, 1951, two of its best players, Gene "Squeaky" Melchiorre and Billy Mann, as well as others, admitted taking bribes from gamblers to "shave points." They were such good players that they could hold down points and still win against other teams. Several teams, including Kentucky and CCNY, were involved in the scandal, and it rocked the national college basketball community, including Bradley, in disgrace.

A year later, Bradley's president, David Owen, resigned, and the next president wasn't appointed until 1954. (Dr. Owen was murdered in Washington, D.C., in 1960.) Between 1952 and 1954, Dr. A.G. "Frenchie" Haussler served as acting president, supported by a leadership group of deans and administrators, including my dad. They were a unified leadership group faced with other issues in addition to the basketball scandal, such as North Central Association (NCA) accreditation.

Most students were oblivious to these problems, but I couldn't be. At times it seemed that the university couldn't make it through it all. And this particularly was the case when the next big bombshell hit my dad personally. As auditor, he discovered that his own boss had been embezzling from the university. He would come home at night and stare out the window, not knowing how to handle it. After having to testify at the trial, which resulted in prison for his boss, he would ask what else would happen to harm Bradley and its future.

I arrived as a student in 1952 when Bradley's worst problems were occurring. The school was still reeling from the scandals, NCA accreditation was on the line, and I had misgivings as to whether I wanted to matriculate there. Financially, however, Bradley was my only option. So I went, and as a student there my experience was bittersweet. Difficult because of all of Bradley's troublesome issues that affected my family, but overall sweet because it also was an enjoyable and productive time for me. I had excellent professors, and although I was George's son, can't recall any of them cutting me any slack.

My friend from high school and Lambda Chi fraternity brother, Warren Goelz, asked me one day if I would be interested in joining him at law school after our third year at Bradley. At that time, in contrast to today, it was possible to enter law school after three years of undergraduate work, and have first year law school credits transfer back to satisfy the additional hours required for a Bachelor's degree. A wealthy Peoria lawyer had left law scholarships in his will for Peoria resident law students, and Warren was going to apply for one. While I was no longer as unhappy as earlier, I was tired of my front row seat at Bradley's difficulties, and this seemed like a reasonable step for me. I couldn't believe that money was available. It seemed too good to be true. But it was, and Warren and I, along with fraternity brother Stan Loula, were accepted to Northwestern Law School, beginning the fall of 1955. Although I was absent from Bradley classes, after my first year of law school I graduated with the class of 1956.

During the next few years Bradley did more than just pull through its problems. It excelled at it. Outstanding new presidents were hired. My dad served under three of them. His contentious tension-ridden challenges ended. He rose from internal auditor to vice president, treasurer, and secretary to the board of directors. He constantly held foremost Bradley's financial strength and improving educational standing. In 1963 he pressed for building a new bookstore to replace an old second floor room that was a disgrace. When built, it was one of the finest in the country. A less popular of his recommendations, particularly at that time among some alums, was to terminate football in 1970. Bradley, he said, couldn't afford to continue it and pay for other sports and a quality educational environment as well. However, whatever opposition there was to the termination died out, and the university was financially healthier because of it.

George Beck was a worker, up and at the office early every morning. He feared retirement because work was his life outside of his family, and he had few other interests except his Masonic lodge, his immaculate yard, and reading history and biography. When Dr. Abegg, formerly Bradley's dean of engineering, took over as president in 1970, Dad was at the normal retirement age of 65. He couldn't have been happier when Dr. Abegg asked him to remain for two years and help him transition into his new position. When Dad did retire at age 67, he found that sleeping later and beginning to travel wasn't so bad after all. Sadly, four months later, he died of a stroke. All in our family were terribly saddened that he had finally realized he would enjoy time outside the office, and as fate would have it, wouldn't be able to.

My dad was not a sportsman. When I was growing up, he did not take me to ball games, teach me how to throw a ball, or express interest in any sport. He was an avid reader, primarily of non-fiction history and political books, and spent hours caring for his lawn and plants. I followed suit by not playing any sport, and for a while resented that he didn't help me by expressing some interest in at least one.

So, how did my dad influence my life? By his own life he taught me honesty and spiritual values. He taught me the importance of finding a path that is enjoyable, and working hard at it. He taught me to be a loyal friend who respected the views of others. And, most of all, he, along with my mom, always was supportive of what I wanted to do. He and my mom, a homemaker (and an excellent one) were my security blankets; I knew that they always were there if I needed them.

Following my dad's death, Myrna and I established the George R. Beck Memorial Scholarship at Bradley, and Dr. Abegg arranged for the University to match the initial contribution. Students have received assistance from the fund's income each year.

Bradley University today is a premier educational institution. I have no doubt that much of the credit goes to the unsung heroes of the leadership group who led it through its dark hours of the 1950s and into the '60s to pave the way for the enlightened leaders that followed. And my dad was an integral part of that group.

Northwestern University School of Law, Chicago, 1955 to 1958

Law School in the 1950s was far different than in 2015. In my class of some 150, three or four were women. In 2013, the American Bar Association reported that almost one-half of law students nationwide were women. They also were treated as a minority in the 1950s. For example, in my Torts class, when we met in the law school's cavernous Lincoln Hall, the professor had a history of calling on the women to discuss the rape cases. One morning when we came to that class, the three women weren't present. So, not to be out fooled, the professor simply moved past those cases to the book's next section. Everybody laughed, and the professor obviously enjoyed himself. But the gals had to return one day, and soon. As they walked in together, the class laughed again. And, they were called on. Can you even imagine this happening today!

Northwestern was known as a great law school. It's even better today, ranked 12th among some 200 in the nation. Although I managed to do okay, I wasn't a stellar student. However, I was glad to be there and in a new venue. I knew that I wanted a law degree, but I wasn't sure what I would do with it. There were possibilities of joining a family friend's law firm in Peoria, but that wasn't certain, and I wasn't fully motivated to practice law anyway.

What came from Northwestern, however, was a respected degree from a leading law school. And it provided me with the essential background to succeed in my life's work of legislative activity and association leadership.

Law school taught me how to think and question. Northwestern, like all top law schools, teaches by the Socratic and Case Methods. Although they are two different things, they are tied together in the law school teaching process. The Case Method teaches how to analyze and determine rules of law by reading and outlining appellate court cases; and the Socratic dialogue is where the professor asks one student questions about the case, rather than simply stating a specific rule of the law. This can be an intimidating experience, particularly when the professor calls on you without warning, and challenges your analysis of the case before the whole class. You must determine the rules by analysis of the case. Although I didn't panic and get sick, as some students described by Scott Turow in his book, *One L*, I worried about when I might be hit with the dialogue and questions. Much of the worry was the strong fear of embarrassment if I didn't get it right.

I enjoyed trial advocacy more than some of the other classes. In trial advocacy, I had to argue cases before Professor Goldstein, who was notorious for frightening students. The Goldstein name was renowned in law school circles for his book on trial advocacy and his ability to produce outstanding trial lawyers. He would stare intensely at you while constantly kicking his bench, trying and often succeeding at distracting you. Before my first appearance before him, I was warned to prepare well because he would distract you with his staring and kicking. So, of course, I was nervous. As I began to speak, and Professor Goldstein began to kick, the first thing that came to mind was Miss Spickard in high school with her tapping pointer. His kicking didn't bother me as I remembered how I had weathered her distraction that day in speech class. Again, thank you Miss Spickard.

Although I didn't qualify for the school's law review, available to only the top four or five students from each class, the law school helped me land a research and writing project with the Transportation Center, located in Evanston. This opportunity provided an invaluable learning and writing experience with various projects they assigned to me.

My new home in Abbott Hall, Northwestern's Chicago campus dormitory, taught me independence. It was my first time away from home on my own. Often along with my roommate, Arthur Neu, I explored almost everything Chicago had to offer, from hockey games to the symphony. I particularly enjoyed exploring Rush Street night life entertainment just blocks away. The father of one of my classmates was a major beer distributor and provider to the bars in the area. Many of us enjoyed that welcomed attention we received on Rush Street, from bouncers to bartenders, because everybody on the street knew my friend. I don't think this was an overriding reason, though, not to be number one in my class.

Overall, law school was an enjoyable experience for me. Some students weren't in awe of it all, and were so confident that they made top grades even if they didn't attend class. There was no intensity with them. Some were uptight all of the time, always worrying about grades and embarrassment. I was in between worry and enjoyment.

Most importantly, my enjoyment came from the lifelong friends I made there, including my roommate, Art Neu*, who returned to his hometown of Carroll, Iowa, to practice law, and for several years served as Lieutenant Governor of Iowa. Richard Wiley, who became chairman of the Federal Communications Commission, and mentioned at other times in this memoir, was in my class when we first met. Ronald Carlson, the nationally prominent holder of the Callaway Chair of Law Emeritus at the University of Georgia Law School, was among them. Those and other friendships have continued over the years, and I cherish them.

Arthur A. Neu

Art Neu passed away unexpectedly on January 2, 2015, of complications from pneumonia. He had served as a distinguished Lieutenant Governor of Iowa, an Iowa state senator, a member of the Iowa Board of Regents, the Iowa Board of Corrections and Mayor of Carroll, Iowa, where he practiced law all of his career. He was a gentleman of sterling character, and known throughout Iowa as fully committed to public service. I will never fully realize that he is gone.

During summer of my senior year in high school, and the summers throughout college and law school, I had to earn money. The hay baling with Uncle Harold wasn't any longer suitable because he had begun using automatic equipment, and punchers no longer were needed. My first job was at Biehl's Laundry and Dry Cleaners, where I worked alongside Mr. Biehl himself, loading dryers. I remember most the stultifying heat in those rooms without air conditioning.

One summer I worked the night shift on the Caterpillar factory floor as a welder's helper, removing beads from metal on the assembly line. This was the dirtiest, hardest job I ever had, but I learned about factories and the people who worked in them.

My most enjoyable summer job was working as a vacation stand-in for the Jewel Tea Company's several delivery salesmen in the Central Illinois region. Jewel Foods started as a household door to door company with sales of coffee, tea and later household goods and clothes. This job was available to me, thanks to the recommendation of my fraternity brother, Bob Thomas, whose father was president of Jewel Tea. The Jewel Tea Company and its brown trucks were ended sometime after the company operated exclusively through supermarkets now known as Jewel-Osco.

While in law school, because of mandatory military service, I served in the Illinois National Guard division located at the Guard's Chicago armory that was across from the school. So that I would not be required to serve longer than necessary after law school, I decided to take Army basic training at Fort Leonard Wood, Missouri, and specialized in armored tank training at Ft. Knox, Kentucky. My first full-time job as a member of the legal profession came in 1959.

CHAPTER TWO

MY FIRST JOB

CHICAGO 1959–1960

American Bar Association

In 1959, I completed Army Basic Training at Ft. Leonard Wood, MO,* and Armored Tank training at Ft. Knox, KY. Next up was the bar exam in early 1960, so I had to take the bar review course in Chicago. I had to find a job in Chicago that would pay living expenses and allow enough time for study. I didn't know what kind of work I wanted. Law jobs were scarce, and my law school grades didn't qualify me for the top Chicago law firms, who took only graduates in the highest ten per cent of their class. Besides that, I was thinking about returning to Peoria to practice with a prominent attorney who was a family friend and who had suggested that he might have an opening when I was ready.

Getting My First Job

Coming to my rescue was Professor William Trumbull at Northwestern. He was a brilliant man who really knew his stuff in "Bills and Notes." He lived alone in a spacious lakeside condo just a couple of blocks from the law school, and unlike most other professors, enjoyed having students over to talk, drink and eat. I was one of the fortunate ones to be invited, so we became well acquainted, and he would give me helpful tips on law school study.

Although Professor Trumbull enjoyed a good time along with the rest of us, he was all business as a teacher, and probably the kindest and most helpful teacher you ever would want. He was everybody's favorite and certainly mine. So, I contacted him for suggestions on where I might find a job.

I didn't have high hopes because, as well as we had jelled socially, he was part of the law school intellectual elite, and his job contacts were primarily with top law firms who hired the cream-of-the-crop graduates. As luck would

28

have it, he told me that he knew of an opening that he thought would work perfectly for me —Administrative Assistant to the Junior Bar Conference (now the Young Lawyers Section) of the American Bar Association. The occupant of that job was leaving to enter law practice. It required a law school graduate because it was necessary to work with member-lawyers on public policy issues. He explained too that there was a lawyer-cultural aspect where the members, themselves lawyers, would consider you more an equal if you had completed law school. Not only would I become well acquainted with many of the best up-and-coming lawyers in America, I could do their staff administrative work on national public policy issues on their agenda and still have time to study for the bar exam in the adjoining American Bar Foundation library.

Professor Trumbull had one request. When you pass the bar, he said, stay in the job at least another year. This was not a temporary or part-time job for only a few months, and his credibility with the ABA could be affected if I left too soon.

My interview was with Kenneth Burns, a junior partner with Jenner and Block, and the volunteer elected secretary of the JBC. I was nervous. The job seemed just right for me, and even though I didn't know what the ABA did, I really wanted it. I knew that there were other applicants, but felt fairly optimistic because Ken Burns was a fellow Northwestern Law graduate who had called Professor Trumbull about it. Although I did plan to stay with it for a while, I still thought that my future as a lawyer would be with a small firm back home in Peoria.

I got the job, and stayed at the ABA until 1980, with four years away with two other organizations, the National Urban Coalition and Common Cause. The ABA was just right for me, and I've often said that I was one of the luckiest people alive to have found it as my life's work. Ken Burns and I became good friends, and as he moved out of the Junior Bar, he advanced to a primary leadership position as secretary of the ABA on the association's Board.

The ABA People and My First Year

My office was at the American Bar Center, located next to the University of Chicago Law School at 1155 E. 60th Street. The ABA has moved its headquarters twice since I left in 1980 to buildings near and in downtown Chicago. I had a one-room office with my secretary, Marilyn Brendel, who sat at a desk near me.

Just across the hall was the Meetings Department; and a girl named Myrna, who would become my wife, sat at a desk just inside the door. (Her sister, Carol, had worked at the ABA, and had helped her get the job when she moved to live with her family in Chicago after leaving Lincoln Christian College in downstate Illinois.) I can vividly remember the happy time I first saw her. We began dating, and every time together was a grand one (she had her first libation at dinner with me, a grasshopper). But she's quick to say that I was off and on as a regular dater, which frustrated her.

The staff of the ABA was small, and several were middle-aged women who operated the machines that stamped out metal address plates, a function unheard of today. The executive director, Joe Stecher, was a lawyer from Ohio; and when I passed the bar, I was the fifth lawyer ever to be on the ABA staff. The total number of ABA staff was 30 or 40, and the lawyer membership was just about to cross the 90,000 mark. Both the membership and staff were small when I joined the staff, compared to growth it had experienced when I left in 1980.

The first months went by quickly, passing the bar exam, and working with top lawyers who were well known in their communities. The JBC's officers and members handled the substance of public policy positions. Although they didn't look to me for policy-making, I learned the ABA's policy-making process, and was responsible for coordinating all of the group's discussions and activities. I liked it.

The ABA staff members were pleasant, interesting people. Joe Stecher, who was in the executive director's position following a career as an Ohio lawyer, had lunch with an office colleague every day at the Windermere Hotel. Occasionally they would invite me along, and our conversations were helpful to me in learning about the association.

One of the finest persons on the staff was Ruth White, the administrative secretary who managed the affairs of the ABA Board of Governors. Ruth treated me like a son, in a way, but also respected me as a colleague. Ruth taught me a lot about "class," because she personified it. Her family personified it. Her older sister was Margaret Bourke-White, a world-class photographer who was the first woman photographer allowed to cover battlefields in World War II. Her own picture adorned the first issue of *Life*, and her photography in and outside of battles was legendary.

Ruth herself was low-keyed, but firm in judgment and efficiency. She taught me not to be in awe of the great lawyers I would meet, but respect and assist them. She was the first to tell me that the "servant-leader" term was the best description of association staff work. "The members expect you to have ideas and use your own best judgment," she would say. "That's being a leader. But always remember that they are the bosses, and they expect you to carry out their will, not yours. This is the hardest part of this work — to find that fine line of knowing when to make recommendations and apply leadership, while also staying in the background and implementing their policy decisions." When a West Virginia lawyer, Bert Early, became the executive director a few years later, that phrase was his guiding principle.

Socially, the best on the staff were the *ABA Journal* editor, Louise Child, and her assistant, Rowland Young. I spent a lot of time with them at lunch and in their office, learning about the lawyer-members and leaders at the ABA. While Ruth never wished to discuss personalities, Louise and Rowland always had time and liked talking about who was who.

They taught me about the politics of the ABA, how it had a history of being rock-ribbed conservative and how changes were underway. Loyd Wright, a recent past president from California, and lawyer to Hollywood stars, had been a member of the John Birch Society, and still exerted some ultra-conservative influence on the association. But times were changing, and new blood was coming along to counter the arch conservatives. The president just preceding my arrival at the ABA was Charles Rhyne who, in 1962 won the *Baker vs. Carr* case (one man, one vote) before the U.S. Supreme Court, and was Richard Nixon's closest law school friend (he told interesting stories about Nixon, like how he always was afraid he was going to flunk out of Duke Law School). Other highly respected leaders were Whitney North Seymour, Sr., one of New York City's most prominent blue-ribbon lawyers and an educational and cultural icon; and Sylvester C. Smith, Jr., senior vice president and general counsel of the Prudential Insurance Company. These men were basically conservative and not liberals in today's sense of the word. But they were progressive and determined to change the ABA from the ultra-right days to a mainstream, influential institution.

Everybody on the staff was not so welcoming. One was a humorless fellow who did administrative work and acted like he was the executive director. He resented me because I didn't treat him like he was the boss. He was so unfriendly that it was difficult to relate to him. I even arrived at my office one morning to find that he had had my filing cabinets removed without my knowing it. I could never understand why he took them other than he thought he might find something to embarrass me.

My encounters with him were so stressful that my upper back shoulders froze, and I landed in the hospital for a couple of days. My favorite visitor was my future wife. When Joe Stecher intervened, that stopped him cold, and he didn't come near me again, other than to sneer when we passed in the hall. He didn't last long after Bert Early, my future boss, became executive director. This was the only personnel problem in my first job. I learned from this, however, that no work is immune from contemptuous colleagues.

As I met the great staff members and ABA leaders, I was becoming a part of the changing ABA. I began to see it as my work home, and thoughts of returning to Peoria to practice law began to fade. I wasn't sure, however, what my future would or could be there beyond the Junior Bar position, and having passed the bar exam I knew that I wouldn't be satisfied in it indefinitely.

Washington, D.C. is in the Works

A few weeks after I started to work, I met the director of the Washington Office, Donald Channell, who was relatively new himself at the ABA. Don was formerly the chief lobbyist of the Georgia Chamber of Commerce. Before he arrived, the ABA Washington Office consisted of two people in two small rooms. One answered questions about the ABA and assisted its members with arrangements with they visited Washington to testify on legislation. The other was exclusively the staff person for the ABA Tax Section, and her work was liaison with the House Ways and Means Committee and the Senate Finance Committee, both of which called on the members of the Tax Section for their tax expertise. All other ABA lobbying and legislative liaison was by volunteer members. The new ABA leadership wanted a savvy lobbyist who would, working with the volunteer members, serve as liaison to Capitol Hill. Don was just the right one for this, with his experience as a lobbyist in Georgia.

Don came to the Bar Center occasionally, and would meet with me to become acquainted with the young lawyers' work. He wanted to enlist them to help him in Washington, and I became his contact for reaching out to them. As we came to know each other, I kiddingly asked him if he could use an extra hand in Washington, and "boy, I sure would like to do that." His response was immediate. He said, yes, he would be looking for another person because the Board of Governors that day had authorized him to hire an assistant. And, yes, he would like me to do it. I could hardly believe this. My reply was that I hadn't even been to Washington, had no experience doing legislative work, and I had been just kidding. Surely he didn't mean it. He said that he easily could teach me the ropes, and that because he already had worked with me, he knew I could do the job. I would add a special value, he said, because I knew the young lawyers and even some ABA leaders better than he, and I knew all of the ins and outs of the headquarters office.

So we headed together to Joe Stecher's office to ask for his approval. He said yes, but it couldn't be immediately. I had to continue helping the young lawyers get ready for the big annual meeting in August, which happened to be scheduled for Washington, D. C.; and I had to give them plenty of time to find a replacement. So, we agreed on the end of 1960, just after the Presidential election between Kennedy and Nixon.

This gave new, vibrant life to my ABA situation. It was bittersweet, though, because Myrna and I were dating, and the move might unhappily change that relationship.

My First ABA Annual Meeting

Most of the summer's work was getting ready for the ABA annual meeting. This was always the year's major event, and the young lawyers had an important role in it, with top-notch speakers and a full schedule of educational meetings.

Flying into Washington for the first time was exciting for me, even an emotional experience. As we approached Washington National Airport along the Potomac River, the entire city opened up before us. Just seeing the real Washington Monument spiraling to the sky was exhilarating, having seen its pictures hundreds of times. It still is.

The annual meeting was Myrna's big event of the year. The staff of the Meetings Department would spend an entire year preparing for it. It required making arrangements for all of the hotels, taking attendee reservations for rooms, allocating suites for officers, section leaders, and on and on. So, while I had to arrive before the meeting started, Myrna and her department colleagues were in Washington even earlier than I.

The highlight of the meeting for me was attending the opening speech by President Eisenhower at the Shoreham Hotel. This was exciting stuff, and it was hard to believe that I was actually there, listening to the president in person; and that I soon would be heading to Washington to live and work.

After the annual meeting, I began winding down my work in Chicago and looking forward to my new job. Myrna and I continued dating, but, as she has reminded me, we did in time "break up" (only to be reunited early the next year). Coming up was the national election on November 6, and this event, particularly after the Kennedy-Nixon debate, was front and center on everybody's mind.

I Learn My First Real-Life Political Lesson

A law school friend, Dick Green, asked me be a Republican poll watcher with him in a Northside Chicago ward. In Chicago, it was difficult to find real Republicans to help in elections.

Although I often had heard through newspapers and talk around town how bizarre Chicago elections were, I wasn't prepared for what Dick and I observed in the November 6th election. From the time we arrived at the polling place until it closed, we were faced with contempt by all of the election officials, including the so-called Republican judge, who treated us with as much hostility as did the Democrat. We were told to stand in a spot by the wall and stay there, or the police would arrest us for interfering with the election.

Policemen would arrive with voters and enter the election booths to "assist" them, all authorized by law if the voter "needed assistance," according to the judges. Most of the violations were by judges not verifying that people were eligible to vote. When they were challenged, one judge replied, "Let them challenge, because it doesn't mean anything anyway." Another judge said that they make their own rules. When Dick told the judges that such blatant illegal conduct like we were observing could lead to prosecution, one replied, "Send me to jail, then."

The local precinct captain was allowed to participate by leafing through the voters' binder, a clear violation of law. When this was challenged, the captain demanded that we be sent out of the building. Fortunately the policeman didn't do it, but the captain continued his illegal activity.

We observed so many irregularities that I sent a letter on ABA stationery, with Joe Stecher's authorization, to the Civic Committee on Elections. I didn't receive an answer.

If anybody ever has questioned whether Chicago elections were rigged over the years, they should have poll watched. They would have seen first-hand the "Chicago Way" in politics, as mentioned frequently by columnist John Kass in the *Chicago Tribune*. Dick Green and I had our best Chicago political lesson that day and learned that, yes, there is a "Chicago Way." It should be noted that local political machines have not been uncommon in America. A look at Tammany Hall in New York, Crump in Tennessee and Pendergast in Kansas City are prime exanples of those.

Soon after the election, I packed up and moved to Washington. Fortunately, one of my best law school friends, Ron Carlson, was serving as an intern in the Georgetown Law School's elite Trial Institute. I was able to share an apartment with him and his roommate, Bob Erickson, on Columbia Pike in Arlington, Virginia. Bob was staff counsel to a House subcommittee that was investigating entertainment rating agencies. The Nielsen Company, which rated TV shows (and still does), was the focus of the investigation. So, from my own roommates I began to learn first-hand how the system functioned on Capitol Hill in 1960.

* A footnote about basic training: My company commander, 2ⁿᵈ Lt. William Hise, who had an interest in becoming a lawyer, and I became friends during my training. Although commanding officers do not fraternize with basic recruits, we did talk occasionally about our mutual interest in law. I disappointed him, however, when I presented arms wrong during the graduation formation. Even after several rehearsals, I managed to use the wrong hand. It was instantly recognized because I was on the front row of the formation, just in front of the reviewing stand. Lt. Hise wasn't happy, to say the least, and he held his head in his hands in dismay. It kept our company from getting first place. However, this embarrassing and consequential mishap did not keep us from becoming good friends, and I was pleased to be a reference for his law school admission.

CHAPTER THREE

MY SECOND ABA JOB
OUR WEDDING
THE BERLIN CRISIS

WASHINGTON, D.C. 1960–1961

After settling into my new apartment on Columbia Pike in Arlington, Virginia, and the office on the fourth floor of 1120 Connecticut Avenue, I returned to Illinois for Christmas. Myrna and I didn't see each other then because we weren't trying to stay together after I moved to Washington.

Myrna and I both were unhappy about our situation, and there always is some uneasiness when confronted with a new work and living environment. Fortunately, Don Channell made the transition easy. Don and his wife, Betty, welcomed me as if I were a member of their family. They invited me to their home, and always included me in parties and even events outside their home. This made my new life immensely easier.

My First Legislative Issue, Which Was Don's Top Priority

Don Channell's top legislative priority was House Resolution (H.R.) 10, the proposed Self-Employed Individuals Tax Retirement Act. At that time there were no tax benefits for self-employed individuals who wished to save for retirement. Corporations, large and small, could establish defined retirement plans (pensions), with funds set aside tax free-for the benefit of employees. No IRAs or 401(k) s were available for anybody, including the self-employed. So lawyers, doctors, dentists, barbers, and all other self-employed individuals did not have the same retirement tax benefits as corporate employees.

H.R. 10, or the Keogh Bill as it was called, would change that. The bill provided that the self-employed could set aside limited tax-deferred funds for retirement. It was similar to today's 401(k) programs. The ABA, American Medical Association, American Dental Association, American Farm Bureau, and dozens of other associations of self-employed united to form a group called the American Thrift Assembly to lobby for H.R. 10. The group had two unpaid co-chairmen, Joseph "Jigs" Donohue, a prominent well-connected Democrat, and Ralph Becker, an equally prominent Republican. In lobbying, it's always important, and often essential, to have active support of prominent individuals of both parties. Both were practicing lawyers in Washington and well known on Capitol Hill. The Assembly hired a director, Robert Ansheles, to work full time, managing the campaign to enact the bill.

You would think such a bill would be a "no-brainer," and that, in fairness to the self-employed, it would be enacted without difficulty. Not true. The labor unions fought it tooth and nail. Their view: The self-employed professional and business people made so much money that they didn't need retirement assistance, and that it would drain the federal treasury of funds needed for social programs. The bill did pass in 1962, and it was an achievement par excellence for the American Thrift Assemby.

Of all the association lobbyists urging passage, Don worked the hardest. It was his labor of love. But the unions, while finally giving up on defeating the concept, did succeed in limiting the yearly contribution per individual; and, if the lawyer (or other self-employed person) set one up for him/herself, a plan must be set up also for all of the lawyer's employees. While most self-employed were pleased overall with its passage, many didn't utilize it because of the relatively small amount allowed and the all-employee requirement. A few years after it was enacted, the Keogh Bill's yearly amount was increased, and it became the hallmark retirement plan for the self-employed. H.R. 10 was the front-runner to IRAs and 401(k)s.

During my first few weeks of working with Don, I went with him to all of his meetings on the Keogh Bill. Representative Eugene Keogh, the bill's chief House sponsor, was the first House member I met (except, of course, Bob Michel from Peoria, whom I already knew). Mr. Keogh was a leading member of the House Ways and Means Committee, where all tax matters in Congress originate. He was a formal, dapper guy, always a fashion piece with a dark suit and heavily starched white collars. As a lawyer himself, he was committed to this bill.

The Senate sponsor was Senator George Smathers from Miami. He too was a dapper fellow, and mentioned by some as "Gorgeous George." He was an influential member of the Senate Finance Committee, and as a former House member with John Kennedy, was one of Kennedy's closest

Congressional friends. Meeting him right off the bat in Washington was an experience. He didn't act with the curtness of Mr. Keogh — he was more down to earth and friendlier, and would give you more time.

Basic Lobbying Principles

Don taught me quickly about principles of Washington lobbying. What did I learn in my first month in Washington? Although not frozen in stone, generally for a bill to be enacted:

1. Have committed, influential lead sponsors in both the Senate and House, preferably members of the relevant Congressional committees where the bill is considered.

2. Have influential people back home who know the legislative sponsors well, and who can convince them to fight for the bill. These might be colleagues, friends and campaign contributors.

3. It's always helpful to have an effective coalition of various groups with constituents who are united in supporting your bill.

4. You must be able to provide the arguments, solid information and data that the legislators can rely on as accurate in building the case. You must never lie to or mislead a member of Congress: that will be sudden death for all time and on all issues that are important to you.

5. It's important to know the staff of the respective legislators, in both their offices and the committees.

6. Do not give up if your cause is the right one. If you can't get everything you want, be willing to compromise. Another time will come to amend the law if necessary or desirable. In other words, get what you can and be grateful. The legislative process truly is like "making sausage." After all the ingredients go in, you're never sure what's coming out at the other end.

Getting Around Washington and the Kennedy Inaugural Ball

My first visit on Capitol Hill was with Representative Robert Michel, the congressman from Peoria. I had first met him when he was the administrative assistant to Representative Harold Velde, the successor to Everett

Dirksen who was in the House before the Senate. Wishing to be a high school Capitol intern, I had applied for an appointment through Mr. Velde. Bob Michel was my contact in Velde's office for this. Bob warned me that my appointment was unlikely because the Democrats controlled the House. He was right. (Later, at Bradley University, Mr. Velde's son, Pete, was my fraternity pledge father and debate partner...the Bradley team was one of nation's best, and Pete and I helped secure that with our wins.)

While Bob Michel worked for Velde, who had been an avid chairman of the House Un-American Activities Committee investigating alleged subversive communists, he didn't carry the Velde philosophy with him as a successor representative. Although he was conservative, he sought bipartisanship when he could. When he later became Minority Leader of the House, he was known for his ability to work well with "the other side of the aisle."

I was proud to know Bob Michel. We both were from Peoria, and had the same Midwestern outlook. He was elected Minority Leader of the House in 1981 because of the especially high regard his colleagues had for him, and because he knew how to get things done. When I arrived in Washington in 1960, Bob had been a congressman for five years. His administrative assistant (an A.A. is the congressman's chief staff) was Jim Cromwell, a congenial, responsive man. We became good friends, and he became my chief contact person when I wanted information from Capitol Hill.

The month of January, 1961 was abuzz with the coming Kennedy inauguration. It was a time of hope and optimism for many, and Democrats couldn't have been more thrilled. The White House had been occupied by Republican Eisenhower for eight years, and the Democrats were chomping at the bit to regain power. While President Eisenhower was a popular person, a hero in fact, the country was unhappy and tensions were high. The country was in a recession, large numbers were out of jobs, and farm income was dwindling. The Soviet Union was an imposing threat, and the so-called Cold War (war of words between the Soviet Union and United States over which country was strongest and best) was raging. The Soviet premier, Nikita Khrushchev, had proclaimed that Russia would bury the United States and its Western allies. The 1950s had been a decade of civil unrest because of segregation in the schools and public places. In *Brown vs. Board of Education*, the Supreme Court had overturned separate but equal schools as unconstitutional, which required public schools to be integrated. The federal government had to enforce the decision with troops in the South, and there were massive demonstrations for equality. But official segregation still was in effect in the South.

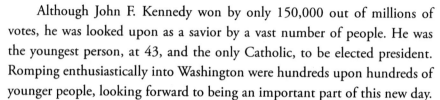

Although John F. Kennedy won by only 150,000 out of millions of votes, he was looked upon as a savior by a vast number of people. He was the youngest person, at 43, and the only Catholic, to be elected president. Romping enthusiastically into Washington were hundreds upon hundreds of younger people, looking forward to being an important part of this new day. I was amazed to be there. Whether Republican or Democrat, it was an exhilarating time to be experiencing a young activist taking over from an elderly father-figure. The time was considered to be "Camelot," after the legendary time of King Arthur, when everything was supposedly beautiful and filled with hope and new life.

Jim Cromwell gave me two tickets to the inaugural ball, and of course this was thrilling just to think about. I was astonished at the mess it was. Our location at the Armory was so noisy and crowded that my blind date and I didn't stay long. It was too crowded to dance, and even difficult to get close enough to hear Frank Sinatra and the cast of thousands who were entertaining. I do remember vividly seeing JFK and Jackie, who were looking out over the crowd from a reviewing stand. We were directly in front of the stand, and it was easy to tell how breathtaking she was in her flowing white evening dress. We heard her say *very softly* to JFK, "There's Bobby," and, turning around, Robert Kennedy was a few feet from us, surrounded by dozens. Yes, a mess. But, hey, I went to the inaugural ball of President John F. Kennedy, and it's something always to be remembered.

An experience that always will stand out was at my first Capitol Hill reception in the "Senate Caucus Room." Every other year the ABA held a reception for senators and representatives in the beautiful Caucus Room of the old Senate office building that later was named for Senator Richard B. Russell of Georgia. Senator Russell was an icon in the Senate, elected in 1931, and the leader of the coalition of conservative Democratic and Republican senators. The Southern Democrats had controlled Congress for years. Before becoming a senator, Richard Russell had been governor of Georgia, and was an arch segregationist. He fought all civil rights bills and frequently led filibusters on behalf of the southern contingent. But he wasn't alone. He was simply one of many segregationists in the Senate at that time; and was respected by most senators, even revered by some, regardless of their politics. Don Channell, as a native Georgian who had known him for some time, introduced me to him as he entered the room with his staff entourage. He was very congenial, and stood with me for what seemed a long time even though many others were standing around to shake his hand. It was like I was the only one who mattered to him, regardless of who was waiting, and this clearly was the mark of an old-time politician, "par excellence."

What I remember most in meeting him was my first Washington experience of "talking in the ear" (my phrase) of a politician. Because of all the loud chatter at receptions, that's what you had to do — get up close and talk into the ear. It was as if you had some very important things to say, and you didn't want anybody else to hear it. Well, Senator Russell talked into my ear, and I felt very important (of course he wasn't telling me anything very important). Then I talked into his, and he invited me to stop by his office when I had a chance. He told me that he respected the American Bar Association and was pleased that his friend Don now had help. That brief time with Senator Russell, perhaps the most influential senator of his time, is vivid with me. I would do a lot of "talking into ears" at future receptions and political fund-raisers, but none as impressionable as that night at my first Capitol Hill cocktail party.

Myrna and I Are Engaged

Myrna and I kept in touch. We wrote letters back and forth, and most of the time I was hoping she could join me in Washington. I didn't know how she would respond if I asked her to visit me. It took me a while to get the nerve to ask her to see me again. But when I decided to do it, I knew that I wanted to ask her to marry me, and sent her a ticket.

It's hard to explain how happy I was when she said that she would come to Washington. I remember well the day she arrived at the (then) National Airport. She remembers it too. She was wearing a hat that was in style then because of its similarity to those worn by Jackie Kennedy, and as beautiful as she was, she didn't look just like I had remembered without the hat. I said something about it, and she hasn't worn a hat since.

I proposed with a red rose over dinner at an Italian restaurant just off Connecticut Avenue. I had planned to put the ring on the rose, but was so nervous that I forgot to do it. Fortunately for me, considering how our Chicago dating became somewhat erratic, and she always felt I wasn't around at gift-giving time, she said yes. So, we were to have a new beginning at our first of October wedding, and happily with three adult children and six grandsons, we celebrated 50 years together in 2011.

Myrna stayed in Chicago during the summer, and we began making our plans — she for the wedding, and I for where we would live.

The Bay of Pigs

While America was filled with hope over "Camelot," and seemingly a "new beginning," the tensions between the Soviet Union and the United States were raging. The Cold War was permeating American life, and always lurking was the threat of nuclear war. It was serious enough for schools to conduct air-raid drills called "Duck and Cover." Students wouldn't file outside, but would drop to the floor, under desks, and cover their heads when the siren sounded. Not that this would have done any good, but it did make us feel safer. The public also was reminded of where to find bomb shelters that had been built during WWII.

Against this background, Fidel Castro, Cuba's Communist dictator, was considered a threat to the United States by the Central Intelligence Agency. After the success of the Cuban Revolution in 1959 with the overthrow of Batista, Cuba was a Communist country on our doorstep. It began to acquire Soviet tanks and tank destroyers, Soviet howitzers and other artillery of all kinds, plus light bombers and jet fighters.

In 1960, before JFK was elected, the U.S. government, led by the CIA, began planning an invasion of Cuba by Cuban exiles. American troops would not be involved, but training exiles would be on American soil, and one of the main bases for that was on Useppa Island, Florida. It was supported by the Joint Chiefs of Staff as a covert operation, and one week after his inauguration, President Kennedy reluctantly gave the go-ahead. But, at its first attempt, the invasion fell apart, the exiles were defeated by Soviet-bloc trained Cuban revolutionaries, and a rebellion of Cubans against Castro did not materialize. The invasion provoked international outrage, humiliated JFK, and led to the removal of John Foster Dulles as director of the CIA.

I cite that bit of history, and there were other situations, to show how tense and unsettled America was during my first year in Washington. Interestingly, though, the Bay of Pigs didn't mean a lot to me or much of the country at the time of the invasion. Nobody knew what was going on until it was over. However, all hell broke loose afterward, and anti-American events around the world got our attention. There were anti-U.S. demonstrations in Latin America and Europe; and JFK was severely criticized at home by Cuban exile leaders for agreeing to such a feeble effort without U.S. forces, and by anti-war leaders who were appalled at the entire idea.

The 1961 Summer

Summers in Washington are hot-hot and oppressively humid. At that time in the 1960s, Congress took many weeks off, beginning in late June and returning after Labor Day. Some staff were still around, and the legislators would come and go, but not much was going on.

Don and Bob Ansheles were not letting up on pressing for H.R. 10, and were working primarily with the staffs of members of the House Ways and Means Committee and the Senate Finance Committee. All federal tax bills must first be considered by the Ways and Means Committee, but it's important also to keep information flowing to the Senate Finance Committee senators and their staffs. In fact, it was generally the informed lobbyists who kept both House members and senators apprised of what each body was doing. I had always assumed that there would be ongoing organized liaison between the respective committees on both sides of the Capitol, but soon learned that wasn't true. *We* were the liaison. So Don and Bob were busy going back and forth, but I didn't have a specific summer legislative assignment.

Meeting Bill Foley: Don suggested that I start making the rounds on Capitol Hill, and introduce myself to key staff members. He suggested that I start with the House Judiciary Committee because he barely knew its general counsel, Bill Foley, and the ABA frequently had issues before the committee. Further, the committee's long-time chairman, Emanuel Celler of New York, wasn't fond of the ABA with its ultra-conservative reputation. Don believed that I could help by asking Mr. Foley to have lunch and tell him about our relatively new office and ABA agenda.

I was surprised when Mr. Foley agreed to have lunch with me. He was not only well known on the Hill; he was considered a strategic mastermind in getting Judiciary Committee bills passed by the full House. (He was Congressman Celler's chief aide on the House floor in managing passage of the Civil Rights Act of 1964. I was awe while, from the House gallery, watching him skillfully maneuver among House members during the debates, giving instructions and information. I would watch him many times.)

Washington then was a martini-lunch town. He and I broke the ice with each other by having a couple of them. We became well acquainted, and from that first lunch on, I was lucky to have the benefit of Bill's advice and insights. He was a master legislative strategist, knowing more than most about how the House of Representatives worked.

I soon learned that business lunches were an everyday affair in Washington, and I suppose everywhere else that business was conducted. Along with them came the martini. When I tried one or two, I would be lethargic in the middle of the afternoon. So, after several months of enjoying my lunch times, I had to lay off of them. It always amazed me, however, that so many others could have drinks at lunch, and it didn't seem to bother their effective work at all. That was in the 1960s, and I think it has moderated greatly over the years.

The Gomiens: I made the rounds on Capitol Hill meeting more staff members, and probably the most notable were John Gomien and his wife, Glee. They were administrative assistant and executive secretary respectively for Senator Everett Dirksen. John had worked for Senator Dirksen since the senator arrived in Washington as a House member, and was as influential a staff member as any on the Hill. John was located in the senator's Senate Office building office, and Glee was in his Minority Leader's office just off the Senate floor.

Because the ABA's office had had such little presence in Washington, I was somewhat of a mystery to John. Because Senator Dirksen was so important as the Republican Senate Leader, he was besieged constantly by national lobbyists and Illinois constituents who wanted access to him. And, to boot, everybody, and I mean *everybody* wanted Senator Dirksen to speak at their meetings. He was the Senate's master of oratory, the Oracle from Pekin, Illinois, and just plain fun to hear. So, at first, John gave me only a few minutes to say hello. He did agree to meet with me, however, and was friendly about it. I thought that was because I was from Peoria, which was in the senator's old House district. To make matters worse in my case, the senator had been angry with the ABA because its Federal Judiciary Committee that evaluates federal judge nominees had given one of his nominations a low rating for service on the bench. It didn't take long to learn that Dirksen wasn't the only senator who had a distaste for the ABA because of poor judicial ratings it gave some nominees. The ratings would be reviewed by the Justice Department and the Senate Judiciary Committee that approved nominations. After all, federal judgeships were political plums. But John did give me a few minutes to get acquainted, and that first meeting began a relationship that I often found helpful. John, a quiet, reserved man, would be friendly to me, but that was about it.

My association with John's wife, Glee, was a different matter altogether. She sat just inside the Senator Dirksen's Capitol office, and was the only person in that small reception area. I called on her occasionally when I was in the Capitol. Neither she nor John was from Peoria, but she always enjoyed hearing tidbits about it. The first time I came face to face with the senator was when I had stopped by one day, and he came roaring into his reception room. He was always in a hurry, and always rumpled with his hair sticking in all directions. He took a quick look at me, grunted hello, and kept going into his office. There was no time for pleasantries. That changed over time, particularly when Myrna and I would attend so-called Illinois Society dinners, where we could talk with him and would have our picture taken together. "Society" dinners are events for Washington-area residents to socialize with others from their individual home state. They are led by prominent Washingtonians who have roots in those states, and are the one yearly event when the entire state's Congressional delegation will attend.

Over the years, many times Glee would give Senator Dirksen a message from me about an ABA position, and I always knew he would see it because of her. She occasionally arranged appointments with him when an ABA officer was in town, but she and I agreed that would be seldom, and then only on an issue that the ABA considered especially important.

Rehoboth Beach: That summer on the East Coast turned out to be more fun than I had expected. Ron, my roommate, had introduced me to several of his friends at the Georgetown Law Center, where he was enrolled in its advanced criminal trial practice program (which led to his national prominence in criminal law at the University of Georgia Law School). These friends were mostly Georgetown law professors, including A. Kenneth Pye, the program's director. Every year these guys rented a house for the summer at Rehoboth Beach, Delaware, and they invited me to be part of the group. While nothing ever got out of hand at these outings, we all acted like children at times because we were so happy to be there. Ken was the moderately serious one on the scene, but fortunately his arrival at the house wasn't inhibiting.

I found an apartment for Myrna and me at the same complex on Columbia Pike in Arlington where I was staying with Ron and Bob. But, as summer ended, Ron's trial practice program ended, and Bob had decided to move back to Oklahoma. Luckily, I was invited by Ken to live in a spare room in his house in Northwest Washington until we were married.

Ken Pye: Ken was another exceptional, indeed brilliant, person who had questions about the importance and even the legitimacy of the ABA as the representative of the American lawyer. He considered it irrelevant. As we came to know each other, he decided to give the Criminal Law Section a try, liked it, and ultimately became a council member. And, as the ABA began to change its approaches with enlightened new leaders, he took an interest in the Legal Education Section.

Ken died of cancer at the age of 62. But no memoir of mine would be complete without saying more about him. Saying that he was brilliant is an understatement. With his close friends, he was friendly with a dry sense of humor. But he was a tough-as-nails, no-nonsense leader as well, admired by all who knew and worked with him. After Georgetown, he served for 21 years with Duke University as professor of law, university counsel, director of international studies, dean of the law school, chancellor, and its acting president. He was heralded as helping transform Duke from a regional school to one of national prominence.

When he went to SMU in 1987 (interestingly, as a strongly committed Catholic) as a college president known for producing results, it was in the wake of a scandal provoked by payments to football players that had been made with the knowledge of the university's board. The football program was banned for the 1987 season and sat out the entire 1988 season.

Ken was credited with rebuilding the university's athletic program while improving its academic standing. I was no longer then with the ABA, and was out of touch with him. But I called him to congratulate him when he took the job, and asked how he, the consummate academic he was, could ever undertake the rebuilding of a major nationally prominent football program. (Of course, at Duke he had presided over nationally prominent basketball.) He simply said that at a school of SMU's worldwide standing and size, football was important for the school's unity and spirit, *and,* with some humor in his voice, its fundraising. He, the academic man, was a practical man as well.

Why do I devote this much space in my memoir to one person like Kenneth Pye? Because he was one of the most uniquely gifted persons intellectually, practically, spiritually, and personally whom I've known. It was my *special privilege* to have known him so well, and to have benefited personally from his friendship and generosity. I also will talk about other gifted individuals I've had the privilege of knowing. In a sense, this memoir is a celebration of the lives of many people whose contributions have made lasting marks on society, and with whom I've had the opportunity to associate.

Congressman Bob Michel and more summer fun: Bob Michel was a singer, and a good one. He sang in a quartet on Capitol Hill, and, while not a professional, could have been. He and his close Congressional friend, Harold Collier of Berwyn, Illinois would sing some evenings at a downtown Washington rathskeller. Jim Cromwell invited me to meet them for dinner and singing, and while I didn't sing with them, they made me feel at home. People would gather around, and sometimes join in, but Bob was so good that most just wanted to listen to him. Neither Harold's nor Bob's wives had moved to Washington, so these were stag evenings.

Getting to know ABA leaders: During this summer I was able to become acquainted with top ABA leaders who lived in or visited Washington. Since the Washington office was so small, it was easy to spend some time with them. The notables I first met were *Charles Rhyne* and *Whitney North Seymour, Sr.*

Charles Rhyne, a Washington lawyer had been the ABA president in 1957–1958 (the term ran from the August Annual Meeting to the next August). Charlie had been the youngest ABA president at age 45. He was particularly noteworthy because although several presidents immediately preceding him were distinguished lawyers and judges, some, like Birch Society member Loyd Wright, were also known as extreme conservatives. Charles Rhyne helped break that mold. A successful corporate lawyer, he spent his career meeting tough challenges that greatly impacted society. Just before I met him, he had argued before the U.S. Supreme Court the landmark case of *Baker v. Carr*, the legislative reapportionment case that established the one-man, one-vote principle. As president of the Bar Association of the District of Columbia, he was able to strike the word "white" from its constitution, and as a new trustee of Duke University, his alma mater, he successfully fought the school's segregation policies. He was particularly interested in world peace through the rule of law, and in international affairs. His ABA hallmark was in creating "Law Day," as a counter event to Russia's "May Day" when armored tanks paraded in Moscow, and he served on many presidentially appointed international commissions.

Having said all of these noteworthy things about Mr. Rhyne, perhaps the most interesting was his close friendship in law school with Richard Nixon. He told about that friendship in a *D.C. Bar* interview:

> While working my way through law school as a carpenter, I ran a nail into the side of my hand that became infected, causing me to miss many classes. I had bone surgery and lost a number of bones in my right hand. In class, we were seated alphabetically and seated next to me was a student from California, who was scared to death he'd flunk out every day, by the name of Richard Milhaus Nixon. I spent most of the year in the hospital, and Nixon said, "You're going to have a tough time, and I will help you every night that you miss a class." And he did, or I never would have gotten through that year.

> *Bar Report, April/May 1998*

Another of notable lawyers was New York's **Whitney North Seymour, Sr.**, who was the ABA president during my first year in Washington. He often would stop by our office when he was in Washington. Just as most who knew him, I was in awe whenever he entered the room. He was stately, distinguished, and dignified; New York Wall Street, but a Midwesterner born in Chicago and educated at the University of Wisconsin. He was managing partner of Simpson, Thatcher and Bartlett, and was known as one of *the* prominent New

York lawyers whose stature nationwide was unquestioned.

Whitney North Seymour was not just a highly successful corporate lawyer. He believed that the unpopular, as well as the popular, should be provided counsel; and throughout his career, carried out that conviction with action. On appeal, he represented a young black Communist who had been convicted of violating a Georgia anti-insurrection law, which dated from Reconstruction. The conviction and sentence of 18 years were based on Communist literature found in the defendant's room. Mr. Seymour won the case before the U.S. Supreme Court on the basis that the evidence didn't support the conviction. That was Whitney North Seymour. He and his wife, Lola, were active in New York City civic life, and his main personal interests were in the *arts* and preserving *historical places* there.

Regardless of how busy Mr. Seymour was in his practice, he was always immediately at our side when we needed him, and, as ABA president, placed high priority on our Washington work.

And Now, a General Observation

So far I've written about many individuals who came into my life when I joined the staff of the ABA. Where else would I ever have lived the work and life I entered when I took that first job as Junior Bar Conference administrative assistant, without even knowing where I was headed? Where else would I have become acquainted with all of these notable and contributive people who, in virtually all cases, were making a difference in national and international life? I held these people and my experiences with them in awe, and still do. It never stopped, from the time I began working at the ABA in 1959 until my retirement from the National Association of Independent Insurers in 1996, and finally my retirement from my last corporate board meeting at Harleysville Insurance Co. in 2007. Throughout my entire working and family life, from Peoria to Washington and back to Illinois, I've been thankful for my good fortune. Not that there weren't difficult days and years. Like everybody else's experiences, there were plenty of those. But, almost by chance, I found the most rewarding and fulfilling professional work possible for me, and that's the story of this memoir. I've never stopped thinking about that. Everybody has a story to tell, and I believe it's not uncommon for fulfilling careers to develop unplanned, just as mine.

Problems in Berlin

While I was having a good time in 1961, planning for a wedding in October, getting to know Washington, and frolicking on the beach, the president of the United States was facing severe problems with the Soviets regarding the status of Berlin. During the 1950s, a steady outflow of refugees from the Soviet occupation zone of East Germany to the West took place. Millions of professional and business people were escaping Communism, most easily through Berlin, and the flow was escalating. Soviet Premier Nikita Khrushchev issued an ultimatum giving the Western Powers in Berlin, the United States, Britain and France, six months to agree to withdraw from Berlin and make it a free, demilitarized city. His objective was to get the Allies out of Berlin so that East Germany could stop the flow of refugees. The Allies objected so strenuously that the Soviets withdrew their ultimatum, and agreed to meet with the Western Powers to try to resolve the issues surrounding Berlin.

By 1961, nothing had been resolved, and Khrushchev issued a new ultimatum that the Western Powers must be out of West Berlin by December 31, 1961. This led to President Kennedy making statements about the United States wanting peace and acknowledging the Soviets' "historical concerns" about their own security in Central and Eastern Europe. He said that the United States wanted peace, but "would not surrender," all of which caused more confusion and an escalating confrontation. While talking peace and some conciliation with the Soviets by wanting to resume talks, he began requesting from Congress an increased call-up of the U.S. Armed Forces and ordered that draft calls be doubled. He requested also the authority to order to active duty ready reserve units and individual reservists. He even requested funds to identify structures that could be used for fall-out shelters in case of attack, and to stock those shelters with necessities.

Standing by its ultimatum and signaling strength, the Soviets and East Germans began assembling materials to build a long, high permanent wall to separate West and East Germany. They saw this as a practical way of stopping the outward flow of the best East German talent. As the wall was being built, the top American military general was recommending that tanks with bulldozer mounts be used to knock down parts of the wall. But Secretary of State Dean Rusk took the position that "Berlin is not a vital interest which would warrant determined recourse to force to protect and sustain." In the meantime, the call-up of troops was proceeding, tanks were being deployed to the wall, and the Soviets and East Germans were increasing their build-up on the east side of the wall.

Although I had been in the Illinois National Guard, and my name was registered with a Reserve control group in Pennsylvania when I moved from Illinois to Washington, I wasn't thinking about being called into the service. The news reported that the armed services were being filled with thousands of new recruits, and this didn't apply to me. Talks were going on, and some political commentators didn't seem overly concerned. The Soviets were known for "saber rattling" (an ostentatious display of force with the threat of using it), and this was merely an example of that. It simply wasn't going to happen to me. But it did, and I'll discuss that later.

Our Wedding

In late September, excitement was building for our October wedding in Chicago. The standoff on Berlin was still taking place, but the National Guard servicemen such as I still weren't seemingly in line for active duty. Sadly, though, five weeks before the wedding, Myrna's dad, Harlan, had a severe heart attack while playing catch with Myrna in a neighboring school yard. It was so bad that he would be bedridden in the hospital for five weeks, and this obviously dampened our spirits. But we were thrilled that he was alive; and fortunately he was able to leave the hospital in time to attend the wedding. Happier yet, he recovered well enough to return to his mail route soon after that.

Our wedding day was warm, with light rain. Everything was in place except that Myrna, at home in her finery, had been forgotten. It seemed that everybody responsible for *getting her to the church on time* was involved in getting Harlan there, and overlooked the bride herself. So, the poor gal wound up arriving at the church in an uncle's dirty old car.

But once she arrived, looking spectacularly beautiful, the day flowed perfectly. Her young cousin, Scott, and my two-and-a-half year old niece, Jane, were splendid in his tux and her fall-colored dress. Myrna's mom, Madge, an excellent seamstress, made all of the bridesmaids' dresses. The church was filled with dozens of friends and relatives from downstate Illinois, and a few, including ABA officials, from Chicago. Myrna's brother-in-law, Don Browning, a distinguished professor at the University of Chicago, and our good friend, Rev. Jim Stockdale, presided. Both were Disciples of Christ ministers.

Considering the times and our family culture then, there was no big cocktail reception with a meal and dancing. Coffee, punch and cake in the church basement were it. But we had a lot of fun, and we were particularly happy that Harlan could be there with us.

Our honeymoon was in Colonial Williamsburg, Virginia, the pre-Revolutionary War reconstructed town near Richmond. We were able to relax there, eat great food, and tour an interesting place.

Service During the Berlin Crisis

On my first day back at the office, I detected something different in everybody's "welcome back." I discovered why when I opened the big armed services envelope on my desk. There were orders to report to active duty. I was to report to the 150th Armored Cavalry Division of the West Virginia National Guard, which had been ordered to Fort Meade, Maryland, on November 1. The heads of all my office friends were peering in the door, wondering exactly what the papers were.

These orders boggled my mind. I had just been married. I was the lowest of Army privates, and had been assigned to a tank unit of what I surmised were West Virginia hillbillies. Going from the Whitney North Seymour culture to this was a jolt, to say the least.

Myrna didn't have a job yet in Washington, so we would have to cancel our apartment lease, and she would return to Chicago. Questions then were flying right and left. Since I had not applied for a Judge Advocate commission after law school, my thoughts about JAG now were changing. Myrna agreed that I should apply for a commission even if it meant three years' active duty.

Fortunately I was acquainted with the Judge Advocate General of the Army, General Ted Decker. He was an active ABA member, and I had met with him and his top aide even before moving to Washington. He, among all the armed services JAG's, loved the ABA, and I had heard that he obtained his appointment with the support of ABA leaders like Mr. Seymour. Surely, I thought, I can get the commission, and soon.

So I explained the situation to the general's top aide at the Pentagon. The general told him that I should immediately file my application, with recommendations, and that he was sure a commission of Second Lieutenant would be offered to me. However, the process would take at least two months from the time it was received at the Pentagon. This was deflating.

It would take at least 10 days to get my six or seven required letters of recommendation; and at least *two months after that* before hearing anything. That would be Christmas!

I had all of my recommendations in hand quickly. Myrna made her arrangements to move back to Chicago. We were grateful when she was hired as a second secretary to the new ABA president in offices just a few steps from her old one in the Meetings Department. An interesting note here, to show how the ABA still was in a state of transition: The president was John C. Satterfield of Yazoo City, Mississippi. Mr. Satterfield was one his state's most prominent and powerful attorneys. He had been active in the ABA for years, and in line for the office of president for some time. He was an arch segregationist. He was a gracious man who warmly welcomed Myrna back to the Bar Center. But as a lawyer who represented interests opposed to integration, he was a sharp contrast to the Rhynes and Seymours, the emerging ABA leaders.

My two former law school classmates who were serving their JAG time in Washington offered me condolences and help. Art Neu, my law school roommate, offered me the couch in his small Arlington Towers apartment until I had to report to duty; and Richard Wiley (who later would become chairman of the Federal Communications Commission), offered a ride to Ft. Meade on reporting day.

Dick's wife, Betty, went along on the ride to Ft. Meade, and best described the atmosphere in the car. She said it was quiet, like going to a funeral, and when I walked away from the car, I looked like the loneliest guy in the world. I guess I was.

It didn't take long to develop some friendly associations with the men of the 150th Division. They weren't any different than I. They were from a National Guard unit in Beckley, West Virginia, where the commanding bird colonel, Colonel Holliday, was the owner of a local supermarket chain. Another, Captain Harlan (Skip) Wilson, Jr., was a local businessman. They had been called out of their private lives just like I. I was a curiosity because I was a lawyer *and* a staff member of the American Bar Association. What was I doing there? Most of them, except the three officers and first sergeant, were not business managers. They were grocery stock boys, construction workers, gas station attendants, hardware store salesmen and mechanics. I waited a few weeks before I said anything to the commissioned officers about my JAG application. When I did tell them, they were supportive and understanding.

Within a few days, Colonel Holliday asked me to serve as his Courts and Boards assistant, which was to handle disciplinary legal issues, of which there were few, and keep him abreast of changing rules from higher headquarters. This didn't relieve me of duties with the tanks, with maneuvers, or maintaining them. And because I had been to Ft. Knox tank training, even though I was a private, I was put in charge of overseeing the work with several tanks. This startled me because not being mechanical at all, I didn't know half as much as the local guys who worked with cars and machinery. However, I did it, and even took charge of helping maneuver out tanks that were stuck in muddy hills.

The colonel gave me a desk in a small office near his. There weren't many disciplinary issues, and none was serious. Personal problems of some of the men did take my time, though. It wasn't the job of the Courts and Boards assistant, but because I was a lawyer and available, Colonel Holliday encouraged them to talk with me if they wished. The problems ranged from marital to money to sick children back home. There wasn't much that I could do for them except lend an ear and give advice; however, twice I arranged leaves for them to return home for a short time. As word spread that this guy who helped get their tanks out of mud would also talk with them at certain hours, I had a few "clients" each week. I think it did some good, but in some cases, I thought they were just looking for an excuse to get out of work.

I had a major embarrassing moment, and it could have been more serious than just embarrassment. One morning at 5:00, all tanks were revving up to parade around the grounds at Ft. Meade. Mine was the lead tank. I was to start the procession. But I couldn't find my keys to the tank. The sound of the revving tanks throughout Ft. Meade was thunderous. We were scheduled to pull out at 5:15 sharp, and my tank sat silent. If I didn't move out, nobody else could either. Talk about a state of shock. I had to run back to the barracks to find them. They were in my duffle bag, where I had put them. We pulled out at 5:15 sharp.

Thanksgiving came and went, and there still wasn't even a hint on whether we would be shipping out to Europe. I don't recall being overly concerned about it. There seemed to be a general feeling that the stand-off of West and East tanks at the Wall would be resolved. But, the confrontation was still full-blown, and the vitriolic words were still flowing between Kennedy and Khrushchev. At Ft. Meade, we received very little information about what was going on. The general public knew more than we did.

Around the middle of December, I received the offer for the JAG officer's commission from the Pentagon. When a commission comes through, it's first an offer. You must accept or reject the offer. Colonel Holliday said that if I decided to accept and leave the 150th, they all would understand; if I decided to stay with the unit, I would be welcomed.

By this time the other men knew that I might be offered a commission, and they were told about the actual offer the day it arrived. But, here's the catch: the day before, President Kennedy announced that the crisis in Berlin was easing, and that it was possible that Army and National Guard reservists would be released sometime in 1962. Now what to do? Do I commit to stay with the West Virginians as a private, or do I become an officer and remain in the Army for three more years?

That evening I was lying on my bunk half asleep. Five or six men at the other end of the room were playing cards, and I overheard them discussing my offer. One said he'd want to do it, and be glad to make the money. Another said that the money wouldn't be much, and he wouldn't. He would stick it out at Ft. Meade for a few more months, especially since we probably weren't going into combat. And so the talking went. One said he'd give anything to be able to be an officer, and it would be a lot better than the life he would return to back home.

I decided to stay with the 150th. Most of these men had become my friends, and those days when I feared the "hillbillies" were far behind. This meant, of course, contacting General Decker and all who had written letters for me. Every person agreed with my decision. Myrna was happy. Everybody was happy. Christmas was a happy time. And, with that, 1961 came to a close.

CHAPTER FOUR

THE NATIONAL POLITICAL ENVIRONMENT
THE AGENCY PRACTICE ACT
THE LAWYERS' COMMITTEE FOR CIVIL RIGHTS UNDER LAW
THE CRIMINAL JUSTICE ACT OF 1964

WASHINGTON, D.C, 1962-1963

When it was certain that Army reservists would be released in 1962, we were allowed to live off base. So, Myrna and I began making our plans for her to return to Washington. We needed a place to live, and she needed a job.

An active Washington ABA member offered us his Capitol Hill townhouse in exchange for low rent and doing some painting and "fixing up." It was an old federal row house, just one block from the Capitol. It needed a lot of attention, but the cost and location were a lucky break for us.

I called on Lee Gomien, Senator Dirksen's assistant, and asked her if she knew of any Capitol secretarial jobs that Myrna could apply for. Her immediate response was that our timing was perfect. Kansas Republican Senator Schoepel had died, and a new senator, James Pearson, had just been appointed by the governor to replace him until the next election. The new senator had asked Glee to find a secretary for him. How lucky was that, to have the "Mother Hen" of Republican senators helping us?

So, Myrna returned to Washington to begin her new job with Senator Pearson, and we moved into the federal townhouse.

Myrna went right to work, helping the senator's administrative assistant and others organize the office for his arrival. She worked for him, gaining valuable Capitol Hill experience, through his election and until 1964, when our first child, Rich, was born.

Although the Berlin Crisis was abating, serious issues continued to plague Washington. President Kennedy, as all presidents, had no time to rest.

Civil Rights Demands Are Real and Urgent

The quest for equality among African-Americans was heating up. Although I wasn't discharged from the service until August 1962, the turmoil in the South over segregation was impacting all of us. It seemed like we were in a state of never-ending crisis because of all the unrest in America, generated by severe racial restrictions remaining in the South. While the civil rights issues weren't affecting me personally, they would by 1963; and Myrna was up close to them through her new Senate work life.

When Kennedy was elected in 1960, it had been six years since the Supreme Court ruled that racial segregation in public schools was unconstitutional. But the South had continued to rebel and stifle the mandate, and segregation reined in most other institutions. In 1960, sit-ins had begun in earnest at lunch counters, and the movement spread rapidly throughout the country, particularly on college campuses.

Over 70 percent of African-Americans voted for John Kennedy, with high hopes that he would bring real change. But Kennedy was reluctant to proceed, because he didn't want to lose Southern senators and representatives on other important issues. So, while he appointed many blacks to jobs in his administration, he didn't move out on civil rights legislation. In due course, however, he did move forward. Freedom riders were being beaten and buses burned in 1961, requiring hundreds of federal marshals to protect them and maintain order. And in 1962, James Meredith caused rioting and some injuries and death when he attempted to register at the University of Mississippi. President Kennedy considered it imperative to send in the National Guard and federal troops to thwart the Mississippi governor, and allow Meredith to enter and attend class. It was a time of high tension throughout the country.

How were these days relevant to me at the ABA? It was because the leaders of the ABA were having a difficult time inside the association coming to grips with the civil rights demands, and I was a close observer of the discussions and small group debates. ABA President John Satterfield (Myrna's former boss), the arch segregationist from Mississippi, was in lockstep with the anti-integration Southern political leaders. The South was heavily represented in the ABA with members and association leaders. The moderate leaders weren't in a position to challenge them openly without tearing the association apart (which none wanted to do), but were constantly talking among themselves about what stands the ABA should take, and the strategies necessary to have a voice. The national organized bar was doing nothing. And, many of them, even though they believed in civil rights for all, didn't want to be seen as supporting civil disobedience and what some perceived as mob action.

With the ABA laying back, in 1963 a group of its leaders led by Bernard Segal of Philadelphia, and including men such as Whitney North Seymour and Charles Rhyne, sent word to President Kennedy that they would assist him in organizing a group of private lawyers who would represent African-Americans in racial discrimination cases. This was an important strategic step for the organized bar in America because it would be a mechanism for lawyers who wanted to promote civil rights and participate in the movement to do it. And, it would be led by many of the same men who led the ABA. In other words, it wasn't to be a "fringe" group of lawyers who were not in the mainstream of the profession. Kennedy responded by inviting dozens of these lawyers to a meeting in the East Room of the White House in June 1963. He asked them to form the Lawyers' Committee for Civil Rights Under Law. The list of invitees was made by Mr. Segal and his friends, and he included Don Channell and me.

Following the president's talk urging the lawyers to get involved, and a response from Mr. Segal that they would establish a Lawyers' Committee, we attended a reception in the White House Rose Garden and met President Kennedy. When he shook my hand, I was struck by three things: he was tall and very rigidly erect because of his back brace; he looked squarely into your eyes, almost piercingly; and had a firm, dominant handshake. I've had three other visits to the White House, and each time felt privileged to be there. But attending a meeting hosted by the president in the East Room, and meeting him later in the Rose Garden, was an exceptional experience.

The Lawyers Committee established a small staff in Washington to coordinate its activities of enlisting lawyers throughout the South to provide legal representation on discrimination issues. It was the legal profession's way of helping with the civil rights cause without alienating the southern lawyers in the ABA, and importantly, the southerners on Capitol Hill. This was such a sensitive time. The ABA saw itself as a house for all lawyers, including those who were against the movement; and even the ABA leaders who ardently supported equal rights for all didn't want to destroy the association over it. It wasn't going to be drawn into the politics of the movement even though in this, the 21st Century, that approach would be considered disdainful if the facts were the same as then.

Consequently, I was not directly involved in the Lawyers Committee's work. The committee was engaged in legal representation, not legislative or other political activities. Bernie Segal handled much of it from his Philadelphia law office. I stayed well informed, and provided information about its work to Congressional offices when I was asked. And, I was asked often why the ABA wasn't involved in what was the most defining issue of the time. The Lawyers Committee, with its long list of ABA leaders on its masthead (14 past presidents and four board members), was a satisfying response in most instances. Everybody on Capitol Hill understood the situation, particularly as it applied even to them. Unless you were from a liberal Congressional district, you too were hesitant and didn't want to alienate half of the Hill. Remember that some of the most important senators, such as Russell from Georgia (the leader of 24 southern senators), were segregationists, and they considered the civil rights movement as an attack on them as well as on the segregated institutions.

But the boiling confrontations over civil rights weren't the only crisis-level issues facing America in 1962 and 1963. The Cuban Missile Crisis was front and center, and the Vietnam War was simmering.

The Cuban Missile Crisis Threatens Nuclear War

It's been said by historians that the Cuban Missile Crisis was the defining moment for the Kennedy Administration; that we came closer to nuclear war then than ever before, and probably ever since. In October 1962, U.S. intelligence reported to President Kennedy that the Soviet Union was secretly and quickly building missile sites in Cuba that could easily deliver nuclear war heads to America. Fidel Castro feared that since the U.S. was defeated in the Bay of Pigs debacle, it might undertake an actual invasion of Cuba. Soviet Premier Khrushchev had his own objective: it was to establish intermediate missile sites close enough to reach the U.S., which he thought would deter the U.S. from attacking the Soviet Union. The Soviets didn't have long-range missiles that could reach the U.S. So, to achieve both objectives, protecting Cuba and Russia from U.S. attacks, he would put nuclear missiles quietly on America's doorstep.

Military leaders wanted to knock out the sites, but Kennedy was afraid that a military invasion of Cuba could lead to world war. Instead he decided to deploy a naval blockade around Cuba, and demand the Soviets to remove their missile sites and back away from its Cuban armament plan altogether. The U.S. Army was put on high alert. The global public was informed, and as some have said, "the next few days literally were hair rising." The public was reminded again that the Cold War with the Soviet Union was a real one; and, just as in 1961, Americans were given instructions on how to build, stock and live in a bomb shelter. *Life Magazine* had devoted thirteen pages to "how to" and these were relevant all over again.

Nikita Khrushchev did back down, but had to save some face, so he obtained from the United States a guarantee that it would not attack Cuba.

U.S. Involvement in Vietnam Is Increased

The United States was involved in the Vietnam War before President Kennedy was elected. President Eisenhower already had assured the South Vietnam government that the U.S. would help it stop North Vietnam's attempt to overthrow it.

Kennedy agreed with Eisenhower that the North Vietnamese must be stopped because their success would mean a communist victory in gaining more territory. So, he escalated U.S. involvement in 1961 by agreeing to send thousands more troops and advisors. By the time he was assassinated in November 1963, the number had increased from 700 to 15,000. This was a big step, but wasn't as momentous at the time as the other issues bearing down on Americans. That urgent time on Vietnam would come later.

My Own First Legislative Issue, The Agency Practice Act
(And my first first-hand lesson in lobbying on Capitol Hill)

Lawyers who represented clients before the Internal Revenue Service were required to file an application to practice and abide by certain standards of the IRS, but they weren't required to take a special IRS-administered bar exam and be admitted to an IRS bar. Traditionally they were authorized to appear before the IRS if they were admitted to the bar of any state.

The IRS attempted to change this by amending the federal Agency Practice Act to require a new IRS examination for all lawyers representing clients before it. The ABA opposed this amendment, and association witnesses were selected to testify against it before Congressional subcommittees. Subcommittees hold hearings and make recommendations to the full committees that decide whether to take the issues to the full Senate or House.

Don delegated the issue to me as a good way to get "my feet wet." I contacted the witnesses, and received an outline of their testimony so that I would know firsthand their arguments. Then I called on the chief counsel of the Senate Judiciary Committee's Subcommittee on Administrative Practice and Procedure, Bernard Fensterwald, Jr. Bud Fensterwald was no stranger to Washington or Capitol Hill and was close to the subcommittee's chairman, Senator Edward Long (D-MO). *Later he unsuccessfully defended James Earl Ray, Martin Luther King's assassin, and formed an organization to investigate the truthfulness and findings of the Warren Commission that investigated the assassination of President Kennedy.*

Bud was receptive to me and the ABA's position. Again, as with so many others on Capitol Hill, he was surprised to see me because he had never had contact with an ABA representative. He, like others, knew about its positions on federal judges, but that was about it.

He told me that he was glad to see me, and not to worry. Senator Long would be friendly to the ABA witnesses and would have many questions for those from the IRS. There was no reason for a new bar examination by the IRS, he said, other than limiting the number of lawyers who could appear before the IRS, which would drive up expenses for clients, and create more government bureaucracy.

Several days later, I met with the witnesses before the hearing and briefed them on how friendly the day probably would be. I told them what Bud had said and suggested that they focus some of their testimony on some of the points he had suggested. He would be sitting directly behind Senator Long, and would be sympathetic to them.

The hearing went well, with only three senators present most of the time, Chairman Long, the ranking Republican senator, and the bill's sponsor. The sponsor tried to help the IRS witnesses with some friendly questions, but the answers weren't very satisfactory. Other senators would come and go, place their remarks into the record, and ask an occasional question. This is how Congressional hearings on lesser matters usually go. No cameras, press or even an audience, except for a few bored tourists who want to see a hearing in action.

After the hearing, I met with Bud again. I made some points that I hoped would be included in the subcommittee's report that would go to the full Judiciary Committee. These reports become an important part of the legislative history of a bill, and for later interpretation, can be as important as the legislation itself. Then he surprised me. He said that the staff's draft of the report would be ready soon, and that I could review it before it was published. That would assure that the report would represent accurately the views of the ABA's witnesses, and he could be certain that it was technically correct. The bill was reported to the full committee with the recommendation of no action.

I learned then, first hand, about one of Don Channell's important lobbying principles: The influence and standing of the sponsor/sponsors is all important. Having the chairman and staff on your side from the beginning is all important. If they are, they will work positively with you.

This was a happy time for me, and in more difficult times to come for me on the Hill, I would think back to Bud Fensterwald and how easy he made it for me. The IRS issue didn't go away completely, but today, in 2015, the IRS does not have a special bar examination for admission to practice before it.

My First Major Issue, the Criminal Justice Act of 1964

In 1938, the Supreme Court ruled in *Johnson v. Zerbst* that the Sixth Amendment to the U. S. Constitution required legal representation in all federal criminal cases. This was the "law of the land," but Congress had not provided funding for the constitutionally required counsel. Lawyers representing those accused of federal crimes had to do so *pro bono* (free) even though they were appointed by the court. The private bar could not keep up with this work, and it was clear that those unable to pay were not getting "equal representation." While there had been many years of study and support for funding by Congress, it failed to act. Although the ABA was one of the groups that supported federally funded legal representation, other than occasional testimony, it never had made a vigorous effort to insist on it.

In August 1962, Sylvester C. Smith, Jr., the general counsel of the Prudential Insurance Company of America, was elected president of the ABA, succeeding John Satterfield. Mr. Smith was familiar with Washington, and frequently stopped by our office. He wanted a vigorous ABA lobbying program to get Congress to enact federal funding for representation of indigents accused of federal crimes. He was outraged that neither the organized bar nor any other group seemed to have cared enough to push for it.

He and Don agreed that I should lead the ABA's staff effort. It was going to take concerted effort, almost full-time, and Don didn't have the time. President Smith told me that he had confidence I could do this, and I was elated to have my first chance to take the lead on a major issue.

Don and I already had had some warning that this would be one of Smith's priorities. He had been active in legal aid work in his home state of New Jersey and had spoken about our inadequate system of legal representation. Because the ABA had testified on this subject, we knew about the bills that had been introduced in the Senate and House; and we also knew that, particularly in the House, a few Republicans and Southern Democrats were either against it or on the fence. Mr. Smith also had done his homework through Prudential's Washington counsel. He told us that it had the enthusiastic support of Senator Sam Ervin (D-NC), the respected former judge on the Senate Judiciary Committee, and Congressman Emanuel Celler (D-NY), and most other Democrats on the Judiciary committees. Senator Roman Hruska (R-NE), a conservative, influential member of the Senate Judiciary Committee, had helped pass former Senate "federally funded" counsel bills, but needed encouragement this time around because the bills always died in the House. Congressman William McCulloch (R-OH), the ranking Republican member of the House Judiciary Committee, was lukewarm or at least not very interested in promoting it. My job (and Don's as well by helping me) would be to get their support with, of course, Mr. Smith's backing.

Mr. Smith had help for us. Mr. McCulloch's best friend and supporter from Piqua, Ohio (his hometown), was Milo Warner. Mr. Warner had been the national commander of the American Legion, and as a lawyer, handled most of Prudential's legal work in the Piqua-Dayton metropolitan area and western Ohio. Mr. Smith had asked Mr. Warner to come to Washington and urge Congressman McCulloch to support and lead efforts to enact the Criminal Justice Act. He would, in essence, be my helpmate, and he surely was.

Milo was an engaging gentleman, as you might expect the former national commander of the Legion to be. Not only as Mr. McCulloch's close friend, but as a convincing trial lawyer, he was the right person for this job. He took a room at the Willard Hotel, and he and I became glued to each other for weeks.

Bringing in Milo Warner demonstrated another of Don's principles of effective lobbying: Enlist the support of close friends and active supporters from back home.

My first step was to call Bill Foley, the House Judiciary Committee's general counsel, with whom I had stayed in touch. Bill was happy about this. Not only did he want a criminal justice act to pass, he was happy to see the ABA getting involved with action, and not just occasional talk. He arranged a meeting for me with Congressman Manny Celler, who also was pleased, and urged me to discuss it with Congressman McCulloch as soon as possible. He said that he could deliver most of the House Democrats, but that the Republicans wouldn't move without Mr. McCulloch. He also said that he believed the Republicans on the Senate Judiciary Committee would move if Senator Hruska would give his renewed support.

Milo suggested that I make an appointment directly with Mr. McCulloch, and feel him out. He told me that the congressman was a solid conservative on virtually everything except civil rights. He was an "equal justice" advocate and very bothered about racism and strict segregation in the South, and "rest of the country, for that matter." However, he was a conservative on federal spending and more federal government activity, and this would be his stumbling block. Milo himself was a staunch Midwestern conservative, but Sylvester Smith had convinced him that this was a project he should take on.

Milo wanted me to have a direct personal relationship with the congressman, and we did not visit Mr. McCulloch together. He, Milo, would come into Washington frequently as a personal confidant and practicing lawyer who could discuss the need for paid counsel in Ohio cases. He believed that Mr. McCulloch's heart was for this, and that his (Milo's) job was to show support from back home.

My meeting with Congressman McCulloch was my first face to face meeting with a member of Congress whom I "lobbied" myself without Don. I was nervous waiting to meet him outside his office. Would he welcome me, slough me off, argue with me, or what? I liked him immediately. He, like Milo, was a small man and very personable. He put me at ease, and we engaged in small talk about small towns in the Midwest and his time in Congress (he was elected in 1947). He said that he understood the issue's importance of assuring equal justice, but its high cost caused problems for him.

He also didn't want federal public defenders on the federal payrolls, creating more federal employees and bureaucracies around the country.

"I realize that I'm pretty old-fashioned," he said, "but I've always thought that private members of the bar should take these cases *pro bono.*" But he would think about it because he realized that the scope of the problem had gotten beyond the private bar's ability to handle all cases for no compensation.

He suggested that I talk with Congressman Arch Moore (R-WV). Congressman Moore was the Judiciary Committee's member who had the most interest in this. He warned me that Mr. Moore could be "mercurial" at times; I remembered he said this because I had to check the dictionary for the word's meaning. I think he meant that Mr. Moore could be difficult and objectionable. He said that we also should talk with Richard Poff (R-VA) who was the second ranking Republican on the Judiciary Committee. He, Mr. McCulloch, would need Mr. Moore's expert leadership and Congressman Poff's support, or he wouldn't be able to convince several other committee members. Mr. Poff was a leader of the House southern coalition of conservatives, and at the time, a leading anti-civil rights legislator. (He later changed completely, and apologized for his anti-civil rights votes, and publicly-expressed pro-segregation views.)

Mr. McCulloch couldn't have been more gracious to me, and invited me to keep him informed of my conversations with others on the Hill, both House and Senate. Even though I had no commitment that he would help as a leader, I felt good about the day. I had had a pleasant first time on an issue face to face with an important member of Congress.

Milo hadn't yet arrived in Washington when I had the McCulloch meeting. He was pleased with what I reported, but said that he hoped Mr. McCulloch would not pass this off to others. If he did not take the lead personally on a bill that was reasonable and compatible with what might come out of the Senate, the legislation could die again. "Without a strong push from the ABA," he said, "this could just die again, as it has before, of inertia." He said that, as the ranking Republican member of the Judiciary Committee, Mr. McCulloch could delegate the hard leg work of drafting to others, but hopefully he would make it clear to all of the members that he wanted it enacted. So, his work (Milo's) was just beginning, and he would be in Washington soon to begin to urge Mr. McCulloch to be the bill's outspoken leader.

"And," he said, "the ABA's and your work is just beginning. Legislation doesn't move without a lot of push from the outside." And, he asked me about the Kennedy Administration's position. "Where is Bobby Kennedy, the Attorney General? Without the Justice Department's support on a criminal justice issue like this, we can forget it." With his practical, down-home political experience, Milo was becoming an additional mentor for me.

My next visit was with Robert Kutak, Senator Hruska's administrative assistant. I wanted to learn first-hand where the senator stood. As conservative as Senator Hruska was, I was hearing that he was a stalwart leader on "administration of justice" issues, and actually had led prior Senate efforts on this legislation.

The meeting with Bob Kutak was one of the biggest surprises of my time in Washington. A pleasant surprise, but a little bittersweet as well. He said that Senator Hruska had repeatedly been a leader, not just a supporter, of a criminal justice act. But, where had the ABA been all of these years on such a fundamental issue of law? I was the first ABA representative to call on him (Sen. Hruska) about this or any other kind of issue involving the administration of justice, and he was the Senate Judiciary Committee's "point man" on such matters. The only times he heard from the ABA were when it opposed a federal judge nomination, and that didn't always go over very well with the senator. After he had finished chastising the ABA, he said that he couldn't be more pleased that the ABA was now at work on this, and that the senator would welcome a partnership with us on the bill.

He said that I should contact Daniel Freed, an assistant to Deputy Attorney General Nicholas Katzenbach at the Justice Department, who was working with him on the language of the current bill. Again, and you as a reader will tire of hearing this, Dan Freed couldn't believe an ABA representative was offering its support on an issue like this. His view of the ABA was a group of stodgy old white ultraconservative men, virtually irrelevant. How many times did I hear this around Washington? Constantly. He welcomed me with open arms and introduced me to the Deputy Attorney General, who was acquainted with the ABA and had met Don. Both the Attorney General and Deputy Attorney General were members of the ABA House of Delegates *ex officio*. Mr. Katzenbach had attended a House session, although Bobby Kennedy had not. He also was point man at the Justice Department for the ABA committee that evaluated federal judgeship nominees, and appreciated the committee's work. Here, all of a sudden, was an ABA friend in Washington.

This was the beginning of a friendship of Kutak, Freed and Beck that would last several years. Together, along with Milo Warner providing the heavy lifting with the House committee's most important Republican, we planned and carried out the strategy that led to the enactment of the Criminal Justice Act of 1964. Also working closely with us, and most importantly, was John W. Cummiskey, the chairman of the ABA Standing Committee on Legal Aid. John was the first ABA committee chairman I worked with, and we became virtually inseparable as colleagues over the next several years. Legal services for the poor and availability of and access to private lawyers for all income groups were front and center subjects during all the years I was with the ABA. John, a staunch political conservative, was our "expert" on legal services for indigents, and had such a passion for the subject of "access to lawyers" by everybody that he was always available with the right things to say at the right time.

We agreed on our various responsibilities. Bob would keep Senator Hruska interested (no easy task with the civil rights issues raging and world affairs so alarming), and continue providing information to Senate offices; Dan would continue perfecting the language of the bill, prepare "General" Katzenbach's testimony at hearings, and continue to inform senators and representatives of the Justice Department's position. I would enlist the ABA witnesses and arrange contacts with key senators and representatives from ABA lawyer-constituents (the Junior Bar Conference made this a top priority), bar associations and legal scholars back home. I would spend most of my time on the House side, attempting to get an acceptable bill from the Republicans, led by Congressman Moore. And, I would arrange through President Smith a strong, fresh resolution of support from the ABA Board of Governors. Don Channell had begun taking me with him to board meetings (board attendance did not become a usual practice among future junior staff), and my first presentation was on this subject. I also took the responsibility of hosting meetings of other groups interested in criminal justice.

Milo's presence in Washington presented a slight problem for me. He was a gregarious person who didn't relish eating dinner alone when he wasn't dining with Mr. McColluch. I frequently had dinner with Milo, who was engaging and enjoyable to be with. What began as occasionally turned into frequently, and arriving home later. Late enough that Myrna would be asleep when I arrived home. One of those nights, she made it clear that that kind of evening couldn't become part of our ongoing Washington lifestyle. She was right. As much as I enjoyed Milo's company, our future dinners together ended earlier. And, when others arrived from out of town, since I had learned my lesson, I was home at a reasonable hour.

With the ABA's and the Justice Department's backing (as well as other interested groups, including the Judicial Conference of the United States), the Senate passed S. 2900 on October 4, 1962. It was not without considerable controversy in the Senate, even with the bipartisan sponsorship of such key senators. There were differences over the per diem to pay court-appointed counsel, the creation of a federal public defender, and whether the act should include defendants who were financially able to retain counsel, but could not hire a lawyer because of the unpopularity of their cause. However, the difficulties were overcome, and it provided funding for a public defender as well as compensation for court-appointed counsel, the two most important components of the act. Its sponsors were Senator Hruska, joined by Senators Norris Cotton (R-NH), Kenneth Keating (R-NY) and Sam Ervin (D-NC). But it was too late in the session for consideration by the House, so it had to be taken up anew in the next Congress. Legislation does not carry over to a new Congress.

Over on the House side, I called on Congressman Arch Moore. Bert Early, a West Virginia lawyer who had just been appointed ABA deputy executive director, knew Mr. Moore and called him to introduce me. I found him congenial. He was, however, very forthright and strong in his views. The congressman supported compensation for assigned counsel, but was adamantly against a new federal public defender. He and Congressman Poff were concerned about the amount of the per diem, and the time it would take to "provide adequate representation," thus driving up the costs. He enthusiastically sponsored the lead bill in the House, but had so many caveats that we weren't certain that the House and Senate versions could be reconciled.

In the meantime, Milo was meeting with Mr. McCulloch, and reported headway, at least on Mr. McCulloch's willingness to provide strong leadership on the bill. He began to take interest in shaping an acceptable bill, and, while he deferred to Mr. Moore as the "expert," made it clear to the Judiciary Committee members that he strongly supported enactment of a criminal justice act. Milo was having success.

I was having some success too. I happened to be a guest at the Army-Navy Game in Philadelphia on December 2, and, coincidentally, sitting directly behind me was Congressman Moore. He was not just friendly… he was smiling and open in conversation. Before I could ask a question or make a comment, he said that I shouldn't worry about the criminal justice act in 1963. "There will be another bill introduced, and we'll get the job done this time."

Dan Freed asked me to meet with him, his Justice Department colleague Herbert Hoffman in the Office of Legislative Affairs, and Deputy Attorney General Katzenbach to discuss the possibility of including our issue in President Kennedy's State of the Union message before a joint session of Congress on January 13, 1963. Everybody in America with an important issue wants their cause mentioned in the State of the Union message. Mr. Katzenbach cautioned us that we would be competing with literally dozens of other issues for special mention, and that it was a long-shot. The Criminal Justice Act, after all, was not at the very top of the president's list. But he would speak with Attorney General Bobby Kennedy, and ask him to put it on a priority list. With the civil rights situation swirling all around the country, he thought the president was looking for related issues to champion, and this might be one that fits that objective. Bob Kutak was elated that we were trying this. "Even with Republicans," he said, "public support by the president before a joint session will give us a terrific boost. And it will firm up any wavering Democrats."

Dan wrote the important memorandum that was given to the Attorney General; then all we could do was to wait and hope for the best. In any event, if anything was said, it probably would be only a sentence or even just a phrase. We would have to wait until the State of the Union address for any bills to be introduced in the new Congress.

When President Kennedy rose to give his address, we three were on pins and needles. Dan had some inside information that it *might* be mentioned. But even so, he wasn't sure how credible his "informant" was, and these addresses are changed right up to the last minute anyway. So, who knew?

It was mentioned. Among his recommendations, the president urged that "the right to competent counsel must be assured to every man accused of crime in Federal court, regardless of his means." We of course were elated, and now it would be "back to Capitol Hill."

Immediately following the address, Senator Hruska, joined by the initial three primary sponsors, Senators Cotton, Keating and Ervin, reintroduced the Criminal Justice Act. In his brief optimistic remarks on the Senate floor, he said that the president's remarks were gratifying, and that they, coupled with the support of the ABA, increased the prospects for passage by Congress.

Bob Kutak, in a *Nebraska Law Review* article about the act's passage, credited the ABA as "instrumental in maintaining the momentum which would prevent the bill from faltering" like it had in the past.

In March, President Kennedy sent to the Senate and House a proposed bill which was almost identical to the Senate bill. In May, the chairman of the ABA Committee on Legal Aid testified along with personages such as Whitney North Seymour, and it was approved by the Senate Judiciary Committee. The Senate passed the bill on August 6, 1963.

It had rough going during the House's May hearings, primarily because of strong opposition in the House (especially by Congressmen Moore and Poff) to a federal public defender office. There were other issues with the bill as well. Congressman McCulloch assured us, though, that a bill would be reported by the House subcommittee.

Arch Moore also continued to assure us that there would be a bill. He introduced his own bill in mid-summer, and it was reported to the full House by the Judiciary Committee. In his bill, Mr. Moore reduced the scale of operations, deleted the public defender office, and changed the method of assigned counsel. So, it was substantially different than the Senate bill. I had arranged meetings with Mr. Moore with John Cummiskey and President Smith to try to improve it before the Judiciary Committee's vote. But, Mr. McCulloch and Mr. Celler both advised us to take what we could get. Celler told us that the majority on the Judiciary Committee would not agree to a public defender, and wished the compensation to be scaled back from the Senate bill. He couldn't do anything more about it.

And, to boot, our bill was now taking a back burner, a big one at that, to civil rights legislation that was the hottest topic on Capitol Hill, and before the Judiciary Committees of both Houses.

The House action didn't take place until January 1964. All of us who had worked so hard, including Don Channell and John Cummiskey, were in the gallery for the debate and vote. It wasn't pretty, and it was evident that both

Mr. Celler and Mr. McCulloch had known how to count votes. The votes were not there for the Senate version, and the views of House members varied. Some members believed the Moore bill didn't do enough, others thought it was just right, still others said that they would not have voted for it if it had created a federal public defender. But when the votes were cast, the bill passed. It was a thrill to meet Mr. McCulloch and thank him in the lobby just outside the House chamber. He was as happy as we were. He and so many of us had come a long way together on this issue. There's nothing quite as enjoyable as shaking the hand of the winning Congressperson in the Capitol lobby after the vote.

The next step was a Senate-House conference for resolving the differences. But it wasn't until August 1964, seven months later, that the conferees met.

Milo's work was over. He had helped enlist Mr. McCulloch's active leadership. He told me later that, as an Ohio conservative Republican who believed in very little government, period, he never would have been lobbying for a public defender bill if he hadn't been asked to do it by Sylvester Smith. "But," he said, "I became a true believer as a lawyer. If you're an American and believe in our equal legal system, of course there should be competent counsel for everybody accused of crime. That's not even debatable." He also told me that he enjoyed the experience as much as anything he had ever done.

John came to Washington a few times during the spring and summer to help prepare for the Senate-House conference. We would take information back and forth to the conferees from the two Houses, as did Dan Freed from the Deputy Attorney General's office. They had agreed on most issues in advance of the conference except the public defender. As hard as the Senate conferees tried, the House members would not agree to a federal public defender. The conferees settled on paying counsel "assigned by the court," and that was what passed both Houses. Language *was* included in the Conference report to invite the Justice Department to continue its study of a public defender's practicality and viability in the future.

John F. Kennedy did not live to sign the Criminal Justice Act. President Lyndon Johnson signed it on August 20, 1964.

After the act became law, Bob Kutak, in the *Nebraska Law Review*, wrote:

The Criminal Justice Act of 1964 goes a long way towards making that idea a reality in our federal court system (equal justice for the accused). By its impact on the administration of criminal justice, it is quite possible that the act will become recognized and rank as one of the major legislative achievements in a decade spanning both the New Frontier (Kennedy) and the Great Society (Johnson) and crowded with Congressional actions.

It has proven to be just that. It was an important step, but only the first in laying the groundwork for a federal public defender system that ultimately had to be authorized. The compensation for appointed counsel under the Criminal Justice Act was at rates substantially below that which they would receive from their privately retained clients. The private bar was overwhelmed with caseloads, and the federal district courts could not keep up with appointments. After a Justice Department study, invited by Congress in the "CJA," the act was amended in 1970 to authorize district courts to establish federal defender organizations. By 2009, more than 45 years since the CJA was enacted, there were 80 federal defender organizations. They employ more than 3,300 lawyers, investigators, paralegals, and support personnel, and serve 90 of the 94 federal judicial districts. (By 1970, Bob, Dan and I had left our respective Washington jobs, and did not participate in obtaining the amendment.)

I've written a long summation of my first major legislative issue for a purpose. I wrote it to explain in detail the actions that Congressional sponsors and their staffs, the federal administration, and lobbyists take together to accomplish a legislative objective. From this experience, I learned how much was involved in fulfilling my wide range of responsibilities, all to be repeated in various ways throughout my advocacy career.

This summation and the stories to follow tell only of my own personal involvement and that of others with whom I worked most closely. Legislative achievement involves many more people than I could write about here. Many others, such as groups interested in equal justice, local bar association officials, law scholars, and on and on were called on to participate, testify, write, and speak. It's the total combination that spells success in any legislative effort. No one person can take all the credit.

Some of those persons involved are more important than others. There always must be a **driving** force to accomplish any political objective. In this case, Sylvester Smith's dream and focused objective of achieving a system of defense for the federally accused came true.

And a final note about the basic principles of lobbying. Compromise if you must to achieve your desired result. It might not, in fact probably will not, be exactly as you wish. But that's all right. The time for improvement will come, just as it has with the Criminal Justice Act.

Bob Kutak later left Capitol Hill to form, with Harold Rock, the highly successful Omaha law firm of Kutak Rock. He was an innovator, and under his leadership, Kutak Rock became America's first national law firm with offices in several cities. From the cynic about the ABA when I first met him, he became a leader in the association and received awards for his groundbreaking work in legal ethics and access to legal services. It was a shock to all of us when he died at the age of 50 of a massive heart attack.

Dan Freed became a distinguished professor of law at Yale. He continued his work in criminal justice and became the country's foremost authority on bail in the United States.

Herb Hoffman later became director of the ABA's Washington Office when Don Channell retired.

After his last term in Congress, Congressman Arch Moore was elected governor of West Virginia in 1969 and served until 1977. He was defeated for another term, but was re-elected and served again from 1985 to 1989. He was prosecuted for corruption, pleaded guilty, and sentenced to five years and 10 months in prison in 1990. He served three years in prison, was disbarred, forfeited his pension, and paid a settlement of $750,000 to the state.

CHAPTER FIVE

VARIED COMMENTS ON OUR NEW WASHINGTON LIFE

WASHINGTON, D.C. 1963–1964

We Loved Our Work, and the Days Got Busier

Summers in Washington are very hot and humid. Just riding around the city reminded Don and me how much we liked our jobs, compared to many others. It seemed like the entire city of Washington was under siege by jack hammers tearing up the streets. Not that wielding jack hammers was an unworthy occupation. It isn't. But on these steamy days, we were glad to be in a cab on our way to Capitol Hill, instead of handling one of those. Don would say, "Don't we have the greatest jobs ever?" I agreed.

Then we would arrive at a House office building for an appointment, and enter that wonderfully cool place. After we would leave the elevator, an old clanking contraption "driven" by some older, patronage beneficiary sitting on his stool, we would laugh and laugh. Up and down that guy would go, all day long, frequently with an attitude that he was a congressman himself. Don and I agreed again that we were happy with what we were doing, and not running an elevator.

The times we went to appointments together were too many to count. If the ABA powers that be had known we traveled around town together so often, they probably would have wondered why it took two of us. But there were reasons: Don was teaching me the ropes, and it was important that the staffs of Congressional offices knew both of us, not just one. We were a team.

As the issues multiplied, and as we became much better known around the Hill and the Administration (Executive Branch), we had a need for more staff. We weren't able to handle the calls and the necessary writing by ourselves. We hired Michael Spence to help us with issues and Harry Swegle from the Chicago office for communications and public relations. They both were welcomed members of our team.

In addition to Mike and Harry, another staff member, Lucy Allen, provided assistance to the ABA Section of Taxation. The Tax Section was staffed out of the Washington Office because of the ongoing association it had with the Senate and House committees responsible for taxes. This section provided advice on technical tax issues to the Hill committees and the Treasury Department, and required its own staff member.

The ABA Did Not, and Still Does Not, Have a Political Action Fund

As we in the Washington Office became busier and better known, particularly after success with the Keogh Act, the self-employed retirement tax bill, we occasionally would be asked if the ABA made campaign contributions. It did not, and still doesn't. It is a nonpartisan, nonprofit organization, and while we lobbied and provided information to the Hill and Executive Branch, we didn't engage in political activities. During my time with the ABA, most of our issues, with only a few exceptions, were oriented toward "public interest" rather than "special interests for the benefit of lawyers."

Myrna and I Are in Awe of Washington

Both Myrna and I loved being in Washington. Not only did we relish our Capitol Hill-related work, we felt lucky to be experiencing the Washington historical environment.

Every time we drove past the Washington Monument, the Lincoln Memorial, the White House or any of the other significant landmarks, we were in awe of them. We were in awe of the Capitol and the surrounding office buildings where Myrna spent her working hours, and I visited frequently. They all were things of majestic beauty and historical importance. Whenever I visited a senator's or representative's office, I would ask myself, "Am I really here? Is this really me who is about to talk personally with Senator Ervin or Congressman Michel?" I wouldn't trade my place with any person I knew.

I Wouldn't Trade Places

Today, in 2015, lobbying is big business for law firms, and is considered a respectable activity of the legal profession. In the 1960s, much professional lobbying was done by public relations firms, and still is. Lawyers lobbied too, but many honest-to-goodness practicing lawyers didn't look upon the work as real lawyering. Instead, lobbying was all about whom you knew on Capitol Hill, and that was about it.

A personal story of mine illustrates what I mean:

At an ABA meeting, I was having lunch with some Junior Bar members who were questioning me about my work. All of them practiced law, and some specialized in trial work. One commented that he didn't understand how I could like my work so much. It wasn't legal work, and instead was all political and kowtowing to senators and representatives. As a practicing lawyer, he, John, wouldn't grovel like that to achieve the result he wanted. Just as I was explaining how I advocated positions like he, a distinguished white-haired gentleman walked by our table, and John jumped quickly from his seat. He eagerly shook the man's hand, and addressed him as "Your Honor." The judge told him in formal tone that he was pleased to see him participating in ABA activities and to "keep it up." "Oh, I will, Your Honor," said John, as he literally bowed before judge.

When John sat down, he said with a satisfied smile, "That's my hometown judge." I couldn't help responding with my own smile that I saw that, and that I never had bowed to a senator or any politician like he did. Who was it who acted so politically?

We Move to an Apartment in Arlington

As much as Myrna and I appreciated the good deal we had living in the Capitol Hill townhouse, after I left the service in 1962 we were ready to move on to another place. Capitol Hill was not the safest area, and we were aware of some nearby break-ins. Most of all, though, we couldn't control the cockroaches in the lower-level living area, and the aging building needed too much work. So we found a new second floor two-bedroom apartment in Arlington, Virginia.

My parents, Hazel and George, happened to be visiting us from Peoria on our moving day. The day was Washington hot and humid, and the moving work was hard. There really *were* some creepy crawlies running around, including in the refrigerator. I said, "I'm going to kind of miss this because you get nostalgic about a place." Mammy said, "There's nothing charming about this place. Let's keep packing and get out of here…fast."

And so we moved. Of course, our commuting changed dramatically. In our small French Simca, we would drive into Washington, and Myrna would drop me off in front of the White House, which was a few blocks from my office at 1120 Connecticut Avenue, just across from the Mayflower Hotel. I would walk from there to work, and she would drive to the Senate Office Building where she had free parking. This was an excellent arrangement.

One evening on our way into Washington, as we approached the Arlington Memorial Bridge over the Potomac River, the steering column came loose from the car. It scared us to death, but fortunately we could re-connect it enough to get it off the road. Warren Goelz picked us up and let us use his car that evening. It was time for a new car. We bought a beauty — a shiny, black two-door Chevy Impala. It probably was my favorite car. In any event, we were happy with our jobs, our new apartment and new car.

We Were Happy With Good Friends, Too

In addition to Dick and Betty Wiley who were in Washington on Dick's JAG duty, Warren and Nancy Goelz (high school, college and law school) were living in the area, not far from our new apartment. Audrie and Ron Whitney, also friends from high school and Bradley days, were long-time residents, and their home was like a second home to us. All of them were great helpers for us in settling into the Washington environment.

We frequently were invited to dinner by my dad's cousin, Irene, and her husband, Durward (Sandy) Sandifer. Sandy had been a top officer at the State Department, where he was key in crafting the charter for the United Nations, and was the department's officer in charge of U.N. affairs. He as-sisted Eleanor Roosevelt when she was ambassador to the United Nations, and through this association, Irene and Mrs. Roosevelt became good friends. Their personal relationship led Irene to write a memoir, *Mrs. Roosevelt as We Knew Her.* When Myrna and I knew them in Washington, Sandy was re-tired from the State Department and teaching International Law at American University. The author of *Evidence Before International Tribunals,* he contin-ued to be an acclaimed authority in International Law. As our only relatives in the Washington area, they would invite us on special occasions such Easter, and these always were special times for us.

Our Sight of Celebrity at the Mayflower Hotel

Occasionally Don and I had lunch in the grill room of the Mayflower. Walking into the grill room the first time, we saw J. Edgar Hoover and his FBI deputy director, Clyde Tolson. They were sitting side by side, looking straight ahead toward the grill room door, with their backs to the wall. While in the J. Edgar movie, DiCaprio somewhat resembled "the man," there was no resemblance between the actor Armie Hammer and the real Tolson. The real Tomson was a big, relatively rough-looking man with a large bulb-like nose. Anyway, they weren't saying a word, their faces were grim, and when they were finished, without saying a word to each other, quietly left the room, and were driven away in their black government town car. Whenever I had lunch at the Mayflower grill, I would always see them there, grim, and unapproachable.

We Move Our Office

As our workload increased and we needed more space, and the rent in the Bender Building at 1120 Connecticut Avenue increased also, we decided that we should look around for another location. Don started exploring, and one day came into my office all excited. He wanted me to drop everything and go with him to a brand new building across the street at 1205 De Sales Street. He said that it was the coolest place, on the short street along the north side of the Mayflower. The office space was the entire floor of a small four-story building. Like the Bender Building location, it was perfectly located. It had private offices for all of us, a nice conference room, and a larger room with an adjoining outside deck for entertaining. I was just as enthusiastic as Don, and we signed the lease. We would use the room and deck for entertaining many times.

Bert Early Takes Hold as ABA Executive Director

In 1962, the ABA employed Bert H. Early as deputy executive director. He replaced Joe Stecher as executive director in 1964. His employment marked a sharp turning point in the life and times of the American Bar Association. He had been a practicing lawyer and general counsel of the Island Creek Coal Company in West Virginia, and was an active ABA member. He knew the ABA well, and it was clear that, as executive director, he would bring fresh insights and direction to it. I could see a future with the association under his leadership, and in a relatively short time, we became close colleagues. Our future together began soon after he was hired in 1962 because he was interested in our Washington work and gave us strong support.

Bert Early considered his work at the ABA to be a "labor of love." He accepted the top ABA staff position so that he could help the organization enter a new era of influential professional responsibility, always considering the public interest first. This was his approach throughout his career with the association.

CHAPTER SIX

ADOPTION OF THE TWENTY-FIFTH AMENDMENT TO THE CONSTITUTION
OUR FIRST CHILD, RICHARD, IS BORN

WASHINGTON, D.C. 1963–1964

In 1963, one of the most important political issues in my career appeared on our doorstep. How many times do any of us have the opportunity to assist in securing the adoption of a United States Constitutional Amendment?

The Inability of the President of the United States...
And Vice Presidential Vacancy

The subjects were the Inability of the President of the United States to perform his/her duties in the event of Disability, and Vice Presidential Vacancy. The U. S. Constitution (art. II sec. 1, cl. 6) provides that if the President dies, the Vice President becomes President.

With regard to Presidential incapacity, however, there was no constitutional provision for the temporary transfer of power if the President of the United States was incapacitated and could not function as President. Consequently, no Vice President had been willing to act for a disabled President for fear that it might be viewed as trying to oust the President.

While Article II does mention that in the case of the President's "... Inability to discharge the Powers and Duties of said Office, the same shall devolve on the Vice President," there were no procedures specified to determine what constitutes a Presidential disability. And, just as remarkably, nothing was mentioned about how to fill the office of Vice President when a vacancy in it occurs. That office has been vacant 16 times in the nation's history, and for four years after the death of President Franklin Roosevelt.

Several times since America's founding, a president was unable to act, causing great concern. Two notable times were Woodrow Wilson's stroke in 1919, and Dwight Eisenhower's series of illnesses. In the Wilson case, the president was so ill that executive affairs were administered by Mrs. Wilson and other members of the White House staff, and 28 bills became law because they were not signed by the president. (A bill becomes law if signed by the president, or if not signed by him within 10 days and Congress is in session.)

The "Brownell Plan" Under President Eisenhower

President Eisenhower was ill at various times, and one time he talked about resigning. After his first heart attack, his administration proposed a new constitutional amendment. It was known as the "Brownell" plan, after Herbert Brownell, the Attorney General. It provided for specified procedures to be followed by the President, Vice President and Cabinet if either the President himself, or the Vice President, considered the President unable to conduct business. It generated so much controversy that neither the Senate nor House could reach agreement.

President Eisenhower became very concerned about the uncertainty in the nation if he were to be disabled. He was so troubled by it that he personally drafted an informal agreement of understanding to be implemented by the President and Vice President in the event the President could not act. After sharing it with Vice President Nixon, the Attorney General, and the Secretary of State, all of whom agreed with it, he prepared this letter which was released to the public:

> *We decided and this was the thing that frightened me: suppose something happens to you in the turn of a stroke that might incapacitate you mentally and you wouldn't know it, and the people around you, wanting to protect you, would probably keep this away from the public. So I decided that what we must do is make the Vice President decide when the President can no longer carry on, and then he should take over the duties, and when the President became convinced that he could take back his duties, he would be the one to decide.*

While this was considered a stop-gap measure to provide some certainty, and also was later adopted by President Kennedy and President Johnson, it was subject to the goodwill of the President and did not have the force of law.

Solutions Were Continuously Attempted and Prevented

For decades, efforts to solve this problem were attempted by proposed legislation and constitutional amendments. Even with the serious illnesses of President Eisenhower, the politics of the situation prevented action, other than President Eisenhower's memorandum of understanding. Entire books have been written on the issue's contentious history, notably by Senator Birch Bayh in *One Heartbeat Away*, and John Feerick in *From Failing Hands* and *The Twenty-Fifth Amendment*.

I discuss here only the role of the ABA (and specifically Don Channell and I who are referenced in the Bayh and Feerick books) in helping to secure the adoption of the Twenty-Fifth Amendment, which clarified the Presidential Inability and Vice Presidential issues. This is not meant to lessen the efforts of so many others inside and outside the organized bar who played important roles. The Amendment has been invoked six times since its adoption on February 23, 1967, and the date of this writing in 2015.

The ABA's First Proposal and Actions

In 1960, the ABA had considered the Presidential Inability issue, and its House of Delegates passed a resolution approving a constitutional amendment to resolve it. The proposal had been developed by a committee of the New York State Bar Association. It was unlike the Brownell plan in that it did not establish a specific procedure for handling Presidential Inability. The ABA resolution would, instead, grant to Congress the power to establish the machinery needed if the President became disabled. I hadn't given it any thought then. In 1960, I was just getting started with the Junior Bar Conference, and it wasn't on my "radar" at all. Even though a few senators, led by the prominent Estes Kefauver of Tennessee, had a long-time interest in the subject, nothing happened on the Hill, and Presidential Inability was not an ABA priority when I started working in Washington.

At the beginning of Congress in 1963, Don had a phone call from Louis C. Wyman, the newly elected congressman from New Hampshire. He wanted to meet with Don about his interest in promoting the Presidential Inability issue in Congress. As the recent attorney general of New Hampshire, Congressman Wyman had been active in the ABA. He had been a leading member of the ABA's Committee on Communist Tactics, Strategy, and Objectives, a committee established in the 1950s (during the McCarthy anti-Communist period) to try to ensure that alleged subversives did not penetrate the legal profession. The anti-Communist crusade of the 1950s wasn't an important issue any more, so Mr. Wyman wouldn't be pursuing that. However, he was interested in Presidential Inability and wanted to take the ABA's position and run with it in Congress.

This was January 1963, the year that our young President was assassinated in November. At that time Presidential Inability was not a priority. There were other pressing national and international problems, and I personally was fully engaged with trying to get the Criminal Justice Act enacted. It was not a priority for Don, but he couldn't dismiss Mr. Wyman. Wyman was an important man, and Don wanted me to work with the congressman because his schedule wouldn't allow it (he claimed).

Congressman Wyman provided my first introduction to the issue of Presidential Inability. I soon learned that he did not need much briefing from me because he knew its history well.

Through my reading and mentioning Mr. Wyman to acquaintances around Washington, I learned that, as the New Hampshire Attorney General, he had taken a hard line against people suspected of being Communist sympathizers, even jailing some unfairly without trial. At least one of his New Hampshire anti-Communist decisions had been reversed by the U.S. Supreme Court. And I was learning more why there was so much frowning in Washington when the ABA was mentioned. Because of the work of the ABA Committee on Communist Tactics, Strategy and Objectives, the association was seen by many as a McCarthy-era organization that was unfairly criticizing the U. S. Supreme Court and favoring laws that resulted in unfairly accusing some lawyers as being Communist sympathizers. Lou Wyman had been an outspoken member of the conservative anti-Communist group.

Lou's background clinched it. It wasn't just that he was a freshman member of Congress with no influence. There was a public backlash in America against the McCarthy tactics on alleged Communist sympathizers, and it would be an embarrassment for him to speak for the ABA on Capitol Hill. This was a jolt to me. I liked Lou Wyman, and we had developed a friendly working relationship. But we couldn't afford having him as the congressman out front, promoting the ABA's solution to Presidential Inability.

Lou became so busy with getting settled in Congress that he put Presidential Inability on his back-burner for a while. Fortunately, this gave us time to think about our next steps.

The Kefauver-Keating Senate Hearings

In the meantime, Senator Kefauver and Senator Keating of New York decided to hold hearings by the Subcommittee on Constitutional Amendments. As leading proponents of an amendment, they sponsored S. J. 35, which was the proposal of the New York State Bar and the ABA. We were going to need an ABA witness. The ABA president, Walter Craig, suggested Lewis Powell, a prominent Richmond attorney who would be the ABA's president-elect in August. This was perfect. Mr. Powell could be the ABA's chief spokesman on Presidential Inability. He agreed to do it, and it solved all of our problems with Mr. Wyman, who continued to have an interest, but had become preoccupied with other issues.

Lewis F. Powell, Jr. was a lawyer of the highest stature and credibility. I divert here to highlight him because beginning with Presidential Inability, Don and I saw him often. When he became the ABA's president-elect in 1963 and president in 1964, he provided recognized leadership on all of the major national issues on our table.

Mr. Powell, who would become an associate justice of the United States Supreme Court, was a southern gentleman who spoke in a measured, thoughtful tone, with the distinctive Virginia gentleman's special inflection. He was conservative, personally and politically, but frequently took positions of a statesman and problem solver, rather than conservative or liberal. A most notable example was his opposition to "massive resistance" against the *Brown* decision on desegregation of schools. He was president of the Richmond School Board from 1952 to 1961, and later the Virginia School Board. While not taking public, outspoken stands, he worked behind the scenes with prominent Virginians to support the rule of law and end massive resistance to the *Brown* decision.

Lewis Powell played a pivotal role in advancing the ABA's influence in national public policy and garnering high respect from governing circles and all segments of the legal profession. Just as in his home state of Virginia, at the national level he had an extraordinary ability to bring people of divergent views together. And probably most of all, he was trusted by his colleagues for thoroughly examining the issues and understanding the bigger picture. Everybody felt at ease with him. While he would speak with assurance, he did not raise his voice excitedly or contentiously. And so, it was Lewis Powell who, at just the right time, would lead the ABA on the Twenty-Fifth Amendment and other significant issues to come.

Hearings were held in June 1963, and shortly after, the subcommittee favorably reported S. J. Res. 35 to the full Judiciary Committee. I then met with Fred Graham, the subcommittee's chief counsel, to determine the future status of the bill. He said the Judiciary Committee's calendar was full at that time, and that he couldn't say what would happen next, but to stay in touch.

Senator Kefauver Dies Unexpectedly
Senator Bayh Takes Over the Subcommittee

Senator Kefauver died suddenly on August 10, following a heart attack on the Senate floor. Because he was the primary mover on the Presidential Inability issue, his death abruptly stopped any further action. Fred Graham, a Tennessee lawyer, had been employed by Senator Kefauver, and was now without a Senate sponsor. And, he was counsel to a subcommittee with a questionable future. In fact, the chairman of the Judiciary Committee, Senator James Eastland, was preparing to close the subcommittee down. Fred was discouraged because he had taken an active interest in the subcommittee's work, and the Inability issue was Senator Kefauver's most important subject on its agenda. So, now the issue would be going nowhere. Fred left the Hill, and took a new position with the Secretary of Labor, Willard Wirtz.

Fred and I stayed in touch with each other after he left the Hill to pursue a distinguished career. After serving as Special Assistant to the Secretary of Labor, he was *The New York Times* Supreme Court correspondent. Later, Fred would become law correspondent for CBS News, and ultimately the chief anchor and managing editor of Court TV.

Although Fred never told me this, Senator Bayh wrote in his history of the Twenty-Fifth Amendment, *One Heartbeat Away*, that it was Fred who encouraged him to talk with Senator Eastland about taking the chairmanship of the subcommittee. Fred believed there were important issues on the subcommittee's agenda, and that it should be kept alive. As it turned out, the subcommittee was continued, and Senator Bayh was made chairman on September 30, 1963. Senator Bayh did speak with Senator Eastland, but because he was such a junior senator, he was surprised when Mr. Eastland told him that he was keeping the subcommittee and appointing him chairman. Because the subcommittee wasn't important to most senators, it was easier for Senator Eastland to give the chairmanship to him rather than a more senior member of the Senate. Senator Bayh was elated because it gave him a chance to deal with issues firsthand at the subcommittee level. Little did he know that in a few weeks, the subcommittee would take front and center in Congress. And little did we at the ABA know that our work lives were about to change drastically.

During October and November, Senator Bayh and his staff began organizing the agenda of the subcommittee, but there was no action. In fact, the subcommittee had no resources and its office space had been taken over by other senators. The senator even had to assign an assistant from his own office staff to review records and establish an agenda.

President Kennedy Is Assassinated, Changing Everything

Then, on November 23, 1963, came the news that President John Kennedy had been assassinated. Just as everybody who heard the startling news, I vividly remember the exact time. I was walking into Don Channell's office just as our phones began ringing, with friends telling us to turn on the radio. CBS newscaster Walter Cronkite was talking about it. We all were in a state of shock. The act of the killing was tragic enough, but also who was responsible for this? Was this an act of war? What would be coming next?

The death of the President underscored once again the inadequacy of America's Presidential Succession laws. President Kennedy died, and President Lyndon Johnson was sworn in as President on the plane trip back to Washington. So, there was no Constitutional crisis. *But, what would have happened had President Kennedy been unconscious for days or even months, and could not have performed his duties as President?*

The Senate Subcommittee on Constitutional Amendments was brought back to life, and suddenly attention was directed to it by the Senate and public alike. If there ever was a need for a constitutional amendment to establish procedures if a President could not function, the time was now.

Members of the subcommittee began meeting, and there were differences of opinion remaining. One group supported the simpler ABA approach of giving Congress power to establish procedures. Senator Bayh and others believed strongly that clear procedures must be set out in the Constitution.

Bayh and his staff began drafting "procedures" language, and developing a strategy to move it forward. The strategy included calling the ABA to enlist its help, although Senator Bayh doubted the ABA would change its view.

Before Senator Bayh's staff called us, Don and I coincidentally decided to call him. We had attended a hearing where the senator was speaking, and understood why Indiana voters liked him. As we rode back to the office, we agreed that it would be a special pleasure to work with him (in contrast to so many others on the Hill who were crusty and arrogant), and that we should offer our assistance. We hadn't realized that he wanted to talk with us, and when Don called him on December 13, we couldn't believe how receptive he was. In his book, *One Heartbeat Away,* Senator Bayh described our first meeting:

> We met the next day (after Don had called him). Don Channell was accompanied by Lowell Beck, his assistant in the ABA Washington Office; and Larry Conrad (the senator's assistant) was with me. Although this first meeting accomplished very little that was concrete, our discussion was the first step in a partnership that was to follow a long, tedious path to eventual success. Channell and Beck were committed to following the course of action specified by the ABA House of Delegates. On the other hand, however, I was convinced that our own proposal had more merit and was not inclined to give ground. But the meeting did prove one thing beyond question. Each of us had one common desire: to find a workable solution to a century-old problem. We adjourned after agreeing to meet again after the beginning of the New Year.

Don and I knew from our conversation with Senator Bayh and Larry Conrad that if the ABA stuck rigidly to its current position, we probably would have little influence with the senator. And, after all, our position might not have been the best. Essentially it had been adopted by the House of Delegates on the recommendation of the New York State Bar Association, and was vigorously promoted by Republican Senator Kenneth Keating of New York; but many others, such as former Attorney General Herbert Brownell, supported procedures written into the Constitution. We needed some kind of a consensus, but how could we accomplish that? It was complicated because Congressman Wyman was on the phone again, wanting to get approval to take the leadership in the House of Representatives for the ABA's position. He not only was the wrong political person to do this, he was committed to the current ABA position, opposed to the Bayh approach, and unlikely to yield to anything else.

We Develop an ABA Action Plan, Beginning With an ABA High-Powered Commission

I stayed awake that night, trying to come up with an answer that would allow us to work with Senator Bayh and at the same time work around Congressman Wyman, who was chomping at the bit to take this over. I think I was in awe of this new situation, maybe even starry-eyed, and wanted more than anything for it to work out well. Senator Bayh was a 34-year new senator, just elected in 1962. So here I was, a youngster new to Washington myself, about to work with this receptive young senator, and one who had no negative history in Washington with the ABA. There would be only good things ahead if we did it right.

I came up with an idea that night. The next morning I suggested to Don that we form a well-balanced ABA group to consider a fresh approach to Presidential Inability by examining and critiquing the merits of the various proposals. We should think "outside the box" of traditional ABA committees, which generally were composed primarily of ABA stalwarts. Why not organize a group with unquestionable constitutional expertise, and others who were politically influential with the ABA House of Delegates? They should meet together as a think-tank group so the member-ABA leaders would "buy" into the proposal as their own, and would speak enthusiastically to the House of Delegates. But, we didn't have much time. We would have to move quickly because momentum was building in Congress for a solution. Selecting the right people, and getting them all together so quickly with the necessary background information, was not going to be easy.

Don immediately bought it, and we asked Bert Early, who soon would be executive director, if he had the time to work with us on the association's strategy. This issue was going to require resources of the entire ABA. Although Bert was busy getting ready to take on his new job, he jumped in. He too agreed that a super committee was the correct approach, and said he would do whatever we wanted to help get it going.

After getting the enthusiastic approval of ABA President Walter (Wally)

Craig and President-elect Lewis Powell, we began thinking about members for it. It would be called the ABA Special Study Commission on Presidential Succession and Disability, chaired by President Craig. Before telling Senator Bayh, we would develop our list of names, and contact them only if he thought the "commission" was a good idea. (This was the first ABA group called a commission instead of a committee. It was because it had members who didn't belong to the association.)

The senator and we didn't waste time. On January 2, immediately after the congressional Christmas recess, we met again and told him and his assistants, Larry Conrad and Steve Lesher, about our idea. They agreed that it was a good one. However, Senator Bayh later told us that he had been slightly concerned, because if the new commission favored an approach similar to his, it would be extremely useful and key to enactment. On the other hand, if the commission came up with something drastically different than his plan, the legislative process could be disrupted, and even halted. Perhaps, however, a different approach than his might at least highlight deficiencies in his plan, and these could be rectified. Messrs. Bayh, Conrad and Lesher were pleased with our list of potential commission members. We set January 20 and 21, just three weeks away, as the meeting dates in Washington. This was a short time to arrange a meeting with any busy people, much less those on our list. But, by what seemed like a miracle, we pulled it off.

We were launching an ABA political effort that was more important than any it had undertaken. It probably was exceeded only by the ABA's role in helping block President Franklin Roosevelt's effort to "pack" the U. S. Supreme Court by adding justices to support his New Deal. While we had knowledgeable scholars on the list, we had to give attention also to the ABA leaders who would contribute to the discussion and who would carry the most weight in getting the approval of the House of Delegates. There would be no politicians on the commission. And, it would be limited to 12 members so that everyone would have a chance to participate.

Heading the list was Wally Craig, the ABA president, who would chair the meetings. Next was Lewis Powell, the President-elect. Third was Edward Wright from Arkansas, the esteemed chairman of the House of Delegates. Fourth was Sylvester Smith, Jr., ABA immediate past president. An important member was Ross Malone of New Mexico, also a former ABA president and former U.S. deputy attorney general under President Truman, who had served without a vice president. All four of these men obviously were important for their insights and their "weight" inside the ABA.

The ABA Committee on Jurisprudence and Law Reform was the group that previously had made recommendations to the House of Delegates, so it was important to include its chairman, Jonathan Gibson.

Next on the list was Martin Taylor, chairman of the Committee of the Federal Constitution of the New York State Bar Association. This committee originated the current ABA position.

After the organized bar leaders were listed, we turned to others who would bring the most knowledgeable and credible thinking.

The first name was Paul Freund, suggested as a "must" by Bert Early, and a friend of Lewis Powell since Harvard Law School days. Professor Freund was a Harvard Law School constitutional law scholar, and considered by a former Harvard dean as "the dominant figure of his time in the field of constitutional law." There was a big problem though. He never had associated with the American Bar Association because he didn't like it. We were concerned that he wouldn't want to have any connection with the ABA. Because of the importance of the subject, and a personal call from Lewis Powell, he accepted. Imagine our jubilation when he said yes. Here was the country's most highly recognized constitutional authority, agreeing to lend his expertise. It was like we already had won a victory.

The next was Herbert Brownell, the president of the Association of the Bar of the City of New York, and most importantly the United States Attorney General when President Eisenhower had his heart attacks. Mr. Brownell had personally experienced the problems of a sitting President with disabilities, and had proposed solutions at those times, all of which would write procedures into the Constitution.

Rounding out the list were: Dean Charles Nutting of the George Washington National Law Center, and a constitutional scholar; Professor James Kirby of the Vanderbilt University School of Law, and a former counsel to the Senate Subcommittee on Constitutional Amendments under Senator Kefauver (he brought invaluable legislative historical insights); and Richard Hanson, a Nebraska lawyer who had written *The Year We Had No President.*

Most importantly was a young lawyer from New York, John Feerick. It's impossible to express enough the contributions John Feerick gave to obtaining the solution to Presidential Inability and Succession. In my own research and preparing for our campaign efforts, I read John's law review article entitled *The Problem of Presidential Inability —Will Congress Ever Solve It?* It was the best written explanation of the issue that I had read, and it demonstrated a profound understanding of the problem. John had graduated from Fordham Law School in 1961, and was a new lawyer practicing labor law with the Skadden Arps firm. He filled the bill perfectly —a brilliant new scholar on the subject.

After Don and Lewis Powell read the article, they agreed that John should be involved. How about asking him to be a paid resource person? After all, he was very young to be a commission member, and we didn't know him like others on the list. I had an uneasy feeling about this. We had no other paid resource persons. Each commission member was an expert in his own right, and how would they accept this new, unknown person as a resource person when they were so knowledgeable themselves? Wouldn't it be better, I suggested, to ask him to sit at the table as an equal? After all, while new to the Bar, he had been practicing with a major firm for a couple of years. And wouldn't it enhance the commission to have a young lawyer who already had developed so much knowledge on the subject? His article was more than just another law review article. He seemed to write it with a passion for the subject. Don and Mr. Powell agreed. John became an invaluable member of the commission.

John Feerick did not stop writing and speaking about Presidential Inability and Succession. His first book was From Failing Hands… the story of Presidential Succession. *His second was* The Twenty-Fifth Amendment, *a comprehensive and scholarly history of the amendment. He became, next to Senator Bayh himself, the nationally acclaimed expert on it. John became dean of the Fordham Law School in 1982, after some 20 years at the Skadden Arps firm. His achievements in the field of arbitration and mediation, and work for the cause of social justice are too numerous to mention here. He was president of the Association of the Bar of the City of New York, and chair of the American Arbitration Association. Probably his highest profile labor dispute was when he was appointed to mediate the NFL's salary cap dispute. As the retired dean of*

Fordham Law School, the school created the Law School's Feerick Center for Social Justice where he now (June 2015) is at work.

Each invitee said yes enthusiastically, and agreed to meet in Washington on short notice. The conference was scheduled for January 20 and 21 in a private conference room of the Mayflower Hotel.

The next issue was whom to invite to speak to the commission. There were no legislators on it. So, we decided to invite members of Congress who had specific points of view, and importantly, who would be most influential in shepherding it through Congress. They included Senator Bayh; Senators Roman Hruska and Kenneth Keating; and Congressmen Emanuel Celler and Louis Wyman.

Congressman Celler lived at the Mayflower Hotel, and, we were told that he would participate because his apartment was just doors away from our meeting room. So we were lucky.

And yes, we included Lou Wyman as a speaker-guest. We wanted him to feel part of the process, and hoped he would agree with the commission's ultimate position.

Deputy Attorney General Nicholas deB. Katzenbach agreed to be a "witness."

Because of their roles with Senator Bayh, his staff members Larry Conrad and Stephen Lesher were invited to attend and continue answering questions and commenting after the senator had left.

Neal Kennedy of Senator Everett Dirksen's staff, with whom I had developed an association, was invited to attend as an observer and make comments. Senator Dirksen was so vital to the eventual outcome that we involved Neal every step of the way. If he came on board, there was little doubt that Senator Dirksen would also. In fact, because Kennedy was such a well-known conservative, his view would be important in both the Senate and House.

This has been a long explanation of the formation of the ABA commission, its members and witnesses. It is described in detail because of my own personal involvement, and to show how much work and attention must go into any successful legislative effort of such magnitude. Throughout these so-called "memoirs" there will be many other situations where you might think you're getting more than you need to know. I hope, however, that all of the explanations will give you a clearer picture of what I did, and, that, most of all, you will have an understanding of the lobbying process. The lesson here is that successful legislation isn't determined by only calling on a few legislators and throwing some money around. You have to call on them, have support from back home, and in many instances, as you'll learn later, contribute political dollars to support the legislators who support your views. **However, the first and most important principle is that the product must be a good one. This is what we achieved with all of the detailed work that went into the enactment of the Twenty-Fifth Amendment.**

The commission heard from all of the witnesses, and except for a couple of members, notably Mr. Taylor of New York, it agreed on a consensus supporting the Bayh approach of establishing constitutionally enumerated procedures rather than simply giving Congress authority to act. Jonathan Gibson, like Mr. Taylor, also wanted to stick with the original ABA position, but agreed to join the consensus because he felt so strongly that a solution must move forward.

Messrs. Craig, Powell, Brownell, Wright and Malone met virtually all night to construct specific language that, after more discussion, would be approved by the full commission the next day. Don Channell and I, along with Don Hyndman, the ABA public relations director from the Chicago office, met with them. We contributed our views of what consensus had been developed during the discussion.

Senator Bayh said of the commission's consensus: "The first step had been taken in the longest of legislative journeys —the enactment of a constitutional amendment."

While Senator Bayh convened two days of hearings beginning the next day to get a sense of how senators were leaning, Don and I went to work to get ready for the House of Delegates meeting coming up on February 17, 1964. It would vote on the commission's recommendation.

Our First Child, Richard, Arrives

In the meantime, Myrna and I were expecting our first child, a momentous occasion to say the least. Richard Lowell Beck was born on February 5, 1964, at the George Washington University Hospital in Washington. This, of course, took my mind completely off of everything connected with work. I took some time away from the office and stayed with "Richie" and Myrna at our apartment on Pollard Street in Arlington.

Myrna had left Senator Pearson's office, not intending to return to work. While it seemed implausible, the senator was unhappy *with me* for it. He relied so much on Myrna that, as I understood it, he was upset that she wouldn't return to work, and blamed me. Fortunately, in time his "brooding" faded away, and he was friendly with me again.

The House of Delegates Approves the Commission's Consensus, and We "Go to Work"

The House of Delegates unanimously endorsed the commission's consensus, which essentially was the same proposal as Senator Bayh's Senate Joint Resolution 139. This was attributable to the careful planning, the work of the commission, and the commitment of the ABA officers.

Don and I were off and running. We now were sanctioned to work with Senator Bayh in favor of his position. We could literally smell success, but were soon to learn that it wasn't going to be all that easy. There were more senators to convince, and we had a House of Representatives leadership group, beginning with Congressman Celler and his Republican colleagues, Messrs. McCulloch and Poff, to enlist.

Remember that this was 1964. A tumultuous year. Senator Bayh was busy (and I mean busy) holding more hearings, which included members of the ABA commission, and promoting his constitutional amendment, S. J. Res. 139 with other senators. Don and I began organizing a grassroots program in the organized bar. The Junior Bar Conference enlisted its members to contact their senators and representatives. Providing organizational support to the young lawyers was easy for me because I knew so many of them. But it was clear that Congress and the new Johnson administration had other priorities. Civil rights events were exploding, and Congress was severely divided on what to do. President Johnson was leading a Presidential transition. The Viet Nam War was escalating. There seemed to be a greatly divided and contentious population on every major issue.

While the Kennedy assassination provided momentum for a solution on Presidential Inability, it wasn't front and center with the general electorate. It simply wasn't an issue that touched a person's bread and butter or direct personal interest. *The issue taught me another basic legislative/political principle which I found applied to every piece of legislation:* **You inspire the overall public's action when the issue is something that affects them, either personally or because of their cause-driven interest.** *You can organize coalitions of groups around an issue common to them all, but only if they* *feel the issue is in their own interest. Consequently, coalitions come and go, depending on the issue.*

We were faced with these facts in trying to organize active support for the Twenty-Fifth Amendment. Outside of the organized legal profession, with its attorneys and constitutional scholars, there wasn't strong public interest in promoting the Amendment even though it was a pressing issue. So, what would we do to build support?

First we decided to build support among thought leaders, such as heads of business and labor. If they would not actively work for it (and most would not, because they had their own "fish to fry" with their own interests), at least they could be educated so that they wouldn't oppose it. So, education of as many groups as possible was our first order of business.

We Sponsor a Washington Conference of Thought Leaders

To do that, we decided to hold a one day conference of as many national groups and thought leaders as possible. The groups invited ranged all the way from the American Political Science Association to the AFL-CIO. We had over 750 invitees.

The panel of speakers would be as important as organizing the ABA commission. First on our list was former President Eisenhower, for the obvious reason that he had suffered some illnesses that could have been seriously disabling. He agreed to be the luncheon speaker, thanks to Herbert Brownell. In addition to the former president, these leaders were panel speakers: Congressman Celler, Senator Bayh, Herbert Brownell, Wally Craig and Ed Wright. Each had a specific role, but we didn't know what Mr. Celler would say. We did know that it was essential to include him in the process if we were going to get his leadership in the House.

To be moderator, we asked LeRoy Collins, the former governor of Florida and chairman of the Democratic National Committee the year John F. Kennedy was nominated. Governor Collins would be just the person to help with media because he was then the president of the National Association of Broadcasters.

Ed Wright, chairman of the ABA House of Delegates, had an especially important role. He was to explain the ABA's position and plans for conducting a nationwide campaign for the Amendment. Its adoption would be no easy task. A constitutional amendment must be proposed by a two-thirds majority vote in both the House and Senate, and ratified by three-fourths of the states. (The other way would be through a national Constitutional Convention, which never had been called.)

The process would require concentrated organization and the support of many groups. We, of course, hoped for little or no opposition.

The conference was held at the Statler Hilton in downtown Washington on May 25. It was the event in Washington that day. We accomplished all that we had hoped for. The press turned out in droves, and President Eisenhower strongly supported the Bayh/ABA proposal. We were on pins and needles, waiting to hear from Congressman Celler. At this point, he was the most important person in the room, and had not hinted how he felt. Fortunately, he said enough positive things to assure us that we could work with him. But, he also said that he hadn't reached conclusions yet.

President Eisenhower received a standing ovation. The crowd was with us. The conference's objectives were met. The public was informed, interest groups had been brought together, and the ABA was demonstrating national leadership. Still hanging was whether Mr. Celler would fully support us. And, when he and the other members of Congress in attendance returned to their offices, they had their hands full with other pressing issues which were knocking down their doors.

I looked forward to meeting President Eisenhower face to face. Just before the luncheon, a few participants met in a small reception room to greet him. But, I couldn't get there in time because of handling last minute details and welcoming attendees. Don, as always, came to my rescue. He took me past the Secret Service to the platform after the speech, and Herb Brownell introduced me to the former president. He was smiling, just as we always saw him, and was very congenial. Of course we didn't become lifelong friends. But I had the privilege of shaking his hand, and this was a treat in and of itself.

We Meet With the Business Council in New York City

An interesting day for me was a meeting with the executive committee of the Business Council in New York City. The Business Council is a formal group of 150 CEOs of America's most important companies from all business sectors. While it doesn't take positions, and is non-partisan, it meets to discuss relevant business, civic and political issues. Herb Brownell was well known by the members, and he asked Don and me to accompany him to present our case. He would do the talking, and we would have five minutes. If there were no questions from the members, we could be satisfied that they understood, and were with us. We would thank them and say goodbye. Don and I were there to show ABA support.

It's difficult to describe the feeling when entering a room with a round-table of CEOs from companies such as GM, GE, Aetna, Hewlett-Packard and Caterpillar, to name a few. Never having experienced a meeting like this before, I didn't know what to expect. They were extremely courteous, obviously so because of Herb Brownell. They listened attentively, all with smiles, and thanked us for coming. When we left the room, Herb said that we had done our job. Although the group doesn't take positions, several CEOs, as individuals, sent letters of strong support to their senators and representatives.

Highlights of Our Actions Resulting in Adoption of the Twenty-Fifth Amendment

I can't describe all of the strategy and the details of our lobbying and statewide efforts that led to success of the Twenty-Fifth Amendment. As I've mentioned, those details are covered extensively in the Bayh and Feerick books. I'll conclude by listing highlights of Don's and my work between the time of the ABA leadership conference on May 25, 1964, and final adoption in February 1967.

Don Channell had a new mission, and put virtually all of his energy into the Twenty-Fifth Amendment. It no longer was a Beck-only situation like when I was trying to work around Lou Wyman (and yet keep him involved), and first met Fred Graham on the subcommittee staff. We all were involved deeply now, from the ABA president, president-elect, House of Delegates chairman, executive director, Don, and I. All of us had plenty to do.

1. My main job, along with John Feerick, was to provide support to the ABA Junior Bar Conference (now Young Lawyers Division). They carried the heaviest load of getting letters and calls made to Congress. We started with targeting key leaders in Congress. While Senator Bayh and his staff seemed never to sleep, always meeting with senators and their staffs, passage of S. J. 139 required massive communication from knowledgeable constituencies back home. We were able to produce those letters and calls. One illustrative result was with Senator Harry Byrd of Virginia.

Senator Byrd's assistant told us: "I don't know what it is, but the lawyers are all over us. Put us down as a cosponsor." Mike Spence, our new staff member, helped me immeasurably, with getting state and local bar associations to respond.

2. I also focused on the ABA Legal Education Section and the Association of American Law Schools to enlist the help of constitutional law professors. Of course, Professor Freund's and Dean Nutting's scholarly reputations couldn't have been more helpful.

3. The media work, contacting national news services, TV and radio stations, was done primarily by Harry Swegle, who had joined us from our Chicago Public Relations Department.

4. With the help of Mike and Harry, I organized meetings of groups with Washington offices, focusing on business and labor. In these small meetings, we found that most other groups were looking exclusively to the ABA to carry this. They were willing to consider it a law organization's issue because of our expertise in law schools and the practicing bar.

5. There still were hurdles to jump. One was getting Congressman Celler's attention. Another was enlisting the support of our Republican friends, Congressmen McCulloch and Poff. Don focused on the Judiciary Committee chairman, Mr. Celler, and I provided information to the two Republican committee leaders. All three of them seemed to favor an amendment, rather than just legislation, which was an important hurdle to overcome; and they also favored something similar to S. J. Res. 139. But they disagreed with 139 over a timing issue if Congress had to act on a disagreement between the President and the Cabinet on the President's fitness. This would be a serious, almost insurmountable "sticking point" to the very end of the joint Senate-House conference, when finally compromise language was agreed to. Don and I had close contact with these three offices, but, again, because of so many other issues on their plates, it was difficult getting their attention. Bill Foley, the House Judiciary Committee's general counsel, warned us not to expect House action during this session of Congress. We understood this, but it dampened the momentum.

6. Although the Senate passed S. J. Res. 139 on September 29, 1964, Congress adjourned in October and the Amendment died. But when Congress convened in January 1965, Senator Bayh introduced S. J. Res. 1, the same resolution that had passed the prior September, and Congressman Celler introduced H. J. Res. 1, the equivalent of S. J. Res. 1.

7. The Amendment, S. J. Res. 1, passed the Senate 72-0 on February 19, 1965, and was delivered to the House of Representatives. It passed the House on April 13, 1965, by a vote of 368–29. My description of our work sounds almost as if, after a few hearings and contacts by Senator Bayh and us, the Twenty-Fifth Amendment was passed easily by the two-thirds required majority in both the Senate and House. But this wasn't the situation. Several senators and House members had reservations and concerns. They expressed them, and in many instances, offered their own amendments to the Amendment.

8. While this narrative of our activities with the Amendment doesn't tell everything, some final vignettes are interesting.

   a. Senator Dirksen, the Republican leader, was friendly with Senator Bayh, but had his concerns about writing procedures into the Constitution. We knew that we had to have his support. Neal Kennedy, his assistant who had been working with us, suggested that Lewis Powell, Don and I meet with the senator. Neal believed that he ultimately would agree, but that he would welcome a visit from the ABA president-elect. The problem was getting a time when Mr. Powell and the senator could meet. Lee Gomien helped. That meeting with Everett Dirksen was one of my most eagerly anticipated meetings I would have on Capitol Hill. Entering his ornate Capitol office with its crystal chandeliers and breathtaking view of the Mall to the Washington Monument was an experience. Senator Dirksen, the great orator, unexcelled by any other then or since, and just as great a "character," greeted us warmly with his booming voice. He expressed interest that I was from his home area, told a story or two, and got down to business. While he didn't commit himself, he seemed sympathetic, and was impressed with all of the thought given the issue. Neal told us that the visit was the right thing to do, and that we probably could count on the senator's support. He was right.

b. We needed the support of President Johnson, and while we thought he would endorse it, we still hadn't heard. Senator Bayh and his staff were concerned. They had meetings with Ramsey Clark, son of Supreme Court Justice Tom Clark, and now an assistant in the White House. Clark assured them that the president was aware of the issue, but couldn't comment on what he might do. In his State of the Union message, President Johnson mentioned Presidential Inability, and said that he would consider it and make a proposal. This concerned all of us. We were so far along with it, and if the President made his own proposal at this point, the entire effort could be thrown off base, maybe for good. As luck would have it, Don and Betty Channell hosted a dinner party at their home, and Ramsey Clark was a guest. At that party, we cornered Mr. Clark, and while we didn't realize it until a few days later, he was responsible for President Johnson's ultimate endorsement of the Bayh bill. Dinner parties can be helpful.

c. When there was a question about how long it would take for the House Judiciary Committee to move on the issue, we (ABA) hosted a luncheon in the Capitol with Senator Bayh and the House Judiciary Committee leaders. Our house scholar, John Feerick, was on hand to stress again the Amendment's importance from a national historical perspective. We did this to keep the momentum going, and invited key media as well. It was another way of keeping the issue out front as well as we could.

d. Some contention arose between the House and Senate after both Judiciary Committees had reported their resolutions. The question was over which body would vote first. The majority leader of the Senate, Senator Mansfield, told Senator Bayh that he didn't want the Senate to delay, and that the Senate should proceed immediately. However, Bess Dick, Congressman Celler's assistant, had told Larry Conrad that since the Senate had already voted on it once, the House should go first. Senator Mansfield was adamant; however, it was because he didn't want the Senate to lose interest, and wanted to strike in that body while the iron was hot. Senator Bayh, knowing that both Don and I knew Mrs. Dick, asked us to see if we "could spread some oil over troubled waters." Don talked with Mrs. Dick. The next day when Larry talked with her, she wasn't concerned about which chamber went first. *This is another example of non-Senate/House individuals providing coordination between both bodies, something that senators and House members and their staffs couldn't always seem to do effectively.*

e.   Finally, a note about how Lewis Powell again helped "save the day." During the Senate-House conference, when representatives of both bodies met to try to reconcile their differences, the Senate conferees agreed to a time limit of 21 days, relenting on their position of no time limit. But the House members wouldn't agree because they insisted on a time limit of only 10 days, and the conference collapsed. It collapsed over *that*, and it was a serious disagreement. From the biography of Lewis Powell by John Jeffries this is the account of what broke the stalemate, leading to the final adoption of the Twenty-Fifth Amendment: "In desperation, Bayh called Don Channell, who was attending an ABA regional meeting in San Juan, Puerto Rico. The next morning's first flight brought Powell from San Juan back to Washington, where he met with Emanuel Celler and all five House members of the conference committee. He then went to see Senator Bayh, who was just leaving for Indiana. Powell rode with him to National Airport, following him inside the terminal to continue the conversation. There Bayh and Powell (accidentally and surprisingly) ran into Celler, who was headed back to Brooklyn for the weekend.

Powell brought the two legislators together on National Airport's upper observation deck and pleaded for compromise. Bayh volunteered to call on Celler early the next week, and Celler agreed to reconsider his opposition to the twenty-one-day limit. In a letter written only a few hours after the event, Powell called the success 'not so much the results of my efforts at mediation as the wholesome effect of *cooling off.*' Whatever the cause, Celler reconsidered, and the House conferees decided they could live with twenty-one days."

This statement, "not so much the results of my efforts…" reflected exactly the modesty of Lewis Powell. It was a modesty that those who knew him, including his colleagues on the Supreme Court, admired so much.

On June 30, 1965, the Joint conference report on S. J. Res. 1 was passed by the House and delivered to the Senate. On July 6, 1965, the Senate passed the report. This was Senator Bayh's account of that emotional moment in the Senate:

> At last the roll call was completed. "On this vote the yeas are 68, the nays 5," announced the Presiding Officer. "Two-thirds of the senators present and voting have voted in the affirmative; the Conference Report is agreed to."

> What followed was a blur to me: the congratulations of colleagues who had worked along with us; the exchange of looks with Don Channell and Lowell Beck of the ABA, who had been sitting in the visitor's gallery hanging on to every word; a smile from Marvella, who also was sitting above; the exuberant walk back to the Senate Office Building with those who had helped guide the amendment to its final passage pummeling me on the back. We had experienced success and failure during the many months we labored through the legislative thicket. But this was a new feeling. Hard as it might be to believe, once and for all the job was done. The final outcome, of course, was in the hands of the state legislators, but for the moment I could relax and enjoy the exhilaration of victory. It had not always been that way. (From *One Heartbeat Away.*)

Congress had acted, and now it was up to the state legislators to ratify. Thirty-eight states out of 50 had to agree. The ABA's efforts for Congressional passage now went into high gear to obtain the votes in the states. Senator Bayh and his staff, in addition to several other supportive senators, began sending letters and detailed information to state leaders, urging them to vote yes as quickly as possible. On July 12 and 13, 1965, just six and seven days after Congressional passage, Nebraska and Wisconsin were the first two states to ratify. On February 10, 1967, Minnesota and Nevada were the 37th and 38th states to ratify, completing the required three-quarters of the state legislatures.

The Twenty-Fifth Amendment to the Constitution now specified procedures if the President could not discharge his responsibilities.

Essentially, under Section 3, the President may temporarily make the Vice President the Acting President with a written declaration to Congress that he is unable to discharge his duties. The Vice President serves as Acting President until the President sends another declaration to Congress that he is able to resume his duties.

Section 4 allows the Vice President and Cabinet to transmit to Congress a declaration that the President is unable to fulfill his duties, and the Vice President assumes the office of Acting President. The President may assert his ability to serve by his own declaration to Congress. If the Vice President and Cabinet disagree with him, Congress would have to decide the issue with a two-thirds vote within twenty-one days.

On February 23, 1967, the Twenty-Fifth Amendment became part of the Constitution of the United States of America when it was signed by the General Services Administrator as required by law. Although the President of the United States is not required to sign a constitutional amendment, President Johnson hosted a formal signing ceremony in the East Room of the White House, and affixed his signature as a witness. He considered the adoption of the Amendment so significant that he wanted to give it his official recognition.

This was my third time as a guest in the East Room of the White House: the first to hear President Kennedy talk about civil rights, and the second, President Johnson's signing of the Bail Reform Act of 1966. Both were auspicious occasions for me, but this, of course, was the most exhilarating. As Don and I were leaving the East Room with coats in hand, Herb Hoffman from the Justice Department, who had helped on the Amendment just as he had on the Criminal Justice Act, ran up to us. "Did you get to shake hands with the President?" he asked. "I think you might have missed him because he's in the little room next to the East Room, where he's greeting Senator Bayh, Congressmen Celler and McColluch, and a few others." We said no, we didn't know about that. He told us to hurry and follow him, and we might make it in time. We did, but just in the nick of time. We were the last ones to come into the room and shake President Johnson's hand. He towered over both Don and me, and I remembered from an earlier time his hand grip of size and strength like I'd never felt with anybody else. We were carrying our coats, and it was obvious we had hurried into the room. Thanks to Herb, we made it just in time.

———————————— ◈ ————————————

Unmentioned in detail during my narrative here is the provision relating to a vacancy in the Vice Presidency. In many instances, this has been as important historically as the inability of the President. Until the Twenty-Fifth Amendment was adopted, the Constitution did not provide for filling Vice Presidential vacancies. The Vice Presidency has been vacant 16 times due to the death, resignation or succession of the Vice President to the Presidency. Often these vacancies lasted several important years as was the case after President Franklin Roosevelt's death when President Truman succeeded him and there was no Vice President for almost four years.

This was changed under Section 2 of the Twenty-Fifth Amendment, which reads: "Whenever there is a vacancy in the office of the Vice President, the President shall nominate a Vice President who shall take office upon confirmation by a majority vote of both Houses of Congress."

The Amendment has been invoked six times since its ratification and now in 2015: four times in the case of Presidential succession and two for Vice Presidential vacancies. When Vice President Agnew resigned in 1973, President Nixon nominated and won approval for Gerald Ford to fill the Vice Presidency. When President Nixon resigned in 1974, Vice President Ford succeeded to the office of President, leaving a Vice Presidential vacancy. President Ford nominated and won approval for Governor Nelson Rockefeller of New York to fill it.

The three brief Presidential inability "vacancies" since the Amendment's adoption were during a somewhat confusing situation when President Reagan was shot, but no formal temporary succession plan was instituted; when the Amendment was invoked in 1985 because of President Reagan's Surgery, and Vice President George H.W. Bush assumed the powers as Acting President; and when, in 2002, the Amendment was used by President George W. Bush who was hospitalized for a few hours, causing Vice President Cheney to serve as Acting President then.

———————————— ❧ ————————————

And so, the work for the Twenty-Fifth Amendment was over. It was the quintessential lobbying adventure. All of the principles of effective lobbying had been utilized, and for an excellent cause. We had a superior product, an effective coalition of support, strong assistance from lawyers and constitutional scholars "back home," the right leadership in Congress, and the support of the President of the United States. We, as ABA lobbyists, had developed trustworthy relationships on Capitol Hill that continued long after 1967, and we had done our job of providing effective communication and liaison between both Congressional houses. It was the experience of a lifetime for a new guy from Peoria who had found his niche.

It was even more of a lifetime experience for Senator Bayh, the young senator who had been raised on an Indiana farm, had gained prominence as an Indiana legislator, and had beaten a senior Indiana senator when the odds were strongly against him. He credited Marvella, his first wife who died of cancer, for encouraging him to enter public life (when they first met at a debating tournament, she was the better and more experienced public speaker). Through all of his years of prominence, he always knew exactly how to accomplish victory through preparation and human relations; and he *never* considered himself better or more important than anybody else.

While he has had many important political successes on important issues in his Senatorial career, and was proud of each achievement, including the Twenty-Sixth Amendment on the 18-year-old vote, and women's rights legislation, even today in 2015, he considers the Twenty-Fifth Amendment to be his crowning success. Senator Bayh "cut his Senatorial teeth" on the Twenty-Fifth Amendment, and has never forgotten that.

A few days after ratification, Don and I hosted a celebration party in our DeSales Street office. Senator Bayh, Congressman Celler, and Congressman Poff were among our honored guests. A good time was had by all, and our office, with its functional ability for hosting happy events, served its purpose well that night.

CHAPTER SEVEN

The Legal Services Program of the Office of Economic Opportunity

WASHINGTON, D.C., 1964

While efforts on the Twenty-Five Amendment took long, persistent work from all of us involved, other major activities were taking place alongside it. One of those was the emergence of a federal program of legal services that was developed by a new agency called the OEO. The OEO was a massive anti-poverty program that President Johnson considered a cornerstone of his administration. In contrast to the Amendment, which was supported and unopposed by lawyers throughout country, the announcement of an OEO legal services program caused loud outcries from individual lawyers and many bar groups. Its development presented the ABA with difficult challenges that couldn't be ignored. It struck at the heart of what many lawyers considered the feared federalization of the legal profession.

The ABA's Involvement Begins With a Newspaper Article

In October 1964, I read an article in *The Washington Post* that vividly caught my attention. It was the beginning of the ABA's involvement at its highest level in creation of a program that changed the legal profession's approach to "legal aid"; and according to Justice Lewis Powell's biographer, John Jeffries, it was considered by Mr. Powell to be his "greatest achievement" as president of the American Bar Association.

The *Post* article was about Edgar Cahn, a special assistant to Sargent Shriver (brother-in-law of President Kennedy and former head of the Peace Corps), the director of the Office of Economic Opportunity. The article described a proposed nationwide system of legal assistance offices that Cahn was urging Shriver to incorporate within an agency of the OEO called the Community Action Program (CAP).

I knew that the OEO had been created in August as part of the "War on Poverty," but it wasn't on my radar screen. While I knew that it was a government department "to eradicate poverty in America," I didn't know anything about its specific objectives. Looking into it more closely after reading the *Post* article, I learned that it was a massive undertaking of the federal government with emphasis on involving the poor themselves in organizing programs to combat poverty. It was to help the poor gain education and jobs, and basically help them function at the highest level of their abilities. To carry out these objectives, a Community Action Program was created within OEO; and the OEO also was the home of programs such as Head Start and the Job Corps, which provided education and skills training to low-income young people. I didn't see how legal services, as I knew "legal aid to the poor," would fit into this program. However, I soon would learn.

Don Channell agreed that we should try to meet with Edgar Cahn and learn about his idea. An entirely new approach to legal services was under consideration by a new federal agency, and we at the ABA knew nothing about it. Not knowing anybody at the OEO, I called Jules Pagano, a friend at the Peace Corps who had worked there with Sargent Shriver. He affirmed with Edgar Cahn that Don and I were "good guys," and arranged for Mr. Cahn to have lunch with us.

Lunch With Edgar Cahn

Over lunch Mr. Cahn didn't hesitate to share his plans. Just as the OEO wasn't on our radar, neither the ABA nor the organized bar was on his. We were from different worlds with different experiences, but the discussion was friendly and constructive.

Edgar's wife, Jean, was an African-American lawyer, well-known in circles active on behalf of the poor. Edgar explained her earlier efforts in New Haven, Connecticut, that were part of a Ford Foundation experiment with neighborhood centers as a means of eradicating poverty. The foundation proposed that one program of the centers be legal assistance; and Jean Cahn opened a legal assistance office in one of them. This office provided legal assistance, like traditional legal aid, to the poor; however, its main function was, through the legal process, to effect changes in institutional structures that were keeping people down, whether they be welfare agencies or government rules.

Jean worked primarily on civil cases, but on one occasion defended a black man accused of raping a white woman. Jean argued that the woman had consented willingly to intercourse, and this caused a public uproar in New Haven. Under intense pressure, the Ford Foundation pulled its funding, and the neighborhood legal assistance office closed down.

From this and some other experiences, Jean and Edgar published in the *Yale Law Journal* their ground-breaking article, *The War on Poverty: A Civilian Perspective*. They wrote that the poor must have access to legal assistance, and that it had to have a "power base" that was not dependent on funding in the local community. They argued that their "civilian perspective" was that the new legal assistance offices should be organized to serve the interests of the local residents, and should not be beholden to any welfare agency or political organization. Lawyers in these offices would be empowered to use the courts to seek redress from any institution that did not act in a just or legal manner toward the poor.

The Cahns concluded by recommending that federal funding for such neighborhood law offices be included in the poverty bill.

Sargent Shriver read this article just before it was published, and according to his biography, *Sarge,* by Scott Stossel, was "powerfully struck by it." Prior to passage of the Economic Opportunity Act in August 1964, Shriver and his War on Poverty task force had been struggling with various issues, including what to do about legal services. He had decided not to include legal services in the Act because he thought the bill's language of approaches to fight poverty was broad enough to include free legal assistance. As the OEO program began to function, however, some form of legal assistance was needed to deal with the problems of the poor, ranging from harassment by landlords to unconstitutional treatment by government agencies. There weren't enough traditional legal aid agencies to do this, and most of them weren't even located in poverty neighborhoods.

However, Shriver and the task force didn't know how best to integrate legal assistance into their poverty program; nor did they know just what its philosophy of operations should be. Enter the Cahn article. Again, according to the Shriver biography, when he read it, he said, "It was like Columbus discovering America, an exciting thing for me to discover... something that captured my mind and imagination. That's the genesis of Legal Services---it's really pretty simple."

Edgar gave us this background, and then explained the work of a task force that Shriver set up after the Act was signed. The Cahns were leading the task force. Its charge was to recommend how lawyers would fit into the War on Poverty. He told us that some in the group did not want any involvement by the ABA or the National Legal Aid and Defender Association (NLADA... the national group of legal aid societies). They saw this new program not as a "legal" program of personal legal assistance to individuals as much as a program to bring about change in the poverty environment. We learned later that most rejected approaching the ABA because it was too conservative and would kill it before it started. Jean and Edgar, on the other hand, with some influential support on the task force, believed that local bar associations must be involved or local lawyers and judges might work against it if they weren't included. They apparently had not addressed the question of the American Bar Association. The task force finally agreed with the Cahns about local bar associations, although unenthusiastically.

Even though they favored involving local bar associations, until my phone call, neither the Cahns nor the other task force members were planning to contact the ABA. However, that changed with our luncheon. Programs like these were not Don Channell's "cup of tea." So, he looked primarily to me to carry the conversation with Edgar. I was troubled as I listened to Edgar. And, yet, considering the ABA's "establishment" history, and its close ties to the NLADA, which was not seen as innovative, I understood. This new idea was "cutting edge," and could face strident opposition locally and nationally as invading the domain of private lawyers and traditional legal aid societies.

I told Edgar that I thought the ABA should have a vital interest in the program; that I couldn't imagine a legal venture of this national magnitude succeeding without at least the ABA's knowledge, if not its support. I told Edgar that I personally supported the idea of cooperation with the OEO, but had to be truthful that I was cautious about my estimate of support by the ABA leaders.

Before the luncheon, I had discussed this meeting with John Cummiskey, chairman of the ABA's Standing Committee on Legal Aid, whom you'll remember was my kindred spirit during the Criminal Justice Act days. He said that whatever I did, keep the contact going for future conversations and possible cooperation. That's just how the luncheon concluded. We promised to meet again after we had met with our respective colleagues.

Edgar Cahn Reports Back to OEO
An HEW Conference Is Scheduled

Edgar immediately reported to Sargent Shriver and the OEO staff that the ABA was tentatively interested in the program. While the staff remained skeptical about any involvement with the ABA, Mr. Shriver was encouraged, so much so that he assigned Cahn to arrange a meeting between President Johnson and ABA leaders. I informed John Cummiskey that a conversation with the OEO had started, and we should prepare for a future meeting, possibly with Shriver. A meeting with President Johnson wasn't timely, however.

Soon after the luncheon, I learned of a conference on legal services that was scheduled by the Department of Health, Education and Welfare (HEW) to be held in November. It was not connected with the OEO program, but OEO people were invited, and Edgar was a consultant. It was to examine the experimental legal service programs such as that in New Haven, where Jean Cahn had worked. Because it seemed that the entire federal government now was looking at how to establish legal services programs, John Cummiskey and William McCalpin, another ABA committee chairman involved in expanding legal services, wanted to attend, but their requests were denied. They were told that this was a narrow conference simply to examine the activities of these agencies, not a program to "persuade bar leaders that these programs should be part of a national federal effort."

I was concerned about this. What was the harm in including them, other than the new legal services activists just didn't want the ABA there? I thought this would be a good time to educate Cummiskey and McCalpin about the new, developing legal services programs, and it would be a missed opportunity if they weren't included.

I immediately called Ken Pye who now was the associate dean of the Georgetown Law Center. He agreed, and obtained two invitations from the conference's leader, Jack Murphy, who was a friend of his. (Jack and I later worked closely together on the developing legal services issues.)

To attend the conference we chose Junius Allison, executive secretary of the NLADA, and Bill McCalpin, chairman of the ABA Standing Committee on Lawyer Referral. Allison was a long-time legal aid lawyer, and McCalpin had little legal aid experience. But, opening better access to legal services to *all* people was McCalpin's ABA agenda, and he was the right person to participate.

The conference speakers were hostile to traditional legal aid offices as not being innovative enough, not being responsive to needs of the poor, and hopelessly unable to reach enough people. In addition, Edgar announced that the OEO would be organizing a new national legal services program; and that Sargent Shriver had appointed his wife, Jean Cahn, to develop and manage it.

Junius Allison was upset. He saw this as a danger to legal aid, and that as federal dollars poured into new entities, established societies would be cut out of the picture altogether. Consequently, the NLADA Executive Committee passed a resolution that legal aid societies could do the full job with adequate funding; that any OEO program would be a duplication of existing legal aid agencies; and that the use of non-lawyers attempting to practice law would raise serious ethical questions.

Bill McCalpin, on the other hand, was not insulted by legal aid society deficiencies discussed at the conference. Instead, he learned about what the poor thought about many of the traditional legal aid societies. He was planning to make such a report to President Lewis Powell and other ABA leaders. He would not fight the OEO's entrance into legal services, as Junius Allison urged him to. In fact, because of the NLADA's antagonistic resolution, it seemed to McCalpin that a greater burden now was on the ABA to openly collaborate and discuss with the OEO. Opposition could come later *if opposition was necessary.*

Supermarkets of Social Service

Before Bill McCalpin could make his report to the ABA leaders, Sargent Shriver announced that the OEO was launching a network of "supermarkets of social service" for the urban poor. Neighborhood centers administered by local Community Action Agencies would provide a host of services, including "homework aides, recreation aides, health aides and legal services for the poor." And these services, Shriver continued, didn't have to be provided by professionals. As far as legal services were concerned, laymen could serve as "advocates for the poor." To lawyers reading this the next day, it meant the federal government would be engaging in the "unauthorized practice of law."

All hell broke loose among lawyers throughout the country. They were writing and calling our Washington and Chicago offices, demanding that the ABA oppose this program. The outcry was loud and harsh. Executive Director Bert Early and I were at the center of all of this, taking calls, and answering letters. But the real work of responding now and setting the ABA's course fell to President Powell and Bert. This was no longer simply a "Washington" issue. Neither believed that outright opposition at that time was the correct answer.

President Powell realized that he had to move fast. Don and I had met Edgar for lunch in October 1964. The HEW conference was November 12. The Shriver speech was November 17, and, now, just a few weeks after we first learned of the proposed OEO program, the intentions for the program were known throughout the legal profession.

Bert and Mr. Powell had been talking for months before Powell became president, about increasing the ABA's efforts to improve availability of legal services. It was even part of the Powell "inaugural address" to the ABA. If handled properly, with appropriate cooperation and collaboration with Sargent Shriver and the OEO staff, the new OEO program could be an excellent vehicle to advance meaningful legal services to the poor. But it wouldn't be easy. The ABA was the organization of establishment lawyers, conservative in outlook and cautious in actions. And the two OEO leaders were the Cahns. They were activist visionaries who promoted and acted on far-reaching ideas. But, from the beginning of this venture, while they distrusted the American Bar Association, they knew nothing about it; they did believe, though, that the program had to have the support of the local bar associations to get started and to survive. To put it mildly, the road of meetings and negotiations was a rocky one, but Mr. Powell and Bert wanted to take that road, hoping that the result would be cooperation, not opposition.

After the Shriver bombshell, our first big ABA planning meeting with Lewis Powell and Bert was held at Chicago headquarters. Bill McCalpin reported that he believed there could be cooperation between the ABA and OEO. John Cummiskey added that the ABA could not retreat from its "40-year old public position of expanded legal assistance to the poor" because of unfavorable mail. It was decided that there would not be an immediate campaign of opposition to the OEO program, and that we needed to find out if and how the ABA might fit into it.

Rather than have President Powell meet with Sargent Shriver at that level, the group decided to ask the Cahns to meet with Messrs. McCalpin, Cummiskey, Channell and me (as President Powell's representatives) in Washington. We would explore the program's objectives and the possibility of active cooperation. I was assigned to help plan the agenda and arrange the meeting.

The meeting was held on the Monday after Christmas. The ABA's 1965 Midyear Meeting of the House of Delegates was to be held February 7, and we had to be ready by then, one way or another. A decision by President Powell had to be made in plenty of time before that date.

The meeting was one of suspicion on both sides. The Cahns expressed how the current system of legal aid did not address the problems of the poor, but only provided limited individual legal services. And, they represented a drop in the bucket in fulfilling needs of the poor. They expressed doubts about the feasibility of cooperation with the ABA because of its conservative nature and its ties to existing legal aid with the NLADA's opposition. They were not expressing just their own views, but also those of most legal activists working with them.

Messrs. Cummiskey and McCalpin stressed that the ABA historically has been a strong supporter of legal assistance to the poor, and the Standing Committee on Legal Aid has been saying for years what the Cahns were saying: that legal aid agencies had to improve and expand their objectives. The Cahns acknowledged that they did not know this, and indeed had never read any of the committee's reports. It was clear from the Cahns that the program would go forward, regardless of the organized bar's support, led by the ABA. However, they were excellent spokespersons and negotiators (although so were John and Bill who were outstanding lawyers: Cummiskey was a tough Michigan labor negotiator for business); consequently, they were careful never to close the door on cooperation. John and Bill responded that perhaps the program could get started without the ABA's support, but it might not last if it ran into the hurdles from lawyers throughout the country who were calling for ABA opposition.

And so it went…for over two hours, without any concrete conclusion, and with a relatively unfriendly atmosphere. This meeting, however, was the beginning of years of close cooperation between the ABA and the OEO program and its successor, the National Legal Services Corporation. Messrs. Cummiskey and McCalpin believed *strongly* that the ABA must find the path to cooperation. And, the Cahns came to believe that ABA support was essential for the program's success, both politically and at the local bar association level. But those hands weren't played by either side at this meeting.

The Final Steps Toward ABA Cooperation With OEO

Time was of the essence if an ABA position could be presented to the House of Delegates in February. Many ABA members were calling for an all-out war against this new "radical" agency, while President Powell, himself conservative by nature, was making availability of legal services to all a major effort of his program. This was supported by Bert Early, who was working closely with Mr. Powell to modernize the ABA as the nationally respected leader of the American organized bar.

After days of internal ABA meetings at the Chicago headquarters and memos and phone calls between the Chicago and Washington offices, Mr. Powell and Bert invited the Cahns to a January meeting with ABA leaders at the Bar Center. My role was not as a speaking participant…this was Lewis Powell's and Bert Early's meeting, buttressed by McCalpin and Cummiskey. Just listening was interesting enough.

Jean Cahn's comments about that meeting, *in a later oral history interview*, explained the opening tone. She said that Edgar was supposed to be with her, but instead had to travel with Shriver for another meeting. So, he left her (not that she couldn't handle it…believe me, she could) to face about thirty-some very old white men sitting around a very long table at the ABA Center who were all dead set against legal services for the poor. My message, she said, was "did they want to be on the outside looking in, or the inside participating and helping the program succeed?"

Commenting further in that later interview, she said that after that meeting, Messrs. Cummiskey, Powell and McCalpin were very supportive, but that "Bert Early and Lowell Beck" were very much in the forefront, working out the politics of how they were going to get the members of the ABA to solidly endorse the program, knowing what the opposition was like at the local level. She complimented Mr. Powell and every ABA president following, saying that everywhere they went "on the road" they helped calm down the local lawyers by supporting the legal services program.

Jean wasn't entirely correct in recounting that meeting. While all of the ABA participants were white men, and I guess that from her perspective they were old, they were not "all dead set against legal services to the poor." But in fairness to Jean, when she entered the walnut-paneled room, with their gray hair and pinstriped suits, she had reason to believe that they were against her. She did not know how Messrs. Powell and Early felt, and could recall our Washington meeting one month earlier that did not end with positive conclusions.

The long meeting of two days, which Edgar joined on the second day, ended with agreement between the Cahns and the ABA leaders. From Lewis Powell's biography by John Jeffries is an excellent summary account of the importance of that session and the efforts to gain support of the House of Delegates at its New Orleans Midyear Meeting just weeks away:

> Although in hindsight the advantages of agreement are apparent, at the time the possibility of collaboration seemed remote. Differences in background, outlook, and politics separated the two sides. And, as Jean Cahn recalled, the "distance to be bridged could hardly have been cast more symbolically than to ask a white lawyer from the ranks of Southern aristocracy leading the then lily-white ABA and a black woman lawyer representing the 'feds' to hammer out a relationship of trust and cooperation."

> But they did. The ABA leadership agreed to endorse the OEO program and to bring the formidable clout of the organized bar behind it. The OEO agreed not to exclude existing legal aid societies from government funding and to accept some shared management of local organizations. The ABA secured the OEO's commitment to maintaining traditional professional standards in providing legal services to the poor, and the OEO gained the participation of the existing legal aid attorneys in a greatly expanded federal program.

> Now came the hard part. Mr. Powell had to persuade the House of Delegates to go along. In committing the ABA in support of the federal program, Powell was far ahead of the prevailing sentiment in the organization. The members of the House of Delegates almost surely would have rejected the idea had they been left on their own, but they were not. In the words of the historian of the OEO Legal Services Program (former director Justice Earl Johnson, Jr.), "no president could have worked any harder or more artfully to influence a decision than did Lewis Powell." He drafted the resolution of support introduced at the midwinter meeting in New Orleans, solicited the backing of

leading ABA members, persuaded the organization's board of governors to endorse the resolution before it went to the House of Delegates, and arranged who would speak on its behalf and in what order. On February 7, 1965, the ABA endorsement that many OEO officials believed an "impossibility" was passed **without dissent**. John C. Jeffries, Jr., *Justice Lewis F. Powell, Jr. (A Biography)*. New York: C. Scribner's Sons, 1994.

Mr. Powell had carefully done his homework. His success was a testament to the enormous respect everybody had for him. After all, we had been on a roller coaster ride for some four intensive months, and in the midst of it all, Mr. Powell knew exactly how to handle it.

Lewis Powell always had been respected highly in the legal profession, both nationally and at his home base, where he was acknowledged as one of Virginia's outstanding lawyers, if not the most outstanding. But his astute manner, with judgment and temperament, on this program gained him praise outside the legal profession as well. He had successfully brought together a working alliance between social and political conservatives and liberal activists, a cooperative alliance between the American Bar Association and an expanded legal services movement that has continued to this day in 2015. Not that there haven't been rocky times, but as contentious political issues arose with the work of many lawyers who were funded by the OEO and later the Legal Services Corporation, the ABA has been there, maintaining that lawyers be allowed to do their independent jobs of representing the poor.

One of the most notable examples of this high respect was the endorsement that Jean Cahn gave Mr. Powell when he was nominated by President Nixon for the United States Supreme Court in 1971. She had left the OEO by then, and she and Edgar had started a law school at Antioch College. Jean Cahn told the Senate Judiciary Committee that Mr. Powell had shown himself to be a man of principle, who pledged his word and kept it. "As a black person," she said, "who has seen many promises made and not kept, it has been all too rare an experience to find a man who not only holds to such a belief---but who is prepared to back that belief with all the resources and stature and skill at his command." She believed that Lewis Powell would "go down in history as one of the great statesmen of our profession."

The Rest of 1965 Into 1966

While the intensity of those first few months were over for me, and all of us at the ABA got back to more of a regular schedule, there were interesting and some consequential days ahead. Being on "location" in Washington, I was involved most of the time when the ABA was scheduled to participate, and was included by the OEO staff in many of their planning meetings at the OEO offices.

- An informal advisory committee of OEO and ABA representatives hammered out guidelines of cooperation. In June, the ABA, the OEO and the Department of Justice co-sponsored a national conference for legal aid lawyers and OEO personnel. Agreements based on the new guidelines were reached between the legal aid community and new government program. Myrna and I hosted a special dinner at our home on the Mt. Vernon Parkway for the 100 conference participants, which included Lewis Powell, other ABA leaders, and most top OEO officials (Sargent Shriver was traveling). Myrna personally cooked shrimp creole for the crowd, a truly remarkable feat.

- After Jean Cahn served for a brief time as the program's first director, Clinton Bamberger, a young Baltimore lawyer with an innovative spirit, was selected as director. Following Clint's service, his deputy, Earl Johnson, Jr., was appointed director. Earl had been an official of the Washington, D.C., Neighborhood Legal Services Project, and like Clint, he had the ABA's strong support. Immediately after they took over, the OEO Legal Services Program was well under way.

My Involvement After the Bamberger Appointment

Following the Bamberger appointment, my role was liaison from ABA to Clint and Earl. We worked together in coordinating the education of the bar nationwide to the value of the program.

Finally, in 1966, I managed a successful legislative effort for the program on Capitol Hill. Although the original language of the Economic Opportunity Act gave broad enough authority to fund legal services, it was not explicit. Don Baker, the OEO's general counsel, decided that specific authority for legal services should be included when the Act was amended in 1966. He asked for our help in taking the lead.

Congresswoman Edith Green, an Oregon Democrat and considered then as the most influential woman in the House, was the second ranking member of the House Education and Labor Committee, which was responsible for the Poverty Act. Don Baker called her and explained the situation. She asked how the legal profession would react if specific language authorizing federal funding for legal services were to show up in legislation. He then arranged for John Cummiskey and me to meet with her; and that meeting began a long-standing relationship between Mrs. Green and me.

She was able to insert this language in the amended act: "the Director (of OEO) shall carry out programs…which provide legal advice and representation to persons when they are unable to afford the services of a private attorney, together with legal research, and information as appropriate to mobilize the assistance of lawyers or legal institutions, or combination thereof, to further the cause of justice among persons living in poverty…"

We had "passive" assistance from Congressman Gerald Ford, the Republican leader of the House. John Cummiskey was, like Mr. Ford, from Grand Rapids, Michigan, and they had been friends for years. When we called on him in his Minority Leader's office, he was laid-back and smoking his pipe. He had not been following the Legal Services saga and was curious as to why the ABA would support it. After John assured him this had been thought through carefully, he told us not to worry. The Republicans would support Mrs. Green.

When the amendments passed, I met Mrs. Green in the lobby just outside the House floor to thank her. She said, "Well, we did it, and thank you for bringing this to my attention." I thought about the word *lobbyist* that day as I stood there, waiting for her to meet me. I thought about its apparent origin in the British Parliament as the place outside Chambers, where wheeling and dealing take place. I had stood outside the American chamber before for what you might say was wheeling and dealing, and would again, but it can also be a place of joy if the vote goes your way, and you're there to greet the sponsor.

Mrs. Green and I kept in touch after that, even after we returned to live in Chicago. When she was on a business trip to Chicago, a year before she retired from the House in 1974, she visited Myrna and me for dinner at our Hinsdale home. But that night at dinner, her views about all federal programs, including legal services, had changed dramatically. She had moved from one of the most active creators of federal social services programs (including the OEO) to a dismantler of them, believing they were inefficient, ineffective and wasteful. She tried hard, through what was known as the Green Amendment, to greatly limit the services of the Legal Services Corporation, which was the successor to the OEO program. Although her amendment became law, its wording did not produce what she had intended. In taking these kinds of actions, this lady, this former liberal congresswoman, known in the House as the Mother of Higher Education, and primary author of the landmark Title IX that prohibited universities from discriminating against women, was looked upon with hostility by many of her Democratic House colleagues.

As with the rest of these "Memories," I could not even begin to cover all of the stories about this subject. The complete story of the OEO Legal Services program is covered in its history by Earl Johnson, Jr., *Justice and Reform: The Formative Years of the American Legal Services Program*. There also are informative chapters in *Lewis F. Powell, Jr.: A Biography,* and *Sarge: The Life and Times of Sargent Shriver.* The *Justice and Reform* and *Sarge* volumes referenced my participation, and I've gratefully drawn on them to buttress my memories of that period.

When the OEO was ended as an umbrella of various programs, a new separate Legal Services Corporation was formed, and that also had the strong support of the ABA. It, however, continued to draw controversy because of its work on legal reform and challenges against established institutions.

As a final comment: How did the OEO program do in its first full 18-month period---from January 1, 1966, through 1967? In his book, Earl Johnson wrote that legal assistance for the poor increased eightfold over the level it had taken the legal aid movement 90 years to reach. .

After leaving government service, both Messrs. Bamberger and Johnson have had distinguished careers. Clint was dean of the Catholic University Law School, and professor of Law at the University of Maryland. Earl taught law at the University of Southern California and was an award-winning California Appellate Court justice from 1982 until 2007. As I write this in 2015, he has published a monumental study of legal aid in America.

CHAPTER EIGHT

The Bail Reform Act of 1966
We Return to Chicago in 1967

WASHINGTON, D.C. 1966–1967

On June 19, 1966, I received a Western Union telegram from the White House which read:

> LOWELL R. BECK 1705 DESALES NW
> AMERICAN BAR ASSN. WASH D.C.
> PRESIDENT JOHNSON CORDIALLY INVITES YOU
> TO THE WHITE HOUSE TO ATTEND THE SIGNING
> OF S. 1357, THE BAIL REFORM ACT OF 1966,
> A BILL TO REVISE EXISTING BAIL PRACTICES IN THE COURTS
> OF THE UNITED STATES. THE CEREMONY WILL BE
> WEDNESDAY, JUNE 22, 1966.
> PLEASE PRESENT THIS TELEGRAM AT THE WHITE HOUSE
> NORTHWEST GATE AT 9:15 AM ON WEDNESDAY. PLEASE CONFIRM
> YOUR ATTENDANCE BY RETURN WIRE TO SHERWIN MARKMAN AT
> THE WHITE HOUSE.
> JOSEPH A. CALIFANO JR SPECIAL ASSISTANT TO THE PRESIDENT

Dan Freed, whom you will remember at the Justice Department during the Criminal Justice Act days, told me that I was on "the list" the department had submitted for attending this ceremony, but you don't know if you'll get an invitation until it arrives. While I had attended a White House event hosted by President Kennedy, this was my first bill signing ceremony. As long as Myrna and I lived in Washington, and as many notable individuals we had come to know, we always were exhilarated by it all. Exhilaration is caused by a White House signing ceremony. I think most people, no matter who they might be, feel the same way. Maybe that's why so many who work in

Washington never leave, or at least never want to. Anyway, we never took the importance and grandeur of Washington for granted.

I received this invitation because of my work in getting the new Bail Reform Act enacted. Most people outside of a narrow group in the Criminal Justice field had never heard of this Act. It's in a highly specialized area of law, and its passage merited only a small article in *The Washington Post.*

I expect that the subject of bail isn't understood by most people except lawyers and those who have to use it. *Bail is some form of property deposited or pledged to the court to persuade it to release a suspect from jail, on the understanding that the suspect will return for trial or forfeit the bail, and probably then be brought up on charges of the crime of failure to appear for trial.*

The ABA Acts on Bail Reform

One of the country's most influential public figures little known to the general public was James V. Bennett, the long-time director of the Federal Bureau of Prisons. Mr. Bennett, who had had been director from 1937 to 1964, believed that prisons had become inhumane and poorly operated, and he pressed for extensive reform. An example was his strong criticism of Alcatraz, for which he led Congressional action to close.

Mr. Bennett was active in the ABA, and chairman of the Criminal Law Section just before he retired from the Bureau of Prisons in 1964. Working with officials at the Justice Department, including Dan Freed (who was a student of bail practices), Mr. Bennett became a leading advocate of reforming the federal bail system. He knew that if that could be accomplished, the states, where reform was especially needed, would follow.

The Eighth Amendment to the Constitution prohibits excessive bail, but gives no inherent right to bail. Consequently the bail system is governed by legislation at the federal and state levels. Prior to 1966, the bail system was focused on the accused having money to be released from jail. The system was not only unjust for many of the accused, but was filling jails needlessly at a great public cost.

Through Mr. Bennett's leadership of the ABA Criminal Law Section, the association endorsed bail reform, and was a leader in getting a law enacted known as the Bail Reform Act of 1966.

Mr. Bennett looked to our Washington Office for assistance. All of a sudden, it seemed like I was meeting with him and Dan Freed one minute, running to the OEO offices the next, and meeting with Senator Bayh and Larry Conrad the next on the Twenty-Fifth Amendment.

At the Justice Department, Messrs. Bennett, Freed and Herb Hoffman and I plotted our strategy. Senator Sam Ervin, the quintessential country judge from North Carolina, chaired the Judiciary subcommittee for this subject, and Congressman Celler was the person to talk with in the House. Neither had to be convinced that there was a problem here, and with Jim Bennett's stature and long-standing experience with prisons, we had good chances of success. At hearings, we had to present examples of abuse and offer expert testimony. We had to call on senators and representatives, as must be done with any legislation. Dan himself was steeped in knowledge about bail in the United States, and had written the landmark book, *Bail in the United States,* with Patricia Wald, who later became a judge on the United States District Court for the District of Columbia, and from 1986 until 1991, served as chief judge.

Together, we drafted the legislation, wrote testimony, arranged for expert witnesses, and called on key members of the Judiciary Committees of both houses of Congress. We arranged for prison officials, judges and lawyers from "back home" to call or write members of Congress.

Essentially the Bail Reform Act of 1966 gave defendants accused of non-capital crimes (i.e., those crimes other than offenses punishable by death) a statutory right, where the constitutional right was lacking, to be released pending trial on "personal recognizance or unsecured personal bond," unless the judge determines the accused to be a flight risk.

The Act was signed by President Johnson on June 22, 1966, in the East Room of the White House. After the president's remarks, we walked to the front of the room to receive a pen from him. A summary of his remarks at the signing tell the story of the Act:

"Today we join to recognize a major development in our entire system of criminal justice — the reform of the bail system.

"This system has endured — archaic, unjust and virtually unexamined — ever since the Judiciary Act of 1789.

"Because of the bail system, the scales of justice have been weighted for almost two centuries not with fact, nor law, nor mercy. They have been weighted with money.

"But now, because of the Bail Reform Act of 1966, which an

understanding and just Congress has enacted, and which I will shortly sign, we can begin to insure that defendants are considered as individuals, and not as dollar signs.

"The principal purpose of bail is to insure that an accused person will return for trial, if he is released after arrest.

"How is that purpose met under the present system? The defendant with means can afford to pay bail. He can afford to buy his freedom. But the poorer person can not pay the price. He languishes in jail weeks, months, and perhaps even years before trial. He does not stay in jail because he is guilty. He does not stay in jail because any sentence has passed.

"He does not stay in jail because he is any more likely to flee before trial.

"He stays in jail for one reason only —because he is poor.

"There are hundreds, perhaps thousands, of illustrations of how the bail system has inflicted arbitrary cruelty:

— A man was jailed on a serious charge brought last Christmas Eve. He could not afford bail so he spent 100 days in jail until he could get a hearing. Then the complainant admitted that the charge that he had made was false.

— A man could not raise $300 for bail. He spent 45 days in jail waiting trial for a traffic offense for which he could have been sentenced to no more than 5 days.

— A man spent 2 months in jail before being acquitted. In that period, he lost his job, he lost his car, he lost his family—it was split up. He did not find another job, following that, for 4 months.

"In addition to such injustices as I have pointed out, the present bail system has meant very high costs that the taxpayer must pay for detaining prisoners prior to their trial.

"What is most shocking about these costs—to both individuals and the public—is that they are totally unnecessary.

"First proof of that fact came because of really one man's outrage against injustice. I am talking about Mr. Louis Schweitzer, who pioneered the development of a substitute for the money system by establishing the Vera Foundation and the Manhattan bail project.

"The lesson of the project was simple. If a judge is given adequate information, he, the judge, can determine that many defendants can be released without any need for money bail. They will return faithfully for trial.

"So this legislation, for the first time, requires that the decision to release a man prior to the trial be based on facts—like community and family ties and past record, and not on his bank account. In the words of the act, 'A man, regardless of his financial status—shall not needlessly be detained—when detention serves neither the ends of justice nor the public interest.'

"And it specifies that he be released without money bond whenever that is justified by the facts. Under the act, judges would—for the first time—be required to use a flexible set of conditions, matching different types of releases to different risks.

"These are the steps that can be taken, we think, without harming law enforcement in any manner. This measure does not require that every arrested person be released.

"This measure does not restrict the power of the courts to detain dangerous persons in capital cases or after conviction.

"What this measure does do is to eliminate needless, arbitrary cruelty.

"What it does do, in my judgment, is to greatly enlarge justice in this land of ours.

"So our task is to rise above the debate between rights of the individual and rights of society, by securing and really protecting the rights of both.

"I am proud now, as a major step forward, to sign the Bail Reform Act of 1966 into the law of the land."

(The message sounded exactly like Dan. He helped write it.)

The Bail Reform Act of 1966 did not allow judges in non-capital cases to consider the danger a defendant posed to the community. In some cases, and particularly in the District of Columbia where local crime was governed by the federal bail law, this resulted in further violent crimes by defendants who had been released on personal recognizance. This was corrected by the Bail Reform Act of 1984, which provided for detention in non-capital cases, as well as capital cases, where necessary for the safety of the community.

We Return to Illinois in 1967

Having begun my Washington work in 1961, I had learned the way it functioned, from the Congress to the White House to federal agencies. Don Channell had taught me well, and had given me free rein to take on many direct responsibilities. I couldn't have had a better situation within the ABA staff, and although I was an assistant director, I was fortunate to be able to function at the highest ABA officer and staff levels. Consequently, I was restless. As much as I valued and enjoyed my association with Don, I felt ready to be in charge. But Don was fully in charge, and would be for some time.

One day in late 1966, a possible opportunity to head my own Washington office appeared. I had been working with a coalition of national retailers and consumer groups on consumer credit legislation, and became well acquainted with the Washington director of the National Retail Merchants Association, John Hazen. The NRMA was the influential lobbying group for merchants such as J.C. Penney, Sears, and Montgomery Ward. John was the quintessential Washington inside lobbyist, and you would never find a friendlier, savvier person. His family owned New Jersey newspapers, and he was a publisher there as well as a Washington heavyweight. He frequently would take me for lunch at the Metropolitan Club, and we would discuss the state of affairs as well as the specific issues on our agendas. We hit it off so well, I think, because he always was interested in the ABA's issues and my role with them.

As we met, our conversations turned to my own future and interests. One day he surprised me when he said he would be retiring from Washington in a year, and return to run his newspapers in New Jersey. He would like me to join him as his Washington assistant, and learn the retail issues so that I could succeed him. You can imagine how I felt. This came at just the time I was wondering what I would do next.

John said that first he would discuss it with the NRMA president at its headquarters office. He wanted to know, however, if I was interested before talking with his president. Of course I was interested, but knew I had to discuss it with either Don Channell or Bert Early before giving John the go ahead. I decided to call Bert first. Our relationship had become so close during the OEO struggles that I knew he would respond constructively. I explained to him that I wasn't leaving, but had this possible opportunity, and wanted him to know that I would like to consider it…could he give me any advice?

Bert's response was immediate. He said that he was just a few days away from asking me to help him create a new Division of Public Service Activities in Chicago. The current director of the division it would succeed, retired Army Judge Advocate General George Hickman, was retiring from that job soon; and Bert wanted me to return to Chicago to form the new division. I was honored. However, I wasn't sure that I wanted to leave Washington where I was gaining such valuable experience and enjoying it all.

He told me to think it over, that he wanted me to join him in Chicago, and here was the "kicker"… "When thinking it over," he said, "do you want to spend the next several years representing department stores, or would you rather make a real difference in peoples' lives by staying with the legal profession and helping the ABA take bold steps in public service programs?"

I decided to move to Chicago. Myrna was happy. Rich (Richie then) needed to be around our family, and we needed a more stable home life than Washington was offering. So, in the summer of 1967, we moved back to Chicago, and I began a totally different kind of day in the headquarters office.

Don was understanding, of course, and proceeded to hire a new assistant, John Tracey, who over the next four to five years, until leaving to join a business lobbying office, was one of the ABA's most valuable assets.

And John Hazen also understood. He too had decided to return home. "You can always come back to Washington," he said. "But people have very few chances to break new ground as you'll be doing with the ABA in Chicago."

A Postscript to 1967…
Admission to the United States Supreme Court

One day in early 1967, Don told me that, before I left for Chicago, he and I should be admitted together to the U.S. Supreme Court. He had spoken with Ramsey Clark, who was the new Attorney General of the United States, and Mr. Clark had offered to personally move our admissions. Of course I was excited about it. As an admitted lawyer in Illinois, and Don in Georgia, we both were eligible for admission to the Court. The next admission day for lawyers to appear in person with their sponsors before the Court would be May 22. The Attorney General told Don that he would be available to attend with us that day.

On the appointed day, Don and I were met at the Court by our mutual friend, Alice O'Donnell, who was Justice Tom C. Clark's assistant. She escorted us to the front visitors' row where several other lawyers, with their sponsors, already were seated. If you don't have a personal lawyer-sponsor to accompany you, at times the Solicitor General would move your admission, and Solicitor General Thurgood Marshall was present that day to do that for five or six lawyers. As Don and I took our seats, Mr. Marshall was speaking to his group in a humorous, casual way.

I had met Thurgood Marshall at a meeting and at a reception. I was aware of his casual side, and enjoyed his brief comments to his six lawyers. Our sponsor, the Attorney General, to whom the Solicitor General reports, hadn't yet arrived, so we were listening with interest to Mr. Marshall. He was telling them not to be nervous; that we must all rise when the Court entered, and that the chief justice (then Earl Warren) would ask him for their names. It would be over quickly, and then they would leave, he said. He said that they were lucky because the Solicitor General's group always went first, ahead of individually sponsored lawyers. Just at that time Attorney General Clark arrived to sponsor us, and an astonished Mr. Marshall said, "Oops, we'll go second." Everybody laughed.

Some interesting facts about the two Clarks: Justice Clark retired from the Court the next month, in June 1967. Some said that he retired so there would be no conflict between him and his son, Ramsey, who was the new attorney general.

Thurgood Marshall was appointed to the Court in October 1967 by President Johnson to succeed Justice Clark.

CHAPTER NINE

WE'RE BACK IN ILLINOIS
OUR SECOND SON, JONATHAN, IS BORN
WE MOVE TO WASHINGTON AGAIN

CHICAGO, ILLINOIS 1967—1968

While Myrna and I both knew Chicago's North Side neighborhoods from days when we were single, the suburbs were unknown to us. Bert and Betsy Early gave us helpful information. When they relocated from West Virginia, their requirements were the same as ours: churches, good schools, safe neighborhoods, and as convenient as feasible to the American Bar Center on the University of Chicago campus. The commute to the South Side wouldn't be easy from any suburban location, but the western ones provided the most direct access by car, and public transportation wasn't available from Hinsdale, where they located, to Hyde Park.

Hinsdale had everything we wanted, beginning with high-ranking schools, but prices were unthinkable for us. Its sister community within the same school district, Clarendon Hills, was more reasonable at that time. So we settled on a relatively small house that had the potential for an add-on at 108 Ann Street, just a few blocks from the charming downtown area.

From ABA Division of Committee Activities to Division of Public Service Activities

The ABA had undertaken several program activities that could be labeled "public service," and Bert wanted that highlighted so that the national organized bar was engaged in public service as well as lawyers' self-interests. Examples of public service were "Youth Education for Citizenship under Law" that promoted public school curricula on the role of law and the courts in maintaining public order and stability, and legal responsibility as citizens. A program created by the ABA and Association of American Law Schools was the Council for Legal Education Opportunity (CLEO) that opened opportunities for minorities in law schools. Law Day USA was an ABA-sponsored program inaugurated by ABA President Charles Rhyne. On May 1 each year, when the Soviets paraded their military might in Moscow, Law Day highlights programs throughout America to promote the rule of law over military force as a national objective.

The ABA staff functions for these and several other programs were placed under the new Division of Public Service Activities, and the Division of Committee Services was terminated. My job was to organize and manage the new division and develop new programs in this area.

Director of the Division of Public Service Activities... *My First Job as a Manager*

Firing an employee isn't fun. As a first-time manager, changing from hands-on doing to delegating, I quickly had my first taste of difficulty. A relatively young lawyer (I'll call him Tom) couldn't communicate without twisting his sentences. Tom had graduated from law school and passed the bar, but simply couldn't communicate effectively enough to do this work. I gave him the benefit of the doubt and discussed it with him several times. But he didn't understand.

I had some complaints from ABA committee chairpersons that they too had problems understanding him and didn't have time to continue trying. Since I had never terminated an employee, I was nervous about it. Bert told me not worry about it. He said that most people really do understand in their hearts if they are unable to do the job and would respond accordingly. He assured me that everything would be okay.

I'm a good sleeper, but didn't sleep well that night. I kept repeating in my mind what I planned to say to Tom, and was hoping for the best. I felt sorry for him because I didn't have any idea what kind of job he could land next.

Well, Tom did *not* respond as I had hoped. If most people take firing passively, Tom was an exception. He objected excitedly. He disagreed with me and urged me to reconsider. When I told him that I had made up my mind, he moved to the window ledge and sat there objecting. He would not take "no" for an answer, and said that he didn't accept my decision. When it was clear that he would not stop objecting, I warned him that if he did not leave, I would have to call security to physically remove him.

The lesson here was that not *everybody* reacts to termination the same way. I guess I knew that, and that's why I hadn't slept well the night before.

Some women lawyers weren't fun either. In 1967, there weren't many women lawyers. And, some in that limited number tried to show that they really were in fact lawyers by being exceptionally strong headed and tough, even in situations where calm and rational discussion were important.

My first encounter with one of these lawyers came early as director of the new division. The staff of the Youth Education about Citizenship under Law program was meeting in the building with a representative of Attorney General Clark, who was interested in providing a Justice Department grant for a new program. Because I was acquainted with the attorney general and had helped prepare the grant application, I decided to attend a few minutes of the meeting. When I arrived, our staff was listening to a one-way monologue by the representative whose vision of it wasn't even close to our program's objectives. She had every right to be challenging and to suggest changes. That was her job. But she had the staff of three, including the director, the able Joel Henning, who was no "shrinking violet," totally intimidated. Her manner was only that she knew best and that she was from the Justice Department *in Washington, D.C., no less* (la-di-dah). She had our staff on trial instead of exploring a simple public service program.

My staff was just sitting there, and seemed dumbfounded by her. When I asked how things were going, she said not well because my staff wasn't responding to her, and this was unacceptable. When I asked her to restate her points, she was so disrespectful that I asked why she was acting like this; that there was no reason to be so confrontational, particularly when we were considering only a simple grant for a worthwhile program. That didn't change her; it angered her. I told her that obviously we weren't getting anywhere, that I too knew the attorney general, and that he wouldn't want his staff to act like that. I told her that I wanted her to leave the building. She packed up and left.

I called Herb Hoffman at the Justice Department and explained the situation. He didn't know this "representative," but later said that she was new at the Department and that he would arrange to have another person meet with us. We got the grant for the program.

About women lawyers today, in 2015: Why do I mention that it was my experience that so many early women lawyers behaved so unnecessarily confrontational when it was counterproductive? To be sure, all of them weren't like that, but so many were and, in this Youth Education situation, confrontation was indeed counterproductive.

It's been said that when a woman lawyer acts tough and mean, she's a "bitch," but when a male lawyer acts that way, he's just being effective. That might have been true then and even today in 2015. But, I mention this case because of how much it's changed from the 1960s, when the women lawyers were finding their way in a world completely dominated by men. I believe their frustrations then grew out of a sense of insecurity as they attempted success in that world. Law school classes now are 50 percent women in many schools, and more in some. The landscape has changed. Some women may still feel insecure, but so do many men. Most now know that there are times to crack the whip and times to soften up to be effective. Some will say that the field of law still is a man's world. This may be true in some areas, but it's not like I remember it when women lawyers were just coming on scene.

Racial Tensions Continue in America Regardless of New Civil Rights Laws

The Watts Riots. Racial riots, in all their fury, began in America in August 1965. The Watts Riot in Los Angeles raged for six days. It resulted in more than $40 million in property loss, and its size and cost exceeded any urban confrontation this generation had seen. It started when a white California highway patrolman arrested a young black driver for suspicion of driving while drunk. A large crowd gathered, and exchanges between police and the crowd grew into violence in this poverty-stricken area of South Central Los Angeles. Cars were overturned and burned, and stores and offices throughout the area were damaged and looted. This riot was so serious that thousands of California National Guard troops were mobilized; 34 people were killed, thousands were injured, and many more thousands were arrested. While some local officials blamed the violence on outsider instigators, a state commission determined instead that it was the result of poverty, general unrest, and unemployment.

Few attempts were made by officials to rectify the problems, and the rest of the country, although shaken for a while, seemed to forget it. As bad as it was, I can remember being concerned, but didn't think a lot about it because it was so far away and I had my own daily interests.

Chicago didn't escape rioting. A year later, in June 1966, the Puerto Rican community along Division Street erupted in rioting. While the duration and damage were not like Watts, it was another example of growing unrest in American urban "ghettos."

Urban riots rage across America in 1967. As tumultuous as urban rioting was in 1965, and to a lesser degree in 1966, it was only the precursor to what followed in 1967. The 1967 rioting was so alarming and widespread that it merits some detailed explanation, and the following is excerpted from *Rioting in America* by Paul Gilje:

> Beginning in April and continuing through the rest of the year, 159 race riots erupted across the United States. The first occurred in Cleveland, but by far the most devastating were those that took place in Newark and Detroit. The former took twenty-six lives and injured fifteen hundred; the latter resulted in forty deaths and two thousand injuries. Large swaths of ghetto in both places went up in flames. Television showed burning buildings and looted stores, with both National Guardsmen and paratroopers on the scenes.

> The 1967 riots were part of the activist political culture of the 1960s. Agitation for civil rights seemed far overdue in America. It was a decade of upheaval and change involving not only black activism but also growing antiwar sentiment, street theater aimed at social change and class conflict, and the beginning of a women's rights movement. Within this mixture of activism, the civil rights movement, led by The Reverend Dr. Martin Luther King, Jr., came into its own as a biracial effort to achieve full integration and political rights in American society. The Civil Rights Act of 1964 and the Voting Rights Act of 1965 would seem to have met the demand, but that was not to be. Black activism remained alive and well, and moved beyond the moderation of Dr. King to embrace the concept of Black Power evoked by militant radicals like Hughey Newton, Stokely Carmichael, and H. Rapp Brown. It was embodied in the Black Panthers as the foremost organizational vehicle for African Americans of the era. Radicalization of the civil

rights struggle — seemingly encouraged by legislative progress under the aegis of President Lyndon Johnson's Great Society — led to the explosions of 1967 in black ghettos across America. Rapp Brown's often-quoted epithet, "Burn baby, burn," euphemized it most famously.

Yet even the destructive component of Black Power should not be taken out of context: the year 1967 ended with a final act of violence in late October, when antiwar protesters from around the country moved on Washington, D.C. Those who gathered at the Lincoln Memorial on 21 October were largely white, largely middle class, largely educated, and formerly mainstream in their politics. But, when U. S. Army units met them with fixed bayonets, they took to the streets of the capital in an outbreak of destructive rioting and constructive confrontation, and 650 were arrested.

So, while 1967 was to go down in history as another major riot year like 1765, 1834, 1877, 1919, and 1931 (rioting and urban violence were not new to America), it should be noted that not all of the riots were outpourings of racial confrontations that year. Violence was in the air in 1967, but so was free political expression as guaranteed by the U. S. Constitution. (Paul Gilje. *Rioting in America*. Bloomington: Indiana University Press, 1996.)

President Johnson Appoints the "Kerner Commission"

In July 1967, President Johnson appointed an 11-member commission, headed by Governor Otto Kerner of Illinois, to determine the causes of the riots that began in 1965, and make recommendations for future action. The commission reported on February 29, 1968. Its findings essentially blamed white America for the black community having a lack of opportunity, and its historic warning was that "Our nation is moving toward two societies, one black, one white — separate and unequal." Recommendations for action included improved federal and state programs for better housing, opening employment opportunities, improving education and "opening suburban residential neighborhoods to Negroes." Changes from public housing high rises to smaller units, scattered throughout communities, were recommended, along with changes in police attitudes and actions.

Interestingly, President Johnson did not agree with much of the report, and there were many critics who believed that riot instigators were excused from responsibility. Others, such as Dr. Martin Luther King, Jr. disagreed with the critics. Dr. King called it "a physician's warning of approaching death, with a prescription for life."

President Johnson had forged ahead with the Civil Rights Act of 1964 and the Voting Rights Act of 1965. He had established the national "War on Poverty" that already was spending millions on inner city programs. He didn't accept the idea that billions more should be spent, and since the Viet Nam War was sapping dollars from the U.S. Treasury, he couldn't justify spending more on urban issues.

Martin Luther King, Jr. Is Assassinated, and Cities Burn

Dr. King was assassinated on April 4, 1968, in Memphis, Tennessee. Following his death, riots erupted again. Large sections of Washington, D.C., were devastated. Thousands of federal troops and National Guard troops were dispatched to assist the local police force. Over 100 cities faced widespread civil disorder, with Baltimore and Chicago facing the most destruction.

I did not experience the fires first hand, even though the American Bar Center adjoined the South Side Woodlawn neighborhood that had some destruction. The most devastated areas of Chicago were on the West Side, where literally block after block of housing and businesses were destroyed. It was so bad that smoke could be seen for miles around, troops were deployed, and food and water were scarce for several days afterward. While some radical blacks were accused of fomenting the rage, it appeared to be primarily a reaction by young ghetto dwellers over Dr. King's murder. Sections of the West Side of Chicago were like war zones, and it took several years for them to recover.

Jonathan Is Born

One month later, on May 4, my and my family's life would change drastically by a call from Washington, D.C., and change even more on May 5 when our second child, Jonathan Everett, was born at the Hinsdale Hospital.

John W. Gardner Is Appointed Chairman of the Newly Formed National Urban Coalition in 1968, and I Consider Writing Him About a Lobbying Job

One evening in January 1968, I happened to read about John W. Gardner's appointment to head the newly formed National Urban Coalition. It was an organization established by a diverse group of some America's best-known leaders to tackle the problems of the cities. These men and women were frightened about the future of the country, and came together at a convocation to try to unite to put their immense influence and resources at work to solve the urban crisis.

John Gardner had resigned as President Johnson's Secretary of Health, Education and Welfare (HEW), and these leaders prevailed upon him to head the Coalition. His three best friends in the group, Andrew Heiskell, chairman of Time, Inc., David Rockefeller, chairman of the Chase Bank, and J. Irwin Miller, chairman of Cummins Engine, urged him to do it.

Bert Early had introduced me to John Gardner's prominence. Bert had read Mr. Gardner's books on excellence and leadership, and held him in the highest esteem. He made a special point of taking me to hear Gardner speak at the American Law Institute annual meeting in Washington in May 1967. Gardner, then HEW Secretary, couldn't have been more impressive, with his long list of credentials in private life, and his achievements in government.

He had been president of the Carnegie Corporation of New York and the Carnegie Foundation for the Advancement of Teaching, the leading foundations for promoting excellence in education; and was responsible for a landmark report issued by the Rockefeller Brothers Fund entitled *The Pursuit of Excellence: Education and the Future of America.* This report was so profound on the need to improve American education that it awakened Americans to our competitive educational crisis with the Soviets, who put their first vehicle, Sputnik, into space in 1958, which was the year of the report.

Several pages have been written in books and articles on Mr. Gardner's prominence and achievements. He received the Presidential Medal of Freedom in 1964, and was awarded the Public Welfare Medal from the National Academy of Sciences in 1966. As HEW secretary, he oversaw the launching of Medicare, and redefined the federal role in education. And, in 1967 he presided over the beginning of the Corporation for Public Broadcasting.

He was the founder of the White House Fellows program, which helped launch many national political and thought leaders such as Colin Powell and Dorothy Kearns Goodwin.

Without acrimony, he resigned from HEW. While he did not announce it publicly, many believe it was because he opposed the Viet Nam War in principle, believed it was needlessly causing too many deaths, and was taking so much funding that was needed here at home.

So, it caught my attention when I read in *Life* about Mr. Gardner and the Urban Coalition. *Note: In addition to Messrs. Heiskell, Rockefeller and Miller, the Coalition's board was made up of many other high-profile business, labor, civil rights, and civic leaders such as Henry Ford II; George Meany, president of the AFL-CIO; Dorothy Height, president of the National Council of Negro Women; Chicago Mayor Richard J. Daley; New York Mayor John V. Lindsay; civil rights leaders Julian Bond and Whitney Young; LaDonna Vita Tabbytite Harris, founder and president of Americans for Indian Opportunity; Edgar Kaiser; Mrs. Theodore Wedel, president of the National Council of Churches; Leonard Woodcock, president of the United Auto Workers; and William Eberle, president of American Standard, Inc.*

Mr. Gardner's picture was on the full inside back page, and an accompanying article told how he *would be hiring* an entirely new group of people to staff the Coalition: lobbyists, public relations specialists, researchers, administrators, fund raisers...the whole works to make a new lobbying organization of such magnitude succeed.

While I was not unhappy in my new Chicago job, I already missed the Washington environment and the immersion in current issues. When I read that John Gardner had begun hiring a staff, including lobbyists, some of that interest returned. I was a good lobbyist, and had been a part of successful legislative efforts. The country was on fire, and this new organization couldn't be more important at this time. Wouldn't it be just right to offer my services to Mr. Gardner, and perhaps even lead the lobbying staff? Yes, it would, so I drafted a letter to him, giving my background and asking if I could meet with him.

After reading the letter to Myrna, and thinking about it overnight, I tore up the draft letter. It was outlandish to think about moving back to Washington. Most importantly, Myrna was pregnant with Jonathan who was expected in May. We had just built a new family room addition. The stars weren't aligned for me to do this; and, after all, I had my hands full at the ABA.

A Surprise Telephone Call

On Friday afternoon in early May, I had a telephone call from a man who identified himself as Chris Mould, the special assistant to Mr. John W. Gardner in Washington. He asked if I knew about Mr. Gardner and the National Urban Coalition, and, of course, I said yes. He was calling because "Mr. Gardner would like you to meet with him in Washington, and consider taking the job as chief lobbyist of the Coalition." This was so completely out of the blue, and was such a surprise that I hardly knew how to respond. I asked him how Mr. Gardner obtained my name, and in particular, why did he seem certain that he wanted me for the job without knowing me. He replied that Mr. Gardner was heading a "coalition" of diverse interests with a board of differing political views, some liberal and some conservative. Mr. Gardner was looking for a colleague who could relate to all of them, and all of the lobbyist candidates so far were too dogmatically liberal or conservative (mostly liberal). He said that Mr. Gardner had "struck out" until my name was mentioned to him by two men who had known me in Washington. One of the men was Allen Pritchard, the president of the National League of Cities, who had been Senator Pearson's administrative assistant when Myrna was the senator's secretary. He was a Republican. The other was Berl Bernhard, a Democrat and prominent Washington lawyer whom I knew as staff director of the U.S. Commission on Civil Rights. They did not know each other, and as Republican and Democrat, suggested me at separate dinner parties in the same week. Mr. Gardner believed that I could be the right person because of the respect he had for both of them.

I told Mr. Mould about the letter I did not send to Mr. Gardner; that it was impractical to move then, and even more so now with a new baby on the way at any time. I was honored, appreciated it, and regretted very much that it just wouldn't work out for me. He didn't press me, but gave me his phone number to call over the weekend if I changed my mind. He would meet me in Chicago over the weekend to go over all details of the job if that would help. I thanked him, and went to Bert's office.

Bert's reaction was, "How can you <u>not</u> take the job?" He said that he knew it would be a great personal inconvenience for Myrna and me, particularly Myrna; but this was one of the best opportunities he had ever known to make a difference, and to become acquainted with some of the most substantial people in America. The urban problems were tearing the country apart, and I would be at the heart of problem solving with a man and a group with the resources and moxie to make a difference. He thought Myrna and I should talk over all of the pros and cons and that I shouldn't just dismiss it out of hand.

Myrna and I Discuss a Possible Move Back to Washington, and Jonathan Is Born

We were a week away from Jonathan's projected birth date, and Myrna wasn't in a mood to discuss a return to Washington. But, being the trouper that she is, she agreed that it was an opportunity, a calling if you will, not to be missed. After some crying by both of us, I called Chris Mould and told him I would meet with Mr. Gardner at his Washington office on Monday morning.

Saturday was a hectic day with continual conversation about the craziness of all of this, and still wondering if it was the right decision. And then, that night, Myrna went into labor, and Jonathan arrived at the Hinsdale Hospital at 1:30 A.M. on Sunday, May 5. This, of course, would have changed my plans to fly to Washington the next day, but Myrna insisted that I go even though she would still be in the hospital with our new son.

So, I met with John Gardner on Monday morning, and was hired to join him as executive director of the Urban Coalition Action Council, the lobbying arm of the National Urban Coalition. We agreed that July would be our moving month because there were so many arrangements to be made before the actual move.

Our house in Clarendon Hills was put on the market immediately. The summer of 1968 was viciously hot, and life around the Beck household wasn't easy. Myrna had the new baby to care for, and prospective buyers were coming and going with Jonathan in the bassinet.

Knowing that both Congressman Bob Michel and Congresswoman Edith Green were well acquainted with Mr. Gardner because of their close working relationship with him as Secretary of HEW, I called both of them to tell them of my new job, and ask for their advice and opinion of him. I was certain that both of them, a Republican and a Democrat, would concur, but if they didn't, there really wasn't anything I could do...I was on my way. They both reacted more enthusiastically than I had expected. Both not only knew him, they had worked closely with him, and deeply respected him. So, this simply reassured me that I had made the right decision. And, they were ecstatic over the formation of the Urban Coalition, with its high-powered leadership and important objectives.

We had to travel back and forth to buy a new house, which we found in Waynewood, Alexandria, a few blocks south of our former residence on West Boulevard Drive just off Mt. Vernon Parkway. While searching for a house, our friends Larry Conrad, Senator Bayh's special assistant, and his wife, Mary Lou, provided their home while they were out of town; and since they had no bassinet, our six-week old Jonathan slept in a dresser drawer. Equally helpful, just as during our first few years in Washington, were Ron and Audrie Whitney, friends of many years from high school and college days in Peoria.

The Moving Day Arrives, But Nothing's Easy

The moving van driver told us that he would meet us in four days at our Waynewood house. As soon as we arrived in the Alexandria area, we moved into a local motel to wait for the van. Four days came and went, and no van arrived. I had to begin work with a man and group of people I didn't know. Myrna had a 4-year old and a 3-month old to care for. And it was Washington hot with no home.

But, still no truck, and the moving company didn't want to tell us why, other than it would be arriving "soon." We soon learned that the company, after loading all of our furniture, had removed it to a warehouse in Chicago to give another customer priority. Living out of suitcases in one motel room, our frustrations couldn't have been deeper. While the delivery was finally re-solved, our former Alexandria neighbors, the Ralons, took pity on us and invited us in until the truck arrived.

So began our new life in the Washington, D.C. area. This, the second time. And with two little guys. And with an entirely new work environment and boss whom I didn't know. It would be just the fulfilling, exciting, stressful and growth experience as I ever could have imagined.

With Uncle Harold, looking at his and Grandpa McMeen's fat hogs. After church that day I wasn't really dressed for the barnyard, but always liked being there. 1941

With my sister Carol, Grandmother McMeen, and my parents, George and Hazel, at the McMeen farm.

Morning WPEO radio broadcast to high school students.

*Summer college vacation sales job
with the Jewel Tea Company.*

*An unlikely tank driver...
but I actually enjoyed it.*

With our parents, George and Hazel Beck, and Harlan and Madge Kohl. June, 1963.

President Kennedy addressing bar leaders on civil rights in the White House East Room. This meeting began the Lawyers Committee for Civil Rights Under Law. I'm seven or eight rows back on the middle aisle (if you can find me). June 21, 1963 (White House photographer Abbie Rowe)

*Former Peoria Congressman Bob Michel, the highly respected Minority
(Republican) Leader of the House when bipartisanship wasn't a dirty word.
Congressional photograph*

*With ABA President Lewis F. Powell, Jr., Neal Kennedy (assistant to Senator
Dirksen), Senator Dirksen, and Don Channell. We were discussing the need for the
25th Amendment on Presidential Disability. Congressional photograph*

Myrna with her boss, Senator James Pearson.
Actually, our son Rich is in the picture also. Congressional photograph

The ABA Commission on Presidential Disability meeting. Senator Bayh is speaking.
His assistant, Larry Conrad, is on his right, and I'm on Larry's right. John Feerick is
on the senator's left. ABA President Craig and President-elect Powell head the table.
January 20, 1964 ABA photograph

We celebrate the 25th Amendment victory at our ABA DeSales Street office. To my left are Representative Poff, Senator Bayh, House Judiciary Chairman Celler, and Don Channell. ABA photograph

With Sargent Shriver and OEO Legal Services director Clinton Bamberger. OEO photograph

*Receiving a pen from President Johnson at the signing of the Bail Reform Act.
June 22, 1966 White House photograph*

CHAPTER TEN

THE URBAN COALITION ACTION COUNCIL

WASHINGTON, D.C. AGAIN, 1968–1970

Arriving at the new office, I felt an unease that was hard to explain. I wasn't any longer in the comforting arms of Don Channell, Bert Early and the ABA. They had been my friends, mentors and brothers, and the ABA my secure work-home.

Everybody at the Urban Coalition, from John Gardner down, was new to me. But I was welcomed heartily by Mr. Gardner and the excellent staff members he already had assembled, some of whom he had brought with him from the Department of Health, Education and Welfare.

The executive vice president of the National Urban Coalition was Peter Libassi, who had been Mr. Gardner's special assistant on Civil Rights at HEW. And, remember, the '60s were the days of turbulent change in racial relations in America. Pete had been Mr. Gardner's right-hand man at HEW during that time, and had managed many difficult situations from school to public facility integration. He had experienced it, from confrontations to negotiations, most of which were emotional and even violent.

The Urban Coalition was classified under Section 501(c)(3) of the Internal Revenue Code as a charitable, educational and research organization. It was exempt from taxation, and contributions to it were tax deductible. However, under this classification, it was subject to limits on lobbying and prohibited from supporting political candidates. The coalition was organized to develop public policy data and positions through research, and its activities were dependent on large contributions from foundations, corporations and individuals.

While the coalition did research and developed policy positions on urban issues, the main objective was ultimately to conduct lobbying on those issues; and for the influencing of legislation, the organizers of the coalition created a separate adjunct organization called the Urban Coalition Action Council. While also exempt from taxation under 501(c)(4) of the tax code, contributions to it were not deductible. Raising money for the action council, therefore, would be more difficult and limited.

The Urban Coalition Action Council was related to the National Urban Coalition, but was a separate organization. Its board members were the same in both groups; and when the board met, it first would conduct coalition business, considering results of its research. It then would adjourn the coalition's meeting and constitute itself as the Action Council board, called the "Policy Council," which would pass resolutions and give the green light to begin lobbying.

Sounds complicated, doesn't it? It really wasn't, but it *was* confusing. It was particularly confusing to some board members who were very busy people and would try to leave the meetings before the policy council convened. Gardner, however, ran tight meetings, and generally could convince them to stay for a while. I mention this structure in some detail so that it's clear where I belonged in the whole thing. As executive vice president of the Coalition, Pete Libassi reported directly to Mr. Gardner, as did I, the executive director of the Action Council. Some 100 people reported to Pete, and six to me. For public relations activities, writing position papers, and all administrative services I needed, I would draw on the coalition staff, and the coalition would be paid with action council funds for their services.

Pete and I worked closely together, often hourly. My other daily associates on the coalition staff were Tom Mathews, unequaled in public relations savvy; Georgianna Rathbun, writer of the most readable newsletters, position papers and general documents that I could have wished for; and Bob Meier, the administrator who was Mr. Gardner's personal assistant at HEW.

My one Action Council legislative associate was John Lagomarcino who, as a fellow lobbyist, became one of my most trusted and helpful confidantes during my entire time with the Gardner organizations. I can't forget my secretary, Barbara Seldon, who did more than anybody to help me get settled in.

The Work Was Hard and Stressful

It took only about a week to learn that this enterprise wouldn't be easy to work with. *It became clear, after only a short time that coalitions of such diverse groups and individuals don't work well if they are organized to function on a permanent basis when there's so much disagreement among the members.*

When the Urban Coalition was organized following the devastating urban riots, the leaders agreed to a strong joint statement of principles for working together on an urgent urban agenda. They were truly concerned and some frightened over what was happening. They all believed that we were living in a time of grave crisis, and that they, as private-sector leaders, were compelled to come together and present a solid front on urban issues to the president of the United States and Congress.

It took several months to get the Action Council going. There was some question, even among board members, about the idea's validity, and funding and staffing were problems from the beginning. It was one thing for leaders of business, labor, minority groups, religions, and mayors to talk unity when the cities were burning; it was another to implement this ideal on a practical day-to-day basis.

Mr. Gardner himself had had a distinguished background in consulting, education, and more recently, government. As Secretary of HEW, he learned the ins and outs of the Washington political scene. However, he came to the political process quite reticently and remained considerably aloof from it. While most members of the Action Council's board (the Policy Council) attended meetings regularly, there was reluctance by many to put the real muscle of their organizations behind lobbying drives on Capitol Hill; unless, of course, the issues were those they supported as their own. So, Gardner's relative aloofness from the process and Coalition members' reticence to pull together contributed to our frustrations.

The Legislative Issues Were Often Controversial Within the Action Council

It was virtually impossible to hold the Urban Coalition together on legislative issues for any length of time. Some of the business members of the board never really saw the Action Council or any part of the Urban Coalition as a lobbying activity. Rather, they had seen it primarily as a way for them to participate in local groups where various segments of the community would come together and talk out issues. By nature, businessmen were quiet lobbyists. They would concentrate their few shots on Capitol Hill in rather narrow ways, focusing only when they felt they needed to, and preferring to work quietly out of the limelight.

And regarding the specific Action Council's legislative issues, they couldn't "buy in" to some of them. For example, its legislative priority was a massive *Employer of Last Resort* program to put thousands of men and women to work in public service jobs with city and state governments, hospitals, schools and park districts. In 1967, unemployment was a key issue, and believed to be the central cause of massive unrest in the big cities. At the convocation creating the Urban Coalition, all of the leaders agreed to a statement of principles that included massive federal employment as a priority; however, the commitment of the business community never materialized to see it succeed as national policy. Gardner himself didn't like the phrase *Employer of Last Resort*---he knew that it was over-promising to suggest so large a government program. So, in its place the Action Council got behind a new Public Service Employment program to finance needed state and municipal jobs. But, while it was supported by all other segments of the Action Council, and pushed strongly by most of them, business executives still saw it as wasteful, expensive, and meaningless make-work. It did not become law.

When a prominent Midwestern businessman, who greatly admired Gardner, learned that Gardner and the Action Council were opposed to the Nixon nomination of Harold Carswell to the Supreme Court, he cancelled a $25,000 check he had sent to us. Carswell was a federal district judge who years before his nomination to the High Court had voiced his support for racial segregation and white supremacy. In his note to Mr. Gardner indicating his disgust with that action, the businessman wrote that he could not understand what the Carswell nomination had to do with urban problems; that he had had faith that John Gardner would spend his money wisely and find answers to urban problems, not oppose nominations such as Judge Carswell. Gardner simply answered him that if he could not understand the relationship between the Carswell nomination and urban problems, he really didn't understand the situation; and that although his money was welcomed and needed, decisions could not be made based on losing or gaining contributions.

Many in the business community weren't the only ones dragging their feet or objecting to the Action Council's positions. One of the most controversial actions of the council, supported strongly by John Gardner, was support of the so-called "Philadelphia Plan." The plan was a Nixon administration federal government order requiring federal contractors to meet goals for hiring minority workers to combat discrimination by specific skilled building trades unions. The labor movement was eager to have the business community, church and civil rights groups press for matters important to them, such as public service employment and the Carswell nomination. But when the council's black members urged support of the Philadelphia Plan, the AFL-CIO was adamantly opposed. Before the council's supportive action, Andrew (Andy) Biemiller, the union's general counsel, called me to his office to tell me in the strongest way that the AFL-CIO did not support it. The civil rights leaders were for it, strongly led by Whitney Young, president of the National Urban League, who told me that the Action Council must support it. So there we were.

It's important for me to highlight another person of great substance and stature that I came to know well. Whitney Young was a gentleman in every respect. As busy as he was, leading the Urban League in four years from a cautious organization to a front-runner in the civil rights arena (from a budget of $325,000 to one of $6,100,000), he always had time to meet with me. I mention him specifically because of the special privilege it was for me to know him. The Urban League had been a moderate organization, with black members, but largely supported by whites. Mr. Young managed to keep the influential white supporters and political leaders while broadly expanding its mission, and organizing programs to help black youngsters prepare for good jobs. Some civil rights leaders criticized him for "selling out" to whites by having close relationships with business leaders like Henry Ford II. Mr. Young responded that they would get nowhere if they didn't work "within the system" for change; at the same time he spoke out boldly for civil rights, for massive "Marshall-like" plans for the inner cities, and was one of the organizers of the March on Washington. Many white business leaders opposed him on this, but he was a man who stood on principles, regardless of what his friends in the African-American or business communities thought. For me personally, his presence helped make my day more enjoyable and fulfilling.

I told Mr. Gardner that Andy Biemiller did not say the AFL-CIO would withdraw its support of us if we backed the Philadelphia Plan, but he might just as well have said it. I had come to know Biemiller well. Knowing the AFL's importance to our program, I worked closely with his staff and met with him frequently. He was a large, formidable man, seldom angry, but tough and no-nonsense. The union had its "own fish to fry" on Capitol Hill, just as most business leaders had, and he would not be on board with the Action Council on any issue that might interfere with success of his own.

What was John Gardner's answer? We had to do what was right, and the Philadelphia Plan was right. We could not say on one hand that we were working for improved urban conditions and, on the other hand, fail to support what, in his mind, would greatly help improve them. So, the Action Council supported the Plan, and we saw less and less of the AFL-CIO's staff.

Urban Visits by Rural and Small Town Legislators Were Eye-Opening to Them

Considering the frustrations that Pete Libassi and I shared over our mutual internal problems and the inertia on Capitol Hill, together we decided that one way of gaining support of non-urban House members was to take them to the big cities and let them see the urban plight for themselves. Ivan Allen, a progressive businessman and Atlanta mayor, and John Lindsay, the former congressman and then New York City mayor, heartily agreed to open their cities to a Congressional tour. Both were members of the Coalition/Action Council boards, and good friends of John Gardner. Both provided their staff members to help with planning and local arrangements.

The tours of New York and Atlanta thoroughly covered the cities' problems. We met in Harlem with local residents, and heard first hand from community residents about the tragic lives due to blight, poverty, discrimination, and unemployment. In Atlanta, we heard civic leaders talk about their efforts to improve the city under the leadership of Mayor Allen, who was leading it into the 20th Century. Mayor Lindsay hosted us at Gracie Mansion, and Mayor Allen had us to his home to discuss what the cities needed from Washington.

Among the several House members who signed up were John Anderson and Tom Railsback of Illinois, Bill Alexander of Arkansas, and Lloyd Meeds and Brock Adams, both of the state of Washington. I mention them in particular because they all worked closely with me after the tours, and Alexander, Meeds and Adams became good friends of mine. Bill Alexander was a first termer when we met, and as a result of the trip to New York City, the Alexanders and Becks met together occasionally for dinner. All of the congressmen took the city tours seriously and cooperated with us when they could.

Congressman John Anderson was a staunch conservative on all issues early in his Congressional career, and ultimately, while remaining conservative on fiscal issues, changed his positions on much social policy. For example, he moved from a conservative to a leader for federal housing legislation. He was a spellbinding speaker, and later ran for President on an Independent ticket.

In fact, housing legislation was an area where the giants in their respective fields, such as Walter Reuther of the United Auto Workers Union, David Rockefeller, and Joseph Keenan of the AFL-CIO Electrical Workers worked closely together to try and mold effective legislation. It was in this area that the Action Council, over its short span, had some modest successes. Working with several groups, we were able to muster support for appropriations for Sections 235 and 236 of the Housing Act of 1968, which provided federal funding and standards so that low-incomers could move into affordable apartments rather than public housing. This success was even with strong foot-dragging from the administration that mouthed support, but didn't help on Capitol Hill. And here, the coalition concept of business, labor and civil rights groups, working together, had a victory.

But We Still Were Getting Nowhere

My work-life, often going late into the evening, seemed like a hopeless cause as we moved past 1968 and '69. While Andrew Heiskell, the chairman of Time, Inc. and one of Gardner's closest friends, was a frequent visitor at our offices, always wondering how things were going and pledging continuing support; and with the staffs of J. Irwin Miller, chairman of Cummins Engine, and the Washington representative of Gardner's close friend David Rockefeller showing interest, the Coalition couldn't seem to hold together. After a little more than a year, George Meany of the AFL-CIO, who had never attended a meeting, sent word that the AFL was unhappy as an Urban Coalition member.

During this time, I was able to add a couple of new staff members. But soon a very able, young Ronald James, who had arrived with the strongest credentials from the African-American community, was taken from me by Donald Rumsfeld, who had just been appointed by President Nixon to head the then beleaguered Office of Economic Opportunity. Ron wanted to stay with us, and was a true believer in our program, but Rumsfeld called Gardner, said that he needed him, and that was that. Ron and I did agree that serving as Rumsfeld's personal assistant was a move up for him. But it was a blow because Ron was such an extraordinary person, and I needed his help.

John Gardner himself was discouraged. He was not a political man, and yet was heading an organization designed to be legislatively influential. He was busy with his widespread personal and professional activities. On many mornings he would stay home to work on his fourth book, *The Recovery of Confidence.* As a trustee of the Rockefeller Brothers Fund, he often would be in New York for meetings of the Fund and other interests. And, he took time off to prepare the Godkin lectures at Harvard.

Having said that, Mr. Gardner seemed to know *everybody* who was anybody. Constantly visiting him at his office were noted columnists and writers such as Elizabeth Drew and officials of the Brookings Institution, the Ford Foundation and most other foundations. Also visiting him were university presidents either seeking his help on changing positions or wanting advice on how to succeed at their jobs. He continued to be highly respected by all who knew him, and in the public eye as well, for his uncommon intellect, thoughtfulness and ability to communicate on public issues through writing and speaking. He was always getting great press. It was only John Gardner's enormous credibility everywhere for his sound thinking and ethical character that kept our doors open.

Mr. Gardner was in constant demand countrywide to speak before large groups. He always appeared on local television wherever he went, plugging the work of the Urban Coalition. In city after city, his speeches were, of course, helpful, but only somewhat to us back at the office. There was one major problem: he would talk much more about the need for political structural change than the individual specific issues we were pushing. The dangers of political money and Congressional secrecy and seniority were his major themes; these, to John Gardner, were the embodiments to solving our problems, and his speeches generated enthusiastic responses to act for change.

John Gardner Wasn't Always "Easy" for Me

While John Gardner and I worked closely together for almost four years, he wasn't always an "easy" boss. I learned very early that he was very independent, guarded his time jealously, and was not going to let me or anybody else waste it or cause him to use it when he simply did not want to. There were times when he and I had tense moments over our differences about his use of time. I was mostly interested in seeing his time used to make the Action Council effective. This was a task. It's not that he didn't wish to use his time effectively for us; we just disagreed at times.

Within days after I first went to work for Mr. Gardner, I had a request from Congressman Bob Michel, his and my friend from Peoria, to help secure Gardner to speak at the George Washington Day Dinner in the central Illinois city. This dinner, a key yearly event in Peoria, drew 1,000 business and professional people. Congressman Michel was a very important member of Congress for us. He was the ranking Republican member of the subcommittee for health, education and welfare matters of the House Appropriations Committee, and was key to any appropriations that we sought in those areas.

Being from Peoria myself, my standing with Mr. Michel hardly would be enhanced if I could not secure John Gardner's appearance. But this made no difference. Mr. Gardner replied that it was difficult to get to that city, particularly in the dead of winter, and he was unable to make it. Just as I expected, the congressman persisted, and suggested that I try again. So I did. I explained to Mr. Gardner that it was vital that he make this trip, and that if he didn't, I would have a hard time facing the congressman again. Mr. Gardner took the letter of invitation and wrote "will attend" across the bottom. He then looked at me sternly and said, "I'll go, but, mister, you've just used up all of your credits with me for the rest of the year."

This was a fine way to get started with a new boss after just a few days on the new job, and it's correct to say that my blood pressure, normally excellent, zoomed up after leaving his office.

I met Mr. Gardner at the small, quiet Peoria airport on a cold, blustery day. We said very little to each other all the way to the hotel. But, as he began his speech, he acknowledged my dad, who was in the audience, and praised his son Lowell; and then proceeded to make his usual articulate talk. Bob Michel was elated, and guess what? He helped us with important Housing appropriations. And, of course, I felt good about the whole thing.

After that episode, Mr. Gardner explained his abruptness to me. He told me that he had come down so hard on me because, as we continued working together, I would be besieged by requests for him to speak. He said that speaking to audiences after dinner or lunches was a complete waste of time. You communicate important messages, he said, through extensive use of the television media and writing. Occasionally public speaking is important, but only on a highly selective, focused basis, and not after dinner or luncheons.

I was asked frequently. In fact there wasn't a week that I didn't think back to that time I learned I had no influence on getting him to speak. All I had to do was tell others that.

The Peoria speech episode wasn't the only time that Mr. Gardner balked at my requests. The first time that I had to arrange an appearance before a Congressional committee, his reaction was hardly that of a seasoned political person who was eager, or even just willing, to enter the fray.

Soon after President Nixon took office in January 1969, he made clear his determination to call off Johnson's War on Poverty. Coalition leaders and Democrats in Congress were determined to preserve the program and its Office of Economic Opportunity. Senator Gaylord Nelson asked Gardner to be the lead-off witness before his subcommittee to support a two-year extension of the OEO.

Senator Nelson's request caused difficulties. Mr. Gardner wanted the war on poverty continued, but as former HEW secretary, he had always believed that many of the OEO's functions should eventually be returned to the Cabinet-level departments, particularly HEW and Labor. He did not wish to advocate a two-year extension of OEO. Instead, he was willing to testify on the broad subject of poverty, and the need to work hard to eliminate it. The first draft of his statement to the subcommittee focused on the need to eradicate poverty. But he was unwilling to say, yes, this is the agency to do it, and, yes, the Urban Coalition Action Council and I support this bill that will keep the OEO going for two more years.

Out of frustration, I asked Pete Libassi to help me. He had been down this road before with Mr. Gardner. Together, he and I explained to him that the senators were trying to keep an agency alive to fight poverty in the face of a hostile new Administration and that a general statement on poverty wouldn't help them. Poverty groups, civil rights groups, and labor unions all had rallied around the OEO, despite its weaknesses, as the one agency that was addressing the problem, and they saw its extension as an essential cause at that particular time.

Mr. Gardner became perturbed with both Pete and me. He said that the OEO was weak, and keeping it going with this Administration fighting it was a losing battle. He had no heart to advocate its continued existence as it was. His position was understandable as a former HEW head; however, it wasn't the right approach for us at the time. I pointed out that if we in the Action Council stubbed our toe in our first testimony before Congress, we would not be taken seriously again. It would destroy our credibility as the leading urban advocate. He still didn't agree.

Eventually Pete and I asked Gardner what his answer would be if he were asked directly by a senator whether or not he would favor continuation of OEO for at least a couple of years more. He replied that he probably would have to answer "yes" because there was no current alternative. That was the best we could get from him, and I passed the word to Senator Nelson's staff. The question was asked of Gardner at the hearing, and he replied as he said he would.

Several days later, I told him that I was the person who planted the question with Senator Nelson. He managed a small smile and said it was okay. I was learning how to relate to John Gardner, but the hard work at that effort didn't stop.

There were other examples of Mr. Gardner's reluctance to deal with legislation in a needed, timely way. He was a very careful and thoughtful man, and one who had to be exactly sure of his footing, and the *importance* of a telephone call before making it. I knew the importance of being prepared, but to me, it was unnecessary to be overly prepared, particularly when you already were familiar with the subject. It was difficult to get him to call a Congressional leader when an issue of concern to the Action Council was hanging in the balance.

Even when the legislative issue was school desegregation, with which he and Pete dealt extensively at HEW, he insisted on receiving a thorough memorandum stating all sides and an oral briefing by staff members before he would call his old friend, Speaker of the House John McCormack. When I explained that time was of the essence on this issue where he already understood its full implications, and had handed him a briefing sheet, he continued to require the complete information he had requested before making the call to oppose the bill. We, of course, did what he asked. And the onerous amendment was defeated. His call to the Speaker was late, and probably made no difference even though the amendment was defeated. But our constituent organizations knew we had made the effort.

I Have a Possible Opportunity to Leave the Action Council

William Paley, the forceful chairman and undisputed boss at CBS, was another powerful Gardner friend. While he wasn't on our board, he supported Mr. Gardner and instructed his Washington office director to cooperate with us. After working with Paley's Washington representative, he told me that he would be leaving CBS for another position, and asked if I'd be interested in being considered for his job. Of course I was interested, but couldn't possibly think about it without Mr. Gardner's blessing.

Mr. Gardner gave it an immediate, absolute thumbs down. He said that I didn't know Bill Paley. Knowing Paley and knowing me, he said that Paley wasn't my type of person, that working for him wouldn't allow me any rest at all, and that I would not like it. He said that since Bill Paley hired and fired well-known celebrities at will, what did that mean as far as I was concerned? Further, he needed me where I was. Well, I wasn't getting much rest as it was, but didn't proceed any further.

Gardner Begins to Change As the Action Council Wanes

Gradually, toward the end of 1969, Mr. Gardner began to show a markedly increased interest in the Action Council's legislative program and to lead it toward adoption of positions that seemed outside the rebuilding-the-cities framework. The Council's decision to oppose the Carswell Supreme Court nomination caused misunderstanding among some of its members. And, its opposition to the billion dollar anti-missile program, the ABM, distressed business supporters and the AFL-CIO alike, which objected to any cut-back of jobs in defense industries.

He had become far more outspoken on issues and willingly would pick up the phone and call a congressman almost on an hour's notice without requiring a long briefing two days in advance. In December 1969, at the National Press Club, even though they were friends, he called for Representative John McCormack's resignation as Speaker of the House. This was a sharp departure from his prior avoidance of personalities in discussing public issues. It seemed almost out of character. In speeches and writings, he customarily took the high road, discussing concepts and proposing remedies, and never name-calling.

The National Press Club had invited Gardner to address one of its lunches. He readily accepted (this was national exposure, different than in Peoria). In staff discussions before the speech was prepared, for the first time he said he wanted to shake up Congress. In a way, the tables were turning, and I was the one most hesitant. Tom Mathews, our public relations guru, was exuberant. This would give the press attention that John W. Gardner needed. I was cautious. As a lobbyist, I feared that "shaking up Congress" could stop what little forward movement we had going on Capitol Hill.

Gardner explained to us: He was distressed at Congressional leaders' continued acquiescence in prolonging the Viet Nam War and their failure to deal effectively with the urban crisis.

To dramatize his point, Gardner decided to single out the seniority system in Congress as a symbol of its lethargy, and to put much of the blame on Speaker McCormack for his lack of leadership.

He told the Press Club that the nation was "…anxious but immobilized. We know what our problems are, but seem incapable of summoning our will and resources to act. Let 1970 be a year of renewal, and during that year let us give our institutions and ourselves a jolting reappraisal and overhaul."

Gardner spoke circumspectly of President Nixon's lack of leadership. He teed off much more dramatically on Congress. "Few institutions in our national life are as gravely in need of renewal as is the Congress of the United States. Renewal requires first of all measures to abolish the seniority system and to curb the abuse of power by entrenched committee chairmen."

Noting that federal judges are required to give up their administrative duties when they reach 70, Gardner proposed that Congress impose the same rule on its own members. "The Speaker of the House is 78. Thirteen Senate and House committee chairmen are over 70, six of them over 75, two over 80. They are full of years and honors. They can serve their country best by stepping aside." In an additional thrust, Gardner called on Congress to stop "tolerating grave conflicts of interest among its members."

After the speech I immediately changed my mind. The press reaction was widespread and complimentary. And it signaled a new interest in our organization's legislative program and our desire to confront Congressional obstacles head on.

Soon after the speech, at a dinner party at Rep. Lloyd Meeds' home, several younger members of Congress (Meeds, Alexander, Adams, and Hamilton) gathered around me and told me how pleased they were. The rigid seniority system barred their paths to leadership roles. By stepping on prominent toes, they told me, Gardner had given them the impetus they needed to seek ways to achieve the Speaker's retirement. Late in 1970, McCormack did retire.

Not everybody in Congress was pleased. Congresswoman Green, with whom I had developed such a warm personal association and a fan of John

Gardner, called me to express her strong displeasure. She believed that elections for committee chairmen would only pave the way for the most "popular" members, and that Congressional memory of the issues was needed in the leaders. In fact, Mrs. Green continued to be cool to me until a few years later when she visited Myrna and me in our home in Illinois.

Most of Gardner's friends and associates were pleased and surprised by the change in style and tone of his Press Club speech. But others on the Action Council Policy Council believed he was inviting too much controversy.

Although Gardner never told me so, I am convinced that by December 1969 he already was thinking about forming an organization of citizen lobbyists and activists, rather than relying on leaders of established organizations. Many of the latter, quite naturally, could not put aside their own organizations' interest for the good of a coalition of interests. *And there is a supreme lesson in politics here…legislative accomplishment is most often dependent on the word from "back home," not just from a few well-intentioned national leaders. Another is that political coalitions are only as effective as the unified personal interests or causes of the entirety of their members.*

While John Gardner's stock was rising as an activist, the Urban Coalition spirit that was so prominent in 1967 following the city riots had diminished. Many members of the Action Council did not like the way Gardner had begun to speak out on controversial issues, and were becoming reluctant to be identified with him so closely. Still others felt the council should not be taking positions that could reflect adversely on them, and money began to dry up. Every day we on the staff were caught in the middle between diverse groups, and had to walk a fine line of trying to satisfy all of them, and in the end, not really satisfying any of them. The Urban Coalition itself, under Pete Libassi's leadership, continued to function effectively in organizing local groups that were trying to come together as coalitions with solutions to local problems. But our small Action Council staff had become dispirited and uncertain about the future. It was now clear that, as first constructed, the Urban Coalition Action Council had no significant future.

I Again Consider Leaving

In January 1970, two Cummins Engine Company officials who were special assistants to Irwin Miller, Cummins CEO and Gardner confidant, approached me about a job. Because I worked closely with them, they were

I FOUND MY NICHE

aware of our problems and pessimism, and asked if I would be interested in a new position they were creating. Cummins did not have a Washington office, they said, and was planning to open one at some future time. It would have two functions: Cummins Congressional Relations, and an office to research and fund public service activities of interest to Cummins.

I not only jumped at this possibility, I was excited about it. J. Irwin Miller, who was personally involved in creating this new office, was not William Paley and was known for his business ability and charitable nature. At their invitation, I flew to the Cummins headquarters in Columbus, Indiana, and met with the company's president. He said that the new position was on the drawing board, but wouldn't be finalized for several months. They were interested in me, but, of course, it was necessary that I have Mr. Gardner's approval and recommendation.

So, for the second time, I told Mr. Gardner about the possibility of leaving, and asked for his blessing. I was upbeat about it, and this time I felt certain he would say that it sounded good. But he didn't. Instead he asked me to have dinner with him that night at the Cosmos Club, an inner sanctum of literary, intellectual and other nationally prominent leaders, where he was a member.

A Gleam in Gardner's Eyes

At dinner Gardner said that he knew the difficulties we were having with the Action Council. He didn't blame me for wanting to leave. He encouraged me to stay, indicating that he had plans that he had not yet discussed with anyone about converting the council into a large, effective membership organization. He was thinking of combining our Washington-based professional lobbying with the back-home support of thousands of members. He said that as he traveled around the country he continually was asked by concerned citizens, "How can I help turn the country around?" Although the Action Council was made up of nationally known leaders who represented millions of members in their respective organizations, they often were reluctant or did not know how to enlist those members in the council's activities.

Consequently he had come to believe that an organization consisting only of top leaders was not an effective answer; but that a strong, spirited lobbying group of citizens from all walks of life could be. The citizens group

161

would draw from all segments of society and would not be confined to the best-known leaders.

He said that he had thought about the possibilities of a citizens' organization many times, even before he was HEW Secretary, but never had a chance to do anything about it. At HEW, his views about the need for such a group increased. There he saw the influence of specialized groups in supporting some programs and blocking others. He learned first hand how the specialized lobbies work, and how Congress was so thoroughly involved in the interests of the groups that financed their campaigns. And, in his view, money and secrecy were primary causes of government *not* serving the public interest.

Now was the time for him to organize a national membership group to engage in citizen action that was necessary to make government accountable to the people.

I responded that I appreciated his confidence that I could help with this new effort, but that I really did not believe he understood what he was getting into; and that having been a staff member of another large voluntary membership association for many years, I had no real heart for it again. I told him that a membership organization could cause us more difficulties than it appeared to be worth; that it would require a large bureaucracy simply to service the members. It would be difficult to get it off the ground, and would cost far more money than probably we could raise.

He reiterated that he had not discussed this with anybody, and that my wish to leave prompted him to tell me now. He had been thinking about it for some time, but he had not defined it specifically. He wasn't sure how to construct it, but he was convinced that he *had* to act on starting a large membership organization to influence public policy through the people back home. He believed that, as the idea developed and was refined, a close-knit continuity with the Action Council should be maintained.

As far as I was concerned, I really wanted to move on to something else, *exactly like the Cummins office.* Just as so many others who were working on a crisis basis for months and even years following the 1967 riots, I was virtually exhausted. The thought of picking up from where we were and building a new national membership organization of activists from all walks of life hardly raised my spirit. Mr. Gardner could tell that I was less than enthusiastic.

Then he clinched the whole thing with me. He needed me, he said, to continue with the Action Council so that it would continue with its policy council and staff during the planning of the membership; and he needed my help in its planning. While I was helping him, he said that he, in turn, could help me more personally if I remained. He said that, as a young man, I had grown in strength and judgment during my time with him, and that my acquaintances and knowledge had broadened immeasurably. "You have grown considerably in this work," he said, "but you have many years of continued growth ahead of you. My question to you is, 'Will you continue to grow more with Cummins Engine or with me?'" I stayed with John Gardner.

The Months to Follow With the Action Council

Very little happened about the new membership group for a few weeks after our dinner. I had agreed to stay, the Action Council was still in existence, and we had a legislative agenda to implement. We also had severe money problems and attempted to solve them as best we could. We could expect little more from former donors, and some, such as labor, were bowing out.

In February, the Action Council was at work on the welfare reform bill proposed by President Nixon, known as the Family Assistance Plan, which was about to emerge from the House Ways and Means Committee. Mr. Gardner had testified in strong support of a bill that would have established a guaranteed annual income. While many council members, including the businessmen, had signed letters of support, it was a practical impossibility to get them to actively lobby for it. The House passed the bill, but the Senate did not, even though Gardner and our staff worked with Daniel Patrick Moynihan, the then domestic affairs assistant to President Nixon, to garner support. Other issues like public service employment, food stamps, and Voting Rights were on our agenda, but the country seemed in no mood to pursue vigorous new social policy.

Moynihan, in his 1972 book on the failure of the guaranteed annual income proposal, highlighted the American public environment at that time. He wrote:

> The world's most powerful democracy had entered a period of assassination, riot, and protest: war abroad and increasingly the conditions, certainly the rhetoric, of war at home. An opposing party seeking office needed to do little more than stress these facts. It was a time to keep things from coming apart: a time to

head off disaster: hardly a time to contemplate a quantum leap in social policy.

While praising Mr. Gardner and the Action Council, Moynihan went on to write that the electorate, in electing Nixon, had voted overwhelming against social change, and many had voted for something like social regression.

Against this background, we were trying hopelessly to keep the Action Council going with social policy proposals. But except for the welfare reform bill, which was specific legislation, we, after almost two years, had a difficult time establishing a meaningful legislative agenda with any hope of success.

Our financial coffers were so low by March that we were living by hand to mouth. The National Council of Churches gave some more, and Warren Lindquist, personal assistant to David Rockefeller, continued to pursue funding for us. Our total needs were some $500,000, and we managed to raise close to $75,000, just enough to keep our doors open.

John Gardner's attention, however, during February and March was not on Action Council business. He was looking ahead to something new, and at the same time did not want to harm the ongoing program of the National Urban Coalition. He proceeded slowly and cautiously after first broaching the possibility of a membership organization with me. He had clear goals in mind, but did not want to desert his friends in the coalition; and further, I suspected that he lacked full confidence that he, a non-politician, could successfully put together an effective political movement, even though he was driven to it.

He had turned down a proffered appointment as Senator from New York after Robert Kennedy's assassination, and when admirers told him he ought to be president of the United States, he dismissed the idea as entirely foreign to his nature. Nevertheless, he confided in me that an estimated 250,000 people had admired his books, articles and leadership in education to an extent that they could be counted upon to constitute a core group who would follow his leadership in an action-oriented citizens' organization. How right he was. When the first rumors, just rumors, because nothing was being said yet openly, appeared in print, hundreds of letters began arriving in the coalition's office, saying, "I've admired your writings and I'm anxious to join the citizens' organization you're forming."

We on the staff had difficulty envisioning the tremendous national response that later would materialize for the "new" action council. John Gardner had foreseen it, however, and in March 1970, told Tom Mathews and me that it was time to seriously start the planning of a broad-based citizen organization. In September, the planning began in earnest for what would become Common Cause.

CHAPTER ELEVEN
The Planning of Common Cause

WASHINGTON, D.C., 1970

In March 1970, Tom Matthews and I began talking about the membership effort, and at first the discussions centered on a direct mail effort for the Urban Coalition itself. In April, the board approved the idea of exploring it.

The initial discussions were primarily between Tom and me, and Tom began conversations with a direct mail specialist, the Guy L. Yolton Advertising Firm. Around May 1, Gardner entered our conversations, and it was decided that, to be politically effective, the new members should belong to the Action Council. At the same time, the Urban Coalition must be left intact because, without John Gardner, its future would be questionable. During the early spring months, nobody within the Coalition structure, including those who were talking with Gardner, Tom, and me about a membership drive, was thinking of it as completely separate from the Urban Coalition.

By May 1, there had been enough discussion, particularly between Gardner, Tom, and me, that a strategy began to emerge. We knew that we wanted a membership, and even thought about Mr. Gardner talking with a prominent reporter to get the word around that membership was in the wind. But, we decided that we weren't far enough along in our planning to say anything publicly. While we were focused only about membership of the Action Council, we were thinking also about a new name for it.

Because the word was out, many on the coalition staff were beginning to question whether John Gardner would stay with the coalition or leave to begin something new. While Gardner was keeping his counsel on this, Pete Libassi, who was now involved in the discussions, Tom, and I were talking about a true membership "action arm" for the coalition, and there was no thought of it breaking completely from the coalition. It would be the old Action Council with a new name and an action-oriented membership.

Everything at this time was still unclear. Although Mr. Gardner was talking with Tom and me, and occasionally Pete, he wasn't talking with anybody else. It appeared to people around the office that something was afoot, and he wasn't communicating about it. John Lagomarcino and Georgianna Rathbun told me that something had to happen soon, that morale around the offices was poor, and everybody wanted to know what was going on.

At John's and Georgianna's urging, I met with Mr. Gardner for long periods to discuss the need for clarity, a timetable, funding, and importantly, regular access to him. If we were going to move expeditiously, we needed his constant attention on the details as well as policy; he agreed. For the first time, we discussed the need for a new and radically different board. And such a board must be able to produce "new blood," and new leadership from its own ranks or from our "membership."

Most of all, we talked about the alienation of youth generally, and the cancerous effect the War in Vietnam was having on our society, which must be a prime concern of such a new organization. We discussed that we must be willing and able to respond to youths' deep-felt disgust toward the current way our society was doing business. The standard "liberal folklore," as John Gardner expressed to me, of better housing, better schools, and more jobs simply wasn't enough. The kids are not "bums," and public figures like John Gardner were going to have to muster the courage to stand up and say so. Lack of empathy and a failure to respond to genuinely held feelings and beliefs are at the heart of many of the problems. *This discussion of youth alienation reflected Gardner's strong feelings.*

Because Gardner, Tom and I had been talking about this "new" Action Council for a few weeks, it was firmer in our minds than in most others. John Lagomarcino and Georgianna were correct, however, that it was not gelling quickly enough, and that very little seemed to be happening. So, I prepared my first specific memorandum on new directions for the Action Council, and met with Mr. Gardner again on May 5, 1970. Basically, the memorandum suggested these approaches:

1. The name of the Action Council should be changed completely. The word "Council" was too limiting, and "Urban" should be deleted since we were moving toward a broader purpose. Some on the staff were working on this.

2. A new, vibrant publication needed to be developed, and Georgianna was preparing a prospectus.

3. Its program and outreach should be separate from, but still closely allied with, the Coalition.

4. While the Action Council was not achieving victories, it was enjoying a degree of respect around the city, and we should capitalize on that respect. We needed to provide a membership from all walks of life, from whom we currently weren't drawing upon, to help in securing legislative victories.

5. Specific additional staff needs were recommended: lobbyists to concentrate on specific subjects like welfare reform, manpower, crime and military spending; a membership campaign manager who also would manage fund-raising; and an issues development manager, working closely with the Coalition staff, but separate from it; and an editor and writers for a first-rate comprehensive legislative bulletin.

6. We needed to enlist key well-known people in local communities and pursue them vigorously to join and lend their names. (*We didn't spend time on this. It wasn't Gardner's view. He was moving away from that and more interested in pursuing the "5%" that he had written about. He said numerous times that about 5% of the people are the movers and shakers, and that they come from all walks of life, all geographical areas, and all occupations. Five percent of those in the ghetto as well as 5% in the business community will reach out and provide real leadership, and these were the people he was after in the new action organization. We would find them everywhere, he said, not just in the establishment, and not just in the inner circles of the business and labor union communities.*)

Mr. Gardner and I discussed the memorandum at length over two days. Out of those discussions came an understanding that we would need a first-rate fundraiser and a very good issues person. He thought it was premature to start talking then about more lobbyists, and he talked more thoroughly with me about the new agenda of government reform of the process. This new agenda had not caught on significantly with me, but thinking back to the

Cosmos Club, I began to realize that government structural change, such as Congressional seniority, money and secrecy, were a higher priority with Mr. Gardner than the traditional urban agenda of housing and jobs, as important as they were. He knew that, as Patrick Moynihan had written, America wasn't in the mood for those kinds of social action issues at that time.

John Gardner Becomes an Outspoken Activist

Speaking out on John McCormack and other senior Congressional leaders was a turning point in Gardner's activities. The second was his decision to speak out strongly against the U.S. "incursion" into Cambodia announced by President Nixon on April 30. This and related events had a profound effect on him, and intensified his planning for a new membership organization. He was besieged by calls from friends asking, "What can we do to bring this war to an end?"

On May 4, Ohio National Guardsmen fired on demonstrators at Kent State University and killed four students. On May 9, an anti-war rally drew 100,000 demonstrators to the Washington Monument. Even more of them spread out all over Washington, and as I was driving into the city, my car was mobbed by several of them, climbing on my hood, banging on my windshield, and pulled away by police.

At the time Mr. Gardner and I were planning the next steps for the new organization, all of these tumultuous events were happening. And, just at that time, on May 13, he was scheduled to speak to the Illinois Constitutional Convention on the relationship between state constitutional reform and urban problems. He had been invited by the respected convention president, Samuel Witwer, who was his strong admirer.

Three days before the scheduled speech, Gardner threw away his draft, and told me he was determined to speak out as an individual, not as Urban Coalition chairman, on the nation's "Crisis of Confidence." The speech he wrote was extremely critical of President Nixon's actions, and urged citizens to let their representatives in Congress know that their constituents wanted forces withdrawn from Cambodia and an end to U.S. presence in Vietnam within a year.

Speaking "as a Republican," Gardner said many Americans no longer believed the promises of their leaders, and felt that "the President is isolated, that he is not adequately exposed to reasonably opposing views." In unusually emotional terms, Gardner wrote, "the nation disintegrates" while fear, anger and prejudice dominate the scene.

When word reached Witwer of what Gardner intended to say in his speech, Witwer called me and withdrew the invitation. This is the thrust of my memo to Gardner the next morning about Witwer's reasons after being up most of the night on the phone with Witwer:

1. They were expecting remarks on state constitutional reform and its relationship to urban problems, and any other remarks were not germane.

2. They did not wish for President Nixon to be criticized at the Constitutional Convention and could not understand the relevance of Cambodia to state constitutional reform. (Some 40 Democrats who were followers of Mayor Daley would be present. The mayor had a hard line policy on the war and rioting in ghettos, and his delegates might interrupt your speech.)

3. The speech could destroy the convention. (The convention delegates were very tense; the 18-year-old vote had been approved by only 10 votes yesterday, and this issue had greatly divided the convention. Several delegates were calling for adjournment <u>sine die</u>.)

Those were Mr. Witwer's reasons. I wrote further in my memo that *Mr. Witwer stressed that he and others with the convention had high admiration for you, and asked that you still come and deliver extemporaneous remarks on specific issues relating to state Constitutional reform. I responded that your speech placed emphasis on making the process of government more responsive to the demands of the times, and you felt your remarks were appropriate.*

Mr. Witwer and I did not argue. We were friendly with each other. He stressed that he desired it that way, and I agreed. He is following through with this. So far his remarks to the press have indicated that our discussion last night was friendly.

We released Gardner's speech to the press, although he did not give it. And from that time on, he devoted almost all of his time to the details of starting the new citizens' organization. Actually, Mr. Gardner came through this scene quite well with his friends, including positive feedback from many Action Council board members. For example, as late as June 25, Warren Lindquist of the Rockefeller staff was still speaking supportively to me and offering his hand to help us raise funds for the Action Council. And, during this period, we all still were pursuing our regular Action Council agenda.

While Mr. Gardner did not receive public criticism from his old friends and supporters, he was picking up new friends and supporters with his heartfelt statements about the country's seemingly insurmountable problems. It was becoming clear that he was pulling away from his more cautious approach to issues, and in turn this meant the beginning of a separation from some of those old friends and supporters. This new John Gardner was noticed by everybody on the Urban Coalition staff and those in organizations who had worked closely with the Action Council for the first two years.

Even with all of this newness, the Action Council was still functioning, and we had a program to implement, including welfare reform and public service employment, both finding roadblocks that seemed impossible to overcome.

Mr. Gardner began to show impatience with Tom and me over what he thought was slow movement toward Action Council membership. His mind was now fully on these next steps, and he was expecting us to provide the first basic approach. I told him that it was impractical to keep the Action Council's program going on one hand and develop a comprehensive new membership program on the other. The outside pressures on the Action Council continued on a day-to-day basis. It was baffling that he didn't express understanding of pressures on the staff in trying to respond to Policy Council members who wanted to know what was going on; the need to continue testifying and lobbying on our agenda; the lack of funds to keep going; and the morale of the Urban Coalition staff that was plummeting.

It was simple. I couldn't manage both, even with Tom's and John Lagomarcino's sage advice and constant attention. I suggested to him that we should not be developing our plans in a vacuum by ourselves; and that if we were to move faster, I should take time away from the Action Council's day-to-day management to develop more specific plans. To move away from our insular planning, I suggested that he authorize me to make the rounds among Washington legislators and lobbyists, talking with them about the possibilities of a citizens' lobby.

I Interview Many People on and off Capitol Hill

To get away from phone calls and activities in my office, I moved to the offices of Maur, Fleisher and Zon, our outside public relations firm. Working out of this office, I visited numerous people: Senators Percy, Bayh, Pearson and

Schweiker; Congressmen John Anderson, Brock Adams and Bill Alexander; John Koskinen, a friend who was administrative assistant to Senator Ribicoff (now 48th Commissioner of the IRS), and Jim Batten of Knight Newspapers. I also called on Andy Biemiller (AFL-CIO), Lucy Benson (League of Women Voters), "Bookie" Bookbinder (American Jewish Committee), Larry Finklestein (Public Affairs Council, an organization of corporate public affairs officers), Marian Wright Edelman (Children's Welfare Rights), Esther Peterson (Consumer Affairs official), and John Gunther and Allen Pritchard (Conference of Mayors and National League of Cities).

While we ran into a good deal of cynicism about the success of a citizens' lobby, we also received encouragement, some strongly. Senator Birch Bayh, for example, said he and others in Congress had been talking of the need for such an effort because of the deep frustrations in the country about how to bring about change. He stressed that we must be very selective in our issues because we would accomplish little if we took on too many. He strongly opposed the word "lobby" in the new name, believing that the connotation was wrong, and would not be received well on Capitol Hill, or even among our potential supporters.

Senator Charles Percy emphasized leadership, because in his experience with fund raising, people give to people they trust and believe in; they do not give to things. He said we should establish a dues-paying membership because this is the only way regular income and active support could be assured each year.

Congressman Bill Alexander from rural Arkansas warned me to do everything possible to preserve John Gardner's credibility, which he said was high on Capitol Hill. Alexander thought the citizens' lobby sounded like a third political party, and that it would need a candidate if it was going to succeed. He was not enthusiastic about the idea.

Congressman Anderson liked the idea and assured us that he would work with us. He had great faith in John Gardner's ability to make it work.

Most of the politicians stressed that it should be "moderate" and not appeal to the extreme on either side. It should appeal to the center and try to develop a better understanding between the center and discouraged, militant young people.

Among lobbyists there was less enthusiasm. But Lucy Benson, president of the League of Women Voters, gave us much good advice. While most of the lobbyists thought an effective lobbying organization had to have a strong political base, Lucy Benson's experience with the League enabled her to warn us of possible pitfalls. She said that participatory democracy in an action-oriented organization was a big problem. If there was too much consultation with the membership, it delayed action. If arrangements were made for swift response to events, the organization might face danger of being captured by overly zealous elements. She had confidence that Gardner could design an effective organization and attract members.

Andy Biemiller wasn't at all enthusiastic. After thinking about it for several days, he told me that the AFL-CIO didn't like the idea of a membership campaign and that it would drive businessmen away from us. It wasn't long after this that the union withdrew its support.

Our Counsel Advises Separating the Coalition and Action Council

The most compelling advice was from our own Urban Coalition tax counsel, Mitch Rogovin. His advice sealed the ultimate decision to start an organization separate from the Urban Coalition. He told us that changes in the tax laws regarding nonprofit groups made Gardner's position, as head of both the largely foundation-supported Urban Coalition, and its non-tax-deductible lobbying arm, the Action Council, increasingly "dicey," particularly if we sought members as "citizen lobbyists." The press and public would have a hard time distinguishing between the tax-deductible research and educational organization (the Coalition) and its lobbying arm (the Action Council membership), Rogovin warned.

In the long run, Rogovin said, the Action Council would have to have a different board. Mr. Gardner, he said, should strongly consider giving up chairmanships of both organizations. All of the press we generate must be for the new organization for its full advantage; and as we begin to get additional press coverage, particularly as Gardner did after the Cambodian situation, the press should not be relating the positions and Gardner's outspoken views to the 501 (c)(3) Urban Coalition. It will continue to be an important urban research organization, and its tax exemption should not be jeopardized.

In time, Gardner resigned from the Urban Coalition, but retained his chairmanship of the Action Council. Clearly he had in mind the Council as the base for the citizens' organization.

In the meantime, Gardner was very encouraged by this feedback from my interviews, and was not discouraged by some of the criticism and skepticism about the new organization. Generally speaking, lobbyists with most groups around Washington were skeptical, even hostile. There was a general feeling that we were taking a pie-in-the-sky approach, and that an effective lobbying organization had to have strong political bases around the country. It would not succeed by simply building a membership of a few thousand, even if they spoke out vigorously.

After spending several days working out of the Maur office, I moved back to my regular office. We got down to serious business in planning, and Tom and I began traveling back and forth between Washington and New York, meeting with the direct mail firm of Wunderman, Ricotta, and Kline. We practically lived with this firm and public relations advisor Bill Ruder of Ruder and Finn. With them, we addressed the organization's name, the direct mail appeal, and the membership fee. All of us, including Mr. Gardner, worked from a late May planning memorandum of vital questions that John Lagomarcino, Tom and Georgianna helped me prepare.

Our Planning Begins in Earnest

While too long to include here, for historical purposes this is the memo's outline:

1. What is the purpose of the new organization?
2. To whom are we appealing? (Liberal to moderate to conservative?)
3. What is the name?
4. Should the board be changed, and when?
5. What changes in incorporation will be required?
6. What do we call the supporters (members?)?
7. Should annual "dues" be established, and how much? Will $10 each pay the way?
8. Do we solicit the views of the membership?
9. When does the membership campaign begin?
10. What efforts should be made to secure members in addition to direct mail and newspaper ads?
11. What will be the program of the new Action Council?

12. What will be the staff requirements?

13. Who will be responsible for preparing the literature?

14. Should (and can) the new Action Council contract with the Urban Coalition Communications Division?

15. How will policy be developed and implemented?

16. How much money is now committed to getting the new organization off the ground?

17. Will a new major fund-raising effort be required in addition to members' "dues"?

18. When and how will the current Action Council executive committee and policy council be asked to react?

At this point in early June, Mr. Gardner began taking an active role in *all details* of the organization. This would be *his* organization. While he looked to all of us on the staff for the basic plans, he began attending to every detail, and this was the way it would be from June 1970 until I left the organization almost two years later. Those closest to John Gardner began to see an entirely new person.

These former suggestions — that we state clearly the purpose of the new Action Council and rename it, that a firm money commitment should be in hand, that we needed regular access to John Gardner, and that a board of new blood should be created — began to become a reality as Mr. Gardner became accessible to all of us engaged in planning, and as he himself set out to raise substantial new funds as front money.

In the late May memorandum, I said the name of the organization was still open (and gave a list of possibilities), but I was able to identify its purpose: "To provide an 'action home' for hundreds of thousands of moderate to liberal to conservative (political center) citizens who wish to play a role in influencing the national political tone and specific legislative objectives to advance the public welfare (such as the Vietnam War, the extension of the Voting Rights Act and the Carswell nomination); who wish to be a part of a movement that will guide individuals on 'what they can do.'"

We would try to bring generations together, rural and urban people, ADA'ers (Americans for Democratic Action), and Jaycees. But we did not know yet if they should be called "members," because that suggested a direct role in determining policy positions, something we wished to avoid. As Lucy Benson had warned, we did not want to open a Pandora's Box of demands from the membership, but we would seek their views by a questionnaire twice a year.

We would keep the membership informed on legislative issues, alert them on the best timing of appeals to their senators and representatives, suggest activities they would undertake in their communities, and advise them on how to become more effective in local activities.

I wrote in that memo that a campaign for members should be ready to move by Labor Day. Looking back, I'm struck by the fact that staff views, as represented in that memorandum, were pretty traditional; they focused on separate and distinct legislative goals. There was no mention of "revitalizing government" or opening up the system to citizens, themes that Mr. Gardner was to stress successfully in launching the new organization.

Decision on a Name

The question of what to name the new organization posed problems. Although he was becoming involved in more details, Gardner took very little time helping with a name. Several of us on the staff suggested names: New America, Coalition for National Renewal, Citizens Action League were some of them. Our direct-mail consultants came up with a longer list: Crusade for a New America, We the People, American Coalition, and Common Cause were among them.

The name Common Cause seemed to be everybody's first choice but mine (although I didn't have a choice…this was hard, coming up with an appropriate name). I'll never forget the hour I heard it. We had been struggling with a name for weeks; and finally Tom went to New York to sit down with the public relations people and settle on one…once and for all. He called me from New York, and in a low, mysterious tone said that he had a name. I asked him in a similar, but questioning, tone, "What is it?" He said in a hushed, drawn-out way –"C o m m o n C a u s e." I said, "You must be kidding. That sounds ridiculous."

I couldn't visualize walking into offices of senators like Pearson from Kansas, or congressmen like Alexander from Arkansas, and displaying my card as Executive Director of something called "Common Cause." This sounded too much on the fringe to me, and wouldn't win any friends for us on Capitol Hill.

Tom told me not to worry. "George Washington," he said, "often used the term 'common cause' in talking about America's fight against the British." He thought that might be traditional enough for me.

The name *did* reflect accurately what John Gardner had in mind. He believed that there were common issues, namely embodied in the revitalization of government, which cut across all political and philosophical lines. It was catchy, different and described Gardner's primary agenda of revitalizing government. In one of our late night meetings, we just decided that would be the name, period. And, once we had settled on the name, we began talking about the contents of the direct mail pieces and an agenda for Common Cause.

The First Test Appeal to Members

In now taking an active role in all details, Gardner insisted, against the advice of the direct-mail specialists, that the annual dues should be $15, not $10. And he was right. A test mailing in July of letters urging membership at $15 a year pulled more favorable responses than did the same letter offering a $10 membership.

Above all, Mr. Gardner insisted on writing the first appeal to potential members himself. We had considered seeking a list of well-known sponsors, including sports and entertainment celebrities, but in the end decided to go with John Gardner alone.

The direct-mail people were not pleased with his letter. It seemed unconventional to them. The enormous response it drew came as a big surprise to them.

In his four-page letter Gardner described Common Cause as a *"new independent, non-partisan organization for those Americans who want to help in the rebuilding of this nation."* He said we must help end the war in Vietnam, renew the attack on poverty and discrimination, shake up and renew outworn institutions. *"We shall never accomplish all that unless we believe in ourselves. We can regain our confidence as a people — but only by a commitment to positive action... We take the phrase 'Common Cause' seriously. The things that unite us as a people are more important than the things that divide us."*

This was typical John Gardner — deep concern about things that were wrong, deep optimism that citizens had it within them to right those things that had gone wrong. Mr. Gardner did not take lightly the preparation of this letter. He spent several nights writing it and rewriting it. And, it finally was becoming evident to all of us closest to him that he was moving away from the old Action Council agenda with priorities on "new solutions in housing, employment, education, consumer protection, etc." to new priorities such as "revitalizing politics and government" and "ending the Viet Nam War on a scheduled timetable." And, as we began working on this agenda, the planning took on "movement" tones.

The test mailings drew an unusually good response; and word of mouth, press stories, and Gardner's appearance on "Face the Nation" moved citizens who trusted him to telephone and write in, volunteering to join his organization and to offer their assistance.

Common Cause Is Launched in August

On July 28, 1970, the Policy Council of the Action Council met to change the organization's name to Common Cause. On August 18, John Gardner publicly launched his new organization at a press conference at the Statler Hilton Hotel.

The Associated Press story of August 18 reported that John W. Gardner formally initiated a nationwide nonpartisan, political movement called Common Cause…to be a citizen's lobby to force action on reform of the political system and solution of national problems. David Broder, writing in *The Washington Post* on August 20, took a cautious, but hopeful view. He said that if Gardner could prove that a constituency existed, he may provide a movement, not based on the quicksand of the college campuses, which can free the nation from the trap of Viet Nam, and turn its energies to the urgent unsolved problems at home.

The first newspaper ad for Common Cause was taken from Gardner's letter and bore a headline he wrote: *"Everybody's Organized But the People."* It said Common Cause would be a "Citizen's Lobby, concerned not with the advancement of special interests, but with the well-being of the nation." Asserting that most parts of the political system had grown so rigid that they could not respond to impending disaster, the ad said that one of Common Cause's aims would be to "revitalize politics and government."

I remember vividly the relief and pleasure with which he received the results of the first opinion poll sent out to the 13,000 members who were first to join Common Cause. The poll asked the membership to choose their priorities among the 15 issues listed as our "Agenda for America." U. S. withdrawal from Vietnam and a reduction in military spending (funds to be diverted to domestic solutions) were the members' first choice. Coming in second, to John Gardner's gratification, was "overhaul and revitalization of government at national, state and local levels to create effective and responsive institutions and processes." Elimination of poverty and protection of the environment came in third and fourth.

Our goal for Common Cause was to gain a membership of 100,000 by the end of the first year. The goal was reached in 23 weeks. On our first official anniversary, September 1, 1971, the membership exceeded 200,000. His estimate that over 200,000 who trusted him from his books and commentaries would join his organization came true.

John Gardner had become a political figure. The public by the thousands came to hear him—in Seattle, Portland and Chicago — to name a few. They filled Constitution Hall in Washington, D. C. I always will relish those experiences of "warming up the audiences" as I traveled around the country with him. Those mass rallies were true love affairs between the main event — John Gardner — and the audiences. They came in droves then because of their trust in him and his new idea, Common Cause, and literally hung on every word. He brought them some hope in a troubled time, and they responded in kind by their enthusiastic applause and by joining Common Cause.

John Gardner, who in past times would hold back from testifying on a specific poverty bill, wasn't holding back any longer. He did display "modesty of spirit," but loved every minute of it, and was providing outspoken leadership.

Now our task was to make the new organization work and, at the same time, completely separate the two organizations so that minimal disruption would occur with the National Urban Coalition. So far, only the name and agenda, not the structure, had been changed...from Urban Coalition Action Council to Common Cause. But now Common Cause could no longer simply be an arm of the Urban Coalition. Each organization would have to stand on its own feet.

John Gardner as I knew him...with his sleeves rolled up. 1970
Urban Coalition photograph

John Gardner (foreground) in a Common Cause "boiler room" telephone blitz.
Tom Mathews is standing in the background. Courtesy of Peoria Journal Star

I lead off a Common Cause "rally" at Constitution Hall when John Gardner spoke about the new organization. Courtesy of Mrs. Aurora K. Reich

In my Common Cause office with a picture of my hometown, Peoria, on my wall. Courtesy of Peoria Journal Star

Chesterfield Smith "breaks me up" after dinner at our home.

Bert Early and I perform at an ABA staff skit.

*With First Lady Nancy Reagan at her White House
anti-drug conference. 1989 White House photograph*

With General McDermott (McD) at an NAII meeting.

With Don Schaffer, Carl Hulbert, and Major General Robert Herres, Ret., USAA CEO, 1993-2003, and former Vice Chairman of the Joint Chiefs of Staff. My handicap helped us win at this NAII outing.

With Senator Bayh at his home in 2012.

The WYCC-TV First From Chicago staff with guest Stan Mikita, the all-time leading scorer of the Chicago Blackhawks, just before my interview with him.

Chicago bus ad for our TV show. 1997

Our son Jonathan, his wife Suzi, and Spencer and Liam Beck. 2015.

Our daughter, Lori, and husband, Richard, with Chris, Ryan,
Stephen and Matthew Andrusko. 2015.

Our son Rich, Myrna and I on the Amalfi Coast, Italy. 2015.

Our family...Rich is a graduate of Grinnell College and Loyola University-Chicago, where he obtained his Masters degree in Social Work. He leads the case management department in a Chicago area hospital... Jonathan and Suzi , graduates of Miami University of Ohio and Middlebury College, respectively, hold law degrees from Vermont Law School. With their two boys, they live in New Hampshire where he provides business administrative services, and she is counsel with a commercial insurance company... Lori and Richard are graduates of Ohio University. She, a hospital RN, and Richard, a chemical engineer, live in Wisconsin with their four boys.

CHAPTER TWELVE

The First Year of Common Cause
Our Daughter Lori Is Born

WASHINGTON, D.C. 1970–1972

From the launch of Common Cause in 1970 until I left it February 1972, I highlight here only those events where I was directly involved. Otherwise, the full detailed story of the first year and a half would fill an entire book in and of itself. A summary of the first year was written by John Gardner in *In Common Cause*, published by W.W. Norton in 1972.

An Increased Staff Is Hired

Two new staff members were immediately required, one to supervise Common Cause's own research and program development, and the other to direct its massive direct mail program. Robert Gallamore, formerly with the Bureau of the Budget, and the Department of Transportation, and with a doctorate in economics and political science at Harvard, was hired as director of policy development. Heading up the direct mail and fund raising effort was Roger Craver, who had extensive experience in fund raising, particularly as a university development director. (Roger had come on board before the August announcement, and was involved in membership planning as well as helping decide the name, Common Cause.) By February the staff had grown to 14, compared with four who reported to me at the Action Council.

John Lagomarcino was named director of legislation. Georgiana Rathbun took on the monthly edition of the new *Report from Washington*. Tom Mathews became the full-time public relations director after leaving the Urban Coalition.

The Urban Coalition/Coalition Action Council Structure Changes

For the first few months, we functioned as before, with only the Action Council's name changed to Common Cause. As we had imagined, it became necessary to disengage altogether from the Urban Coalition and operate exclusively as a separate 501(c)(4) organization. John Gardner resigned as chairman of the coalition, and his friend Sol Linowitz, the former chairman of Xerox, and former U.S. Ambassador to the Organization of American States, succeeded him.

While Andrew Heiskell, the chairman of Time, Inc., and some other members of the former Action Council board (Policy Council), remained on the Common Cause board, several others, including David Rockefeller, opted not to remain. During 1971, the board reconstituted itself with a nominating committee and election by Common Cause members.

The Common Cause Issues Are Controversial and Not for the Faint of Heart

Welfare Reform known as the Family Assistance Plan

On August 8, 1969, President Nixon announced his proposal on welfare reform called the Family Assistance Plan. It would have eliminated the old welfare system that had been in effect for years, and would have provided a minimum guaranteed income for poor families. It included work requirements, and also provided benefits for millions of working men and women whose incomes were insufficient to lift them above the poverty line.

The F.A.P.'s architect was Daniel Patrick Moynihan, who at that time was Nixon's Assistant for Urban Affairs (later senator from New York), and a friend of John Gardner. The plan was opposed by Nixon's most conservative advisers, although a guaranteed minimum income gained some acceptability among conservatives when economist Milton Friedman recommended a negative income tax to provide a safety net for the poor while also rewarding work. Perhaps the clearest definition was a *New York Times* commentary by Peter Passell when he wrote: *"It would meet the most irksome of American problems — poverty — with the most direct and radical of solutions: money. All families with children would be eligible for a minimum stipend; no longer would the absence of a 'man in the house' be a precondition for welfare."* It would protect mothers and children by exempting from work mothers with children up to six years old.

Passell went on to write, *"A Republican President, elected in significant measure out of distaste for the dependent poor, thus proposed the adoption of a guaranteed income. F.A.P. was a kind of domestic trip to China, a triumph of pragmatism over ideology...not until the Peking voyage was a Nixon initiative to receive such wide enthusiasm."*

During his time as HEW secretary, John Gardner had taken a strong interest in welfare reform, and, according to Moynihan* in his history of the F.A.P., *"much of the Nixon proposal was based on planning that had begun in HEW when he was Secretary."* Gardner and the Action Council moved immediately to support the proposal. A new staff member, Jack Moskowiz, was employed to focus primarily on welfare reform.

Because he was traveling in November 1969 when the House Ways and Means Committee held its hearings on the F.A.P., Mr. Gardner wrote insightful testimony in support, which was presented by former Ambassador George McGhee. Because Gardner was away often during that time, he believed it would be helpful to enlist the help of another prominent individual who was well-known and respected around Washington. He decided to bring on board, as his personal consultant, his old friend George McGhee who had recently retired after years of various highly visible Foreign Service positions.

Ambassador McGhee would testify when a high-profile person was advisable, and help us gain more entry on Capitol Hill, where he was well known and respected in both parties. He had gained great wealth as an oilman before WWII, and had a distinguished military career on the staff of General Curtis LeMay, for which he was awarded the Legion of Merit. After the war he worked for the State Department, disbursing aid to Greece and Turkey, and served as Ambassador to Turkey. He held diplomatic positions under President Kennedy, and was Ambassador to West Germany from 1963 to 1968 when, he retired from the Foreign Service and joined the boards of Mobil, Proctor and Gamble and Trans World Airlines.

I welcomed George McGhee with open arms. He was an unflappable man, with great self-confidence, and yet not pretentious. He took a strong interest in the Action Council, and always gave reassuring words that we were on the right track.

He was exactly the right person to present testimony on behalf of Mr. Gardner. Members of the Ways and Means Committee couldn't have received it better. According to Patrick Moynihan, the Gardner statement made it clear that he knew a guaranteed income when one was proposed, and he was sufficiently a student of federal social policy to recognize the emergence of an important family policy. His testimony began by acknowledging both:

First, we would offer a general word of praise for the emphasis on children that is at the heart of the proposals under discussion. It's about time.

Second, we would emphasize that, if the proposals are accepted, the federal government will for the first time in history accept responsibility for providing a minimum level of payment throughout the nation and for financing it. I would have been very proud had I been able to establish that principle during my tenure as Secretary of Health, Education and Welfare. It is an historic step. All the details of the present proposals fade in significance compared with that major advance in federal policy.

He offered on behalf of the Action Council some recommended changes, including clarification of the job standards and work requirements, and that provisions be included for job creation.

After the hearings, we began calling on House members and their staffs; and enlisting the support of Policy Council members, asking them to contact legislators also. We published material that detailed provisions of the Plan, and added the names of the many mayors, civil rights leaders, labor union officials, college presidents, business leaders and church leaders who supported it. It was a major undertaking, with dozens of well-known individuals signed on as supporters.

However, as is generally the case on Capitol Hill, most congressmen and women look to "experts" to help them out because they know so little about the intricacies of the subjects they are voting on. It wasn't long before some experts began denouncing the Plan from both the left and right, with arguments as to whether the work requirement for mothers was too stringent to whether the F.A.P. payments were too high or too low.

Controversies swirled and emotions were extremely high from the time of the November hearings until March 5, 1970, when the Ways and Means Committee voted 21 to 3 to report to the House the Family Assistance Act of 1970. All Committee Republicans voted for it, and three Democrats were against a guaranteed income of any kind. On April 16, the House passed the Act by a vote of 243 to 155. 63 percent of Democrats and 59 percent of Republicans voted for it.

Controversial emotion was exploding. Threats were made by the National Welfare Rights Organization, an organization of welfare recipients. Its first vice-chairman, appearing in opposition before the Ways and Means Committee at its March hearings, threatened: "I am going to tell you right now, we are going to disrupt this Senate, this country, this capital, and everything that goes on…"

It takes numerous pages for the full history of the F.A.P., which is the subject of Moynihan's 1973 book, *The Politics of a Guaranteed Income… The Nixon Administration and the Family Assistance Plan.* But, in the House of Representatives, many members voted on blind hope that there was good in it, and far better than the present welfare system, which most labeled a mess. Congressman Wilbur Mills from Arkansas, the respected chairman of the Ways and Means Committee, surprised everybody on the House floor by his emotional support…he called the Plan the "only ray of hope" for ending the "welfare mess." The House members trusted Patrick Moynihan, the many organizations and leaders who supported it, the Ways and Means members who heard the testimony, *and* John Gardner.

To my own personal delight, conservative Illinois Republican Harold Collier, a friend of mine, and a member of the Ways and Means Committee, rose on the House floor to speak succinctly, giving the reason that he and most Republicans were for it. He said, "I urge every Member of this House to give welfare reform a chance. To do anything less is to accept the present program, with all of its present shortcomings and its inevitable social doom." Moynihan singled out Collier's statement as a "respectable, if not conclusive, argument." I couldn't have been more pleased with Mr. Collier's support and statement. The congressman had told me that he would support it, which he did in both the Committee and full House vote, but hadn't said he would rise and speak as he did.

But wait. It passed the House, but that was only the beginning. Opposition strengthened, and controversy did not subside. As it moved to the Senate, disagreement arose over whether this Plan was the answer to shedding the old Welfare System. More experts and organizations, both liberal and conservative, began opposing it for different reasons: Liberals because it didn't provide enough money for welfare recipients and work requirements for mothers were too rigid. Conservatives because they opposed anything that smacked of a guaranteed income. The Senate hearings were venomous.

While Senate Finance Committee hearings were being held in the summer of 1970, the Urban Coalition Action Council was changing to Common Cause, and all of us had our hands full with that. But John Gardner, and consequently the staff of the Action Council/Common Cause, didn't let up on its support of the F.A.P. While I was primarily busy with the change-over, I worked closely with our lead staff man, Jack Moskowitz, and John Lagomarcino, in talking regularly with the Moynihan office, and in particular Robert Patricelli, who was the point man on the bill at HEW. We worked with Patricelli, who had been a key staff man in the Senate, on amendments that might help make the F.A.P more palatable to both liberals and conservatives. Pete Libassi, who was knowledgeable on welfare reform from his HEW days, was an important participant.

The Senate experience was nothing but frustration. Hearings began in April, and no Republican supported the bill. The Democratic Southern conservatives had piercing questions, many of which HEW Secretary Robert Finch seemed unable to satisfactorily answer, and Patricelli was called to answer. Some senators weren't interested, others had difficulty with provisions that the NWRO disdained, and others might have opposed it because they didn't want Nixon to have a victory.

And so it went. The NWRO passed a resolution that called the F.A.P. an act of political repression. Its leader, George Wiley, said that the Nixon plan must be defeated. On the other hand, the Democratic mayor of Cleveland, Carl Stokes, an African-American, representing mayors throughout the country, supported it with passion while speaking on the plight of the cities.

As the year was ending, because of constant efforts to revise the draft bill and persistent lobbying by the administration, most of the Finance Committee's members seemed finally ready to support it. John Gardner, the new HEW Secretary Elliot Richardson, and Pat Moynihan decided that Common Cause (newly named by then) would be most helpful by hosting a meeting of all the organizations supporting the legislation. The meeting was planned for November 17, just three days before the scheduled Senate vote, at a downtown hotel. Richardson would describe the revised bill up for the vote, and ask for a massive lobbying effort during the next several hours. Each group was invited to bring up to three representatives, and it was anticipated that some 150 persons would attend. George Wiley wanted to bring 150 or more welfare mothers to present the NWRO position. He had called our office to reserve those places. When our program planner told him that wasn't possible, he said he would be over immediately to talk with John Gardner and me.

Gardner wasn't in the office, so I prepared to meet with him. I had never met George Wiley, but knew him by reputation. He was known as a militant African-American who had strongly advocated aggressive tactics to accomplish his goals.

George Wiley earned a doctorate in organic chemistry from Cornell University. He taught chemistry at the University of California at Berkeley, followed by teaching at Syracuse University. Prior to Syracuse, Wiley had led voter registration drives and counseled student activists taking part in sit-in protests. While at Syracuse, he become active in the drive for civil rights and started work for the Congress of Racial Equality. He left CORE and organized nationwide protests by welfare recipients in what became known as the "Welfare Rights Movement." He founded the NWRO in 1967, and then began invading welfare offices, demanding more money. He demanded $5,500 per year for every American family with four children, and set up local chapters to accomplish that. By 1969 he had enlisted thousands of members and 520 chapters.

Because Wiley's career in welfare rights was filled with bullying and intimidation, I braced for what to expect when we met.

Mr. Wiley arrived in his flowing, wide-sleeved African robe. It might have been called a grand boubou. It was strikingly beautiful. And George was a beautiful person. He couldn't have been more pleasant with me. Gentle, almost. He wanted to see John Gardner, but seemed pleased to talk with me. He said that the welfare subject was at the heart of everything his organization did, and that it was important that the people most involved — the welfare mothers — be present at our meeting to explain their point of view. I told him that Mr. Gardner and I agreed, and that he and his representatives were invited to attend and speak; but each group was limited to an appropriate number of attendees and a limited amount of time to speak; that should apply to the NWRO as well. He responded that 150 welfare mothers would arrive in Washington tomorrow from around the country, and they were expecting to be admitted. The meeting ended in disagreement, but courteously.

I liked George Wiley. I thought that he was a genuinely fine person, truly concerned about the plight of the poor, especially mothers with children. I also felt that, counterproductive or not with the general public, he believed that his unconventionally strident tactics of confrontation were the way to get the attention needed to solve poverty problems. Strong, unbridled ego, yes. But sincerity, also yes. (In August 1973, he was reported missing, and it's thought that he drowned in Chesapeake Bay. To me this was a sad tragedy, and I felt it personally. Not just because I liked him, but because, whether you agreed or disagreed with his tactics, he was a formidable, genuine presence for the good.)

As pleasant as Wiley was to me, we at Common Cause knew that he was planning to disrupt our meeting. He didn't want it to be successful, and wanted the publicity of dozens of welfare mothers objecting loudly to the bill and the HEW Secretary's presentation. If the meeting were held, even if only three mothers had been admitted, the remaining 147 would be outside in front of the cameras, aggressively attacking the bill. It was agreed by everybody involved that the meeting should be cancelled.

Between November 20 and December 16, 1970, more efforts were made to get the bill to the Senate floor and pass it there. Several more changes were agreed to by the administration at the request of Senator Ribicoff (D-CT), who had hoped to get a bill passed.

On December 3, Common Cause held a meeting of supporting groups (this one more low-key than the first futile one) to listen to Secretary Richardson's positive response to Ribicoff and some other senators. He had accepted most of their proposals, and hoped this finally would allow passage. The NWRO still was opposed, and this seemed to be the straw to kill the bill. But, as Patrick Moynihan reminds us in his book, *Again, not quite.*

Senator Ribicoff and Republican Bennett (R-UT) had the cooperation of the Senate leadership to get their amendments before the full Senate for a vote there. But, on the day of the vote, a filibuster took place over a bill that some thought would sanction the Cambodian incursion, another filibuster was planned by opponents of import quotas, and organized labor found problems with the Ribicoff-Bennett F.A.P. amendments.

The Senate was in such upheaval that it could not pass the F.A.P. The Majority Leader Mansfield told the Senate that they had made a spectacle of themselves. There were a few days left in the session, but not enough time to consider it again. It was dead.

The defeat of the F.A.P. was especially disheartening to many because it was such landmark legislation, and had such large bodies of support from mayors to civil rights groups to business leaders. While many believed that the income maintenance proposal was inadequate, they also considered it was a true reform of the welfare system, ranging from helping families stay together, to work incentives and requirements. We continued to the end with high visibility, including Senate testimony by our vice chairman, Bill Eberle, the chairman of American Standard Inc. But conservatives and liberals alike, in the long run, joined to defeat it, although for different reasons. As it turned out, it later provided the foundation for two major acts. President Reagan supported an "earned income tax credit" which, in effect, returns money to certain low and moderate income workers whose tax rates are negative; and in 1996 a Republican Congress passed a landmark Welfare Reform bill, signed by President Clinton.

———————————— ଏ ————————————

I've written extensively about the F.A.P because the Action Council, and then Common Cause, were so heavily involved in trying to enact it into law, only to see it go down in defeat; and it was the primary Common Cause legislative effort when I was personally involved from planning to lobbying. While during 1971 I testified on campaign spending reform and limits, and participated in the planning of other lobbying efforts, such as our campaigns to end the Viet Nam War and to adopt the 18-year-old vote Constitutional Amendment, most of my time was devoted to getting Common Cause going with advertising and direct mail, hiring new staff members, and focusing on organizing some local offices. Virtually from the day Common Cause was announced, our staff members who had the legislative responsibilities did most of the direct, day-to-day lobbying work on Capitol Hill.

---

* Much of the specific detail of the House action and Senate deliberations are, even though uncited specifically, from Patrick Moynihan's thorough account of the history of the F.A.P., *The Politics of a Guaranteed Income (the Nixon Administration and the Family Assistance Plan)*, Random House, 1973. I could not have recalled this account as thoroughly without it. My own involvement in the effort is recalled by my personal recollections and notes, as well as references in the Moynihan book to Mr. Gardner, me, the Action Council and Common Cause.

The Vietnam War

While abuses in campaign spending, the Congressional seniority system, and other topics were key issues for Common Cause, the principal activity on Capitol Hill in the spring of 1971 was to promote enough interest and support for an end to the Viet Nam War and complete withdrawal of U.S. troops by the end of the year. The war wasn't specifically an "urban" issue such as employment, poverty and housing, but it was draining the country's spirit and finances so much that little else could be considered seriously. That was one reason John Gardner began speaking out against the war before Common Cause was started.

To engage in the "end the war" activity, in April we undertook a massive campaign among our Common Cause members to enlist House members, most of whom had given almost no attention to popular pressure to end the War, to sign a statement of purpose calling for total withdrawal from Indochina. Two statements, one for Republicans and one for Democrats, were prepared by David Cohen who was hired to give the campaign national prominence. David had been an aide to Walter Reuther, president of the United Auto Workers, and knew his way around Capitol Hill with both parties. Four Democrats, led by Speaker Tip O'Neill, sponsored the statement for Democrats and five Republicans, led by Rep. Charles Mosher of Ohio sponsored theirs.

Ending the War was not simply a Republican/Democratic issue in 1971. It had become mainstream with the public and was at the top of our new members' priority list of issues to be tackled by Common Cause. A strong majority of the American public opposed the war, making it all the more surprising that it had such little organized attention in Congress.

A telephone bank of 14 phones was set up in the Common Cause conference room. Volunteers made calls all day and into the evening to Common Cause members, asking them to call and send letters to their respective Congressional representatives. We asked them also to contact friends and relatives to do the same thing. Many of them were asked specifically to either call or visit their representative's local office. If the Congressperson's local office manager received even a dozen or so such contacts from constituents, that would have serious impact.

The walls of the phone bank room were covered with charts giving the names of all House members and a tally of how many Common Cause members agreed to call or write. Volunteers signed up from all over the Washington area to make calls, under the day-to-day guidance of our phone volunteer leader, Ruth Sax. Volunteers would be a mainstay of Common Cause's work from its beginning. Our members responded by the thousands, urging their respective House members to sign the statement sponsored by their respective party leaders.

These signed statements didn't have the force of law, but they were meant to say publicly to the President that U.S. House members wanted him to act, and soon, on Indochina.

They did not succeed in ending the War on the timetable we had urged. And while dozens of House members signed them, we didn't get the majority we had sought. Fred Wertheimer, a top Capitol Hill Republican legislative aide who joined our staff to assist David on the campaign, and to focus on campaign spending, later said that his feedback from the Hill was that the Common Cause effort had made "very significant advances...among more conservative members of both parties." My own feedback was that, while no Congressional action of any kind on the War had been considered seriously before our campaign, the letters and calls from our members heightened Congressional interest in doing something about it. I was told by some of my Capitol Hill friends that they were hearing from middle to upper income voters... men and women, mostly white and business and professional people... a constituency the Congress seldom heard from before in such large numbers. This made a special impact. We were giving these people, our members, a new vehicle to express their personal public policy views directly to members of Congress, and they were responding.

History tells the story. After years of growing public discontent that reached a climax in 1973 and tens of thousands of deaths of Americans and Asians, the United States did leave Vietnam. This was not a Common Cause victory as such. It was the result of pressures and advocacy from numerous sides, with Congress and the President finally acting. But Common Cause had shown that it had muscle, and that a vehicle such as it, one that allowed and promoted citizen action, could be effective.

Note: While we at Common Cause were criticized by the White House as being partisan and ultra-liberal for working so hard to end the war, this criticism was incorrect. When we engaged in our End the War campaign, the public was strongly against the war. The opposition had gone "mainstream." Starting in 1965, a Gallup poll found 61 percent agreeing with the war, but only 28 percent in May 1971. After years of fear of nuclear war and turmoil over race relations, America continued in turmoil. Mass protest rallies numbering in the tens of thousands were being held around the country and in Washington. They didn't stop. In 1970 Kent State University students protesting were shot, and this was followed by 100,000 demonstrators converging on Washington. Killed in the war were 58,220 U.S. service members, 800,000 to 3.1 million Vietnamese, and hundreds of thousands of Cambodians and Laotians. It was time for this war, which most considered a useless, devastating venture, to end.

The use of the "boiler-room" telephone bank for calling Common Cause members worked. Led by our staff members of John Lagomarcino, Peter Edelman and Jack Moskowitz, we had formerly used it for calls to end the *Congressional Seniority System*, when we had helped make a dent in that autocratic practice in the House. While it didn't seem like a lot at the time, it was a major breakthrough for Congressional reform. As reported in *The New York Times* on January 20, 1971, "the rigid seniority system of members rising automatically to power" was changed to "the selection of committee chairmen will be subject to approval by party caucuses." Common Cause used the telephone bank to augment visits to House members and their staffs; radio and TV discussions of seniority; discussion of seniority at church, club and political meetings; even at a Sunday School class; and, of course, letters to the editor. This victory showed us that our members were indeed interested in governmental "process" issues like Congressional Seniority, just as they would be on issues like the Vietnam War.

And now our campaign was against the war; and while we didn't have immediate success with that, we had made change begin to happen with the Seniority System, and most of all we had provided an organized vehicle for thousands of citizens to express their views in an effective way to members of Congress. In time, the War ended; and in time, the Seniority System and closed committee meetings on Capitol Hill ended too.

The 18-Year-Old Vote

We used the same technique of telephone banks plus extensive work in local communities to urge ratification of the Twenty-Sixth Amendment to the Constitution.

In 1970, Congress and the U.S. Supreme Court created a chaotic situation for the 1972 elections. Congress passed a bill, signed by President Nixon, which lowered the voting age in all federal, state, and local elections to 18. In that same year, the Supreme Court, in *Oregon v. Mitchell,* ruled that this could apply only to federal elections, leaving it to the states to determine their age qualification. This meant that 18-year-olds in all states could vote for federal officials, but not in state elections. Forty-seven states were in the illogical and costly position of having to implement this new voting arrangement unless they immediately changed their state and local laws to conform to the federal law. If all did not, there would have been a chaotic hodgepodge of voting requirements for 18-year-olds throughout the country. The more direct and preferred method was to amend the United States Constitution to lower the voting age.

By March 1971, the Twenty-Sixth Amendment was proposed by the Senate 94-0, and the House 400-19. Common Cause played a major role in securing rapid Congressional action by hiring Jan Keefer and Ian MacGowan, who had been the leaders of the Youth Franchise Coalition, a coalition of interested groups that had successfully lobbied the first bill. From the Common Cause office, they marshaled again all of the interested groups; and the issue was so popular that new Congressional hearings weren't even held. Because the campaign now would shift to states for action, Jan and Ian were already at work with Common Cause to lead the efforts to secure ratification. Ratification would require three-fourths of the states to agree. Some states were balking; others were simply dragging their feet.

While several organizations, led by the Youth Franchise Coalition, were driving forces behind Congressional passage, Common Cause had the in-place mechanism to reach voters to lobby their home legislatures and governors. On March 22, 1971, a day before final Congressional approval in the House, a full-scale ratification lobbying process was kicked off by a Common Cause press conference, with several prominent state officials participating. The effort *was* full-scale and had to be swift. Under Jan's and Ian's leadership, states were pinpointed that needed heaviest attention from phone bank calls to our members or even personal visits by our staff to organize state-wide efforts. Common Cause members, when knowing when to contact their state legislators and governors, came through in grand fashion. The Twenty-Sixth Amendment became part of the United States Constitution on July 1, 1971, and ratification was completed quicker than any amendment in history.

Why was lowering the age so popular, and why did it sail through a unified Congress so fast? And why was it adopted by the states more quickly than any other amendment? Many were saying that it was because so many of that age were dying in the war, and others pointed to the violence on the college campuses. But it wasn't that simple. There were many reasons as reported in the March 1971 *Common Cause Report from Washington:*

Of the 11.5 million persons age 18–21, 4.1 million are in the labor force, 800,000 are in the armed forces, 4.9 million in school, 80 percent of the total are high school graduates, 46 percent, college graduates. A high percentage of these young people have begun paying taxes on a regular basis, yet are precluded from the basic participation in the government they are helping to finance.

Persons 18 years of age are treated as adults by the legal system and by insurance companies. The Federal Government permits youths to enter the Federal Civil Service when they reach 18, and — as is well known — young men of this age are subject to military service; a sizable proportion of the American troop commitment in Vietnam falls within the 18–20 age group and most of these are draftees. If they are required to risk their lives for the system, they should be allowed to participate in it.

There can be no doubt that today's 18-year-old knows more about what is happening in the nation and world than the 21-year-old of earlier years. This is the result not only of more education, but also of the vastly expanded supply of information that today reaches all Americans.

Much is made of campus violence recently. But of the 2,300 U.S. colleges and universities, less than one percent have had serious disturbances, and less than two percent of their students have been involved in violent behavior, according to the staff report of the Eisenhower Commission on Causes and Prevention of Violence.

I had had the unique privilege of having a key role in securing the adoption of two Constitutional amendments. While my participation with the Twenty-Fifth was direct lobbying and strategy with the Senate and House sponsors and their staffs, I was involved with in-house planning and the staff operations in the campaign for the Twenty Sixth. This involvement in campaigns for adoption of two U.S. constitutional amendments far exceeded whatever I had expected to do in my career.

Once again, when talking about legislative success, it's essential to have lobbyists at work, talking directly with legislators and their staffs about the need for action, and providing valuable information. This must be coupled with voters back home who contact those legislators and make their voices heard. The voters can be acquainted with representatives…this obviously is very helpful. But often, it takes much more than that…it takes people organized back home to make a difference, and this is what Common Cause was created to do.

John Gardner Becomes an Even More Outspoken Activist My Workload Continues to Increase

In early 1971, the membership was growing by leaps and bounds. We had far exceeded growth expectations. By December 15, 1970, 60,000 members had signed up; and six months ahead of our projected schedule, Common Cause went over the 100,000 mark on February 19, 1971. When John Gardner returned from a speaking engagement in Hawaii, some 100 volunteers and staff members welcomed him back with the news. Volunteer Joe Kelly, on behalf of the group, presented him a replica of a 100,000-member graph to celebrate the achievement.

We did indeed have a "movement" of people who by and large didn't join movements, but were disillusioned with the way the country was going. They were disgusted with the process, wanted the war to end, wanted solutions to our pressing problems, and trusted John Gardner to help solve them. Many of them had read his books, knew of his keen intellect, and admired his work in public service.

The "movement's" early success brought happiness and exhilaration to us at work on it. For me, in addition to that, it meant all day and into the night. The kind of rapid change was all-engaging for all of us who had cut our teeth on what now seemed like rather peaceful days at the Action Council.

Within the operations of Common Cause, the board was changing. From organized labor, AFL-CIO head George Meany had left, and only Joseph Keenan of the International Brotherhood of Electrical Workers remained. Gardner stalwarts J. Irwin Miller of Cummins Engine and David Rockefeller had decided to pull away (although John D. Rockefeller III had sent Gardner a check for $25,000). Among top businessmen, Andrew Heiskell, chairman of Time, Inc., Bill Eberle, president of American Standard, Inc., and Donald MacNaughton, chairman and CEO of Prudential Insurance Company, remained.

We were gearing up to have our first election of board members by Common Cause members, and names for nomination had to be selected. Several remaining board members chose not to run for election, and resigned.

John Gardner himself had changed, and eagerly began appearing at mass Common Cause rallies around the country, preaching his message of changing the processes of government so that decent, intelligent citizens would want to hold political office as their public duty. The political system itself, he said, was at the heart of our national inability to deal honestly with solutions, and act on them rationally and in a timely manner. Unless we opened the system for new blood in politics, lessened the need for money in elections, and made political decision-making more transparent, as a nation we would continue to stumble along.

At the beginning of these trips, I accompanied him to "warm-up" the audiences and introduce him. In Portland, Seattle, Atlanta, and Constitution Hall in Washington, D.C. where we were on the platform together, the rallies drew thousands because of their trust in him and his new idea. They literally hung on every word. He brought them some hope, and they responded in kind by their enthusiastic standing applause, and by joining Common Cause. He wasn't holding back any longer as the "private man" he was known to be. He loved every minute of it, and was providing outspoken leadership. I relish those experiences of "warming up the audiences" for John W. Gardner, and observing the true love affair between him and the audiences. I was happy for him that his dream of an influential citizens' group, one that would make a difference in our political life, was coming true.

As much as I enjoyed my travels with him, I couldn't keep them up and manage Common Cause's operations as well. We functioned like an ongoing political campaign. The only difference was that political campaigns eventually come to an end. Our Common Cause organizational efforts and advocacy never ended. In addition to issue research, direct mail activities, boiler-room telephone banks, fundraising, membership polls and service, and ongoing advocacy on cutting edge issues, we began implementing our plans for opening local offices in key states.

Our first effort was a *pilot project in Colorado* to determine if "citizens of Colorado run their state." Craig Barnes and David Mixner, both political activists and later authors and leaders on citizen access to government, led the project with a bipartisan group of prominent Coloradoans and volunteers. They advocated new laws such as those to make access to government easier for citizens, and citizen involvement in regulatory agencies that decide anti-pollution policies or set utility rates. Some of the bills were "right to know" bills, requiring lobbyists to register and disclose expenses and the companies and interests they represented. Other bills required state elected officials and judges to disclose their financial interests. Although the Colorado legislature did not pass the proposed legislation at the time, the local organizing effort was significant and proved that Common Cause members in a state would join local efforts for change. This prompted us to begin planning the creation of state Common Cause offices.

Our name was *Common Cause*. Practically every group with a "cause" in the environmental, equal rights, anti-poverty, and other fields too numerous to mention came knocking at our door. They would seek endorsements or want to become affiliated with us for the use of the Common Cause name. Many wanted money, thinking that Common Cause or John Gardner himself, who was known for his fund raising ability, would help them. We met with them all, and at first this often fell to me as executive director. It wasn't long before I had to delegate these meetings to others. Eventually we were forced to be highly selective, and finally prescreened them by phone. This of course left some of them very unhappy, some contending that we weren't at all interested in their good works.

Our Daughter, Lori, Is Born

We indeed had a movement going. We did not have a president. Mr. Gardner was chairman and I was executive director. There were times when I yearned for Ambassador McGhee to be back with us, but full time. George McGhee had provided needed in-house maturity and public awareness and strength that I did not have the experience or stature to provide. But we also needed somebody with the ability and "savvy" to help John Gardner lead a movement. I wasn't a "movement" person, and at the age of 36, felt at times literally overwhelmed, even out of place, with all that was required to make this work effectively.

And, in the midst of it all, our third child, Lori Kay, was born in February. This added to the pressures on my life and the need to pay more attention to my home life while managing a wildly bucking horse. All of these circumstances combined meant that I needed a help-mate, and probably a boss, if you will, to make this venture succeed. I discussed it with Mr. Gardner. He not only understood what I said, but he explained that he was aware of my workload, and had already begun thinking about another person to join us. At the same time, he reminded me of our dinner together at the Cosmos Club, and thanked me for sticking with him during the successful transition from Action Council days. He hoped that I would be re-energized with a new co-worker on board. He mentioned Myrna and Rich, Jonathan and Lori, and didn't want me to have to ignore them because of my workload. As busy as he always was, he had tried to make time for his wife, Aida, and his daughters, and didn't expect anything different than that for me. By this time in our relationship, I had felt his appreciation many times, but now I was experiencing something different from him. When I left his office I was feeling the emotion of his understanding and warmth about my personal life, and was grateful for that.

A New President Is Selected

John Gardner already had been casting his net for an individual to fill the role of president, a position yet to be created. While he hadn't discussed it with me before our conversation, he began sharing names that had been suggested to him. The one name that kept appearing was Jack Conway, president of the Center for Community Change, a non-profit group which worked to strengthen community organizations. He had been chief assistant to the United Auto Workers' late Walter Reuther, and a federal housing and anti-poverty official. His public policy and citizen organizing skills seemed what were needed to complement Gardner's background as educator, foundation executive, and Cabinet Secretary.

Jack Conway seemed to me to be the person to fill our need. My only concern, after meeting him, was the striking difference between him and

John Gardner. I realized that we did not want a carbon copy of Gardner, but this man Conway couldn't have been more different in both physical stature and personal manner. He was indeed a community organizer, and had been Reuther's chief assistant in growing the UAW and professionalizing its staff. He had served in high government positions as well, including deputy to Sargent Shriver at the Office of Economic Opportunity.

I was certain that Conway would be "head-strong," one who insisted on doing things his way. Of course, that defined John Gardner as well, and I could visualize them as two roaring bulls at times, each sticking to his own ground. And, this was John Gardner's organization. He owned it, and nobody else did. I didn't worry about this, though, because Jack's strengths seemed to be what we needed to carry Common Cause into its next phases. (On one occasion I did uneasily witness, in the privacy of John's office, the two bulls sticking emphatically to their own ground. Emphatic probably is too mild a word.)

Conway himself did some soul searching before agreeing to take the job. He told the *National Journal* that "he wanted to be sure he wasn't getting into a powder-puff atmosphere where a call from the White House or a call from somebody turns things off." He learned quickly that threats didn't deter John Gardner, and that we were serious about commitment to achieve victory on important issues. In late March 1971, the position of president of Common Cause was created, and Jack Conway was named to fill it.

Immediately upon arriving, Jack plunged in. To him, the Vietnam War was the major perfect Common Cause issue to fight. Common Cause members overwhelmingly opposed it, as did the American general public. And yet, as a serious issue, it still was being fought out on the streets with massive rallies and demonstrations. "It's time," Jack said, "to move the war from the streets to the Congress." He assigned David Cohen, his colleague in former positions and now on our staff, to lead the campaign. And, with this move alone, I began to feel relief. That was a huge turning point for me.

Jack began focusing on field operations, and in July appointed David as director of field operations for Common Cause. Small offices were opened in San Francisco, Denver, New York and Boston, with more on the way. So, Jack Conway was off and running, with his ability to organize legislative campaigns and his field operations experience.

Charges of Partisanship Are Made

With the arrival of Jack Conway, who had held high positions in the Democratic Party, and our campaign to move the war from the streets to the halls of Congress, some Republican Party leaders began accusing Common Cause of being "liberal Democratic," and anti-Nixon. The charges were that Common Cause claimed to be nonpartisan, but was not.

Gardner hit back vigorously. He pointed out that, while there were Democrats on the staff, "no reference is made to the fact that during its first six months the two top officers (the Executive Director, Lowell Beck, and myself) were both Republicans....reference is avoided to the fact that Common Cause has been the chief citizen organization backing President Nixon's Family Assistance Plan, that I (John Gardner) fought actively in support of the Administration's Philadelphia Plan while losing Democratic labor union backing, and have publicly supported the President's plan for federal agency reorganization." Further, he said, our efforts to end the war had a strong majority backing of the American people; and our support of the 18-year-old vote was also supported by the full Congress and the President himself. He pointed out that he worked closely with many officials of the Nixon administration such as George Schulz at the Labor Department, Elliott Richardson, Leonard Garment who was White House counsel, and Melvin Laird who was Secretary of Defense and had been chairman of the House Republican Conference. These and others, such as Patrick Moynihan, Nixon's urban affairs advisor, were Gardner's good friends, and he communicated with all of them frequently.

Gardner also stressed that the principal purposes of Common Cause were to bring changes to the governmental system, such as seniority, campaign spending and closed legislative meetings. How, he asked, could those issues be considered only "Democratic liberal"?

The partisan charges didn't deter our efforts. The membership kept growing, and Common Cause's reputation for pressing for good government kept increasing as the media learned more about it. And as Gardner also said, "If we in fact had been partisan, it would be insane, and we might as well close our doors. The nature of the efforts would cause us to continue to be subject to attack. Undertaking changes in the Congressional seniority system could be seen as an attack on Democrats, since they controlled all of the committees on Capitol Hill." And so it went.

My Last Several Months at Common Cause

With Jack Conway on board, and the arrival of David Cohen and Fred Wertheimer to assist John Lagomarcino, I was able to focus more on operations and again some policy issues.

Fred focused on abuses in *campaign spending*, which became his first love and still is, 40 years later. He and our issues director, Bob Gallamore, assisted me in preparing testimony on campaign spending that I presented to the Communications and Power Subcommittee of the House Interstate and Foreign Commerce Committee on June 9. Under the direct mail campaigns led by Roger Craver, we were growing by leaps and bounds, and at that point were up to 167,000 members. We felt that this continuing unprecedented growth in new membership was giving us new clout, and that we could now begin to focus more seriously on one of our most important issues, political campaign spending.

Essentially, my testimony called for measures to reduce expenditures, such as free or reduced costs of television time for candidates for federal office in general elections. Candidates often paid the highest rates in both broadcast and print media, and we asked Congress to remedy this. We also urged limits and caps on giving and spending; and incentives that would encourage candidates and parties to return to their grassroots for financial as well as electoral support. We urged Congress to enact these incentives, I said, because the current system, with all its loopholes, made it easier to raise money in big chunks from outside sources than to engage in the tough work needed to raise local money in small amounts. This Congressional action would enlarge the contributor base to political campaigns, and campaigns financed by many are "clearly more democratic and desirable than campaigns financed by a few."

We didn't get very far that year with changes in the campaign funding system. But, over the years of Common Cause's history, that subject always has been a top priority, perhaps its top priority. It is a situation of moving ahead a few steps with positive Congressional action, and moving backward with the recent (2010) case when the U.S. Supreme Court in *Citizens United* gave Constitutional approval to unlimited corporate and labor union political contributions, calling them "persons" under the law.

As the summer moved on, we were entering our "next phase" at Common Cause, and my personal "next phase" as well. The initial organization was behind us, and we now were an activist membership movement. New staff members and dozens of volunteers were coming on board. The workload was shifting from headquarters organization and issue development to organization in the field, a function that I was not participating in any longer. While I continued to be executive director with plenty to do, I knew that my future could not be with Common Cause. There were now others more capable of leading "movements" than I.

I vividly remember discussing my situation with Anne Wexler, a friend of Jack's, who had been temporarily hired by us to organize a Voters Rights Project, a drive to identify and rectify obstacles to voter registration in the states. She became like a big sister to me and visited with me often in my office. She had had several years of political campaign experience, and was fascinated that here I was, after years with the "establishment" American Bar Association, organizing and now managing what in effect was a national activist movement. Smiling, I replied that I really wasn't any more "establishment" than John Gardner when we took the Urban Coalition chairmanship. But I admitted to Anne that while I always had been oriented toward public interest issues, I felt more at home promoting them from an "establishment" base. I confided in her that I had not wanted to take on a new membership organization like this, but did it to help manage a smooth transition from the Urban Coalition Action Council to Common Cause; and now that I had done it, I wouldn't change the experience for anything. I told her that I had favored all of our policy issues, except I was uncomfortable with our opposition to the funding of the SST (supersonic commercial transport) because I didn't feel we at Common Cause had the expertise to enter that fray. (Common Cause opposed the billions to fund it because it was considered wasteful and unnecessary federal spending when domestic needs were crying for attention....this was a successful effort by a coalition of environmental groups supported by Common Cause.)

Having told her that, I said that I thought it was time to leave. It was no longer "my" organization as it had been from the beginning; and with my growing family, I needed a more stable long-term situation.

She was curious about the large aerial picture of Peoria on my office wall. What city was it, and why was it there? I replied that central Illinois was my home, and that I always felt that that picture represented the "real world" more than the elites who populated Washington; that real power came from the Peorias of the world ("If it plays in Peoria…") instead of the pristine drawing rooms of Georgetown; and the picture was there to remind me where I personally and real political power came from.

I went on to tell Anne that as much as I would like to make a change by leaving Common Cause *and Washington,* there were staff members still here who were my special teammates. I didn't feel obligated to John Gardner any longer, but did feel hesitant when it came to leaving the staff from Action Council days and some new staffers whom I had brought recently into Common Cause. One in particular was Dick Tempero whom I had hired at the ABA, and had brought to Common Cause from Chicago. Another was Bob Gallamore, a personal friend I had hired to head research and policy development. There were others as well. They had helped me more than I could express, and I didn't want to leave them in the lurch now. She replied that they and the new people were fitting well together; and from her observation, each had the confidence of Jack Conway. Besides, she said, each one of them shines with ability, and they would succeed wherever they went.

"You need to do what's best for you and your family," she said. "And if that means taking them home to Illinois, you should do it. Everybody would understand." I had realized that, but it always helps to have some reassurance, and I appreciated her comments. *(Anne Wexler, a Democrat, later formed her own Washington lobbying firm with a well-known Republican friend. She was the first woman to found and head such a major successful firm, and became known around the Capital as one of the most powerful individuals in the city.)*

A few nights later, Myrna and I were on ladders painting Lori's room. As I looked at her and the two boys, I knew that I wanted to move; that they should be around grandparents and other relatives; that in Illinois we still had family on farms that they would enjoy visiting; that we could concentrate more on having some fun with friends instead of simply spending so much time at dinner parties, *always* talking about the big issue that would come and go, and who was doing what to whom. Not that there's anything wrong with discussing issues at parties…but some diversion from them would be nice.

From my ladder, I asked Myrna what she thought. What if we packed up and moved back to Illinois? Would she like that? She was elated. While we had talked about it occasionally, she was surprised. She was concerned that I would miss Washington, like after the first move back to Illinois. But after a long talk about it, she was convinced that this time I was ready.

The only problem, and it was a big one, was that I didn't have a job to move to this time. There was no CBS vacancy or new Cummins Engine office to consider. But for some reason, both Myrna and I had faith that everything would turn out okay.

The next morning I told Jack Conway about my decision. He was very responsive, and we discussed it at length. He wondered if, for some reason, I felt that I was not a welcomed part of the newly arriving group, and wanted to emphasize that he considered me an important part of his team. I explained the situation just as I had with Anne. He assured me that I should take my time; that there was no need to hurry.

Following that conversation, I knocked on Gardner's door, and told him my decision. I stressed to him that this time I had decided to move the family back to Illinois, and had no intention of seeking another position in Washington. And, as with Anne and Jack, I explained the whole situation. His answer was interesting. "This is the third time," he said, "that you've come to me about leaving. After three times, I can't say no, and I'm grateful that you've stayed with me until now. But," he continued, "be certain that you are doing the right thing about moving back 'home.' It won't be the same. It won't be like you remember it. Parents age and die, siblings move away, and you're left with a life you hadn't anticipated." I responded that I still thought it was best, particularly for our young family. We ended the conversation with his offer to help me in any way he could.

The next step was to start looking for another job in Illinois, so the obvious place to start was with Bert Early at the ABA. I wasn't thinking of the ABA as the place to work, but instead asked Bert if he could help me with leads, particularly in a public affairs position with a major company or association. He did better than that. "Why not come back to the ABA," he said. "I've been discussing a number-two position, as my associate, with Leon Jaworski (that year's ABA president), and he has agreed to recommend it to the board. Knowing you as he does, I'm sure he would agree that you would be the right one for that position. Think about it."

I was stunned. I hadn't planned on this, and wasn't even thinking of the ABA because I couldn't think of a position I would want there anymore. And, another membership organization? Hadn't I said many times that I didn't want that again? This was a different situation, though. Helping Bert manage this entire organization that was growing in numbers and national influence would be a huge step forward, and put me back into the work of the legal profession.

Myrna was elated again. Neither of us could believe that my job situation was solved so quickly, and that both of us would be going home again, in home location and workplace. I called Bert the next day, and he said he would call me back after he had spoken with President Jaworski. His call, saying Mr. Jaworski had approved, came that afternoon; and Myrna and I began making plans to move in February 1972.

Another Issue Pops Up

All of my work wasn't finished, though, even as I was disengaging from Common Cause and arranging to move to the Chicago area. In October 1971, President Nixon announced that he would nominate Lewis Powell for appointment to the U.S. Supreme Court. This took the country by surprise because Lewis Powell was unknown to the national public, although esteemed by the legal profession. Those who knew him were surprised as well because he had previously refused the nomination offered by Nixon.

John asked me what I thought about him. After all, two southerners already had been nominated by Nixon and turned down by the Senate. Common Cause had participated in the opposition to the Carswell nomination because of his anti-civil rights history. What should we do this time if opposition developed? I was horrified at the thought of opposing Lewis Powell, this extraordinarily insightful and decent man. Common Cause could not do that. John then asked me to go with him to an afternoon meeting at the Sheraton Hotel, called by Joseph Rauh, Jr., a prominent Washington lawyer who was an active civil rights advocate and leader of the opposition to Carswell. He had called a meeting of civil rights groups and others interested in the nomination to discuss Mr. Powell's nomination. I told John that there was absolutely no way Common Cause could participate if other groups decided to oppose it. I don't believe that John had seen me as animated about anything as this. He told me to calm down, that he understood what I was saying. "Let's go to the meeting and you can tell them what you think (after you have calmed down)." We did that. Common Cause did not oppose the nomination. The support for Lewis Powell was so strong that he was confirmed by the Senate 89 to 1, and began his tenure on the bench until he retired 15 years later.

After leaving Common Cause, I was elected to its board and continued participating as a board member for a few years longer.

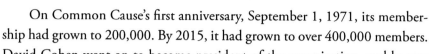

On Common Cause's first anniversary, September 1, 1971, its membership had grown to 200,000. By 2015, it had grown to over 400,000 members. David Cohen went on to become president of the organization, and he was succeeded by Fred Wertheimer. It has local offices in 35 states, and places high priority on sunshine and open meetings laws at the state and local level. It has continued to be hard work, and has led the way for reform at all levels of government. It is carrying out its mission just as John Gardner had planned and hoped.

It was founded and brought to maturity by a man, once a college professor, and later a "reluctant" lobbyist, who had sensed a craving among ordinary, thoughtful citizens for participation with others in rebuilding their government into one they could trust. He created an organization to give them a powerful tool to do that, and some 43 years later, it continues to fight for improvement in government at all levels.

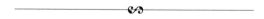

In this commentary on my some four years with John Gardner, the Action Council, and Common Cause, I was unable to mention all of the names who helped make the ventures a success. With my everlasting gratitude to them, I repeat their names given in a tribute that Mr. Gardner gave all of us "co-founders" at Common Cause's 10th Anniversary Luncheon in Washington on September 5, 1980. As he said, we were indeed "staunch teammates," and we could not have pulled it off if we hadn't been.

Remarks by John W. Gardner:

Thanks...many, many thanks...from the heart.

I must give due credit to the 22 staff members who were co-founders. I'm going to read their names.

Lowell Beck, Bob Meier, Tom Mathews, Georgianna Rathbun, John Lagomarcino, Hal Levy, Dave Dawson, Roger Craver, John Wood, Bob Gallamore, Connie Greene, Wendy Burdsall, Bill Davis, Barbara Collins, Mary Hanson, Holly Swan, Salena Quarles, Lee Wilcox, Barbara Seldon, Richard Clark, Mary Turner, Daladier Miller.

I'm going to ask Lowell Beck to stand up because he was my strong right arm. He really made most of the crucial decisions.

They were staunch teammates. There were very few of them to carry the heavy load of those early days. But the proverb says "God gives burdens, also shoulders." They had great shoulders.

The first members and volunteers also deserve mention, though it isn't feasible to name them. There is an Ashanti saying that "No one tests the depth of a river with both feet." But as we approached the launching of Common Cause, we knew there was no way to test the depth of this river prudently. It was both feet or nothing. The first members and volunteers pulled us out of the river.

But you know my view of these things. Organizations and institutions die unless, after creation, there is continuous recreation. Since the founding, Common Cause has been recreated many times. So, strictly speaking — or loosely speaking — there has been a continuous line of founders, right down to the present Chairman and Board and Staff. They also have great shoulders.

John Gardner died on February 16, 2002, at the age of 89. Unfortunately, I deeply regretted that I was unable to attend his service. But Fred Wertheimer gave remarks, and the best tribute I can give John is to repeat some excerpts from them. They are my sentiments as well.

… John embraced and pursued change all of his life. He saw change as a way to make things better for individuals, for institutions, for government and for nations.

… John was a man of fearless integrity. He said his mother was his moral compass, and he served as a moral compass for our nation. He once wrote in National Renewal: "The identifying of values is a light preliminary exercise before the real and heroic task, which is to make the values live. Moral, ethical or spiritual values come alive only when living men and women recreate the values for their time, by living their faith, by caring, by doing. It is true of religion; it is true of democracy; it is true of personal ethical codes."

…He was a great moral force of our times.

…He was a great role model and mentor.

…Justice Louis Brandeis once said, 'The most important office in our democracy is that of a private citizen.'

... John Gardner was the citizen of his times.

———————————— ∾ ————————————

A few days after I left for Chicago, John sent me his picture with the inscription, *To Lowell Beck, from his friend and partner, John Gardner.*

A year later, in his new book about citizen political action and the founding of Common Cause, he sent me one with his inscription on the inside cover:

> *To Lowell Beck, The Godfather of Common Cause,*
> *from his devoted friend, John Gardner.*

I am forever grateful that he had given me the opportunities that prompted these words.

And I am even more grateful that I was lucky enough to know him as an inspiring mentor and teacher, in addition to knowing him as a friend. Yes, John, you did indeed help me grow.

By the way, though, you weren't right about moving back home to Illinois. It was the absolute correct thing to do.

CHAPTER THIRTEEN

RETURN TO THE AMERICAN BAR ASSOCIATION
MANAGEMENT RESPONSIBILITIES
WATERGATE AND "NO MAN IS ABOVE THE LAW"
THE SUPREME COURT ALLOWS LAWYER ADVERTISING
THE AVAILABILITY OF LEGAL SERVICES

CHICAGO, ILLINOIS, 1972–1980

When I entered the American Bar Center in Chicago as the new associate executive director, I had some nervous anticipation. Would the rest of the staff welcome or resent me, coming in like this as the number-two staff officer, and having been away for so long? Had I really made the correct decision to leave politically issue-oriented Washington and once again be primarily a manager/administrator instead of a hands-on lobbyist? I had thought all of this through, but still the anticipation was there.

The fact was that I was ready to get back to the Midwest and what I perceived to be a "normal" family lifestyle. And, with this new job I still would be keeping my hand in Capital affairs since I now would have management responsibility for the Washington Office. So, I would have the best of all worlds: I could work in Washington occasionally, keeping my taste for it, and fly home to Illinois without having to worry about pounding the Congressional marble floors the next day.

With regard to staff resentment, Bert had assured me there was nothing to worry about. David Hayes, the assistant executive director, and I were friends, and he told me that he welcomed me to help relieve him of an exceptionally heavy workload. He and I had kept in touch, and he assured me that he was pleased in that I knew the ABA so well, and was known by many of its leaders and staff.

Fortunately, he and Bert were correct. After my first day back, it was almost like I hadn't left. Everything, from the offices to many of the staff members, was familiar. Of course, during four years away, there had been several staff changes, and many board members and committee and section heads had changed. The learning curve of returning didn't take long.

What Is the ABA? What Does It Do?

Until the 1960s, the ABA was primarily a society that debated and took public policy positions. However, it did some important activities in addition to taking policy positions.

Through a special evaluating team, it conducted reviews of law schools, and gave them either a stamp of approval or non-approval.

The ABA created the American Bar Foundation to conduct scholarly research on the legal system and "administration of justice." While affiliated with the association, and structurally under the jurisdiction of the ABA Board of Governors with a mandate to provide research relating to ABA policy interests, it was an independent research entity.

The ABA's Board of Governors and House of Delegates debated and voted on hundreds of public policy issues ranging from the Twenty-Fifth Amendment to the U.S. Constitution to Federal Election Reform. Most of its policy positions, however, concentrated on issues specifically related to the legal profession and judiciary. For example, it promulgated a code of professional ethics that was adopted by most states; the ABA continually examined the federal and state judicial systems, and took positions for improvement by promulgating judicial standards.

The association developed a system for evaluating nominees to the federal courts, and presented its findings to the U. S. Attorney General, the President of the United States and the Senate Judiciary Committee.

Through its Section on Taxation, the ABA provided technical advice to the Congressional committees dealing with federal taxation.

In the 1960s, the ABA continued in these activities, but added much more. For example, historically it sponsored only a few legally related programs such as teaching youth in the public school system about our legal and governmental system. This changed in the 1960s with programs ranging from the affiliated National College of the State Judiciary (provides practical education for state judges) to the Council on Legal Education Opportunity (to promote and support increased minorities in law school). Most of the new programs were funded by grants from foundations and government, and not members' dues.

Prior to the 1960s, while the ABA sponsored some educational conferences through its specialty sections ranging from Corporation, Banking and Business Law to Family Law, the association's role in continuing education was conducted through the American Law Institute. The association's direct role was minimal. This began to change during the '60s and '70s as most of the specialty sections began giving continuing education their high priority, and education became one of highest priorities of the Association.

The ABA's leaders focused continually on the availability of legal services and whether the entire population was being served adequately. It supported the federal OEO Legal Services Program and the creation of the Legal Services Corporation for indigents, but struggled almost endlessly during the '60s with how to provide and deliver legal services economically to the non-poor, yet non-wealthy. Lawyer advertising was not allowed until a Supreme Court decision in 1977, and with the ability to advertise, the legal delivery system began to change with an expansion of neighborhood legal clinics, and ultimately group legal services provided through union and employer and other benefit programs. But creating new delivery systems faced many roadblocks.

In the '60s and '70s, the ABA grew into a multifaceted, highly complex organization. It was difficult to fully comprehend its wide scope of activity implemented, coordinated and managed by its non-paid volunteer members, leaders, committee and section members, and paid staff. As I look back over my years with the ABA, I feel overwhelmed myself by thinking about it, and couldn't begin to discuss here all that went into managing it every day.

Note: As an important resource for this memoir, I've had the benefit of the ABA's annual report for each year I was with the ABA. Each report is a volume of over one thousand pages of reports of the Board of Governors, House of Delegates, sections and committees and some twenty ABA-related organizations such as the Association of American Law Schools, the Conference of Chief Justices, the Federal Bar Association, the National Association of Bar Executives, the National Bar Association, the National Association of Women Lawyers, and the National College of District Attorneys.

Management/Administrative/Policy Duties Blend Together

During this second time with the ABA, as the number-two staff member, I did very little lobbying. The Washington Office handled that, with only my occasional involvement. This chapter, therefore, focuses on the ups and downs of managing the association, which continued growing into a large, influential professional association.

Managing the ABA doesn't mean just performing administrative duties such as hiring staff and giving them direction. Or planning events like the annual meeting that draws 7,000 lawyers, judges and guests, along with their families, in August to different major cities each year. It means all of that, but also means collaborating with the elected, volunteer officers, particularly the president, president-elect, chairman of the House of Delegates, secretary, and treasurer in fulfilling their responsibilities. With the president and president-elect, it means working alongside them on their programs, and helping decide which ones might be newly initiated or eliminated. It also means advising them when they need you on policy matters, and giving them recommendations on committee member appointments.

Bert Early best explained the volunteer/member – staff relationship in a report to the House of Delegates. Essentially, he said that it is the staff's responsibility to provide continuity through managing an efficient organization with a relatively low profile. It is the members' responsibility to provide leadership, visibility, resolution and inspiration. It is our joint responsibility to assure that the association and legal profession are responsive, innovative, and dedicated to giving our "highest aspirations to promote justice for all."

Bert drummed into all of us on the staff that our role was servant/leader. Provide efficient administrative support, and keep a low profile in working alongside the volunteer members. The ABA is the members' organization; they make the policy decisions and are the association's public spokespersons. At the same time, be innovators, make recommendations with new ideas, and speak up on ways to advance the ABA and the rule of law.

It is in this context that I worked at the ABA in the 1970s. This narrative obviously will not recite the day to day practice of administering the ABA over my next eight years, but will focus on a few notable highlights.

Tragedy Strikes

In December 1972, Bert and I attended a meeting in Washington at the Mayflower Hotel. On December 8th, the meeting adjourned in time for us to make an earlier flight back to Chicago. As we were leaving the hotel, a judge stopped us with some questions that turned into a long conversation. So, we couldn't make the earlier flight. On arriving at the airport, we were confronted with massive delays and cancellations, with no planes leaving for Chicago. United Flight 553 from Washington to Chicago Midway Airport had crashed on a Midway runway and into the surrounding neighborhood. This was the earlier flight we had hoped to take home. We couldn't believe it.

But, what about our colleague, Roger Moreau, who was ABA's director of meetings, and his two assistants, Nancy Parker and Delores Pendry? They had been working at the Mayflower event, and were scheduled to be on Flight 553. We heard the crash was a major one, but we couldn't get information at the Washington airport. So Bert called our Chicago office while I stood next to him at the public pay phone. I had this terrible feeling. Why were flights delayed and even cancelled if disaster hadn't struck? While still talking, Bert gave me thumbs down. Roger had been killed. Miraculously, Nancy and Delores had survived. Forty people, including the three-man crew, out of 55 on the plane, were killed. Five houses were destroyed, three were damaged, and three people on the ground died.

I cried there in the airport. I couldn't believe it. Roger had been one of my closest friends at the ABA. He arrived to run the Meetings Department soon after I joined the staff in 1959, and was Myrna's boss in the department. Myrna and I always called him our personal "cupid" because he insisted that we were just right for each other (he was right).

We both had affection for Roger. He had an engaging personality, *with extraordinary skills at managing meetings, large and small.* To give some perspective on Roger's responsibilities, the ABA midyear and annual meetings were large and complex. The 300-member House of Delegates met in February and August. Its membership encompassed the whole of the legal profession, ranging from "State Delegates" (delegates elected by ABA members in each state), to affiliated legal organizations such as the Federal Bar Association, the Judge Advocates Association, and the National Legal Aid and Defender

Association, to delegates from each ABA section, to state and major bar associations, to the U.S. Attorney General.

While the February meeting was held for the House of Delegates to consider policy, in August, the ABA membership, sections and committees met in addition to the House. Each section held its own annual meeting and dinner. Prominent guests attended from legal circles all over the world. Major speakers and entertainment had to be lined up.

Only a few American and Canadian cities could accommodate an ABA annual meeting. With its attendance of some 7,000 lawyers, and many with families, first class hotel and meeting rooms for all of the sections and affiliated groups had to be obtained. Many cities could host much larger mass meetings than the ABA's. However, while the ABA annual meetings didn't require mass assembly halls, they did require dozens of meeting rooms for its numerous sections and committees, and all first-class accommodations for its members. The planning of each meeting had to be undertaken many years ahead; then, when the time came for the actual event, the implementation was a monumental task. Roger Moreau was a champion at making these and dozens of other events throughout the year work smoothly. He didn't miss a beat: the finest details were his hallmark.

After the close of my first annual meeting since returning to the ABA in 1972, I looked for Roger to praise him for his outstanding work. The attendees were marveling at how well it had gone. People were leaving, and the hotel was going silent. In a room with boxes piled high for shipping from San Francisco back to Chicago, I found Roger sitting alone looking out the window. He didn't seem his upbeat self. I told him how much everybody appreciated his work, and what a success the meeting had been. I hoped that he too felt as good about it. He didn't. He said that I was the first one to say that, and that he was weary of it all.

I said, "Roger, you know how much everybody thinks of you and appreciates you. We are all a family here, and you're an important part of it." Roger was indeed part of the ABA family, and in the year 1972 it was just that: a big family with the member/leaders and staff alike. He was single, and frequently was invited to members' homes for special holiday events. He always would be invited into members' homes when he was away from Chicago. "I know you feel like that, and I appreciate it," he said. "But, I don't think you understand what a lonely job this is. Tomorrow you'll fly home with Myrna and the kids (our children always were with us at annual meetings), and pick up again as a family. I'll be on a plane to Honolulu to begin the details of the meeting there two years from now. Everybody thinks I have the most glamorous job in the world, going from city to city and to exotic places like Hawaii. But it isn't."

I couldn't stop thinking about it, because in the few months since I had resumed working with Roger, neither I nor anybody else had seen him down like this. When he returned from Honolulu, he told me that Hawaii had rejuvenated him; that everything went well there; and that there was no need to worry about him.

That was just four and a half months before the crash. I hadn't seen any relapse in his spirit. I liked to think that he was in that positive frame of mind leading up to his death. But I did think about something important from our conversation that last day of the annual meeting. It's probably true that, as Thoreau said: *"The mass of men lead lives of quiet desperation..."* Roger was always one we thought of as happily full of life. But obviously, he had been holding in his distress. I think this is true with many more people than we realize, including some we know well. Life has a way of getting you down, and others might not notice it at all if it's your nature to be a positive, upbeat person. Since Roger did not have family members in Chicago, Bert and I were called to identify his body. We were warned that it would be difficult. He had been sitting in the front of the plane, and it was evident.

Roger had life insurance through his ABA employment. Out of the deep respect and affection we had for him, both Bert and I took the check to his family in Maine, and attended the memorial service. The ABA was a family.

No Man Is Above the Law

My phone at home rang on Sunday afternoon, October 21, 1973, with Bert telling me that Chesterfield Smith, the ABA's president, wanted us to come to his office at the Bar Center by 5:00 that day. Mr. Smith was extremely disturbed at what was called the "Saturday Night Massacre," which had happened the night before, and was a result of the Watergate Scandal dating back to June 1972. He believed that the country was in deep crisis, "perhaps unparalleled" in the nation's history, and wanted to issue a statement on it. He wanted our help in writing it, and touching base with other ABA leaders.

The Watergate Scandal was the name given the break-ins at the Democratic National Committee's headquarters at the Watergate Hotel/

Office complex in Washington, D.C., and the resulting attempted cover-ups by the Nixon Administration.

Five men were arrested for the burglaries, and cash found on them was traced to a fund of the Nixon campaign. While everybody in the Nixon organization and at the White House was denying any involvement, after several months of accusations and denials, there were enough substantial questions about the president's and his aides' involvement to initiate a Senate investigation with Senator Sam Ervin chairing the committee. The entire country was on edge, and the episode was occupying the daily attention of the media and public.

In April 1973, when it became clear that two of Nixon's most trusted White House aides, H.R. Haldeman and John Ehrlichman, were implicated, Nixon asked for their resignations. They ultimately both were sentenced to prison. He fired White House Counsel John Dean, who had also been implicated, and who then testified before the Ervin Committee as a key witness against the president. Several others, having been pressured by the president to deny everything, committed perjury and were also sentenced to prison.

Even though the sitting attorney general seemed to have no involvement, hoping to erase any suspicions, Nixon then appointed a new attorney general, the respected Elliott Richardson, who was the former HEW Secretary, and whom I knew from Common Cause days. Nixon gave Richardson the authority to appoint a new special counsel to investigate the Watergate issues. The special counsel was to be independent of Justice Department oversight. He appointed Archibald Cox, the noted Constitutional authority at Harvard Law School, and formerly U.S. Solicitor General under President Kennedy.

Bob Woodward and Carl Bernstein of *The Washington Post* were writing articles about what they were finding, but Nixon dismissed their work and the rest of the media as simply unfounded media attacks. He, after all, was President of the United States, and the public would be behind him as they always were, regardless of the media's criticism.

By now and throughout the months of 1973, the American people were even more glued to their television sets than in 1972. As the Senate hearings and the Cox investigation progressed, the television networks covered the hearings live every day. Was the president involved or not? Had he, as many in his administration, committed crimes, or not?

In July, before live cameras, it was revealed by a White House assistant that there was a taping system in the Oval Office. This was a break-through of monumental implications if anything incriminating was on them. Cox immediately subpoenaed the tapes of recorded conversations in the Oval Office, but Nixon would not release them. He cited executive privilege. Cox, however, would not drop the subpoena issued by Judge John Sirica.

The Ervin Committee also had subpoenaed the tapes, and Nixon knew that the public now would not be satisfied with his refusal to release them. If he wasn't guilty of anything, what was he trying to cover up? So, he attempted to set up a compromise that hopefully would satisfy the Senate in particular. On Friday, October 19, 1973, he proposed that Senator John Stennis (D-MS) study the tapes and report a summary of them to the Congress and special prosecutor. That day, after rejecting Nixon's so-called "Stennis Compromise," Cox held a press conference and accused the White House and Nixon of violating the law. He assumed there would be continued legal maneuvering, and had no idea what would happen next.

The next day, on Saturday, October 20, it was clear that the president was not going to accept the subpoena of Judge Sirica. That night he ordered Attorney General Richardson to fire Cox. Richardson refused, and resigned. Then he ordered Deputy Attorney General William Ruckelshaus, and he too refused and resigned. The next person up was the Solicitor General, Robert Bork, who was quickly taken to the White House, sworn in as Acting Attorney General, and after some hesitation, fired Cox.

That was the Saturday Night Massacre, the event that caused us to gather with Chesterfield Smith on Sunday evening to prepare a statement that he would issue as ABA president.

Chesterfield Smith stood out brightly as an ABA president. While each president brought his special skills and achievements to the one-year elected office, Mr. Smith dared to provide outspoken leadership for change in his Florida law firm, the legal profession and the ABA itself. He hadn't always been a fan of the ABA. He considered it too reserved, and not willing enough to face the future realistically. It wasn't bold enough to say and do the things needed in this changing world.

As president of the Florida Bar Association, he became acquainted with ABA President Lewis Powell, who appointed him chairman of the ABA's new committee to examine ways to make legal services more accessible to everybody. Chesterfield loved his committee members and their commitment to the committee's work, and through it became well acquainted with the ABA's leaders and staff. His efforts, as committee chairman, ultimately helped lead the expansion of "pro bono" legal work, develop group legal services and create the National Legal Services Corporation.

In his Florida law practice, he argued cases for gay and lesbian rights. He directed the rewriting of the Florida Constitution that established the one-man-one vote rule. In building the Holland and Knight law firm into an international giant, he was a pioneer in hiring women and minorities. He had built a mammoth financially lucrative clientele, with a monopoly on advising the Florida *phosphate* industry. When asked by a reporter, when he was elected ABA president, how he could in good conscience represent the phosphate industry when he worked so hard on public interest activities, he replied that everybody is entitled to excellent legal representation, even "cruds." While that didn't set well with the industry, they stuck with him as their counsel. He didn't pull any punches, and was just as lively and flamboyant as you might expect from reading this description.

It wasn't any surprise, then, that Chesterfield was troubled and outraged, as a citizen and lawyer, by President Nixon's flouting of the law. He was even more outraged when we learned that the FBI, under Nixon's orders, had entered Cox's office and taken it over. He told us that even his 20-year old son, hearing on television about the FBI incursion, called him and said that he was scared, and maybe there would be some kind of a revolution here if the FBI started taking over courts and government by force. Chesterfield didn't think there was a revolution brewing, but had no doubt that flouting the law by the President of the United States was dangerous and unconscionable.

On the night of the "Massacre," Chesterfield was in Chicago. Chesterfield and other ABA officers had been meeting on Friday, and all were bothered by how Nixon was defying a valid court order. On Saturday, he stayed in Chicago to work at the Bar Center, and attend the Bears-Patriots football game the next day. All Saturday evening, he couldn't get the unprecedented firing and resignations out of his mind. The story fully occupied the news programs. This is how later, in an American Bar Foundation interview, he recounts his day on that Sunday:

"The next day (Sunday) I went out with Bill McBride, who had been a law student, and who was a special assistant of mine. We went out to a Chicago Bears-Boston Patriots football game. It was a sorry football game, and I kept thinking of that thing. I started scribbling on the back of a program some of the things that I might want to say about it. We got out of the football game, and I called Bert Early and told him I wanted to make a statement on it as president, and that I'd like him to meet me at ABA headquarters, and to get Louis Potter who worked for me, and Lowell Beck, and Chris Whittle (ABA director of public relations), and whoever else (he thought should be there). We got a cab and went and got my wife from the football game, and went out to the Bar Center."

When we arrived at the Bar Center at 5:00, Chesterfield told us that he was compelled to speak out publicly about this miscarriage of justice. He thought it was a national crisis, perhaps even unparalleled in our national history, particularly in law and governing. He simply couldn't sit by, as the nation's top "legal spokesman," without saying how outrageous this was, and that, even though he was President of United States, Nixon could not get away with violating Judge Sirica's subpoena and flouting the law this way. Chesterfield had decided to call for another special counsel, this time to be authorized by Congress.

He said that time was running out since it was 5:00 and he wanted to issue a statement the next morning. He wanted our immediate help in writing a statement and making urgent calls to other ABA leaders. He wasn't looking for consensus because he was going to issue a statement, but he hoped for support from as many as possible. Maybe we would have to hold an emergency meeting of the House of Delegates if we wanted to give it added importance, but that would require a 40-day notice. He would go ahead and issue a statement, and then hold a special meeting of the Board of Governors, hoping its members would ratify it.

Chesterfield quickly gave us some background on why he felt so strongly about this. He reminded us that his ABA predecessor, Robert Meserve, and he himself as president-elect, had been speaking out publicly since the Watergate burglaries took place. As the illegalities were revealed, committed mostly by lawyers, they had spoken out vigorously about the problems of professional dereliction, and were considering making recommendations to restructure federal law enforcement agencies such as the IRS and Justice Department so that they would not be used for political purposes. Most importantly, the ABA had called for the appointment of an independent special prosecutor to investigate and prosecute matters related to the so-called Watergate affair.

Both he and Mr. Meserve had had a role in the appointment of a special prosecutor. Speaking on behalf of the ABA, both had publicly urged that one be appointed. Mr. Meserve, a fellow Bostonian with Attorney General Richardson, had made multiple recommendations. He, Chesterfield, became well acquainted with Mr. Richardson and Deputy Attorney General Ruckelshaus, and knew them both as outstanding public servants

On the other hand, he didn't have the same feelings about President Nixon, although, even as a Democrat, he had voted for him. He could not believe that Mr. Nixon knew nothing about the break-ins and cover-ups. It didn't make sense to Chesterfield that virtually all of his closest aides were involved, and the president himself never knew anything. So, he was lying, and his lies were not only thwarting justice, but also, through them, he was attacking the ethical men who were trying to obtain justice. Chesterfield became louder and louder about it, even emotional. He told us that he was emotional about it, that he didn't want his emotions to overtake his reasoning, but knew he was right to criticize President Nixon, and call for the immediate appointment of a new special prosecutor, this time to be authorized by Congress.

Chesterfield began calling the top ABA leaders while Bert and I, Lou Potter, David Hayes, and Chris Whittle went to separate rooms and called other Board of Governors' members. Chesterfield wanted them to know that he was preparing a statement, and wanted to know if they had suggestions.

He personally focused on two staunch Republicans, ABA Secretary Ken Burns and ABA President-elect Lawrence (Ed) Walsh. Burns was a close friend and advisor to Donald Rumsfeld, and Walsh was a supporter of Nixon who had been Deputy Attorney General and a federal judge. Burns was beyond outrage. He thought Chesterfield's statement should be stronger than even Chesterfield himself was planning. Mr. Walsh, after consulting with some of his closest colleagues, including William Gossett (general counsel of Ford Motor Co. and former ABA president), wrote a statement deploring Nixon's action, but it wasn't strong enough for Chesterfield. Mr. Gossett, however, called with his draft, and some of his was included in the final product.

Because so many bar leaders now knew about Chesterfield's plans, the word was getting around. Calls began coming in. Elliott Richardson himself called. Ralph Nader called, primarily to urge the ABA to say something, and then happy to hear that it was being written that minute. Senators called. Chesterfield and the rest of us couldn't take all of the calls. This was a big deal.

Four hours later a statement was finalized. It was strongly worded, headed by "No Man Is Above the Law." It was critical of the president, stating that all indications were that he personally had committed an illegal act by refusing to comply with a court order to release the tapes to the Special Prosecutor, and violated the law by ordering that the Special Prosecutor be fired. It concluded by calling for Congress to immediately authorize a new Special Prosecutor, to be completely independent of the executive branch. It was a strong statement of rebuke to the President of the United States from the country's leading legal spokesman.

We went to work reproducing the statement and issuing it to the press that night. When Chesterfield and his wife, Vivian, arrived at their Near North Side apartment, the television cameras were there, the phones were ringing, and newspapers were preparing to print it the next morning. Newspapers throughout the country printed the statement on their front pages, and editorials praised it. Chesterfield was in demand to speak about it everywhere he went.

In the days that followed, the Board of Governors met, ratified the statement, and specifically called for Congress to authorize an independent prosecutor to be appointed by judges, not the president. It was not an easy meeting. Some members couldn't attend on such short notice. Some opposed the statement, saying the ABA had no business entering this fray. Some agreed that Nixon had done the wrong thing, but thought that the statement was too strident and emotional. One member left the meeting. But when a vote was taken with a slim quorum present, Chesterfield prevailed.

Lawyers and bar associations around the country reacted with highly mixed reactions. Some were vehemently opposed, saying the president of the United States should be supported, not attacked. However, an overwhelming number applauded and praised Chesterfield for having the guts to speak up and uphold the rule of law. On the day Chesterfield was to testify for the new independent prosecutor before Congress, it was announced that President Nixon had appointed a new prosecutor. The new prosecutor was Leon Jaworski, who had just served as ABA president.

Chesterfield and Leon were the best of friends, and Chesterfield greatly respected Leon Jaworski. But he opposed the process of the president appointing the next prosecutor. If the prosecutor found that the evidence favored the president, the public would say that he was just protecting the man who appointed him. He opposed the appointment of Jaworski because of what the process could ultimately do to his "dear friend." The appointment had been made, however.

Leon Jaworski accepted, and built an airtight case against Nixon on the Watergate issues and other corrupt activities of the administration. The U.S. Supreme Court unanimously ruled that Nixon had to release the tapes to the prosecutor. He complied.

The tapes implicated the president, revealing all that he knew and how he attempted to cover-up so much of what had taken place in the burglaries. After the tapes were known to the public, the reaction of legislators and public alike became one of absolute revulsion. People could not believe that the president was so profane and vulgar, and "so contemptuous of the United States, its institutions and people," as the *Providence Journal* wrote.

The tapes revealed Nixon's disloyalties such as agreeing to an aide's suggestion that Attorney General John Mitchell was the "Big Enchilada," and thus should be the fall guy for the whole episode even though he was an old friend. He was a racial bigot by reportedly calling Judge John Sirica (who tried the "Watergate burglars") a "wop," and telling aides to stay away from anything to do with the arts in his re-election campaign because "they're Jews, they're left wing." The *Chicago Tribune*, a conservative newspaper and Nixon supporter, observed that Nixon left a devastating self-portrait on the tapes, one not previously known by the public. It said, "He is humorless to the point of being inhumane. He is devious. He is vacillating. He is profane. Indeed, the transcripts are regularly dotted with excisions marked 'expletive deleted.' "

Threats of impeachment were so serious, even among Republican legislators, that President Nixon resigned on August 8, 1974. The vice president, Gerald Ford, succeeded him.

While impeachment proceedings in Congress were dropped, Nixon still faced the possibility of criminal prosecutions. Chesterfield, addressing the ABA's annual meeting in Honolulu that August, called for a pardon for Mr. Nixon. He thought it was in the best interest of the country. President Ford thought the same thing. He pardoned Nixon on September 8, 1974.

The controversy and emotion throughout the country simply wouldn't go away. While the pardon saved a humiliated former president from going to trial, there was such a public outcry against it that many believed it was the main cause for Ford's loss to Jimmy Carter in 1976.

And, Chesterfield once again, having spoken out for the pardon, was at the center of attention. And, again, it would be necessary to convene an immediate meeting of the Board of Governors for the consideration of Presidential pardons. Some board members favored Chesterfield's remarks as ABA president, even though they were unauthorized by an ABA governing body, and others were unhappy about them. So, what should the ABA say about it? The board met in Chicago on September 12, 1974, and adopted the following statement:

> The Board of Governors of the American Bar Association is concerned with the public reaction resulting from the pardon granted to former President Nixon, and from reports indicating that consideration may be given to additional pardons. The Board of Governors recognizes the constitutional power of the President to grant pardons is a part of the procedures for the administration of justice, and further recognizes that the pardon of former President Nixon could involve considerations not present in other cases. However, the Board believes that one of the lessons of Watergate is the need, in general, for adherence to regular judicial processes.

> The American Bar Association is committed to the fair, just and impartial application and enforcement of the law. In order to avoid the possible erosion of disrespect for the law, the Board of Governors of the American Bar Association recommends that, in the absence of extraordinary circumstances involving public interests of great magnitude, the pardon power should not be exercised with respect to any individual until appropriate judicial processes have been followed.

I cited that statement to highlight how the Watergate mess didn't go away soon, even after all of the legal and political considerations were behind us. I cited it also to show how frequently the ABA leaders and we on the staff were called to be involved in pressing public issues. In this case, we had to straddle a carefully honed line on when presidential pardons were and were not appropriate. Instead of my former work of direct lobbying, planning for and helping prepare a statement like this was part of my job now. We were involved directly in matters most people simply were learning about in the news.

Did the Chesterfield Smith statement and ABA action overall have an impact on the Watergate saga? We never knew for sure. Many other organizations and prominent individuals outside the legal profession were calling for action, and the pressure on Congress from all around the country had become unrelenting. But, yes, it must have had an impact. With all of the lawyers involved in the planning and cover-ups of the break-ins, it must have meant something to the president and legislators when the ABA president and board spoke out. The appointment of Leon Jaworski so soon after Chesterfield's statement, and media events that followed, told us that Nixon was listening, and thought he could pacify the ABA by the appointment. The record shows that he did not.

One result we knew for sure. Regardless of any ABA action that had come before Chesterfield's Saturday Night Massacre statement, that statement called the strongest attention to the ABA as a national leader. It never would be an obscure organization in the public's mind again. Chesterfield himself was in such demand for speeches and television appearances that he regretted he couldn't give the attention he had planned to ABA affairs.

What did we learn from the experience of the Watergate Scandal, a tragic time for our fair system of laws in a nation that depended on them? I think we learned that right can and does prevail. Our individual freedoms rely on rules and laws that guarantee fairness and common decency in human relationships. When those rules are broken, regardless of by whom, the freedoms of all of us are diminished. It requires courageous and right-minded men and women to be vigilant and willing to work hard to maintain those rules and norms of society. I agree with Bill Ruckleshaus who said that right did prevail in 1974 because many right-minded people did something about it. But it took the action of those men and women to bring about a favorable result.

My association with Chesterfield Smith was another highlight of my professional life. It was because of what, who and how he was.

As much as he liked ABA people, and could easily relate to even the most conservative of them, at times he would become impatient with the people and the organization. He wanted it to be more "cutting edge." I seldom found fault with my employer, the ABA, and when I did, I didn't express it. Let's face it, the ABA was becoming a massive organization, difficult to manage, and generally slow to act. But, it was on the move, doing important things, and yes, I did like it, liked it a lot, and felt intimately a part of it. But, once he said to me, "Beck, you like the ABA too much. It isn't healthy to like any organization as much as you do."

Most of all, Chesterfield treated me like a special friend. Of course, I wasn't alone in being his special friend, and being included in his circle. Many people were, everywhere he went. Tom Brokaw mentioned this in his portrayal of Chesterfield as a notable national leader in his book, *The Greatest Generation*. Brokaw talked about two of Chesterfield's close colleagues who felt that Chesterfield always was thinking about how he could make their lives better, even when he was shaving in the morning. But they also felt that there were thousands of others also convinced that he was thinking about how to make their lives better.

I was one of those thousands. When my father died in February 1973, Chesterfield told Bert that he wanted to drive from Chicago to Peoria with him to attend the funeral. When the two of them walked into the funeral home, I couldn't hold back some tears. At my parents' home after the service, he said, "We drove through a lot of flat land coming down here. It sure was black. I liked it." Regardless of the other thousands, I felt like I really was special.

Managing Can Be Grungy Work

Occasionally in one's work life as a manager you have to do something you hate. In my case, it was making changes in the Washington Office that involved its director, Don Channell. He had been my mentor, soul mate and friend. When I returned to the ABA, he and I picked up personally as friends where we had left off, except that now the office was my overall responsibility and times were changing. In 1974, we were attracting sizeable government grants to develop law related programs in various fields, from federal law enforcement and corrections to housing and urban development. Other grants were in the works, such as one on the legal rights of the mentally disabled. ABA committees with Washington-oriented activities, such as Election Law, were better served out of Washington than the Chicago headquarters. This meant new staff members in the Washington Office, and a larger, more efficient office space.

The Section of Taxation had been staffed out of Washington for several years, and some other sections were considering it. The fact was that so many of the ABA's activities were focusing increasingly on Washington, and this was in addition to the increased necessary legislative and federal agency liaison.

Don was a lobbyist. He wasn't interested in the movement of so many activities to Washington, and considered them an interference with his Hill work. When we told him that he had to begin looking for new offices, it was difficult for him to consider leaving 1705 DeSales Street, and yet we had no choice but to do it. He acknowledged that the bigger management role falling on him was not easy, and he didn't fit into it well. In addition to the management problem, he preferred to work primarily with Capitol Hill, and couldn't see the need to begin relating closely with federal agencies like the Law Enforcement Assistance Administration that administered one of our largest law enforcement grants. Even with the Justice Department, where the linkage between Hill and department was vital for us, he preferred to have others on his staff do it.

In short, the Washington Office wasn't providing the level of service now needed to manage relationships between the federal government, the ABA, state and local bar associations, and the increasing number of Washington-related funded projects housed in the office.

I met several times with Don in Washington about the "new day" at the ABA, and the changes in Washington in particular. It was difficult for both of us, because there we were, I, his former assistant and close brotherly friend, telling him about our newly increasing needs, and Don, my former boss and mentor, expressing so much difficulty with it. He suggested that a way to solve it was with two separate offices, one as the Congressional liaison, which he would continue to head, and another office with the committee and project support staff. The two would collaborate when necessary, but even might be in separate locations. The point was that the ABA would have two top managers in Washington, one for legislation, the other for projects and committees, and both would report directly to me.

His suggestion wasn't feasible. To begin with, the Watergate situation had given the ABA newly heightened public exposure, with increased pressure for advice and assistance in Washington. Agencies were coming to us with funding opportunities for their projects. They and legislative staffs were seeking information and policy support like they never had before. This increased activity required more public relations attention in the office. We needed a person who was qualified to oversee all of it on an integrated basis, and two separate offices with two equal directors would be too cumbersome and expensive. I knew this wasn't workable, but didn't have the stomach to tell him that day. Instead I said I would discuss it with Bert, and talk with him soon.

Of course, Bert thought we had to have a new overall manager, and that a change had to be made. I agreed. We decided to offer Don the legislative liaison position under a new manager, but he would have to accept the new Washington Office director as the person in charge. We knew this would be hard for him, but we had no choice.

This was grungy work, having to confront such a close personal friend and mentor on this important change. Offering Don a position lower than his current one, where he had performed so well over many years, wasn't a happy situation. But, we wanted to give him a choice.

I was the top staff officer responsible for Washington, but Bert offered to talk with Don in my place. He knew that I was hurting. More than anything, though, he wanted Don to know that this was his decision as well as mine; and felt that he owed it to Don to discuss it with him. Don had reported directly to Bert for years. Don preferred to resign.

After he and Bert had talked, Don and I met again in Washington. He asked me if this was my decision as well as Bert's. I told him it was. He was displeased, but told me that he felt no ill will toward me. I needed this conversation because I needed the closure, and he knew it. It was the measure of the man to be willing to say this to me when he was hurting so badly.

Don had a severance package from the ABA, and obtained a few consulting jobs for a while. However, one night, while crossing a dark road near his home at Lake Barcroft, Virginia, he was struck by a car, and was in a coma for several months at Veteran's Hospital in Washington. He had been strikingly disfigured and responded to nobody. When I wanted to visit him, his wife, Betty, told me that he would not recognize me, and that I should be prepared for a very difficult few minutes when I saw him. Seeing him lying there was difficult, but the result of the visit was positive for me. As I talked quietly into his ear and held his hand, I told him who I was and that I loved him. Without opening his eyes or moving, his hand squeezed mine. And, it was true...I did love him, and hope that he loved me too.

1975.... The Washington Office Is Reorganized and Moved

1975 was especially important from a management and program stand-point. In 1974, we hired Herbert Hoffman from the Justice Department to head the Washington Office. Herb had many years of service in the depart-ment's Office of Legislative Counsel, and had had extensive experience on Capitol Hill. He now was faced with the tasks of finding new office space, becoming oriented to the ABA, and managing the ongoing legislative efforts. In addition, he oversaw the staff liaison to six ABA committees and one com-mission with Washington-oriented activities. ABA section and committee members were beginning to flock into Washington to testify, and there were appointments to be made for the ABA president and president-elect.

Because of all the new challenges facing Herb, I began visiting him fre-quently. He didn't need help conducting governmental relations, but needed briefings on how the ABA functioned, and how best to serve all of the mem-bers visiting Washington on ABA business.

While, in my Chicago management role, I no longer had been testifying or even calling on senators or representatives, I did relieve Herb by working with the ABA's coalition of bipartisan lawyers to obtain increased compensa-tion for federal judges. Chief Justice Warren Burger had urgently requested the ABA to advocate this, and his administrative assistant, Mark Cannon, provided us with information and back-up support. This was the beginning of my association with Mr. Cannon, and through him, the Chief Justice, on various matters of mutual interest in judicial administration. Chief Justice Burger was well known for his tireless efforts in support of improvements in judicial administration, and was always an advocate for federal judges.

At its board meeting in September 1974, the ABA urged Congress to act on increased federal judicial salaries such as those recommended earlier by a federal commission on federal salaries. Congress had not acted. In 1974, the resignation of United States federal district judges had reached unprec-edented proportions, and inadequate compensation was cited as the reason by more than 80 percent of them. Federal judges had not had an increase since 1969, and the CPI had increased 42 percent, while the income of lawyers generally had increased 43 percent. While the position of Federal District Judge was an honor, it was increasingly difficult to interest the best-qualified lawyers to accept appointment.

Former Attorney General Brownell and former ABA president Bernard Segal of Philadelphia headed the coalition. Knowing both Mr. Segal on ABA judicial administration matters (I was at the Urban Coalition when he was president), and Mr. Brownell from Twenty-Fifth Amendment days, it was especially pleasant to work with them. With the Washington Office's Craig Baab as my colleague, we helped develop a strategy, which included favoring increased Congressional salaries as well. The salaries of both federal judges and members of Congress historically ran together, and it was unlikely that Congress would act unless they also gave themselves a raise. So, Messrs. Segal, Brownell, Baab, dozens of other lawyers from around the country, and I began our calls on members of Congress. I drew on my former lobbying days by speaking with Senators Bayh, Hruska, and Pearson; and calling on Representatives Michel, McCulloch, and Anderson, to name a few. It was fun. Telling congressmen that we favored increases for them (while we also urged increases for judges) couldn't have caused more positive reactions. Making the rounds on Capitol Hill was like the good old days, and exhilarating to be back "in the fray." I had the best of both worlds now. I could live and work in Chicago, and come in and out of Washington when I was needed.

The Chief Justice was elated over our work. In time, federal judicial salaries were raised (for legislators too of course), and he credited us with good work. With Mr. Segal, one of the top Supreme Court lawyers in America, and Mr. Brownell at the helm, the "Chief" knew we had the right people advocating.

As Herb Hoffman quickly took hold, I was careful to stay out of his way. There's nothing more frustrating to a Washington office director than having a boss from out of town plunging into Washington and wanting to second-guess everything. Even more frustrating is that out-of-town boss wanting to visit this or that senator, ostensibly to "show the colors," but primarily to be able to say, "Yes, I visited Senator So and So when I was in Washington."

Herb and I worked closely together on planning the new office location. I myself had some emotions over leaving our building on DeSales Street. I remembered the excitement of moving to that little street along the north side of the Mayflower Hotel; the planning and strategies there, as well as the receptions in our conference/reception room, and the prominent visitors whom we would greet. It was more charming than most other offices, and memories of the times there came flooding back.

In July 1975, the new offices were moved to 1800 M Street, just a block and a half from the DeSales location. They were spacious, with everybody housed on one floor. Herb Hoffman, his legislative staff, and a growing new staff of project directors and ABA committee liaison were off and running.

The Mainstay of the ABA,
the Division of Professional Education, Is Launched

No year can go by without at least some controversy in most work situations. You would think that continuing professional education for lawyers and judges, as a priority activity of the ABA, would not cause any disagreement. Wrong!

After a long history of the American Law Institute serving as the primary agency for professional education for lawyers, in January 1975, the ABA created its own staff Division of Professional Education. The new division was activated to provide within the ABA the staff resources for "taking on a responsible and dynamic role in continuing education…." This new high ABA priority was the result of several years of edging into continuing education by the association, political jockeying among bar leaders, and ongoing negotiations with the American Law Institute. It wasn't easy getting there because of the concerns of various lawyers, including some top ABA leaders, who preferred to keep the ABA's professional education activities in joint collaboration with the ALI. They were concerned that major efforts in that field by the ABA would jeopardize the relationship, which they believed should be continued.

The American Law Institute, located in Philadelphia, was and is the leading independent organization of lawyers, judges and law professors producing scholarly work to clarify, modernize and improve the law. With an elected membership of 4,000, its work of drafting, revising and publishing Restatements of the law, model statutes and principles of law is influential with courts, legislatures and legal scholars.

In 1947, when the ABA had few members and limited resources, the ALI agreed to lead efforts in continuing education for lawyers. The ABA assisted in the program by approving the formation of the ALI-ABA Joint Committee on Continuing Education of the Bar. The Committee's members consisted of seven from the ALI and seven from the ABA, with the ALI president and director and the ABA president and president-elect serving as Ex officio. This joint committee oversaw nationally sponsored continuing legal education through its own programs and promotion of "CLE" at the state level; however, all of it was managed and administered exclusively by the ALI.

When Bert Early took the ABA staff reins, he saw immediately that the ABA was missing opportunities in the continuing education field. He believed that it wasn't fulfilling its responsibilities to the legal profession by not engaging in education programs of its own. The ABA sections of all the law specialties were ready-made entities to provide ongoing education in their respective fields, but were not being utilized for that. So in 1966, with his recommendations, a new system of National Institutes was organized. By 1967, some ABA sections began sponsoring a few educational "institutes," all approved and under the auspices of the ABA Board of Governors. At this point, the ALI noted that a cordial working relationship continued between the ALI and ABA. However, the seeds had been planted for the ABA to conduct its own CLE programs without assistance from or joint collaboration with the ALI.

Some leaders of the ABA were concerned about these developments. Because of the strong intellectual and academic orientation of the ALI, they thought the ALI continued to be the best avenue for sound professional education. Even though these men were active leaders of the ABA, they did not want to jeopardize the ABA's close ties with the ALI. Some of them seemed to have closer allegiances to the ALI than the ABA, and this was particularly true with some ABA representatives who served on the Joint Committee.

Bert didn't let up, however. He argued that providing ongoing education to its members should be the highest priority of the ABA, conducted out of its own offices. Not only did the association have the responsibility to its members, it had the responsibility to itself in gaining new members and sources of income, thereby adding to its overall strength.

When I returned to the ABA, the debate over its role in conducting CLE was in full swing. Agreements between the ALI and ABA were approved by the House of Delegates. However, they only edged the ABA closer to providing full-service educational programs, and its role still wasn't defined and approved by the House.

I was drawn into it immediately as the new staff leader responsible for all programs, including continuing professional education. It was clear by now that most of the ABA leaders favored a full-service education program, implemented through the substantive law sections, but final decisions like this didn't come easily. They also favored a new agreement with the ALI that would free the ABA to proceed as it wished without ALI cooperation or collaboration.

So much information was needed, and so many bases had to be covered in the organized bar before recommendations could be made to the Board of Governors and House of Delegates. They had to be sound ones based on the needs of the bar, and while the ABA's self-interest was important, that could not be the primary consideration.

To gain the information for formulating the ABA's role, the ABA Committee on Professional Education, headed by John Cummiskey, whom I knew so well from Washington lobbying days, sponsored a series of hearings in Chicago, Cleveland and Washington, D.C. in 1972 and 1973. Working with John, I planned and coordinated these meetings. Representatives of ABA sections and other related bar groups gave their views, and from them we knew that the consensus was overwhelming that the ABA should enter professional education on its own as a top priority.

From that consensus, in 1974, John was able to recommend slight changes in the ALI and ABA relationship in providing professional education and leading to the creation of a new ABA staff Division of Continuing Education. The new arrangement officially codified the freedom of the ABA, as the national organization of lawyers, and the ALI-ABA Committee to conduct their own separate CLE activities, each without obtaining the approval of the other. While this was a welcome step forward, particularly in light of some ABA leaders still wanting the ALI to remain predominate in CLE, it was troublesome for a major reason: the ABA continued to be official sponsors of two organizations proving such education.

This major effort was Bert Early's baby. He personally had provided the vision for the new program, and for advancing it through the various necessary committees and the Board of Governors. I worked closely with Bert, helping edit his drafts of recommendations and position papers, and talking with our volunteer leaders. Bill Kleindorfer, the staff director of the Division of Legal Practice and Education, and head of staff support of section activities, worked closely with us. For months leading up to the new division's activation in 1975, putting the right touches on the new, enhanced program was a consuming exercise for us. Politically within the ABA, we had to walk a fine line of producing a separate ABA program, while co-sponsoring CLE programs with the ALI as well. Our charge by the House of Delegates was to produce a program that would satisfy the Association's "duty…to provide vigorous and responsible leadership in the field of continuing education." That was the ABA's newly mandated role. And yet the ALI-ABA Committee, with its staff in Philadelphia, was still functioning with some of our own ABA leaders who were taking active roles in its work. How were we to reconcile these respective responsibilities and operate without overlap or conflict?

The ALI-ABA Committee had performed admirably over its many years of existence. The ALI was an organization of the highest standing with the judicial and legal practicing and educational communities. We at the ABA didn't have pedagogical standing. But we did have the practical expertise available through the specialized law sections of the leading legal specialists in the country. This was perfect for conducting CLE programs for lawyers directly from the ABA, rather than the ALI.

In January 1975, the first ABA director of professional education was appointed. Joel Henning was already on the ABA staff, and had excellent credentials from directing and building our well-known department of Youth Education for Citizenship, a mission to help young people understand our political and legal system. Over the next few years, Joel built the new division into a first-rate educational operation, bringing new vitality and importance to the sections as they concentrated on producing practical education for their members.

The relationship with the American Law Institute continued, and the programs of the new ABA division and the ALI-ABA Committee were conducted separately. There were overlapping tensions at times, and some confusion among lawyers since both were seen as ABA activities. But we had achieved what had been Bert Early's dream…to make continuing professional education a "mainstay" of the ABA. **This story provided real-world lessons on working in the political atmosphere of a voluntary association, understanding the political necessities of accommodating many differing views, while achieving worthwhile objectives as well.**

In 2012, the joint work and collaboration of the ALI and ABA in continuing legal education were terminated. Today, in 2015, continuing legal education is the 'mainstay' of the American Bar Association.

Why did I devote so many pages explaining the ALI-ABA relationship in continuing education?

I wrote it because I consider it, with the enhancement of the ABA Fund for Public Education, the pivotal actions of my employment with the ABA as associate and, later, deputy executive director. Without this new program activated in 1975, the ABA could not have continued as the major nationally recognized organization of lawyers. It could not exist simply as a public policy debating society, or even as a major purveyor of public service activities. It had to provide a substantive service such as education to its members, and had to it on its own. In properly serving its members with education, and in gaining and retaining members, it had to provide them with practical self-interested reasons, not just public policy conferences and resolutions. The ABA, as the national organization of the legal profession, had to take its own major role in education.

In writing this, I also wanted to convey that association staff efforts, resulting in achievement, take vision and persistence. In this case only a few volunteer officers either were lukewarm or outright opposed to the ABA going on its own. But they were powerhouse leaders, with strong influence in ABA decision making. Fortunately, other powerhouse lawyers favored the action. But the primary motivation came from behind-the-scenes staff leadership. This is what the staff was expected to do: provide vision and leadership, but in a low-keyed way. In other words, we were "servant/leaders." It seems at times that, in association work, the meetings and the position papers, hammered out with the staff and volunteers working together, and finally the governing body debates and actions, go on forever. But it's worth it.

Our Finances Hit a Snag

At its 1974 midyear meeting, William Falsgraf, chairman of the Board Finance Committee, and later the ABA president, reported that the cost of upgrading the American Bar Center had run in excess of the amount budgeted. He reported also that a number of budget reductions were being executed to cover the overrun. I remember the unpleasant day Bert told me about this. How could this have happened in that Bert himself had selected new furniture, and had led the planning and execution of refurbishing? Based on the receipts and financial reports he was receiving from our financial office, he thought he was within the budget.

I had helped Bert plan the new building configuration, and visited some furniture stores with him. But, because my responsibilities then did not include finance and accounting, I couldn't help with an answer. The primary problem seemed to be deficiencies in the financial reporting system, and I was as equally surprised as he by this. Consequently, over the next year and a half, the financial reporting system was completely revised under the direction of Robert Easton, a new staff financial officer. While we had to reduce some important expenditures, including additional staff, the income from dues and foundation and government grants were sufficient to continue without much disruption. Although operations weren't seriously affected, for a while it was an unwelcome diversion, and created an unfortunate atmosphere of "how could this have happened?" It had taken this event to focus on the financial reporting system, which had not kept up with the rapid changes in association growth and programs.

Other Groups Come Knocking

As an association grows and its importance increases, other groups come calling at its door. That's what was happening at the American Bar Association. State and local bar associations, their executive directors, and numerous other bar-related groups were calling on us for attention and services.

Some non-legal groups, such as the prestigious American Assembly of Columbia University, came knocking as well. In 1968, the Assembly and ABA co-sponsored the American Assembly on Law and a Changing Society. It focused on anticipated societal changes and how the legal profession should respond to them. The Assembly proposed to us another such conference to be held in 1975.

The American Assembly was founded in 1950 by Dwight D. Eisenhower as an affiliate of Columbia University. As president of Columbia, and then a private citizen, he was concerned about the heavy social, economic and political quandaries facing America after World War II. He wanted to bring together people from all sectors of society to address the difficult issues and propose solutions. As university president, he devoted much of his attention to the creation of this organization, and it continues today (2015) as an influential public affairs forum.

The difficulty with this proposal was that, with all of the business on our platter, we didn't have the staff or the mechanism to respond. Additionally, we needed a much better staff organization to relate to all of the outside groups that we needed to serve. Our former director of Public Service Activities,

David Ellwanger, on an assignment with an ABA special commission, was finishing his work with that group. With this work winding down, David would be an excellent "fit" to organize a new department to meet the growing demands and opportunities we faced with the outside groups. We created the Office of Relations with Other Organizations, folded the department of state and local bars into it, and appointed David to head it. So, another activity was dealt with in 1975.

We went ahead with the American Assembly on Law and Society II. It was a major undertaking, held at Stanford University Law School in June, with some 100 world-class leaders from various disciplines, including U.S. Attorney General Edward Levi. Working with the ABA-Assembly planning committee, David and I concentrated on preparing the agenda and recommending the names of participants. While it was limited to 100, the selection of diversified, knowledgeable participants was a time-consuming, but enjoyable, undertaking. Because of the high-profile nature of the event, and the necessity of selecting the highest caliber participants who would agree to attend, other matters on my agenda had to take a back seat for several weeks. The conferees discussed and debated technical and societal changes that would impact the law and presented consensus as best as they could. The report received wide attention in the media and the Bar, and helped form ABA action for some years following.

The Annual Meeting That Could Have Been a Disaster

The August 1975 annual meeting of thousands was scheduled for Montreal, Canada. When, three to four years earlier, Montreal was selected as the annual meeting city, the number of lawyers with their families and guests attending was underestimated. And, to boot, first-class hotel rooms scheduled for updating weren't ready. Whatever the reason, on March 1, the Board of Governors imposed a moratorium on all registrations. Those then trying to register would have to find their own accommodations. It doesn't take much imagination to know what the outcry was. Talk about tensions on a staff. What were we going to do?

Fortunately, David Hayes and John Donohue, who did operational planning, saved the day. After many trips to Montreal with the meetings department staff, they found alternatives. The alternatives weren't the traditional downtown hotel rooms, but served the purpose well. They included using a cruise ship in the harbor as a floating hotel; downtown apartment hotels; and for those driving their cars, resort hotels in the nearby Laurentian Mountains. Shuttles and trolleys were provided from the various locations.

Over 7,000 lawyers attended. This was a special meeting. The 200,000th member was presented. Secretary of State Henry Kissinger, Justice Lewis Powell, Judge John Sirica of the Watergate saga, U.S. Attorney General Edward Levi, and Secretary of Housing and Urban Development Carla Hills spoke. A special highlight, where the audience sat in rapt attention, was a prayer breakfast address by Rev. Billy Graham.

This was the first annual meeting to which Myrna and I had taken our three children, Rich who was 11, Jonathan, 7, and Lori, 4. Montreal, with its Old-World environment, was a different and special place for them. It was like stepping back into an earlier time, with unusually friendly and welcoming people. They would travel with us to various events many times after that, but this first one in Montreal was an especially enjoyable time for them.

Booz Allen Hamilton Is Hired for Management Consulting

The year 1975 had pushed us to the limits in adding new functions, some involving controversy and dissension, but mostly with positive outcomes. It hadn't been a year of all peaches and cream, however, within the internal operations of the staff.

We had completed a staff management study in 1974, to be implemented in '75. In 1973, our growth was so strong, and new programs with staff components were activated so quickly, that Bert believed a full study of staff management, with emphasis on how it would best serve the volunteer officers and membership, was needed. He told me that he was planning to hire Booz Allen & Hamilton, the internationally known management-consulting firm. I disagreed with him for two reasons.

First, I didn't believe that Booz Allen, as recognized as it was in business management consulting, had the expertise to help us. Corporate management effectiveness was their business. The ABA and organizations like it were completely different animals. The objective of corporations is singularly "bottom line." You begin with a CEO, and everything flows down from that officer. You, whether executive or line employee, have one boss to whom you report, and you are evaluated on how you help the "bottom line." In professional and trade associations, the staff must deal with many objectives, generally reporting to more than one boss. The line of staff authority runs from the executive director down, but you, as the staff member, must also accommodate and "work for" several others, whether they are association officers, or section or committee leaders. It's a balancing act to respond to all of these people. There is no "bottom line," results are subjective, and are difficult to define quantitatively. "How," I asked Bert, "can a Booz Allen consultant, whose clients are mostly corporations, help us? How can a Booz Allen consultant, with no practical experience in association management, help us? From your and my own long-time association experience, we both know much more than a business consultant would."

Secondly, I said, the staff doesn't have time for this. We can hardly get through the day now with our travel schedules, meetings to conduct, and being on constant call to our "volunteer bosses." To begin giving up hours a week to meet with a consultant and his chalkboard will play havoc with us. And, I bet him "everything" that virtually every one of our staff members knew more about how to do their jobs in this professional association than any corporate consultant.

He disagreed. We had to figure out ways to be more staff-efficient, and bringing in this firm was the best way to do it. It wasn't cost effective to keep adding staff as programs were activated, and at the rate we were going, we wouldn't be able to anyway. We wouldn't have the money.

So, the Booz Allen consultants arrived, and we began meeting at the Kellogg Center for management training a few blocks away. I had a virtual staff rebellion on my hands. The consultants tried to be responsive, but just as I had suspected, they learned more about our unique work from us than they were able to offer themselves. Much of what they said obviously would apply well to the corporate environment, but we weren't a business corporation. We were often frustrated with how to be the most effective in an ego-driven volunteer organization with the best legal minds in the country, but the Booz Allen advice didn't apply to our work. The problem was intense for me because the management staff had to attend, and often at the most inconvenient times.

When the Booz Allen report was issued, I had to admit that I was surprised. While it had virtually no helpful advice on individual staff management functions, it did contain recommendations on internal structural changes for saving money and greater efficiency. There were recommendations for restructuring some of the staff divisions and creating office pools, all of which did save money and produce some staff reductions. One of our first steps was to house together the executive staff and president's assistants, and consolidate all of the secretarial functions in this office. This provided more efficiency and fewer people.

My administrative assistant, Norbert Wegrzyn, organized and managed the new secretarial center. The executive offices became known throughout the building as the "green carpet area" because of the new carpet's color. Generally the staff members who came to our offices referred to it like that: "Well, I've got to go to the green carpet area now."

So both Bert and I were correct. Good things did come from the study. But I still maintained, although Bert never conceded even one inch, that it didn't help us at all in managing our daily workloads and multiple relationships with the volunteer leaders and members. The report did recommend new "staff training" on relating to the volunteers. I thought this was a copout because, supposedly, the consultants were hired to do that. Recommendations also included long-range planning, and setting clear-cut, understandable individual staff objectives, with a uniform staff evaluation process based on the objectives. They were good, relevant recommendations, based on good "corporate" business principles. I had to acknowledge that we hadn't been good at setting written, clear objectives for each staff member, and evaluating them on those objectives. We implemented those recommendations, and they were helpful. They even helped with staff morale because it's elementary that when personnel know specifically their objectives, and are evaluated on them, their work is easier and results are better. And yet, we had not been doing this.

Over the years, as association and lobbying groups have multiplied, consulting groups have emerged to focus on them. It has become big business. But, it wasn't then, in 1974 and '75. It was, and still is, a fact that non-profit association and trade association management and corporate management aren't the same. This doesn't mean, though, that the non-profit world can't be run more like businesses, with appropriate cost controls and management objectives through long-range planning; and human resources principles of individual staff objectives and evaluations, compensation ranges, hiring and firing, and benefit packages. They must, or they can't survive. So, Bert, you

were correct again. The Booz Allen consultation was helpful. But I was too…
well, sort of.

A New President Arrives, Presenting New Difficulties

The president-elect in 1975 was Judge Lawrence E. Walsh, a noted Wall
Street lawyer, former federal district judge, U.S. deputy attorney general,
and U.S. representative to the Paris Peace Talks with the rank of ambassador.
While he had been a member of the House of Delegates, he was not well
known in ABA leadership circles. He had been chairman of the association's
Committee on the Federal Judiciary, the prestigious committee that evaluated federal judicial nominees and gave their qualifications either thumbs up
or down to the Justice Department, the President and the Senate Judiciary
Committee. Because of its extreme sensitivity, the committee functioned on
its own, without the ABA staff's services. While he had served on the Board
of Governors for two years, he had not been active with the staff, so he didn't
know us well.

Because of the large number of ABA members from New York, it was understood that a New York lawyer would be president every 10 years. 1976 was
New York's "turn," and Judge Ed Walsh was elected. He was one of the country's most distinguished lawyers and deserving of his new ABA office. When
he became president-elect, he immediately began visiting the Bar Center to
meet with Bert and me. He wanted to become well acquainted with the staff
operations and the association's procedures. There was a big problem, though.
For reasons that neither Bert nor I could understand, Ed Walsh would not
relate well with Bert. It was even worse than that…he began looking to me as
his primary contact instead of Bert.

While I had responsibility for the association's program staff, and worked
closely with the officers and board, all presidents looked to Bert as their principal staff contact and colleague. Several times when I asked Mr. Walsh if
"he had discussed this with Bert," he would say that he didn't have to. "Why
should I call Bert first, when I know you'll be the one taking care of it?"

This was a difficult situation for both Bert and me. It put a heavy burden
on both us because I was now consumed by responding to Mr. Walsh, as if I
were his personal assistant, and my day-to-day management responsibilities
were beginning to suffer. It was just as hard on Bert because it caused confusion among staff members, and they were beginning to wonder who actually

was in charge, Bert or I. It was wearing on us for more than just a few weeks. It began when Mr. Walsh was president-elect, and continued after he became president in August 1976. Neither Bert nor I could determine how to handle it other than to let it run its course until the new president, Justin Stanley of Chicago, took office in 1977. Mr. Stanley and we knew each other well, and his way of working with us was entirely one of understanding and cooperation. As president-elect, Mr. Stanley knew the situation with Judge Walsh, but believed it wasn't his place to try to change it. He thought his involvement would make matters worse.

Things changed between Thanksgiving and Christmas of 1976. Earlier, the U.S. Supreme Court had agreed to hear a case about lawyer advertising which would be decided in 1977.

The case involved two young lawyers in Arizona, Messrs. Bates and O'Steen, who began advertising their legal clinic's service of "routine legal matters" for persons of moderate means. Advertising by lawyers violated the Code of Professional Responsibility of the American Bar Association, which was followed in each state, including Arizona. Consequently the Supreme Court of Arizona found Bates and O'Steen in violation of the state regulation, and prohibited them from continuing to advertise.

The case became the new major issue at the ABA. What were the legal implications? Did the Canon that prohibited lawyer advertising violate the Sherman Antitrust Act and the First Amendment as Bates and O'Steen were claiming? The Canon had been in effect for decades. The ABA believed then that advertising by lawyers was unprofessional and would put lawyers in a bad light. It also could generate thousands of claims that had no basis. Advertising legal services, if you could call it that, was limited to law directories and business cards. So, this was a big deal for us.

Around Thanksgiving, Ed Walsh told me that he wanted the ABA to sponsor a high-powered conference on lawyer advertising. He wanted to conduct it soon so the profession would know it was high on the ABA's agenda, and was receiving our immediate attention. He wanted the best minds in the profession to examine the pros and cons, which would help us decide how to frame our current position. He wanted it held before Christmas.

Before Christmas? Just a month away? I told him that this wasn't just difficult to do; we couldn't do it on such short notice. Not only could we not drop everything else for it, which we would have to do, but identifying the participants and finding them available during the holidays was just not feasible. He disagreed, and wanted me to proceed with it because it was such a pressing issue. I asked Bert if he would talk with Ed because the timing was impossible, and he wasn't listening to me. He responded that he could not; that I knew myself that Ed wouldn't listen to him.

What was I to do? I knew that we couldn't pull it off, but convincing Ed Walsh didn't seem possible. In all of his positions as a large-firm partner, federal judge, and deputy attorney general, he was used to his associates working overtime when they were told to, and was expecting that from me and the staff. This was different, though. It was not just working into the night to plan and select conferees. We could do that. But finding a venue with rooms available over the holidays, getting the invitations out, and getting all of these top people to change holiday-period plans, all in addition to the operational support needed…all together, I simply couldn't do it.

That Friday night, I went home, sat down on the stairs and began to cry. I was sobbing. Myrna was frantic because she didn't know what was going on. I told her that I didn't know either. In between sobs I tried to explain that I hadn't ever felt like this; that I couldn't think straight, and felt that I didn't have enough energy to move, even into the other room. I couldn't put my finger on why. It wasn't just the advertising conference. We could do that if we absolutely had to. It wasn't just Ed Walsh. He was always a gentleman with me; after all, I had dealt with other demanding men before. I had had other pressing assignments that hadn't caused this ill feeling. Maybe I just wasn't up to doing my job. I didn't know. And that was my biggest concern. No one thing seemed to me to cause this problem.

Myrna and I thought a good night's sleep would take care of it. But it didn't. I was worse the next day. Monday I was no better. I wasn't still crying, but had no energy. Myrna and I decided that I should see our family physician. While explaining how badly I felt, I began to cry again. Dr. Agnoli sat and simply listened. He said that he couldn't help me; that I seemed depressed, and should seek counseling, probably from a psychiatrist.

I couldn't believe that a psychiatrist was needed, and decided to wait another day or two before discussing it further with anybody. Myrna called Bert and told him that I wasn't feeling well, had the flu or something, and wouldn't be at the office for at least or day or two. I spoke with our minister, Rev. Herb Knudsen, who had counseling experience, and began crying again. When he heard this, he responded that I needed solid professional help, something that he wasn't qualified to give.

I was fortunate to have a friend from our days together at our Washington area church, Dr. Charles Boren. After serving as a Navy psychiatrist, Charlie moved to West Hartford, Connecticut, to head a nationally known clinic there. He had advice for me. He wanted me to meet a good friend of his. I thought that seeing him would be more attention than I needed, but Charlie didn't agree. He said that we didn't know what was causing this prolonged depression, and he didn't want me to go to a "shopping mall" psychiatrist. He arranged for a meeting the next day with his friend. Not having seen a psychiatrist, I didn't know what to expect.

When I entered the doctor's office, before I even sat down, he asked me abruptly what I was doing there. He said that Dr. Boren had told him that I was terribly depressed, and it was urgent that I see him immediately. He said that I didn't look depressed to him, and that I should see some of his patients in the hospital just a few rooms away. They felt so badly that they were in bed, unable to move; that one, for example, was a well-known trial lawyer who was in bed now, but tomorrow would be trying a case before a jury. By making this "urgent" appointment, I was taking his valuable time away from his patients who were in fact very ill.

I didn't know how to answer this other than to tell him I was sorry, and that Charlie believed I should see him. He then invited me to tell him my story, and surprisingly became friendly and understanding. He wanted to know, first, whether there were pressing family issues, ranging from finances to relationships. There weren't. Then we moved to the workplace. I explained the difficult environment there, and how it was hard just to get through the day, but hard work and contentious times weren't new to me.

He went right to the heart of the matter. My problem, he said, wasn't hard work. It related to the relationship between Bert Early and Ed Walsh, and my frustrations with that had finally reached a boiling point. Neither Bert nor Mr. Walsh understood the tensions they had caused with me, and that had to be resolved, or I wouldn't feel better. Mr. Walsh didn't understand my workload, and Bert, to whom I actually reported, couldn't give me the support I needed. I had nowhere to turn, neither to Bert nor Ed, and had reached a brick wall, causing depression and inability to function.

The doctor explained that I wasn't sick at all; that I didn't know what to do in my work, that I had become overwhelmed without the understanding of my superiors. Bert and Ed both were making demands on me, separate from each other. Bert wasn't any more helpful than Ed. He would hold staff meetings that I simply didn't have time to attend, and often were irrelevant to me. Two men who wouldn't speak to each other, and each expecting performance as they wished, were causing a conflict that I couldn't resolve.

He said that he would give me some advice, and guaranteed that I would feel better soon.

First, I should stay home for a while, maybe even a couple of weeks. If I felt better, maybe only a week. But stay home and take time to separate myself from the causes of the problem.

Second, he said that all of life consists of making decisions based on options that we have. In my case, I had options, and when I decided on one, I would feel better instantly. The options were:

- Ask Messrs. Walsh and Early to meet with you together, and explain your situation to them. They can't keep separately making demands on you, and there must be a clear-cut line of authority managing you. And, that Mr. Walsh must understand your full range of management responsibilities, which he did not, before asking you to drop everything else to do as he wishes.

- Meet with Messrs. Walsh and Early separately in their offices and tell them the same thing.

- Suck it up and live with the situation. Even though it's hard, realize that these particular frustrations will end at some point.

- Because Bert can't help you, and because of that the situation is getting worse, try to have him fired.

- Quit.

He said that once I had settled on one of these options, I would feel better. Go home, think about it, and come back to see me in a week with the one you've decided. He then told me to notice people on the sidewalks when I left him. Look at their faces, and how they're walking. Many of them are suffering some kind of frustration. Some will be experiencing depression, even if it's mild. What you're experiencing now is common to all of us. Sometimes it takes hold of us more than other times. He stressed that there were forms of depression that only medication and counseling would help, but that was not my kind. "If you make a decision in dealing with it," he said, "you'll see the change."

I did what he said. Some of the people I met on the sidewalk looked pretty down in the dumps. I went home, and decided to see Bert and Ed separately. I felt better just deciding an option. I was back at the office in less than a week, talking with Bert. He couldn't have responded better. He agreed that he would be more sensitive to the demands on me, and not expect me to take time meeting with him and reporting to him as well.

I flew to New York, and decided to take Rich, now 12, along. We would make the trip a little fun. Ed couldn't have responded better either. In the meantime, he had thought about the advertising conference, and agreed with me. In fact, he said that a conference wouldn't change the outcome of the Court's decision anyway, and that we would wait until after the decision to sponsor some conferences, maybe around the country, to help state bar associations implement it. Rich and I went to old comic book stores because comic books were his hobby then, and saw the musical, The Threepenny Opera. It was a good trip.

Both Bert and Ed told me to take some more days off. I didn't submit medical bills to the Personnel Department because I didn't want anybody to know I had visited a psychiatrist. As far as the staff knew, I simply wasn't feeling well. I don't hesitate being open about it today. Many people do experience something like this, and whether they know it or not, would feel better if they just knew they could decide which option to take, and take it.

I told Charlie that he had caused me big trouble by telling his friend that I was so sick and that he needed to see me right away. Why did he make it sound so terrible? "Because," Charlie said, "he's so busy that he wouldn't have seen you if I hadn't."

Ed and Bert continued their standoffishness, but they seemed to at least slightly communicate after that. I was able to get back to business as usual.

Soon after this experience, I was named deputy executive director. Both Ed and Bert agreed that I had shown that I could lead the program side of the staff without Bert's day-to-day supervision. While my responsibilities didn't change materially, it was welcomed recognition of my position.

During this period, and following, three good friends on the ABA Board offered me welcomed support. David Andrews, the treasurer, Herb Sledd, the secretary, and Arthur Leibold, who would become treasurer, kept in close touch with me, with assurance that everything would turn out all right. They understood the situation perfectly, and said the other officers did also. I suppose they didn't even realize how helpful they were as individuals I could turn to in confidence.

A note about Ed Walsh: In 1986, Ed Walsh was appointed federal independent counsel to investigate the Iran-Contra matter. He and his office brought indictments against Oliver North, John Poindexter and Casper Weinberger, among others, but some convictions were overturned on appeal; and President George H.W. Bush pardoned others. Judge Walsh died in Oklahoma City at the age of 102.

The Supreme Court Acts on Lawyer Advertising

Because advertising by lawyers was in violation of a rule of the ABA Code of Professional Responsibility, and the validity of the rule adopted by the Arizona Supreme Court was in question, the ABA filed an amicus curiae brief in support of Arizona. The U.S. Supreme Court ruled on June 27, 1977 that it did not agree with the Arizona court, and that the First Amendment to the U.S. Constitution permits lawyers to advertise. It further stated that regulations adopted by the states were appropriate and expected to restrain false, deceptive and misleading advertising. While the decision sent shock waves, and even anger throughout the legal profession, most leading lawyers expected it. They believed that the bar did have an obligation to do more than the Code allowed to provide sufficient information for the public to make informed choices on legal services. In any event, we at the ABA were preparing for it, and the House of Delegates and board created a commission to establish guidelines for assisting state courts, regulatory agencies and bar associations in adapting to it.

We did indeed, after the decision instead of before, have hearings on lawyer advertising. From those hearings, the commission made recommendations for amending the Code. Interestingly, the use of television was the most debated issue then.

Television became the most common form of lawyer advertising. While I understand the Supreme Court decision as a First Amendment right of speech, I question whether it has helped the public make "intelligent decisions" in hiring a lawyer.

Is a short TV commercial with a lawyer simply saying the firm is "for the people" helpful to the layman needing quality representation? It can bring in clients, but is it informative?

Or how about the constant, never-ending line of TV ads by so many different law firms saying the same things, without differencing themselves from each other, on the same station.

And how about this one that aired in Wisconsin soon after the Bates decision? A middle-aged man emerges from a swimming pool surrounded by beauties in bikinis with hands and arms laden with strings of pearls and other jewelry, and exotic music blaring. All of this is simply to tell you that that law firm will produce riches for you. Helpful, right?

Sometimes All Good Things Come to an End

From 1977 to 1981, inflation was almost 15 percent and interest rates were as high as 18 percent, startling when considering today's (2015) figures. All of us, personally and in the workplace, were feeling the impact. The ABA wasn't exempted from it.

Nonpayment of member dues was higher than anticipated. Grants from outside sources were down. The drop in income was significant enough in 1977 for the Board of Governors to apply some stringent budgetary constraints, including no additional staff. Before the board action, we already had begun taking steps to trim the number of positions and consolidate some staff functions. From the years of significant growth, we had entered a new period of little growth, and doing with less.

Having to "trim" staff, whether in a business or nonprofit organization, always can be unpleasant and even painful. In today's world of 2015, staff reductions have been the norm over the past few years. However, letting people go or even saying "no" to requests for additional people was not our modus operandi at the ABA because of our growth in members and programs.

So now that the times had changed so drastically, our daily attention moved from starting new efforts to living with our new financial limitations. At the same time, new issues requiring new ABA commissions and special committees had to be dealt with. Where could we cut to make room for the new? Budget management became my number-one priority, and it wasn't popular.

A staff episode that I vividly remember was a staff director's request for a new addition to his department that turned out to be a very unpleasant situation.

I had to deny his request for a new position in his department. He then came to my office to tell me that he had spoken to the committee chairman with whom he worked closely. Through their close working relationship, they were good personal friends. The chairman agreed with him, he said, and would call the ABA president to secure the new staff member that I had denied.

I pulled my chair up to his, and told him that, as much as I respected his work and wished to support him, a new staff position for his department was not in the budget. It was my job to determine the staff priorities, and he simply would have to make do with what he had. I told him that I too knew his committee chairman, and had known him long before he came to work at the ABA. If he ever went around me again to a volunteer leader in a situation where I had responsibility, he should prepare to leave the association.

I immediately called the committee chairman. He said that he had agreed that a new position was needed, but would not call the president over my head; that he understood my situation, and regretted that I had been threatened like this. We both agreed that the staff member was an excellent performer in his field, but must understand that I, not the committee chairman, managed the staff. A couple of years after that, my colleague David Hayes told me that he just had the same conversation with this staff director. He again had gone over our heads, this time to a new committee chairman. I told David to tell him to clean out his desk and leave the building. If David preferred not to, I would. David did.

This might seem harsh. I hated this part of the job. But in the association world, particularly at the ABA, the staff/member relationship can be difficult and sensitive for the top staff leaders to manage. The line staff can, and many do, develop very close working relationships with the volunteer section and committee members they assist. They know each other almost like in a family. But, at the same time, there's a clear unwritten rule that the top staff officers, such as Bert, David and I, were charged by those same volunteers to manage the place. It would be administrative chaos if every staff member at every level could, without hesitation, go to their volunteer leaders and ask them to veto our decisions. Fortunately this was an isolated situation, and virtually everybody worked within the necessary boundaries.

The ABA Fund for Public Education Is Front and Center

Obviously your job is much happier when the organization is growing and the money's flowing in. That's when you can create, produce constructive results, and make a difference through your work. It's not fun when you have to say "no" all the time, and yet expect ongoing programmatic effectiveness. It's particularly troublesome when the expectations of the member lawyers and judges have been raised so high. Beginning in 1975, only about three years after I came back to the ABA, it became more difficult to fund the programs that were desirable and even necessary if we were going to meet our obligations to the profession and public. The work of the organized bar ranged from public policy on criminal correctional facilities, to fair elections, to the law of science and technology, to education for state trial judges.

Curtailing expenses was not our only option for solving our financial dilemma. We decided to increase substantially the fundraising efforts for the public service and educational programs of the ABA. We would do this through the ABA's Fund for Public Education, which was created in 1961 as the entity for soliciting and accepting 501(c)(3) tax-exempt grants for ABA law-related public service and educational activities. The funding was primarily through grants from foundations and government, and by 1976, the Fund had received grants and other revenues of over $9 million. Some 80 programs of lawyer-volunteer efforts and professional staff were supported by these funds.

Tax-exempt grants to the ABA Fund for Public Education, as it was called then (it has been changed to ABA Fund for Justice and Education) for our public service and educational activities had been encouraging, but were fewer because of cutbacks everywhere in foundation and government grant making. Further, we had not attempted to seek contributions from law firms, individual lawyers and corporations to supplement the grants. These were potential contributors virtually untapped.

The activities of the FPE became one of my major priorities over the next two years. David Andrews, in his role as ABA treasurer, and I worked together for several months to hire a new professional fund-raiser to direct the FPE.

In 1977, our search led us to J. William Straughan, the chief development officer at Wake Forest University. Bill Straughan was a lawyer and an ordained Baptist minister who had special skills at organized fundraising.

His first recommendation was to create an Office of Resource Development, which we immediately implemented. This office consolidated and coordinated fundraising efforts for the ABA FPE, the American Bar Foundation (the research arm of the ABA) and the National Judicial College (the ABA-sponsored training school for state court judges).

Bill's next recommendation was to establish the "Second Century Fund," the entity to receive lawyer and other contributions for the ABA Fund for Public Education. It was created in 1978, the ABA's Centennial Year, as a way of heralding the association's second one hundred years. This was an unprecedented approach for fundraising by the ABA, and began with charter memberships of $10,000 that first were filled by past and present officers and board members. During its first year the SCF had 2,500 ABA members participating, and had raised over $2 million. It was on its way to being so successful that ABA President Leonard Janofsky said, "…the Second Century Fund is the sine qua non for the continuation of the quality and scope of vital activity that has become our hallmark in recent years."

Bill Straughan, David Andrews and I walked a journey together on the push to energize the Fund for Public Education, and get it on its way through grants and solicitations. In 2014, its successor, the ABA Fund for Justice and Education, provided the ABA with over $50 million annually in support of some 200 public service and educational programs, thus relieving the pressure on the operating budget that is dependent on dues.

Our Management Functions Are Split

In early 1979, a major staff change that involved Bert and me was instituted by the two of us and the Board of Governors. While Bert remained in the position of executive director, and he and I continued close collaboration, our functions were split into two distinct management areas. Bert would take on full-time Long-Range Planning and advisor to the president. I continued with the title of deputy executive director, but now with full responsibility for all of the staff operations, which included administration and finance as well as program activities.

The urgency for long-range planning now required Bert's full-time attention so that we would not flounder into future activities. He would work with a new Long-Range Planning Council of the ABA's top leaders. Further, because of the ABA president's increasing public exposure, he required Bert's constant attention, with advice and assistance. I would be directly responsible to the board for the operations of the staff, with Bert available as help-mate, but with minimal involvement.

Managers Always Face Contention

While I was not responsible for the association's directional Long-Range Planning, we needed full-time operational planning with a strong hand to lead it, and that fell to my department. From an association-wide perspective, did we have the correct number of staff members? Were we spending the correct amounts on travel? How could we take advantage of newly emerging video conferencing?

My administrative assistant, Norb Wegrzyn, was well qualified for this role. We decided to make him the director operational planning. This in turn created an opening as my administrative assistant, which following the requirement of our affirmative action plan, we posted for all employees to see. This was an important administrative, not a secretarial, position. It required knowledge of the operations of the association and the ability to speak in my behalf.

To our surprise, the team leader of our executive offices secretarial pool objected to the posting. I'll call her 'Mary Smith'. Mary claimed that she was first in line for my assistant's position, and that under the affirmative action plan, posting the open position was not required because she worked in my staff area. Therefore, she claimed, the act of posting for anybody to apply was to keep her from obtaining the job, and discriminatory because she was African-American. Posting was in violation of the plan, she claimed.

The ABA employed many African-Americans. Located on Chicago's South Side, we were close to homes of many minorities, and they filled many of our important staff positions, ranging from division director, to the head of the personnel department, to administrative and secretarial services. When, in 1976, affirmative action programs were being considered by employers everywhere, and had become mandatory for federal contractors, we at the ABA were leaders in drafting and implementing one. I took a strong personal hand in writing the plan, working closely with the Personnel Department (now Human Resources). While it was required of us as a federal program grantee, it also was the correct thing to do, and we went further in its provisions than we had to. One of the provisions involved posting open positions.

Posting open positions, so that all ABA staff would have a shot at apply-
ing, was an important provision of the plan. It required managers to post any
job that would be filled by somebody from outside their respective departments. However, it allowed a manager to promote a qualified person in his
or her area without posting; and did not require posting for a reassignment
within a department. The program was well received by the staff at all levels.

It didn't even occur to me to not post my administrative assistant's open
position. Mary Smith was not qualified to succeed Norb. Just because she was a
part of my "staff area" did not mean she was in line for the position. It had nothing whatsoever to do with race. Norb, to whom she reported, explained this to
her, and suggested that if she really thought she was qualified, she was welcome
to apply like anybody else. However, she wouldn't do it because she insisted
that she was entitled to the job, and should not have had to apply under the
posting provision. She called in the federal Equal Employment Opportunity
Commission and the Department of Labor. After their investigations, which
found nothing wrong with the posting, she was given a "right to sue" letter, and
brought a lawsuit against the ABA and me in federal district court.

More than a year later, U.S. Federal District Judge George Leighton
dismissed the case for failure to state a prima facie case. He admonished Mary
Smith and her attorney for bringing the suit to begin with, stating that he had
never heard of such a ridiculous charge that, by posting, our plan and federal
law were violated. In fact, he said, it was the other way around. Posting for all
to see, in and of itself, is anti-discriminatory.

One of the first persons to apply was Margaret Rhinehart, the assistant
to our director of administration and finance. Margaret was highly qualified,
having worked on the association's budgeting and program priorities. She
personified everything I needed, and I couldn't have gotten along without her.
She was African-American.

Why do I talk about this? It's because of how important it is to know that
in managing any organization of any size there always will be distractions that
take your time away from the important substantive work. Many will have
the ability to sap your strength by the end of the day. The hours this claim
gobbled up with lawyers over depositions and explaining to staff and officers
alike were legion. Mary's initial lawyer bowed out, and she started over with
another who held "Defend Mary Smith" fundraising rallies in South Side
neighborhoods. Because of the staff's interest in what was going on, I held an

all-staff meeting to explain the facts. Mary had it secretly recorded by another staff member, hoping I might say something that would help her in the trial. Fortunately, there were only positive reactions to the meeting from the staff, which included numerous African-Americans.

The lawsuit cost the ABA close to $100,000 for something that turned out to be nothing. It's especially interesting, I think, that even your best intentions, like implementing an affirmative action plan, can be turned around to bite you. Whatever Mary Smith's motives were for her claim, I didn't know. Whether they were honest and well meaning, or she simply was hoping to extract some money from the ABA, makes no difference. They confirmed that she was not the person for the job.

The Chief Justice of the United States, Warren E. Burger

Warren E. Burger was Chief Justice of the United States from 1969 to 1986. It should be noted (for the sake of it) that the title is not Chief Justice of the Supreme Court because the duties of the office are more than that. And, because of his official role and intense interest in improving the Judicial System in America, Chief Justice Burger had a special relationship with the American Bar Association. He looked to the ABA to help him carry out many of his ideas and recommendations.

Many people do not realize that the Chief Justice's responsibilities go beyond his role as one of the Justices in deciding cases. Unlike the other Supreme Court Justices, he is the head of the federal court system, and this carries multiple responsibilities. Judge Edward Tamm and Justice Paul Reardon wrote in the 1981 *Brigham Young University Law Review* that some reforms were attempted over the years, but it was not until Warren Burger was appointed Chief Justice of the United States that sustained progress in the administration of justice began to be made on a national scale.

Chief Justice Burger relished this role which was a labor of love for him. During his nomination hearing, he responded to a question by Senator James Eastland:

Mr. Chairman, if I were to be confirmed by the Senate, I would conceive my judicial duties to be...deciding cases. Above and beyond that...the Chief Justice is assigned many other duties, administrative in nature. I would think he has a very large responsibility to try to see that the judicial system functions more efficiently. He should certainly be alert to trying to find these improvements...And I would expect to devote every energy and every moment of the rest of my life to that end should I be confirmed.

During his time as Chief Justice, he did all that he could to fulfill that pledge; and the American Bar Association responded when he called on it for help. If it was something like omnibus judgeship legislation, our Washington Office would go to work. If it was judicial standards, our Judicial Administration Division and various ABA judicial committees would respond.

In his address at the 1976 ABA annual meeting, the Chief Justice stated that "in no comparable period of seven years had so much been done by any one profession to improve the administration of justice," and he complimented the ABA for its work on various fronts from its sponsorship of the National Judicial College of the State Judiciary, its support of the National Center for State Courts, its creation and funding of the ABA Commission on Correctional Facilities, and the creation of the Institute for Court Management, to the association's review of the standards of judicial conduct and of judicial administration. He spoke of the litigation explosion, and the efforts by the ABA to add more "badly-needed" federal judges, as well as the need for "impact statements on the courts" for each bill adopted by Congress.

The relationship between the Chief Justice and the ABA was ongoing, and I was one from the ABA who stayed in contact with his office about our activities of mutual interest. Although I spoke with the Chief Justice occasionally by phone, or in person at ABA meetings, my primary relationship was with his administrative assistant (now that position is Counselor to the Chief Justice because of its many varied duties), Mark Cannon, who was an astute professional in his own right. Mark was a prominent political scientist, with an ability to understand broader aspects of society, and an excellent administrator, who handled many of the Chief Justice's administrative duties at the Court. He immersed himself in judicial administration issues ranging from judicial education and judicial compensation to "what kind of disputes can be resolved thoroughly, more swiftly, and less expensively outside the framework of traditional judicial processes." Mark would serve as a go-between for me and the multitude of others who communicated with the Chief Justice, and always would efficiently arrange conversations between us when they were necessary or desirable.

After a few years of communicating with the Chief Justice, he sent me his picture inscribed,

For Lowell Beck, Esq.
With appreciation for support in our common efforts. Warren E. Burger

It could not have been a more satisfying experience than to have had an association with Warren Burger through my position at the American Bar Association. The mutual relationship between him, Mark Cannon, and several of us at the ABA was so close that it was like we were members of the same team. Actually we were. He provided us with the initiatives to get moving for constructive change, and with his stature and our leg work, together we accomplished improvements in the both the federal and state judicial systems.

The Chief Justice continued throughout his Court career to be a harsh critic of the legal system, which he diligently worked to improve; and at times the legal profession itself brought harsh words from him. In his "annual report" to the ABA in February 1984, just two years before his retirement from the Court, he highlighted the sharp decline in the public's confidence in the profession according to opinion polls. Here is an excerpt from that address:

"Does this decline in the standing of lawyers relate in some way to the high cost of legal services and the slow pace of justice? Does it come from a growing public opinion that our profession is lax in dealing with the incompetent lawyer or the errant and dishonest lawyer? The criticism of our profession is not casual or irresponsible."

The Availability of Legal Services and Group Legal Services

The Chief Justice's admonition about the high cost of legal services brings me to that subject. While the ABA fostered legal aid to the poor, and later the OEO Legal Services Program and the federal Legal Services Corporation, it had a difficult time over many years concluding how to effectively serve people of moderate means. We constantly were asking and studying how to provide appropriate access to legal services at costs the average person could afford.

The association devoted innumerable amounts of time, through its committees, sections, the Board of Governors, and House of Delegates, reviewing, discussing and debating what could be done to improve access and costs. Access to lawyers and costs of their service always have been an issue for persons of limited means, most of whom never have met a lawyer. For a will, divorce, or other personal legal issues, how do average persons find a lawyer, and how do they determine a lawyer's competency? And when they find one, maybe through a friend or relative, or by calling a bar association's lawyer referral service, how do they know what the lawyer might cost? These were serious issues when I was with the ABA, and they continued after I left. If you have an auto accident, your legal fees will be "contingent," based on the monetary recovery, if there is one. If there is no recovery, generally speaking the lawyer does not receive a fee. But if you wish to sue for actions such as divorce or child custody, the fee arrangement can be troublesome. Neither you nor the lawyer may know the final amount until the work is completed, and, depending on the number of hours that might be required by the lawyer, it might be considerably more than you can afford.

From 1972 until 1980, much of my attention was on the twin questions: how can lawyers be more accessible to the public, and how can they be affordable to the persons of moderate means? Several committees had agendas of dealing with separate parts of the questions, and a Consortium of five committees, ranging from Legal Aid to Lawyer Referral was created to provide coordination among them. By 1980, the committees dealing with the delivery of legal services had grown to nine. Conferences and meetings of bar associations, consumer groups, labor unions, and many others were held continuously to seek workable answers.

"Group legal services" and certification of legal specialists were examined many times. ABA conferences had names such as "Second National Conference on Legal Services and the Public," and "The Role of the Lawyer in the 80s." Prepaid and group legal service plans are highly varied. They may be plans that provide group rates to individual policyholders who join an organized group, and the plan coverage functions like insurance policies. The policyholder buys a "group-rate" insurance policy that covers the lawyer's expenses, depending on the complexity of the case.

Group plans may be offered by employers, labor unions or others with a prepaid legal services feature paid by payroll deduction, or offered free to group members as an employment or member benefit.

While these kinds of plans have expanded over the last few decades, their emergence didn't come easily. Some outside the profession opposed them as self-serving ways for lawyers to make more money. Many lawyers and bar associations opposed them because they feared the small general practitioner would be driven out by unethical or incompetent groups of lawyers tied into the respective group organizations. Others just felt that it would unnecessarily and detrimentally change the nature of the profession and, in particular, the independence of the lawyer and the confidentiality between lawyer and client. Aside from this opposition, they weren't accepted by the overall public as a necessary personal expense. In other words, "why would I ever need a lawyer anyway, and why should I prepay for legal services?"

The new plans also faced regulatory, legislative, taxation, and even code of ethics hurdles because they were insurance and/or employee benefit programs. One major hurdle was taxation. To be successful as a union collectively bargained benefit plan, as well as all employee plans, contributions to the plans had to be exempted from federal taxation. Provisions for a helpful exemption were included in the 1976 Tax Reform Act through the urging of the ABA and other interested groups.

There were antitrust concerns as well, and uncertainty as to whether plans were insurance or fringe benefits. In some states, insurance commissioners would not attempt to regulate the plans, nor did they allow them to operate even on an experimental basis. However, bar leaders like Bill McCalpin, Chesterfield Smith, John Cummiskey, and Martha Barnett (a Chesterfield colleague who became ABA president) overrode the opposition inside and outside the organized bar, and the ABA developed a program to provide technical support and encouragement to bar associations, unions and consumer groups wishing to organize them.

During the 1970s, the ABA created an affiliated organization, the American Prepaid Legal Services Institute, to assist in developing these plans and fostering their growth and successful operations. When it first was recommended, the House of Delegates deferred it. Interested bar leaders and ABA staff, including myself, had a lot of additional background work to do for the Institute finally to gain its approval by the House in 1975.

It took most of 1976 for us to get the Institute underway. The ABA Board of Governors initially appointed its board, and its staff director was a member of the ABA Legal Services department. Its director, Alex Schwartz, helped bring the Institute to maturity. It is functioning today, still an ABA affiliate, as a clearinghouse and technical assistance source for prepaid legal services and group legal services entities. Today, some 40 years later in 2015, many are served through these plans to gain immediate access to lawyers at fees for basic legal services set by the plans. Millions of others still obtain services of the general practitioners who don't utilize the plans.

ABA attention to access and costs for the middle class began in earnest in 1965, with the appointment of the Special Committee on Availability of Legal Services. Bill McCalpin served as its chairman for five years. The committee's members were some of the best and forward-looking thinkers in the legal profession, including Chesterfield Smith, who as a new ABA participant, credited the other committee members with "selling him" on becoming active in the association. Virtually all of the ABA's leaders continued seeking practical and workable ways to provide legal services to everybody, not just the poor and wealthy. The report of the Prepaid Legal Services Committee in 1976 summed up the atmosphere among most ABA leaders the first year of the Prepaid Institute's operations. Essentially, it said that, since 1965, the availability of legal services at affordable costs must be a reality for all Americans; that organized plans had merit, and that the legal profession, unions and consumer groups had a responsibility to make them work. It concluded by reiterating that the ABA would continue to work for improvements of all systems providing legal service, with the public interest as its clear guide.

While I gave ongoing attention to the "legal services" subject, the real workers in the vineyard were David Hayes and David Ellwanger who assisted the first "Availability" committee, and Director of Professional Services Terry Kramer and his staff, along with Alex Schwartz of the Institute, who provided leadership for several years.

More Changes Were Coming

During the coming year, 1980, the Beck family would experience more change which seemed to be a normal situation for us, and that change, along with my final years at the ABA, is the subject of the next chapter.

CHAPTER FOURTEEN

FINAL DAYS AT THE ABA
MOVE TO THE NATIONAL ASSOCIATION OF INDEPENDENT INSURERS
SOME FINAL THOUGHTS ON ABA DAYS

CHICAGO AND DES PLAINES, ILLINOIS, 1980

At a Christmas party in early December 1979, given by Bert and Betsy Early, I met Arthur Mertz, the president of the National Association of Independent Insurers. We compared experiences of association work, and found that they were similar. The Bert Early phrase of "servant/leader" was applicable to the staffs of both the ABA and NAII. There were some major differences, however. In the business trade association world, the board of directors sets policy, but expects the staff to provide expertise to the association's committees and board, and serve as public spokespersons. They were not considered to be "low profile," such as the staff of the ABA.

Secondly, the NAII, as a business trade group, represented the business interests of its more than 500 member property and casualty insurance companies in the state and federal legislative and regulatory areas, and in the public arena. The ABA also, in some situations, promoted public policies that would serve lawyers, such as allowing lawyers and other self-employed to establish tax protected retirement plans. But, mostly, the ABA focused on improvements in law, programs that were considered "public interest" such as the Twenty-Fifth Amendment on Presidential Succession, and legal representation for the poor and middle class. And, its professional expertise was provided to the federal administration and Congress in areas such as the quality of federal judges and federal tax policy.

Art Mertz told me that he was planning to retire in another year. Shepherding united public policies for 500 companies as diverse as Allstate and the one-state only Tennessee Farmers Mutual had become wearing for him. I told him about my experience, and how "wearing" at times the ABA was for me also, primarily because of the constant changing of association presidents, each with his own agenda that we were expected to promote, regardless of how it would interface (or interfere) with other ongoing programs. I said that actually being "in charge" with a set agenda, such as at the NAII, sounded good to me. With all of our shared frustrations, however, we agreed that we were in the right work, and enjoyed it, perhaps more than anything else we could do.

The next day I received a phone call from a man named Joel Spangler, who was conducting the search for the new NAII president. He said that Art Mertz suggested that he call me. Would I be interested in being considered for the job, he asked? Another candidate was under consideration, and the NAII wanted to make a decision soon; but while he had insurance expertise, he did not have association or lobbying experience, which was a negative for him. My problem was that, while I knew how to lobby and manage an association, I didn't have an insurance background. Spangler said that he didn't think my lack of insurance experience mattered, and that association leadership and lobbying experience were more important. The best of both worlds, of course, would be an insurance specialist with lobbying and association experience, but they had not found a candidate like that. I told Spangler that I would like to be considered.

The Job Interviews Begin

After meeting with Messrs. Spangler and Mertz, I was encouraged. I wanted this new job. The NAII headquarters office was in the Chicago area, so there was no need to move the family again. I was 46, and if I was going to make a change up, the timing was right. And, with this position, I'd be back in the public policy, lobbying fray, without leaving home. But, it wasn't a sure thing. I learned that my competition was the CEO of an NAII member insurance company from Nebraska, and he was well known to both the NAII board and staff.

Within a couple of days I met with the NAII board's executive committee in Chicago. Some of the members were Gen. Robert McDermott, CEO of USAA; Don Schaffer, senior vice president and general counsel of Allstate (the only non-CEO on the board); Joe Lancaster, CEO of Tennessee Farmers Insurance (farm bureau); George Walker of Concord (NH) Insurance; and Frank Barrett, CEO of Omaha Indemnity. They were all friendly, and some seemed encouraging even though the questions were right on target. They were particularly interested in Common Cause because it seemed left wing to some of them (the name, after all, wasn't at all conventional). I explained that it was nonpartisan, and that most of the positions it took while I was there were in support of Nixon public policies and improvements in political processes.

The most insightful question related to the ABA versus NAII staff functions. Two NAII executive committee members were lawyers, and knew how the ABA operated. They wondered if I, having been virtually subservient to the ABA elected officials, could lead an organization as the public spokesman and guiding officer. In direct contrast to my role at the ABA, they as businessmen didn't want to give speeches, testify, and appear in the media. That was the NAII staff's role.

The NAII committee didn't seem concerned about my lack of insurance expertise. That was abundant already on the staff, and certainly in the company membership. They all were welcoming, but that didn't tell me anything except I knew I would like working for them.

Days of Waiting

Surely you know what it's like when you're waiting to hear about something you want, and don't hear a thing. Why aren't they making a decision, or at least calling me with information about the process? That's how it was after my interview, and it was particularly frustrating because Art Mertz had said that a decision would be made before Christmas. When you're waiting like this, it's the most important thing on your mind, and it's hard to realize that the decision-makers aren't also thinking about this every waking minute. Art told me that it was taking longer than he had anticipated, and he would be in touch with me. But, he didn't call, and I didn't want to badger him.

While I was waiting, decisions had to be made before January 1 about my participation in ABA events. Leonard Janofsky, the new ABA president, asked me to accompany a group of ABA board members to meetings in Taiwan in February as guests of the Taiwan Law Society. He then wanted me, with a board member, to proceed from Taiwan to Japan and Singapore to invite leading Asian economic officials to speak about the Asian economy at the 1980 ABA annual meeting in Hawaii.

Further, Mr. Janofsky had been invited to speak at the August meeting of the International Law Society about the new American rules on lawyer advertising. It would be in Berlin, and because he was unable to attend, wanted me to do it. Under this arrangement, Myrna and I, after the ABA's Hawaii annual meeting, would attend the extension of that meeting in Sydney, and then travel to Berlin from Australia.

These Taiwan, Hawaii, Sydney and Berlin trips had to be nailed down; and, of course, a new job would cancel them all. So, I had to agree, but was urgently hoping to get some word from the NAII.

At the same time, Bert, David Hayes and I were immersed with former ABA President Justin Stanley in plans for moving the ABA headquarters from its University of Chicago location to the Near North Side of Chicago. This was delicate and confidential work because of the politics of changing locations, the selection of the new location and the costs. The report was to be presented to the ABA board in April, and I couldn't wait much longer without telling the ABA if I was leaving.

Art was embarrassed. He did not understand why the committee was taking so long, and understood my dilemma. Just before Christmas, he called to say that the committee had selected the other candidate, Ben Nelson. Nelson, who later became Nebraska governor and U.S. senator, had insurance experience, and that won out over my lobbying and association background. I suspected that I hadn't passed muster because of Common Cause, but Art assured me that wasn't the case. Instead, he said, the committee members liked that. They liked the experience I had had with such high-level people, and on nationally important issues. Two members were admirers of John W. Gardner. One member, a staunch conservative, thought that anybody who could weather successfully the internal politics of the American Bar Association could easily manage the NAII. Art confided that it wasn't a unanimous decision, and that some had argued strongly for me. Although I was disappointed, I could now get on with my ABA work. I knew I had interesting and enjoyable days ahead at the ABA.

Clark Wadlow, the ABA board's assistant secretary and youngest member, and I made the trip together to Japan and Singapore after Taiwan. We were successful in Tokyo in enlisting a prominent Japanese official as a speaker, but our visit to Singapore was just that: a nice visit. We couldn't arrange a meeting there with the right officials. Since we were so close to Bangkok, Thailand, and neither Clark nor I had been there, Mr. Janofsky told us to visit there also as a little bonus. All in all, it was a "trip of a lifetime," one that I never would have had if I had been offered the NAII job.

A Great Surprise

The ABA 1980 April board meeting was in Charlotte, North Carolina, and I wasn't very happy. As the staff officer now with full responsibility for staff management, I was locked in disagreement with the president-elect, Reece Smith, on staff salary increases. Reece, who had been an officer of the Junior Bar when I first was hired, and a good friend of mine, was insisting on drastic staff funding cuts. He was adamantly against any substantial over-all salary increase, and considered my recommended increase of about three percent, to be substantial. I argued that it wasn't substantial at all, that some staff would get less than that, and that some high performers had to have more. At the ABA then, three board committees reviewed staff salaries, and each committee agreed with me over Reece's objections. He told me that I should be well prepared at the full board meeting because he would oppose me there as well. I said, "Reece, I've won this in every committee meeting, and those committee members make up a strong majority of the board. Why are you continuing this, and it doesn't come across well that you and I can't get together on something like this, particularly when I've won each time?" He responded that it was the principle, that we couldn't afford it, and he was going to oppose me.

I had two primary responsibilities when the board convened. One was to assist Mr. Stanley with his presentation on relocating the headquarters office, and the other was to present my staff salary recommendation. During the break following Mr. Stanley's successful presentation, I was at my seat putting the final touches on the salary comments. All of a sudden, Myrna appeared to tell me about a phone call waiting. Spouses never entered the "inner sanctum" of ABA board meetings, so I was startled to see her. She said, "Joel Spangler, the search firm man, is on the phone, and wants to talk with you right away. He said that the NAII board is meeting in Key Biscayne, Florida right now, and that Mr. Nelson has decided not to take the job of NAII president. They want you to take it, and want you to come to their meeting now. Can you take his call?"

I was stunned. Yes, I wanted the job, and it couldn't have come at a bet-ter time. I told Myrna to tell him that I couldn't take the call now, but that I would take the job, would call him after the board meeting adjourned, and would fly to Florida the next morning.

I won the salary vote, with only two against me and one abstention. The real story here, though, is that, with the new job in hand, I gave the most brilliant presentation of my career. I hadn't ever spoken better and haven't since. Several board members complimented me, and the staff members who heard me were happy that we had so much board support. None knew that I soon would be leaving.

The ABA Response Was Supportive

Immediately following the board meeting, I asked President Janofsky, Reece Smith and Bert to meet with me. Reece was like my big brother again. Within minutes, the acrimony of the salary increase was already behind us. All three of them were understanding, and wished me well. Most of all, they complimented me on a new position where I would be fully in charge, and also with opportunities for greater compensation. In the 1980s, business trade groups paid their top staff executives more than professional associations. They felt that, if I was going to make a change, I was at the right age, and that opportunities like this didn't come along every day.

So, the next morning, I was on a plane to Miami and the Key Biscayne board meeting of the NAII. What was to come was an even greater surprise to the NAII staff than it had been to me.

The Top NAII Staff Was in Shock

When I arrived at the Key Biscayne Hotel, I couldn't imagine what the future would be like. While I had met the NAII executive committee members, the rest of the board members would be entirely new to me. On the staff, I knew Art Mertz, and had met Gene Bagatti, the chief administrative officer, but no others. How would the other staff members, many experienced "long-timers," respond to me?

Perhaps most of all, what would it be like to leave the ABA again, my employment "home" for so long? We were like a family... the board, committee members, and staff, working together and traveling together. I had grown up there, and this NAII would be a new world to me. And, after all, the ABA was *the* American Bar Association, a nationally prominent organization known by virtually everybody. It was an organization I had helped build and gain national prominence. The National Association of Independent Insurers? Who, outside the insurance business, had heard of it?

When I expressed some concern to Art and Gene about the staff's potential reaction, they told me not to worry. They supported me, and, in particular, it helped to hear that from Gene, a long-standing no-nonsense staff officer who was highly respected by the board and staff alike. As I understood it, he had been a party to the decision.

The meeting with the board, in executive session without staff present except Art and Gene, was friendly and receptive. The board members seemed genuinely pleased to have me with them, and several expressed that view privately to me, as well as in the board meeting.

The reaction of the staff, however, wasn't exactly an overwhelmingly welcoming one. They were expecting Ben Nelson to be the new executive vice president who would take over as president in a year. They knew Ben Nelson. He chaired NAII committees. He visited the headquarters office. He was one of them, and a respected CEO of an NAII member insurance company. From their standpoint, he couldn't have been a better choice to succeed Art Mertz, and they were expecting him to walk in the door any minute. Instead, it was a guy named Beck, a non-insurance person whom they didn't know at all. And, to make matters worse, he was directly out of the American Bar Association. Insurance people disliked lawyers. One staff member questioned whether Lowell Beck actually was being hired to be the next president. Maybe the board had decided, he said, to have a new executive vice president, with the new president to be decided later.

But that wasn't the case. Art and Gene were already ahead of curve. To make it clear that I was Art's replacement, I was named Executive Vice President and President-Elect.

When the shock wore off, most staff members appeared welcoming, even if some were having a hard time accepting what had happened. I have to say, though, that, overall, most took it pretty well. One had applied for the job, and unfortunately his disappointment tended to carry over for a while. Another, Washington, D.C. Vice President Darrell Coover, had strong reservations because he was certain I was too liberal. Darrell was a staunch conservative. He was known as such in Washington, and had been the chief staff assistant to Senator Barry Goldwater. The senator had been Darrell's best man at his wedding. Darrell, however, gave me the benefit of the doubt. He probably was more shocked than anybody by my appointment, but couldn't have been more welcoming, and was the quintessential person of quality and grace. He made it clear that he would assist me in every way, and he stuck by it for all of our many years together. He was particularly pleased that the NAII would have a president who understood Washington and what he did there.

Even Our Children Were Surprised

Our children, Rich, Jonathan, and Lori, knew life in the ABA. They traveled frequently with us to ABA meetings, and knew the children of other staff and officers. They had met famous people, and always seemed pleased that their dad worked for a well-known and *prestigious* organization. Even Justice Lewis Powell knew them, and would ask about them by name. But, again, the National Association of Independent Insurers? What was that? The abruptness of this decision was also a factor. They had had no warning that I was even thinking about a change. But, after all, one was a teenager and the other two younger, so after we discussed it, they went on with their lives.

July 1 Was My First NAII Day, but Some ABA Days Were Still Ahead

I didn't begin my work at the NAII until July 1. This had come too quickly for me to close shop immediately at the ABA. There were management decisions yet to be made and work to complete, such as that of the headquarters relocation committee. As much as I had worked on moving the ABA headquarters to a more convenient and desirable downtown location, I wouldn't be around to enjoy it.

One major decision would depend on the NAII. Since I would be officially at the NAII in August, would Myrna and I be able to say an "official goodbye" at the ABA Hawaii annual meeting and keep my engagement to speak at the International Bar meeting? Art Mertz and the NAII executive committee approved the trip, and agreed to pay for it. How could we have wanted anything more welcoming than that?

I'll always remember the day I closed my desk drawers, said goodbye, and walked to my car in the bar center's parking lot. I had finished my work and been roasted unmercifully at a staff party. I was leaving the place I knew so well, spanning some 20 years.

That evening, I received a phone call from Bernard Segal, the former ABA president who was president-elect when I joined John Gardner at the

Urban Coalition in 1968. He said that he remembered when I left then, and how he had assured me it was the correct thing to do even though he had relied on me. He and I worked closely together when he was president-elect. I met with him in his Philadelphia law office to help him prepare for his year as president, and held him in high esteem. He was the first Jewish president of the Philadelphia Bar Association and the first Jewish president of the ABA. It was a privilege to accompany him to dinner at the Philadelphia Union League Club on the day he became its first Jewish member.

Bernie Segal was one of premier lawyers who argued cases before the U.S. Supreme Court, with more than 50 appearances. He was the ABA leader who convinced Attorney General Brownell and President Eisenhower that the federal administration should look to the ABA to evaluate the quality of nominees to the federal bench; and he spearheaded the Lawyers Committee for Civil Rights for President Kennedy. He was one of the great lawyers.

Just before and when he was president-elect in 1967 and 1968, it was nothing to him to call me at home near midnight, or even later, to discuss his agenda of the week, and sometimes the conversation would go for at least two hours. At that time I was developing the ABA's public service programs, and next to judicial administration, public service was Bernie's highest objective for the ABA. When I returned to the ABA in 1972, he was still an active leader as a former ABA president, and resumed his phone calls. I finally told him that I had to get to sleep, but that seldom made any difference to Bernie. This was the time he did his ABA work. He just didn't sleep.

This time his call was to wish me well with the NAII, and also to tell me how my timing for a major career move was perfect. I was 34 when he told me it was the correct move to work with John Gardner. Now I was 46. Making a move to a top position by age 50 was, to him, the right time. After that, he said, the opportunities at the top became fewer and fewer. This timing allows you to bring years of experience to the new job, while at the same time starting a new life of many years with new experiences. I've always remembered that phone call as a highlighted personal conversation, not only because of who called me, but because of what he said.

My Last ABA Annual Meeting, and Our Trip Around the World

The entire Beck family went to Hawaii in August 1980 to attend our last ABA annual meeting. It was our ABA last hurrah because of the friendships that Myrna and I, and even Rich, age 16, and Jonathan, 12, had made with the officers and their spouses, children and grandchildren. While I already had left the association, in June, to my surprise, Bert had announced his resignation, effective September 1, 1981. It was my swan song, and Bert's wasn't far away.

Bert introduced me to the House of Delegates for brief remarks. I thanked its members for the privilege of serving the association, and mentioned my optimism about its future. In his introduction, Bert mentioned his own decision to leave in a year and said:

> *The American Bar Association has grown and changed dramatically during the past decades as we have adapted to the changing needs of the legal profession and the society we serve. The departure of your two top staff officers now presents a further opportunity for change.... During the two decades Lowell and I have been with the ABA, we have seen and participated in the transformation of the American Bar Association from a small, provincial fraternity into the national voice of the legal profession.*

President Janofsky, in his report to the House, thanked me and mentioned my responsibilities. He recounted all of my positions with the ABA, and concluded with...*He has made enormous contributions to the legal profession and to this Association through his long years of loyal and devoted service.*

It was heady stuff for me.

After the annual meeting, our children left for home with Myrna's mom and stepfather, Madge and Pete Tani, who had accompanied us to Hawaii. Myrna and I then flew to Australia for the extended leg of the meeting with Australian lawyers. From there, we flew to Taiwan, where we met with Taiwanese lawyers and their spouses. In Hong Kong, we stayed with a college friend, Ron Erickson, and his wife, Gaby, a lovely Chinese who showed us around the city with more knowledge than any tour director could possibly give. After a visit to Bangkok, we flew to Berlin through New Delhi, and while we didn't depart our plane there, we felt the stultifying Indian August heat rushing through the plane's open door. We can still feel that heat, and wonder how anybody survives it.

The delegates to the International Bar Association listened to my talk on American advertising with rapt attention. Advertising by lawyers was unheard of in other parts of the world. It was considered unprofessional, and tainted as being too commercial, just as it had been for years in the United States. The First Amendment was not an issue in other countries. After I explained the history of lawyer advertising in America and the rationale of the Supreme Court decision, I showed a brief film of examples of the new advertising. When my favorite, a lawyer with beautiful scantily clothed babes emerging from the swimming pool with strings of pearls and diamonds dangling from their necks and arms, popped up, the entire room broke out in laughter. They couldn't believe that we in America allowed such a thing.

That talk was my last official ABA act. While I did serve on the ALI-ABA Committee on Continuing Professional Education as an ABA representative, and on a special committee on insurance regulation from which I debated a regulatory issue before the House of Delegates, I did not remain active. I didn't have time. What was to come next at the NAII was all-consuming.

Final Thoughts on the ABA Years

These chapters on my years with the American Bar Association were not an ABA history. Such an effort would take volumes, and is contained in the printed annual reports of the association. The chapters aren't an attempted accounting of everything I did there. They're the story of some of the highlights of my role that give a "flavor" of what each day was like. I couldn't recount all of the administrative decisions or programmatic recommendations I made, and even if I could, nobody would be interested. I mentioned some difficult personnel situations because they were examples of what happens in managing any organization. Managers of other groups, particularly non-profit associations, will identify with them.

Just as I can't discuss all of the programs, I can't name all of the people, volunteer lawyer-leaders and staff as well, whom I respected and either assisted or relied on. I regret this because there were so many for whom I'm everlastingly grateful. And I haven't been able to highlight, or even mention, all of the public leaders, ranging from U.S. Senators to U.S. Representatives to Judge Advocates General of the Armed Forces whom I had the privilege of knowing. The years at the ABA were a privilege for me, for which, again, I am forever grateful.

To conclude the discussion of the ABA, I offer some statistics and comments about the changes that occurred in the association during my span of 20 years there. This information, most of it from the 1980 ABA Annual Report, places its growth and importance in full perspective.

When I joined the staff in late 1959, the association crossed its 90,000-member mark. When I left in 1980, its membership had grown to over 250,000. In 1963, there were 62,000 members in 18 dues-paying Sections. In 1980, there were 256,000 members in 24 dues-paying Sections. The Young Lawyers Division had 34,000 members under the age of 36 in 1966, representing some 35 percent of the total ABA membership of 121,000. In 1980, the division had 131,000, representing 51 percent of the total membership of 257,000. In 2014, the ABA's membership stood at some 400,000.

In 1959, there were few program activities conducted by the ABA. In 1980, its committees, commissions, sections and divisions conducted scores of programs, including more than 85 public service and educational programs funded in whole or in part by the association's Fund for Public Education. In 1960, the staff numbered less than 50 people, many stamping out metal name/address plates. By 1980, to support its myriad of program and legislative activities, a staff of 460 was located at the American Bar Center, a new annex office in downtown Chicago, and in Washington, D.C. When I was hired, I was the seventh lawyer in its history to work for the ABA. When I left, some 40 lawyers were on the staff. In 1960, the ABA's annual income was less than $2 million; in 1980, its combined income from dues and grants totaled $34 million.

While the number of committees had not increased significantly, the concept of ABA commissions to include various non-lawyer disciplines in the deliberative processes and program activities was created. In 1980 there were ten commissions, addressing such topics as Law and the Economy, Legal Problems of the Elderly, the Mentally Disabled, and Reduction of Court Costs and Delays. The number of ABA meetings for all programs and public policy purposes was almost incomprehensible. By 1980, ABA entities were conducting more than 2,000 meetings each year, and at the 1979 annual meeting alone, more than 1,000 meetings were held over a period of eight days.

Of special note is the work of the Commission on Evaluation of Professional Standards, a 13-member interdisciplinary group chaired by Robert Kutak, formerly the administrative assistant to Senator Hruska of

Nebraska, and founder of the Kutak Rock law firm in Omaha. With the legal profession under attack after Watergate, the "Kutak Commission" proposed Model Rules of ethical standards relating to lawyers and law practice. These rules, sensitive and controversial, addressed such issues as lawyer/client confidentiality, advertising and solicitation, and conflicts of interest. After overwhelming approval by the ABA House of Delegates, they were adopted in a great majority of states.

One of my proudest acts was to introduce Bob Kutak to the ABA when he assisted Senator Hruska, and to see him become an active leader in the association. He initially was unaware of its work, and later became one of the heralded member / leaders.

My close friend from law school, Dick Wiley, former chairman of the Federal Communications Commission and founder of the Wiley Rein law firm in Washington, became an active ABA leader through my encouragement. He was elected chairman of the Young Lawyers Section, accepted appointment as chairman of the ABA Special Committee on Lawyers in Government, and later as chairman of the Board of Editors of the American Bar Association Journal. *Dick was interested in working as a volunteer in the first Nixon presidential campaign, and I was able to introduce him to Charles Rhyne, who was chairman of the national volunteers for Nixon. Charlie appointed Dick chairman of the national young lawyers volunteers, and from that post he developed his highly successful, distinguished career. As chairman of the FCC, he was responsible for farsightedly mandating High Definition television, which was baffling to most people and controversial at the time. In private life, he became one of the leading communications lawyers; and Wiley Rein, under his leadership, became the premier communications law firm in the country.*

Yet another good friend, John Feerick, while serving as dean of the Fordham Law School after his work on the Twenty-Fifth Amendment, continued his activities with the ABA as chairman of the Special Committee on Election Law and Voter Participation that produced landmark recommendations in those fields. I also highlighted some of his achievements and high honors earlier. John's predecessor Election Law committee chairman was Talbot (Sandy) D'Alemberte, whose committee leadership led him into the ABA's officers' chairs and the ABA presidency.

I could not conclude the section on the American Bar Association without a special mention of my good friend and colleague of so many years, David Hayes. David was the stalwart and enduring staff executive of the American Bar Association, having served on the staff for some 30 years. As general counsel of the Illinois State Bar Association, he was recruited by Bert Early in 1963 to head the departments of unauthorized practice of law and ethical standards, and soon after that was made assistant executive director. He and I served side by side, and his leadership was evident in virtually all ABA activities. He was appointed executive director in 1990, and served as the ABA's chief staff officer until he retired in 1994.

With all of growth of activity and the fulfillment I was experiencing at the American Bar Association, why would I want to leave it? Because it was time. I had worked in that vineyard long enough. It was time for a fresh start with new challenges at, according to Bernie Segal, the right age.

A MEMORIAL TO BERT EARLY

After retiring from the ABA, Bert Early entered the business of searching for lawyers. He founded and headed the country's leading search firm for law firm partners and corporate general counsel. He died on August 4, 2013, at the age of 91.

Most of us, to succeed in the workplace, and life in general for that matter, need a helpmate, mentor and friend... somebody who takes a personal interest in you and provides opportunities for you to grow and succeed. Bert Early was that most important helpmate, mentor and friend for me. I was privileged to be asked to give comments at his memorial service. In tribute to him, I spoke about his indisputable achievements as the quintessential executive director who brought the American Bar Association to maturity. He did this with the help of his wife, Betsy, at his side, who was hailed by association leaders as the Leading Lady of the ABA.

The "Early Era" was best described by former ABA President Charles Rhyne, who said, "When I first met Bert, I knew he was a leader. I knew that if we followed where he led, his dreams would become our dreams and would be accomplished. And they have been. He is recognized throughout the Nation and throughout the World as one of the great men of the law of our day."

I can only say to that..."Amen."

CHAPTER FIFTEEN

The National Association of Independent Insurers
Management Responsibilities
The Advent of Vehicle Airbags
The Natural Disaster Crises and Liability Crises

DES PLAINES, ILLINOIS, 1980–1996

Just as my narrative of the ABA was not a history of it, this chapter isn't a history of the NAII either. The history is captured in a book titled *The Story of an American Insurance Revolution*, published in 1995 for NAII's 50th anniversary. So, as with the ABA chapter, I'll discuss only situations that continue in my memory as having a lasting effect. Except in highlighting a few personnel situations, seemingly unique to professional and trade organizations, this chapter focuses on my role with specific programs and public issues as executive vice president, and then as CEO and president of the Association.

What Is the NAII? (Now the Property Casualty Insurers Association of American, known as PCI)

The question still asked today is "What is an *independent insurer?*" The term stems from a 1944 U.S. Supreme Court decision *(Southeastern Underwriters)* and the 1945 enactment of federal legislation known as the McCarran-Ferguson Act. Prior to these actions, the property and casualty insurance industry was run by a cartel of large Eastern companies such as Aetna and Travelers who set their rates in lock step through an industry-owned "rating" bureau known as ISO (Insurance Services Office). These rates were enforced by the states, and companies could not deviate from them. These large bureau companies did not consider themselves subject to federal antitrust laws, and they operated accordingly in setting rates and stymieing innovation in insurance products. Consequently, competition in the industry was miniscule, causing higher than necessary rates; and vast segments of the market, such as farmers, small business people, motor club members and military personnel were either underserved or not served at all if the large giants would not sell to them. And Aetna, for example, might not consider it profitable or convenient to sell a liability policy to a Tennessee farmer or a military officer, but their lock-step rates and business practices would prevent entrepreneurs from entering the marketplace.

Examples of "independent" companies were the upstart and fledgling State Farm and Allstate companies. State Farm was trying to sell to rural people with products and rates unavailable among the giants. Allstate was a subsidiary of Sears that was beginning to sell insurance in its stores. Both were considered outcasts by the industry's leaders, and were looked upon as unprofessionals who couldn't be depended on. They wanted to go their own respective ways, as *independent companies*, by setting rates lower than those issued by the rating bureaus and mandated by the states.

The Supreme Court decision ruled that the industry was subject to federal antitrust laws, and consequently had to refrain from rate setting in lock step. Further, insurance companies could not engage in *any* practices that involved rate sharing. Congress realized that insurers could not operate (sharing data, developing rates, pooling resources on large risks, for instance) without a limited exemption from the antitrust laws; so it enacted the McCarran-Ferguson Act, which did not allow joint rate-setting, but gave insurers a narrow lane of safety from antitrust restrictions in which to operate. The Act also delegated to the states the authority regulate insurance, acknowledging that the best insurance regulation is that closest and most accessible to the people.

In this period of uncertainty and turmoil in the insurance industry, the NAII was formed to be the voice of the small companies that were trying to succeed. Leading its founding were officers of State Farm and Allstate, fierce competitors, but also united in wanting to develop their own individual insurance products and their own rates without dictation by others. Nor did most of the founders want to sell through agents other than their own. They were "direct writers" who sold to policyholders without a middleman agent like the giant companies retained, and this was a way they could lower rates.

Other companies were attempting to establish themselves the same way in the insurance business. Farm bureaus in the various states and motor club companies were examples.

As a youngster, I can remember my dad talking about his automobile insurance. State Farm's headquarters were (and are) in Bloomington, Illinois, just a few miles from Peoria. I don't know how I can remember this now, but I do. Dad said that he would continue buying Travelers' auto insurance instead of changing to the new State Farm "just down the road" because he didn't know if State Farm could be depended on to stay in business.

That was why the NAII was created: to give the small and middle-sized property casualty insurance companies a national voice to advocate their independence from the large Eastern companies in both rates and products; and to vigorously support state regulation of insurance, which Congress had delegated to the states. A revolution had been created in the insurance industry; and consequently those small insurers who created the NAII grew, over 50 years, into the dominant personal auto and homeowners insurers in America.

With this drastic change came the need for companies to meet new state statistical requirements for which many of them were unprepared. While collective rate-making was prohibited under the new law, companies and state regulators were allowed "a window" to collect and disseminate information to assist companies in making their individual rates. Within two years, the NAII established the Independent Statistical Service as a department to collect statistics and cooperate with state regulators in formulating statistical plans, and serving as statistical agents for companies. This service supplemented the NAII's advocacy mission by giving the independent companies a way to adhere to state-required statistical plans by not having to work with the detested insurance rate-making bureau, ISO. By the end of 1947, 31 state regulators had approved the new NAII-sponsored plans. There was no longer a need for reliance on any other industry statistical service, and the "independents" were on their way, thanks to the leaders of the new NAII.

The NAII was founded by 39 insurance companies. By 1995, its company membership had grown to over 500 member insurance companies. From an NAII informational brochure, here is what the NAII does:

Our staff of about 180 includes attorneys, legislative and regulatory analysts, experts in all phases of insurance operations, statisticians, researchers, and public relations practitioners.

We are first and foremost an advocate on both state and federal levels for our members before legislatures, regulatory and other government agencies and, increasingly, the courts.

We monitor Congress and the federal agencies and all the state legislatures, tracking thousands of bills and proposals annually, and delivering formal testimony on hundreds of them.

In the role of mediator, we furnish data, expertise and company viewpoints to regulators, legislators, and agencies of the state and federal governments.

To our members, we provide a broad range of political advocacy, statistical support and technical assistance.

With conferences and seminars, numerous publications and daily personal contact, we keep members current on developments and alert them to threats, issues and new ideas. We also help our members communicate with their policyholders and the public.

We serve as a rallying point for our companies, organize grass roots efforts, maintain a political action committee, and file amicus briefs on their behalf.

We work closely with, and financially support, numerous groups within and outside the insurance industry, in fields of safety, research, and political activity.

A president appointed by the elected Board of Governors heads the staff. The board sets NAII policy. We focus on members' views and resolve problems through more than a score of committees, which tap the reservoir of talent and skill in our membership. All members of the NAII, regardless of size, have one vote on voting matters.

The NAII headquarters are in Des Plaines, Illinois, outside Chicago. We maintain a Washington, D.C., office and regional offices in Annapolis, Maryland; Atlanta, Georgia; and Sacramento, California.

A Year of Learning and Beginning to Manage the Staff

I would not take over as CEO and president until Art Mertz retired at the NAII's annual meeting in 1981. So for the rest of 1980 and until November 1981, I became acquainted with the staff and board members. I began personal visits to several board members; and the first was with the 1980 NAII chairman, Joe Lancaster, head of the Tennessee Farmers Mutual Insurance Company. He and his wife, Betty, invited me to stay at their home in Columbia, Tennessee, and this welcoming hospitality told me the NAII was a person-friendly workplace. Joe's company was affiliated with the Tennessee Farm Bureau, and wrote insurance only in Tennessee. It was one of the most highly rated insurers in the country, and I soon learned that state regulation, instead of federal regulation of insurance, was vitally important to companies like this. Federal regulation, far removed from the local level and more adaptable to large interstate companies, could have been the death knell to Tennessee Farmers and dozens of other insurers who wrote in one state or in one region. The public that relied on these companies would suffer if the companies were strangled by federal regulation under the rubric of "one regulation fits all."

Joe Lancaster and I developed a strong personal relationship that has lasted throughout the years. He was my first teacher in the insurance industry, and one of the individuals who most made my NAII life so enjoyable. Whenever the large company elites of the East would look down their noses at the small guys as unimportant in the insurance industry, I pointed to Joe Lancaster and Tennessee Farmers to prove them wrong. Here was an insurance executive of impeccable personal integrity, who ran a company with top claim and policyholder service, and an A.M. Best rating of A++ (Superior) for financial strength.

Joe and I didn't focus together only on business matters. He and his teenage son, Ed, both outstanding athletes, wished to learn to ski. Soon after we became acquainted, they joined my young son, Jonathan, and me at Alpine Valley, Wisconsin for lessons (from professionals, not the Becks), and a few days on the slopes. Not that Wisconsin provided the most advanced skiing, but it was fine for us.

Joe and his company exemplified a primary reason I was glad to be with the NAII. Most of my career had been devoted to issues in the public interest and continuing education arenas. While I always would consider them of primary importance, I had come to feel that advocating for business was also crucial. From my experiences with the ABA, and particularly working with the ABA's Commission on the Law and Economy, I believed there were too many wasteful and overlapping laws and regulations facing businesses, as well intentioned as they were. So it was easy for me to be an enthusiastic advocate for NAII member companies…to try to help them operate as competitively as possible under necessary, but minimal, regulation of the individual states, and not the "one fits all" of the federal government.

That first visit to Joe went so well that it prompted me to begin visits to the hometowns of other board members. Later, the visits would broaden out to non-board member companies where I would discuss issues with their CEOs and executive staffs. These visits were essential to learning about insurance operations and the concerns of the highly diversified group of NAII member companies. (The NAII is a cross-section of the insurance industry.

Its membership comprises every type of company, including stock, mutual, reciprocal, Lloyds and other high risk "surplus lines" insurers; and every type of marketing system including direct writer, independent agency, mail order, independent contractor and telemarketing.)

Most of all, I was the representative of the NAII staff, and knowing the executives of our members on a first-hand basis by meeting with them in their home offices was a top priority of mine during my entire time at the NAII. This paid off constantly with cooperative working relationships.

Helping at my side during the learning period and until his retirement shortly before my own, was Bob Wegenke, the NAII senior vice president and secretary. He had joined the staff in 1962, having been a Wisconsin insurance agency owner and a researcher with the Wisconsin Insurance Department. He was a walking encyclopedia of insurance company operations, and knew the member companies inside and out. At the NAII, as secretary, he managed the agendas and meetings of the board, and handled member relations and recruitment.

Staff Issues Were Similar to the ABA's

In November 1980, soon after I was ensconced at the NAII, the MGM Grand Hotel in Las Vegas was hit with a devastating fire, and 85 people died. The MGM Grand had been reserved as the site for the NAII's November 1981 annual meeting. We had to hurriedly arrange for a different hotel in a different city, and this was not easy. While the NAII's annual meetings were not as large and complex as the ABA's, it drew more than 2,000 participants, and all first-class rooms and dozens of meeting rooms were needed. The NAII annual meetings were grand insurance "bazaars" of reinsurers meeting with "primary" insurers to arrange reinsurance contracts for the coming year. Along with the business of arranging reinsurance contracts, it was the largest meeting in the insurance industry where insurance public policy and national political issues were discussed. Dozens of vendors came to display their products. Hotel sites for meetings of this size were always finalized long, sometimes years, in advance.

The only remaining available hotel suitable for the 1981 meeting was the Sheraton Waikiki in Honolulu. Going to Honolulu presented problems because money was tight, and insurance company expenditures were under the watchful eyes of their own executives, the public and state insurance commissioners. Going to Hawaii was considered by some as an unnecessary luxury and wasteful expenditure. But we had no other choice if we were going to accommodate all who needed to attend.

To keep expenses at a minimum, we had to reduce the number of staff members who normally would attend an annual meeting. We decided to take only those who had either an essential role in managing the meeting or in addressing the most current public policy considerations. By early 1981, I was fully in charge of staff operations, and it was my job to decide which staff members would go.

After we had informed the staff of who would be going, I received a phone call from the chairman of one of the association's committees. He said that his committee's staff member had asked him to call me to ask that I allow him to go to Hawaii. The chairman said that the committee would hold a short meeting there, but acknowledged that staff attendance was unnecessary this time. He simply was calling because the staff member was so outstanding, and it would be nice for him since he hadn't been to Hawaii. He also told me that, as a CEO, he would respect my decision, and that he understood the situation. I told him that I couldn't change my mind.

Déjà vu. Hadn't I had this situation before? This staff member was nationally recognized in his field, and we were fortunate to have him at the NAII. I was sorry that we couldn't take him, but if we did, there were others eligible as well. He was deeply apologetic when we discussed it. Nothing more was said after that, and he continued his admirable work. But the word got around that it was best not to try getting volunteer members to override my management decisions. I didn't have this situation again. Various staff members didn't always agree with me, that's for sure. But they would deal face-to-face with me and not try to change my decisions through the volunteers.

The National Association of Insurance Commissioners (NAIC) Takes Front and Center

The National Association of Insurance Commissioners is the standard-setting and regulatory support organization governed by the individual state insurance commissioners. Through the NAIC, state insurance regulators establish standards and best practices, and coordinate their regulatory oversight. It is a forum for the creation of model laws and regulations governing insurance. The NAIC does not regulate insurers or approve rates and individual state regulatory practices. However, as a central resource, it is very important to each company because it coordinates the national system of *state-based* insurance regulation, which affects each state's individual system of regulation.

The NAII staff *and* insurance executives have to pay close attention to the work of the NAIC. Regulatory standards promulgated by the NAIC generally were adopted in individual states, and these regulations would affect the conduct of the business of insurance companies. While many regulations were necessary, new ones would pop up that companies considered too rigid, and consequently impede service to policyholders. The NAII staff had to be vigilant in assessing proposed regulatory standards and alerting our members to their potential consequences. If necessary, the staff would testify either in opposition, support or with alternative ideas.

Participating in the deliberations of state insurance commissioners at their quarterly national NAIC meetings was not one of my priorities during the first couple of years. The meetings concentrated mostly on regulatory standards for adoption by the individual states, and the NAII legal staff, led by our general counsel, Paul Blume, Sr., and his associate, Pat McNally, was well suited for representing us on those issues.

State insurance commissioners generally were (and are) political personalities, some elected by the public, others appointed by governors. It was an advantage to have an individual on our staff who was especially skilled at personal relationships and could generate trust among these policy makers. From 1953 until he retired in 1978, that key personal liaison with state regulators was Spalding Southall, a former Kentucky insurance commissioner who was well known and respected in regulatory circles.

Although Spalding had retired, when I arrived at the NAII, he was still employed to remain in contact with a handful of commissioners he had known well for years. He and I quickly became friends, and although he had moved from Chicago back to his home in Kentucky, he was a frequent visitor at our Des Plaines office. I knew no commissioners. He still was known among them as an "ambassador extraordinaire." He understood the regulatory environment, and had served on the executive committee of the NAIC. Most of all, Spalding was the consummate Southern gentleman with a known reputation for integrity and candor.

I brought Spalding back from retirement, and reinstated many of his responsibilities as our ambassador to the NAIC. Although he didn't move back to Chicago, and didn't return as a full-time staff officer, we broadened his workload to interact again with more than just two or three commissioners.

Spalding was successful because he loved his work and thrived on personal communication. Making a phone call or writing a letter wouldn't suffice for him. If the issue was worth his attention, he would travel directly to the state to get his point across.

And, he was the quintessential social host. He hosted NAII annual cocktail party/buffets near State Capitol buildings for legislators, commissioners and their staffs. These events were different than any I had ever seen. They were known as the Southall "raccoon" parties. Spalding would bring dozens of ready-to-cook raccoons dressed by a friend in Arkansas, and serve them along with roast beef and southern fried chicken. I had never known you could eat raccoon. But for many years they were eaten as a matter of course by many Southerners, and tasted much like the dark meat of chicken or turkey. It wasn't bad, but I relied on the beef and chicken to complete my meal. These events were legendary in various states, including Arkansas, Tennessee, Mississippi and Kentucky. I attended some of them, but the guests weren't very interested in me. They wanted to talk with Spalding.

Spalding's good graces carried over to me several times, as both a supporter at the office and as a friend. Some of the best times that Myrna and I experienced at the NAII were with him and his wife, Alma. As a former high-ranking Kentucky office holder, Spalding owned a box at the Kentucky Derby, and twice we were treated to the mint juleps and those wonderful seats at Churchill Downs. His guests at the Derby always were officers of NAII member companies, and with us he included executives such Mr. and Mrs. Wayne Hedien, CEO of Allstate; Mr. and Mrs. Don Schaffer, Allstate's senior vice president and general counsel; and smaller company CEOs like Bud Inhofe of Mid-Continent Casualty in Oklahoma and Mike McCrary of Transport Insurance in Houston. To Spalding, keeping NAII member executives happily in the NAII family was an important part of his job, and his Derby box helped with that.

Almost as thrilling as the Derby itself were our visits to Claiborne Farms and Spendthrift Farms near Lexington, Spalding's hometown. And, of course,

Spalding arranged nothing less than a private visit at Spendthrift where the Triple Crown winner, Affirmed, was brought out of his stall to welcome us. These trips were highlights for Myrna and me; and perhaps even more so for two of our close personal friends whom Spalding invited on one, Connie and John Riemer. Connie, a lover and owner of horses, continues to say that the festive weekend in Louisville and Lexington was one of the most enjoyable times of her life.

I'm writing all of this about Spalding because he added so much more to my life than being a business associate, as good as he was at that. His graciousness even reached to our 14-year old son, Jonathan. When Spalding learned of Jonathan's love of fishing, he invited us to fish with him and some down-home friends in waters near the Arkansas rice fields. If you ever desire the experience of catching legions of big-mouth bass, line yourself up with a native of the rice field country of Arkansas.

Now it must be said that Spalding Southall did much more than host at his Derby box, hold "raccoon" dinners, and take guests fishing in Arkansas. The best example is when a crisis hit the NAIC's management soon after I took over as NAII president. The entire property/casualty industry was stunned to learn that the staff at the NAIC's Brookfield, Wisconsin, headquarters was developing an insurance data base that apparently had not been authorized by the NAIC's executive committee. It appeared that this system would collect centralized information that could be used for eventual NAIC direct regulation of insurance companies. If some state commissioners did intend to move the NAIC in that direction, the industry had a fight on its hands. Centralized regulation, whether state or federal, was anathema to most in the industry, particularly small and regional companies whose successful operations depended on tailored regulation best suited to their locality.

The first we heard of this was from Ken de Shetler, an officer of Nationwide Insurance Company. He had information from Nationwide's data division that suggested the NAIC could be changing course. Nationwide Insurance, one of the NAII's largest members, was a fiercely independent company, and opposed any form of centralized regulation. A former state commissioner himself, he was outraged that the NAIC central office staff appeared to be planning a possible new role in regulating. He said that "stopping this" would be my first big test as president of the NAII; and that advocacy like this was the primary reason Nationwide belonged to the association. Of course, most

NAII member companies looked to us for advocacy.

My first step was to have our Legal Division and Rate Advisory and Technical Services Department review the information. They agreed that something was different, and had no idea why the NAIC central office needed to create its own new system of compiling data that insurers provided elsewhere. The State Farm and Allstate NAIC representatives agreed, and urged us to move immediately.

Spalding, our Legal Division, R.L. Jewell (the NAII's rate advisory and technical services professional), and I organized a plan of first contacting the NAIC executive committee (comprised of state commissioners), and then, if necessary, all of the commissioners. Spalding contacted two executive committee members with whom he had a particularly close working relationship, Johnnie Caldwell, the long-time Georgia commissioner, and Bill Woodyard, a much younger Arkansas commissioner who considered Spalding a mentor. John Graham, of the Kansas Farm Bureau Mutual, was asked to contact Fletcher Bell, the Kansas commissioner who was the NAIC president that year.

Messrs. Caldwell and Woodyard said they were surprised and would look into it right away. Commissioner Bell, however, didn't take our view quietly. He replied that all we were doing was attacking the NAIC staff. Consequently, he said, we were attacking him and the rest of the executive committee as well. He became so angry with me, as the new NAII president who "organized this attack," that he told other commissioners the American Bar Association was an "unethical" institution for even having had me on its staff, much less making me a top staff officer. He called me to say that if I didn't back off this unwarranted effort I would not be welcome at NAIC meetings.

To conclude this saga: The NAIC executive committee concluded that the new data bank had not been authorized and was not consistent with NAIC objectives. Its development was stopped, and much to our surprise, it was soon announced that the NAIC Central Office would be moved from Brookfield to Kansas City.

Upon hearing the news, one of my first phone calls was from Laura Sullivan, the State Farm representative to the NAIC. She had worked closely with us in reviewing the new ill-fated system and in contacting commissioners. She was happy and complimentary, and this issue began our long-standing working relationship, just as if State Farm had continued as a member of the NAII.

Note: Although State Farm had been one of the leading founders of the NAII, it had withdrawn from the association in 1970. The reasons for leaving were never clearly stated; however, it was presumed that its sheer size as the country's largest writer of automobile insurance led it to handle its legislative and regulatory work on its own.

My entire 16-year experience at the NAII was one of cooperation and friendship with State Farm, including in particular CEO Ed Rust, Jr, Laura Sullivan, and Kim Brunner who became chief legal officer and executive vice president.

The NAIC's executive vice president left soon after the move to Kansas City. Commissioner Bell never told me the industry was correct. At NAIC meetings, he was pleasant, but not overly so. But at his retirement dinner as Kansas commissioner in 1991, he asked me to attend and speak. I happily did.

That's only one story about the NAIC. There were hundreds. The work of the NAIC would occupy hours of my time. However, after a few years as NAII president, I attended fewer NAIC meetings because of so many national issues facing us. Spalding continued working at them, and the Legal staff and R.L. Jewell represented us well.

The Honolulu Annual Meeting

The 1981 Honolulu meeting, when Art Mertz retired, and I succeeded him as CEO and president, was a success. Although attendance was somewhat less than usual, member companies didn't stay away, and the reinsurers who came to do business with the primary insurers came in droves.

The meeting was, in a way, pivotal for me. I was still the unknown new guy, having to prove myself as a substantial enough leader to replace Art. Art had been with the NAII since 1953, when he was hired as a staff attorney. He worked his way up to general counsel, and finally president. He became the leading expert on the insurance industry's antitrust issues. As NAII president, he led a multi-industry massive effort for affordable auto repair parts and state-of-the art facilities for auto body repair when the new revolutionary "unibody" auto construction design was employed.

Just as importantly, Art Mertz could play the piano, and he didn't just "play." He didn't read music. He could play virtually anything by ear, and could he ever pound out the sounds. At NAII board meetings, after dinner Art would head to the hotel bar-lounge and begin playing. Everyone would gather around and sing, and this talent, along with his warm personality, helped maintain camaraderie on the board.

So, I had big shoes to follow. Not only did I not have an insurance leadership track record, I didn't play the piano. *When our family was preparing to attend a retirement party for Art, our 10-year old daughter, Lori, began crying and said she didn't want to go. When asked what was wrong, she said that she would be so embarrassed because I couldn't play the piano, and wouldn't be good at taking Mr. Mertz's job.* ☺

I had two positive situations working for me at the time of the annual meeting. From a lobbying standpoint, we were succeeding at convincing NAIC leaders to scrap the new data base design. And, as this annual meeting's keynote speaker, I was able personally to obtain the former Deputy Secretary of State, Warren Christopher. I was acquainted with Mr. Christopher because of his leadership at the ABA before he served in the State Department under President Carter.

Getting Mr. Christopher to agree to come to Hawaii was important because of his near-celebrity stature at the time. He was in demand as a speaker; and traveling to Hawaii, particularly for a world traveler who had visited there many times, could be a burden.

Mr. Christopher's unsought national stature was because of his role in negotiating a settlement to the Iran hostage crisis in 1980, and Iran's release of the hostages in January 1981. We always live with crises, and indeed it was one for the United States when Iranian students belonging to the "Muslim Student Followers of the Imam's Line" broke into the U. S. Embassy in Tehran on November 4, 1979, and held hostage 66 American diplomats and citizens for 444 days.

This was at the beginning of the period in which the United States was considered the "Great Satan" in Iran, the Shah of Iran was removed, and the Imams led by Ayatollah Khomeini took power. The holding of the hostages and the invasion of its embassy was a humiliating blow to the United States. The American public and the entire world lived with this seemingly endless saga. It was even more humiliating and inhumane because of the tortuous treatment of the hostages, many of whom were paraded with blindfolds in public for the world to see.

Negotiations for their release, and even attempts to rescue the hostages, failed repeatedly over the long period of some 400 days, but finally, due to

Mr. Christopher's effective skill as negotiator, and various international events that were taking place, they were released. Mr. Christopher's name became known across America. Because the annual meeting was just a few months after the January 1981 release of the hostages, both our outgoing and incoming elected chairmen, Frank Barrett and Sol Tversky, suggested Mr. Christopher as the perfect speaker. The meeting attendees would be interested hearing first-hand about the hostage taking and release events, and the implications of the drastic changes taking place in Iran. (In 1993, Mr. Christopher became Secretary of State under President Clinton.)

I was surprised that he agreed to attend, but he did, and the ballroom was overflowing, including many meeting registrants who normally wouldn't attend a keynote speech. It was important for me personally because it was another indication that I, as the new NAII president, was associated with leaders and events on a national level.

To add some merriment to the meeting, Paul Blume, our general counsel, enlisted his old high school friend, Bob Newhart, to entertain at the annual dinner. It was especially fun when he came to our hotel suite afterward. We couldn't stop laughing, and you know why. That deadpan expression never went away.

Face to Face With the "Babe Ruth of Insurance"

Although GEICO was an active member of the NAII, and its executive vice president served on the NAII board, I had not met its CEO, John (Jack) Byrne. Soon after I arrived at the NAII, he called to welcome me, and I spoke with him a few times after that. He stressed that I should run the NAII like a business. He told me that he served on many non-profit boards, and most were managed poorly, as if there always would be money. He said that I had a reputation from the ABA as a good manager, as well as a public policy leader, and it was important that his company's dues were well spent.

He knew of my public policy work, and urged me to help broaden the horizons of smaller and mid-sized company executives. He said that he knew and loved those smaller company executives, but many of them thought narrowly about the industry's future and the changing needs of the public. I had a big job to do, he said, to widen outlooks.

I was able to tell him that we had a new program of operational planning under way, were setting clear objectives for all staff members, and had a chief financial officer, Gene Bagatti, who was one of the best for keeping costs in control and reserving funds for future needs.

I was in awe of Jack Byrne, and even more so when he and his wife, Dorothy, showed up at the 1981 annual meeting. He was a large, imposing man, and while he was known as a tough, astute businessman, was funny and enjoyable to be around. He had a legendary history with saving GEICO from bankruptcy, and interestingly, the NAII was a primary factor in his success story.

The New York Times credited Mr. Byrne with saving the nation from financial trauma if GEICO had gone under. Additionally, the political fallout from such a large insolvency would have been devastating to the insurance industry as a whole.

GEICO (Government Employees Insurance Company) was formed to offer government employees auto insurance at reduced rates because they had fewer accidents. It worked well, and even better when its markets were opened to private sector white-collar workers as well. But in the 1970s, GEICO struggled for various reasons ranging from over-expansion, to inflation, to its own questionable accounting. In 1975, it suffered an unbearable loss of $126 million.

Jack Byrne, who was looking to leave Travelers Insurance where he was executive vice president, agreed to take over at GEICO. He cut costs drastically by employee layoffs, withdrawing from unprofitable states, raising rates, and eliminating high-risk drivers as policyholders. He drastically improved GEICO's service, something he considered just as important to a successful company as a solid bottom line.

At the same time, 27 NAII member companies entered into an unprecedented agreement to infuse capital into one of their major competitors. They knew that it was in their own best interests to save GEICO, and also had faith in Jack Byrne for doing it. Several CEOs invested their personal money in restoring GEICO, and consequently, made millions of dollars of their own as Mr. Byrne turned GEICO around.

The NAII played another GEICO-saving role when its president, Vestal Lemmon, convinced the Insurance Commissioner of the District of Columbia, to forestall the company's liquidation until the agreement could be implemented. This decision gave Jack Byrne time to seal the deal. One year later GEICO had $176 million in capital, enough to continue its operations.

Together, Jack Byrne and the NAII saved GEICO, and the entire industry was spared a disastrous situation.

Over dinner in Honolulu with our wives, Mr. Byrne told me that he had been telling other insurance CEOs that he considered the NAII's management team, under my leadership, to be the best among the industry's various associations, and recommended that they join us. While Jack did not join the NAII board, and continued leaving that role to another, from that night on, we communicated frequently, and GEICO representatives participated in all association functions. We stayed in touch after he left GEICO to lead Fireman's Fund, and then continued to help other troubled companies.

Note: When Mr. Byrne offered the public GEICO preferred stock, Warren Buffett began purchasing it, and by 1995 Berkshire Hathaway became the sole owner of GEICO. Jack was so respected in the insurance and financial industries for his turnaround of GEICO, and, later, Fireman's Fund and other organizations, that Mr. Buffett called him the "Babe Ruth of Insurance." Forbes said that he "made insurance look sexy."

Whoever Said the Insurance Industry Was Boring?

My concept of insurance was "boring." I soon learned, however, that there was nothing boring about it. Some said that if I had had any idea of what faced me, I "would have been forgiven for dropping the proffered President's gavel like a smoldering ember."

During my first year at the NAII, the property and casualty insurance industry's "combined loss and expense ratio" was hovering around 100 points. It soon exceeded 100, which moved the industry into potentially dangerous financial territory. I didn't know what that meant, but I soon learned that the industry had become attached to the practice known as "cash-flow underwriting." Essentially, this meant that companies were charging premiums that were less than needed to pay their claims and expenses. They would charge less to attract more customers, but even though their claims costs and expenses exceeded revenue, their cash flow could be used for investments, such as high interest paying bonds, which in turn would produce profits. Interest rates at that time were producing double-digit returns. But, under this scenario, what would happen when interest rates declined at the very time claims were skyrocketing?

That's what happened. This was also a time when claims were escalating relentlessly because, according to many insurance experts, "the public was in love with bringing multi-million-dollar lawsuits against insurance companies." A severe insurance "availability" crisis took hold, and many doctors, manufacturers, school sports programs, day-care centers and municipalities found it difficult or even impossible to obtain insurance.

In personal auto and homeowner lines, some companies began to withdraw from various markets, increasing the disgruntlement of an already angry public. By 1985, many insurance companies were under water and going out of business. And, to make matters worse, under the guise of tax reform, Congress was taxing the industry more. At the state level, California was seething with unrest over insurance. This eventually, in 1988, would lead to a voter initiative, called Proposition 103, to roll back insurance rates to prior-year levels. The proposition also restricted insurers' ability to underwrite selectively and charge prices that were associated with the expected claim cost of their coverage.

The "availability" crisis seemed to be the only insurance issue on politicians' minds. When I testified at hearings before the U.S. House Ways and Means Committee on tax reform proposals affecting the insurance industry, not one committee member had any interest in discussing taxes with me. Each angrily challenged me on why their constituents couldn't get insurance. Nor were they interested in the reasons I offered, such as frivolous and unduly expensive lawsuits and restrictions on pricing freedom by regulators. Without understanding the complexities of the insurance industry (in our opinion), and regardless of its financial difficulties, Congress imposed higher taxes on it.

The Industry's "Bedrock," the McCarran-Ferguson Act, Comes Under Attack

With the insurance availability crisis seemingly on everybody's mind, some members of Congress undertook an attack on the McCarran-Ferguson Act, the federal law that delegated insurance regulation to the states. Strident calls for federal regulation to replace regulation by the states were emerging. Congressman Jack Brooks (D-TX) chairman of the House Judiciary Committee, introduced legislation to amend the act; and Senator Howard Metzenbaum (D-OH), an ongoing, outspoken insurance industry critic, held hearings that attacked state regulation as outmoded and ineffective. The day

I testified before Senator Metzenbaum's subcommittee was filled with acrimony. The senator wouldn't let up on pronouncing insurance companies as anti-consumer, and angrily considered no other issues such as frivolous lawsuits as causes of the industry's problems. Senator Paul Simon (D-IL) was kinder, but urged us to get on board with federal regulation to help shape it. "Get on board now," he advised, "because the train is leaving the station." One of my young lawyer associates, Bob Zeman, was with me that day. It was his first Congressional hearing, and he later told me that he couldn't believe how harsh the politicians could be when they opposed you. I don't think Bob has forgotten his first taste of a Congressional hearing where the politicians could be so harsh if they opposed you.

Actually, we weren't overly concerned about Congress abolishing the McCarran Act. Our Washington vice president, Darrell Coover, assured us that neither the House nor the Senate would seriously consider the calls for federal regulation. The votes weren't there in either body. Darrell himself was an important part of the reason. I soon realized that Darrell was the quintessential lobbyist, and I was fortunate to have him as my Washington colleague. He came to the NAII in 1968 following positions with Senator Goldwater and the American Medical Association, and lived and breathed the principles of helping small and medium sized companies succeed with limited regulation.

Darrell was known around Washington as one of the most effective insurance representatives in the city. Through Darrell, I came to know Senator Orrin Hatch (R-UT), Senator Alan Simpson (R-WY) and Congressman Henry Hyde (R-IL). All were more than mere acquaintances of Darrell's. They were close friends of his, and as influential members of the Judiciary committees of the Senate and House which had jurisdiction over the McCarran Act, they agreed with the need for state regulation of insurance. They agreed so much with that position that they would speak in its favor whenever the subject raised its head in Congress, either in committees or on the chamber floors. Darrell was always there, providing the information to help them make their case.

A note about Senator Hatch and Senator Simpson: Senators Hatch and Simpson met with us at informal meetings and for dinner at various times. They both spoke at NAII meetings. I make special note of them because they were strong conservatives on policy principles, and at the same time, gave priority to working with senators on "the other side of aisle." For example, Senator Hatch and

Senator Ted Kennedy were close friends, and cooperated on various issues, particularly legislation involving the welfare of children. Senator Simpson, as assistant Republican leader of the Senate, was known for seeking common solutions in the interest of the country. They always will stand out for Myrna and me because of their charm and graciousness and personalities that combined serious thought with low-keyed humor. Well, Senator Hatch was low-keyed, Senator Simpson not so much. It was fun to sit with them at dinner, and be treated to their warm and enjoyable personalities.

While Darrell never wavered from his conservative views, he knew, like Senator Hatch, how to relate to "both sides of the aisle." He had personal close ties with many senators and representatives and their staffs of all political stripes. He was trusted by everybody who knew him, and ranked by *Regardies,* a lobbyist magazine, as one of the top lobbyists in Washington.

Darrell had an army of NAII member company supporters behind him. The voices of small and regional company executives spoke louder than the big company guys. These small ones, who were the backbone members of the NAII, knew their senators and representatives personally, and could make a convincing case for their point of view. That was one of the beauties of the NAII's effectiveness on Capitol Hill.

Judiciary Committee Chairman Brooks got nowhere with his effort to amend the McCarran Act, and Senator Metzenbaum couldn't get the votes to move his bill out of the Judiciary Committee. Senator Simon was wrong. The train didn't leave the station 20 some years ago, as Senator Simon predicted. The insurance industry is involved with the federal government in various ways, depending on the size and structures of insurance companies. However, overall, on a daily operational basis, insurance still is regulated by regulators in the individual states, who continue to accommodate to their states' various circumstances.

The NAII PAC (Political Action Committee)

The first NAII Political Action Committee to raise political dollars for federal Congressional candidates was established in 1976 by Vestal Lemmon, the first NAII president. Prior to then, the association had relied only on its members, working through its Washington Office, to advocate its views before Congress. The NAII did not contribute campaign funds to legislators.

However, it was becoming increasingly difficult to gain support for its positions on Capitol Hill because Congress was leaning more toward anti-business and anti-insurance legislators. These newer members were supported primarily with campaign funds from organized labor and plaintiffs' attorneys. In recommending the PAC to the NAII board, Mr. Lemmon said that increasing numbers of new Congressional members were "seeking and winning elective office, many of them with the considerable financial aid of a strong ally that has long known what political action is all about — organized labor." He continued, "It is a fact today that while organized labor represents a minority of the people in this country, it elects most of our lawmakers, and thereby helps to create the economic and regulatory climate in which the insurance industry must work."

Vestal further pointed out that union PACs outnumbered those of business and the insurance industry by almost two-to-one, and that the NAII had to go into the field, using the same technique. So, NAIIPAC was established, and Darrell Coover, for the first time, had some campaign funds to contribute to legislators whose basic principles coincided with the NAII's.

Although NAIIPAC had been established, Darrell had very limited funds to work with. When I took over as president, it had about $75,000 in the bank, not nearly enough to reach a large enough number of legislators who wished to support our legislative positions and speak forcefully for them. One of his first requests to me was to make PAC fundraising one of my top priorities. To be successful, political fundraising from member company executives had to be led by the NAII president. At that time, prior to the 2010 Supreme Court ruling in the *Citizens United v. Federal Election Commission* case, companies, as corporate entities, could not contribute to the PAC. The contributions had to be made by individuals, and this meant having to raise the PAC's profile among CEOs, who in turn would give it their high priority.

I had had no experience with political money other than to either oppose it in principle or limit it, as espoused by Common Cause; or to not raise any at all, as was the case at the American Bar Association. In fact, it was somewhat unseemly to me at first. However, my views about it changed after listening to various legislators whom we invited to speak at our conferences.

These legislators made cogent statements, and asked the simple question. We support your position of state versus federal regulation, we support your ability to function in a free marketplace, we believe in private companies instead of government insurance except in areas of flood and disaster where catastrophic losses are too large for private insurance companies to supply coverage. But, if we are going to defend the industry on these principles, we have to get elected, and getting elected takes campaign money to cover the costs.

How could these points be denied? The need for campaign money, and lots of it in populous market areas, was a fact of life; and how could the NAII expect any legislator to become expert in our field, take the time and effort to speak vigorously on our shared beliefs, and even provide leadership in Congress on those principles if we didn't support them in their campaigns? To me, it became as simple as that, and I made PAC fundraising a top priority. This meant telling the NAII's member CEOs that we were in a new political day, and that we needed their help with individual contributions from them and each of their top executives.

We provided modest financial support to some candidates who agreed with our positions to begin with. Over my 16 years with the NAII, I made numerous visits to member companies to urge their support of our PAC. As time went on, and the PAC began to grow into eventually the largest PAC in the property and casualty insurance industry, we held special dinner events at major NAII meetings to recognize the contributors. We highlighted in publications those contributors who went above and beyond even what we asked. Asking for money for our PAC was tedious work, primarily because the money had to come from individual pockets for a cause that didn't provide a direct benefit to the giver.

When I left the NAII in 1996, the PAC balance was over $300,000. This was enough to provide some meaningful, but limited, contributions to legislators who supported industry positions on Capitol Hill. But, it literally pales in comparison to the massive amounts that are pumped into the political system today by giant national "Super Pacs." Today it's $300,000 or more to this candidate, and a similar amount to another candidate. Are these super pacs buying votes that would not be cast without these massive amounts of money? Or are they providing support to candidates who agree in principle with their views? And, regardless of which it is, are these giant sums helping elect candidates who don't act in the "public interest," and consequently are corrupting the system? I suppose it comes down to your own view of the public interest. Studies show that a majority of Americans believe the system *is* corrupting politics; and that the campaign funding system, with its vast new amounts of money, seems virtually now out of control. Perhaps if a different Supreme Court changes the First Amendment view on political campaign money, the system can be improved. It probably will require that, however, unless Congress can enact a program that will meet that test.

Vehicle Passive Restraints and Air Bags

The issue of whether automakers should be required by the federal government to install air bags in all cars was a long-standing one. It was presumably resolved by a 1966 act of Congress that directed the Secretary of Transportation to issue motor vehicle safety standards that would meet the need for vehicle safety. The National Highway Traffic Safety Administration (NHTSA), an agency of the Department of Transportation, under the act's mandate, issued its first standard in 1967. This rule required only installation of seat belts in all automobiles, but it soon was apparent that the public's voluntary seatbelt usage was too low to satisfactorily reduce traffic injuries.

After some 60 rulemaking notices where the standard had been imposed, amended, rescinded, and reimposed because of auto company opposition and changes in Department of Transportation officials, Secretary Brock Adams issued a mandatory passive regulation known as the Modified Motor Vehicle Safety Standard 208. This mandate required that motor vehicles produced after September 1982 be equipped with "passive restraints" to protect occupants in the case of a collision. Passive restraints were devices that did not require action by the vehicle occupant except to operate the vehicle. They were automatic seat belts and air bags. These two devices satisfied the standard, and the choice of which to install was up to the manufacturers.

However, the controversy over passive restraints wasn't over. In addition to the automakers, various groups fighting any new federal regulation were fighting this one, and the Pacific Legal Foundation sued the Department of Transportation in the United States Court of Appeals. The Standard survived because the Court upheld it, and it also passed muster in Congress.

While the auto industry had begun installing automatic seat belts, and even some air bags, and was preparing to comply with the full Modified Standard 208, in July 1980 NHTSA reported that thousands of lives were being saved and injuries prevented with these devices. It said also that when all cars were protected with the automatic systems, each year some 9,000 more lives would be saved and tens of thousands serious injuries would be prevented.

However, in February 1981, a new Secretary of Transportation started the process all over again by having NHTSA reopen rulemaking on Standard 208. The reasons, he said, were "changed economic circumstances and, in particular, the difficulties of the automobile industry."

Prior to my joining the NAII, the association had lived through all of the ups and downs of fighting for passive restraints, and primarily air bags over automatic seat belts. Although the NAII was hardly a fan of federal regulation, this was seen as an important, if not essential, public safety issue that could be dealt with only by regulatory mandating. The inexhaustible Donald Schaffer, senior vice president and general counsel of Allstate Insurance Companies, and NAII board member, led the effort for over a decade. He never let up, and if it had not been for Don's leadership and persistence, the air bag might have gone by the wayside. Air bags in automobiles were his passion. He admitted that saving lives and preventing injuries would benefit the auto insurance industry by saving it money, but he made it even clearer that he knew the auto industry had the technology to save lives, and it was this humanitarian reason that motivated him the most.

Don was so passionate about auto safety that some of his colleagues occasionally tired of his constant talk about air bags, and would refer to Don as "Mr. Air Bag." It wasn't always intended as complimentary. It's an understatement to say that he was outraged when, after over a decade of fighting, winning, losing and fighting again through the Transportation Department, NHTSA, the courts and even Congress, that passive restraints were up for grabs once again.

It was at this point that I entered the picture. On a Saturday night in 1981, Don called me at home. He said that he was scheduled to testify on Monday at the NHTSA hearing on passive restraints, but wouldn't be able to do it. As the new NAII leader, I should do it. When I explained my ignorance of the technical and factual points favoring passive restraints, he assured me this wasn't a problem. My testimony would be prepared by one of his staff lawyers, and both he, Don, and the lawyer would be with me. We would spend Sunday night at the Allstate condo in Washington, and I would have plenty of time to prepare.

I wondered why Don, all of a sudden, couldn't testify when he would be there with me. Although he never mentioned it to me, I was told later that the CEO of one of the automakers insured by Allstate had asked the Allstate CEO to pull Don from testifying.

This was never verified, and Don never told me. But he was there with me. I was up most of the night pondering the written statement that had been prepared for me, and going over it again and again. And, there was a big problem: it was brilliantly written, and technically and factually correct, if not fully understandable to me. But it didn't come close to suiting my delivery style, and it was *too* technical for me, the non-expert, to deliver as written. So, I had to completely rewrite it, challenging the automakers on their contentions that their technology was insufficient, and citing the need to save lives.

This would be my first public testimony for the insurance industry, and I had to do it well. The Washington press corps, auto representatives, other insurance representatives, and a variety of consumer groups would be there, all conversant with the pros and cons of passive restraints, and all having strong, even emotional, views.

When we entered the Transportation Department auditorium, I caught sight of Ralph Nader, who would immediately precede me in the witness chair. He was the public face of air bags. There were personages such as Joan Claybrook, the consumer/safety advocate, spokespersons for the auto industry, and groups wanting the regulation thrown out altogether. Nader and I shook hands, but interestingly this was the only time I would be face to face with him again. Occasionally, we would speak at the same conferences, but never at the same times.

Even though I had had virtually no sleep, I wasn't tired. In fact, I was wide awake with exhilaration, and some fear, as I waited my turn. I'd often wondered how nervous trial lawyers were when they made their cases to juries. Because, as often as I spoke before large audiences, I was always nervous just before speaking. Generally, however, if I was well enough prepared, once I began to speak, I was okay. Others who speak or "plead" in public have told me that, regardless of their long experience, they felt the same way. That nervous edge is a good thing…it focuses your concentration, and heightens your energy level.

Because I focused more on the public's need from a humanitarian standpoint, and less on whether the automakers could or couldn't produce safe air bags, I felt that I did pretty well that day. It started me down the road of advocating safety as the NAII's new leader. And it established me in the minds of everybody present as the new guy who would join Don Schaffer as the insurance industry's passive-restraint spokesman.

Ralph Nader left immediately after his testimony. He wasn't interested in what I had to say, and didn't like the auto insurance people anyway. On the other hand, Joan Claybrook welcomed me to the group of passive-restraint advocates, and thought my testimony was very helpful. She remembered my name, she said, from Common Cause days, although we had not met.

NHTSA did not agree with us. After the hearings, it issued a rule rescinding the passive restraint requirement in Modified Standard 208. It said that it was no longer able to find, as it had in 1977, that the requirement would produce significant safety benefits. We at the NAII were stunned. Earlier NHTSA had hinted at possibly rescinding or modifying Standard 208, but we didn't think it would take a step that extreme. It didn't make sense other than on purely political grounds because we thought NHTSA's actions simply were not legally viable.

State Farm officials and we at the NAII decided immediately to file a lawsuit in the U.S. Court of Appeals, challenging NHTSA's action. Taken in part from *The Story of an American Insurance Revolution* this is the story of the months following announcement of the lawsuit and leading up, ultimately, to the Supreme Court's decision in favor of our position. Nothing is ever easy in the political/regulatory environment.

The filing of the NAII's and State Farm's lawsuit against NHTSA was announced at a hastily called press conference in Washington, D.C., the day before Thanksgiving, 1981. The timing of the announcement was considered crucial by the NAII, for Thanksgiving week is generally regarded as one of the slowest news weeks of the year, and the very idea that a large segment of the insurance industry was suing the federal government was certain to whet the appetite of the press corps starving for an important story. And, indeed, it did.

The passive restraint, or air bag, issue which had been debated in virtual obscurity for more than 10 years prior to the NAII/State Farm legal action against NHTSA, was thrust into the public spotlight for the first time. "Insurance Industry Seeks Court Order to Keep Rules on Auto Air Bags" was typical of the front-page, banner headlines that appeared in just about every major newspaper in the country on Thanksgiving Day.

Leading the Washington press conference for the NAII were Don Schaffer of Allstate, Raymond Rasenberger, the attorney who represented the NAII, and I. We issued a joint statement to the press that clearly laid the foundation for the Association's action. In part, it said:

> We contend that the decision of the NHTSA administrator (Raymond Peck) was arbitrary, capricious, an abuse of discretion and not in accordance with the National Traffic and Motor Vehicle Safety Act of 1966 because NHTSA had insufficient basis or evidence to support the decision.

> The NAII is taking this extraordinary legal action because of a strong dedication to the underlying policy of the National Traffic and Motor Vehicle Safety Act of 1966, under which the rule was originally adopted. The intent and purpose of the Act is to reduce motor vehicle accidents and the death and injuries which result from them. It directs the Secretary of Transportation to issue performance standards which will further that policy, and it is our view that the recently rescinded rule does further that policy, and that the decision to cancel the rule in fact contravenes it directly, and is thus illegal.

> The passive restraint rule was the result of almost a decade of substantial deliberations. The rule was supported by Congress and was upheld by the United States Court of Appeals. Full implementation could save as many as ten thousand American lives each year and prevent tens of thousands of serious injuries.

With the stakes in human lives so high, one might have expected a public outpouring of support for the NAII's position, but it did not turn out that way at first. Automotive trade publications, auto writers for the daily newspapers, and a fair number of private citizens expressed vigorous opposition to the notion that automakers should be forced by the federal government to take safety into account in the design of their products. (One well-known national auto magazine columnist criticized me harshly for not knowing anything about cars, and being so presumptuous as to telling automakers what to do.)

Even the nation's corporate insurance risk managers, responsible for the insurance covering their companies' fleets of vehicles, were opposed to the federal passive restraint standard. Responding to a *Business Insurance* magazine survey, they called mandatory air bags "a lot of hot air."

Such major newspapers as the *Chicago Tribune* said the government standard requiring passive restraints in new automobiles amounted to "active coercion." Asserted the *Tribune*: "The government's obligation to protect our safety should extend only to things we can't control ourselves, such as foreign aggression, poisoned food and dangerous drugs, jerry-built housing, and crime." The paper further contended that, "one has the right to expose himself to risk knowingly and voluntarily."

Of course, not everyone was opposed to the NAII's stance. While radio talk shows were not in vogue at the time, many private citizens voiced their support in the only way they knew how, with letters to the editor. One such letter-writer, responding to the *Tribune's* editorial, observed that "Passive restraint systems, such as airbags or seatbelts that must be worn, are not the product of a condescending government protecting one person from his God-given right to innocent folly; actually they protect one person from another's stupid and reckless behavior. This is essentially the duty of governmental organization and legislation. The grandiose notion that the right of our citizens to run their own lives extends to all manner of risk requires a huge leap of reason." (This particular letter-writer was Eric Zorn, who became a prominent columnist with the paper he sharply criticized.)

For their part, and notwithstanding their previous opposition, at least two major auto manufacturers held the view that the government *should* be active in vehicle safety and *should* be promoting the newest technology and the most effective systems to prevent injury and save lives. In Congressional testimony delivered in the same year that the NAII filed its lawsuit against NHTSA, Ford Motor Company clearly stated that vehicle safety requires regulation "because there was no direct market force that would accomplish these goals; yet competitive pressures make unilateral action by any one manufacturer impractical." General Motors expressed essentially the same view. (At the invitation of GM officials, I led a small delegation of insurance executives to GM's Detroit headquarters to hear about the company's progress on developing "safe" airbags. GM was concerned about the injuries that air bags themselves could cause, leading to millions of dollars of liability lawsuits. Experts at Allstate and State Farm agreed that this could be a problem, but contended that the technology, while perhaps not yet fully developed, should not be used an excuse not to proceed. Actually, GM agreed.)

Despite the fact that both Ford and GM agreed eventually to offer airbags voluntarily as an option, the new safety device did not capture the public's imagination. Primarily, this was because air bags were not aggressively advertised, and the cost of installing them piecemeal was more than most car buyers were willing to pay. Many dealers refused to even mention the avail-ability of such an option to would-be buyers. As Ford and GM seemed to agree, however reluctantly, in their Congressional testimony, the only way to resolve the competitive problem they faced, and to bring the cost of airbags within reason, was to invoke a standard requiring their installation, and thus their mass production, in all automobiles made and sold in the United States. Mass production was the only certain way to reduce the unit cost of airbags to an affordable level.

With the public debate having been firmly joined, the NAII knew it had a tough job of education to do, for by now opponents were spreading all sorts of unfounded fears about air bags. For example, opponents contended that air bags were likely to be activated unexpectedly when cars hit a bump, causing drivers to lose control of their vehicles. The bags' inflation required gas that was toxic. The noise the bag made when activated could rupture a person's eardrums. The force of the rapidly exploding bag could lacerate and permanently scar an individual's face.

To counter these arguments, the NAII organized its trained cadre of insurance CEO television spokespersons, including Jim Tulloch of Dairyland in Arizona, Mike McCrary of Transport in Texas, John Bubolz of SECURA in Wisconsin and Bud Inhofe of Mid-Continent in Oklahoma. They carried the association's case for passive restraints to the public in most media mar-kets. Op-ed pieces and letters written by me were published in such major papers as *The New York Times*, *The Los Angeles Times*, the *Chicago Tribune* and *Chicago Sun-Times*, among many others. Allstate and State Farm advertised the air bag story nationally.

Meanwhile, the Court of Appeals issued an opinion agreeing with our position. But the seemingly endless battle wasn't over yet. Although Ford and GM had testified that, if there were to be passive restraints, they should be federally mandated, the Motor Vehicle Manufacturers Association (MVMA) appealed to the U.S. Supreme Court. James Fitzpatrick argued the case for State Farm and the NAII, and I was on the NAII brief with Ray Rasenberger who was our lead counsel. Once again, this time in 1983, the final ruling was in our favor. *Motor Vehicle Manufacturers Association of the United States, Inc. et al v. State Farm Mutual Insurance Co. et al*, 463 U.S. 29, 103 S.Ct 2856, 77 L.Ed.2d 443 (1983). Finally, the passive restraint battle was over. Finally, we were able to rejoice!

The battle over passive restraints was won, eventually leading to bags that are in all new cars today. The automatic seat belts didn't last long as a solution to the passive restraint requirement. They were too cumbersome, broke often, and the public rebelled against them. The automakers finally realized that air bags were the only way to go.

Efforts on Automobile and Highway Safety Continue

Drinking and driving is an age-old problem. Just as Don Schaffer was passionate about air bags as an automobile safety measure, Brig. General Robert McDermott, retired, the CEO who led United Services Automobile Association (USAA) into an insurance behemoth, was passionate about drinking and driving. He, Chuck Lorenz, NAII's senior vice president of public affairs, and I spent weeks outlining an association program to combat drinking and driving, particular among young drivers. General McDermott, known as McD, was the NAII's elected chairman during 1983–1984, and following the successful passive restraint effort, wanted us to continue fighting hard in the safety area.

Many others, such as Mothers Against Drunk Driving (MADD), already were waging national legislative campaigns to raise the drinking age, so we joined in their work without taking the lead on state legislation. Robert Plunk, CEO of Preferred Risk Insurance, and an NAII board member, was our active liaison to MADD.

We did, however, under Chuck's guidance, take a national leadership role in public education by producing two widely acclaimed motion pictures aimed primarily at teenage audiences. We thought we could be most effective by concentrating our program on limited, but highly focused and high quality educational efforts. The movies we produced were titled "Danger Ahead: Marijuana on the Road," and "Just Along for the Ride."

Narrated by one Hollywood's leading actors, Jason Robards, "Marijuana on the Road" was a documentary featuring individuals who had had troublesome experiences with how the drug affected their driving, frequently with tragic circumstances. The film was shown to high school audiences throughout the country, and the U.S. military purchased copies for use at military bases in the United States and throughout the world.

Because of our Robards film and publications in support of anti-drug efforts, on behalf of the NAII, I was invited to a White House recognition luncheon given by First Lady Nancy Reagan in 1989. Mrs. Reagan had started an anti-drug program called "Just Say No," and she made it a priority to recognize groups involved in such efforts.

As well as the marijuana film was received, "Just Along for the Ride" was one of the most successful of its kind ever produced. It was not a documentary. It was a fictional, but vividly portrayed, story of a teen drinking party that ended in tragedy on the road. Young professional actors, some of whom went on to mainstream TV success, played out the story of an accident that was emotionally riveting, with the inebriated handsome, popular young high school student ramming into another car, and killing his own girlfriend who was in it. It was seen by millions of high school students over several years.

The film was so successful (one could not hold back tears) in its treatment of the consequences of drinking and driving, that we held a preview for the media in Washington, D.C. where I introduced it and explained its use. The next day it received such a laudatory review by *The Washington Post* that the *Post's* syndicated column appeared in hundreds of newspapers.

The Public Relations Society of America considered "Just Along for the Ride" so important and well produced that it received the Society's coveted Bronze Anvil Award in the Best-of-Show category, and it was presented to me at the PRSA's 1984 annual convention in New York.

While we at the NAII were proud of our efforts in the safety field to help save lives and contain automobile insurance costs, Ralph Nader and some consumer-oriented groups continued to criticize the insurance industry for not doing enough. To be sure, Nader and consumer groups performed valued public service by highlighting problems in these areas, and he was one of the earliest eager supporters of air bags. But it was aggravating because to many of them, or it seemed to me, we in the insurance business could never do enough to satisfy them. To counter this ongoing criticism, in a speech delivered to an insurance industry audience, I said:

"We were always there, usually far out in front, in every campaign. We were there through lawsuits, lobbying, award-winning films, constructive discussions and dialogue with parties of differing views, such as automakers and body shops. We were there vigorously, and we are continuing to be there. In the safety field alone, we work with no less than 24 groups and coalitions, from the Head Injury Foundation to Mothers Against Drunk Driving. It's a record that we are proud to stand on. We are second to none in the insurance industry in our commitment and enthusiasm for this work. The NAII will continue to seek out effective ways to promote safety and serve the needs of the consumer in the future."

In that speech, I filled in the details of actions we had taken and continued to take. While the general media didn't cover this conference, we sent my talk to papers all over the country. No paper picked up anything I said that day. Sour grapes on my part? Maybe. But, while occasionally we were recognized for "doing good," such as the positive review by *The Washington Post* about our award-winning film, it was frustrating as a representative of insurance companies that, overall, our good works seldom were acknowledged by the media. When I called a Chicago reporter about why this was the case, he replied that the press shouldn't be expected to report a party's work if it's something it should be doing in the first place. That wasn't news, so why report it?

Well, anyway, whether recognized or not, the reward of the NAII's safety work was is in the reduction of injuries and deaths.

The Insurance Institute for Highway Safety, and the Insurance Research Council

The Insurance Institute for Highway Safety. The NAII's work in vehicle safety didn't stop with its own activities. In 1959, it was a founder of the Insurance Institute for Highway Safety, and its support didn't waver. The Institute focuses on reducing vehicle crash losses, ranging from vehicle crash worthiness to truck driver fatigue to safety belt use. Its members are insurance trade associations and individual vehicle insurers, and its board is comprised of representatives from some of these groups. As NAII president, I was an ex-officio board member and an active participant in the institute's work.

The institute's work best known to the public is its crash testing and safety ratings of vehicles. In 1992, IIHS built its own state-of-the-art testing facility in rural Virginia, where it conducts the crash tests that result in its vehicle ratings. These ratings are important to many consumers who want to buy the safest cars. It was an exciting time for those of us on the IIHS board who agreed to build the facility, and witnessed the first crash demonstration there.

Because the manufacturers performed their own crash tests, they weren't enthusiastic about this new, unbiased crash testing and ratings. They knew it would influence their design and sales. However, as IIHS ratings became respected as reliable and favored by the public, most of the manufacturers do consider them in designing their products, and some even feature them in their advertising.

Insurance Research Council. The IRC was established in 1977 to conduct research on public policy matters that affect insurers, customers and the general public. This is research that one trade association or company could not conduct itself. As an independent research organization, the IRC provides a forum for insurance companies and associations to jointly perform data collection and analyses. It conducts surveys of public opinion on insurance issues, and studies trends in loss experience and claiming behavior in various geographic areas. This information is useful to associations, companies, regulators and legislators in improving company operations and framing public policy. It does not advocate public policy or engage in lobbying efforts.

Just as with the IIHS, the insurance trade association presidents were ex-officio members of the IRC board. While I took a strong interest in its work, I didn't participate actively in it. Because research and data analysis were so important to the NAII and its companies, an association Research Department had been created the same year as the IRC, headed by Terrie Troxel, who held a doctorate in managerial services and applied economics from Wharton. Terrie was a leader in the IRC's research program. With his experience and knowledge as our representative on the council, there wasn't a need for my active participation. He called on me occasionally to attend meetings and present the need for a particular research project. Because the NAII was one of the largest financial supporters of the IRC's work, I was updated regularly on the budget, agenda and findings. I mention specially the IRC because of its importance to the industry's joint deliberations and the NAII's active role through Dr. Troxel.

The IRC later was merged into the American Institute for Property Casualty Underwriters under Terrie's guidance when he became president of that organization.

About Brigadier General Robert McDermott, Retired (McD)

As I've previously mentioned, throughout my career with the American

Bar Association and my time with John W. Gardner, I've had the privilege of becoming acquainted with many nationally accomplished leaders. In some cases they and their wives became close friends of Myrna's and mine. Joining the NAII was no exception. One such individual was Brigadier General Robert McDermott, Retired, who was CEO of the United Services Automobile Association (USAA), in San Antonio. When he took over as CEO of USAA in 1968, the company was important in its mission, but relatively unknown to the public, and even many in the insurance industry. USAA initially sold automobile and homeowners insurance to military and former military commissioned officers exclusively. It was a personal lines insurance company, providing coverage to military officers throughout the world. These were people who either couldn't obtain insurance through "mainline" insurance companies such as Aetna and Travelers, or were charged unusually high rates because of their mobility and supposedly high risk. In fact, these individuals were not high-risk overall, and were easy to insure at reasonable rates. As a class, they were excellent prospects for reasonably priced insurance policies from a company willing to insure them.

When McD retired in 1993 as its CEO, USAA was the fifth largest personal lines insurer in the country, and had grown from an automobile and homeowners' insurance company to a major financial institution with its own national bank, and offering a plethora of financial products ranging from mutual funds to life insurance. Its rapid and excellent service, along with its early groundbreaking entry into the use of technology to write policies and provide service, was legendary. The policyholder base remained military; however, it was expanded to include non-commissioned personnel in addition to commissioned officers, and their adult children and grandchildren.

McD had had a distinguished Air Force career, ending as the first Dean of the Faculty at the Air Force Academy in Colorado Springs, Colorado. He had received many top honors and decorations as a World War II combat pilot and operations officer.

USAA had been an NAII member for years. It was one of those small companies that initially looked to the NAII for support and encouragement. When McD went to USAA, he followed his predecessor on the NAII board. He was a different kind of board member, though, because he wasn't an "insurance" man, and his perspective was broadly international as well as national, regional and local.

I learned confidentially soon after arriving at the NAII that McD, as an NAII executive committee member, was one who, from the beginning, supported me as NAII president. He thought I would bring a forward-looking perspective to the association. McD stood out in presence and position. He was respected by most of the board members who headed smaller companies. However, some who made up the association's core base thought he wasn't as interested in their welfare as they would like.

It was clear to me that one of my first company visits should be to McD at his home office in San Antonio. Gene Bagatti and Bob Wegenke urged me to do it soon. They both told me that there were some unspoken tensions between McD and two or three board members, and they didn't want those tensions to build into something bigger.

They explained that some disagreements on the NAII board began in the late 1970s, when an insurance group called the Property and Casualty Insurance Council (PCIC) was created outside the NAII with McD's help. The effort was led by several of the nation's largest property/casualty insurance companies as a vehicle to get the largest and "most important" ones around the table to discuss public policy decisions that were most important to the largest companies in the property and casualty industry.

It was a complicated situation because there already were four primary insurance company trade groups with their own differing and sometimes overlapping constituencies, two insurance agents associations, and a group called the Insurance Information Institute (III) that "communicated insurance industry information to the public." And there were many large companies such as State Farm, AIG and CNA that were not affiliated with any trade group.

The association presidents I worked most closely with were: American Insurance Association, Larry Jones followed by Bob Vagley; Alliance of American Insurers, Paul Wise, followed by Frank Nutter; and Insurance Services Office, Dan McNamara (while the NAII had a history of opposing the work of ISO as a rating bureau, that opposition had subsided, and my relationship with its president was one of cooperation, and support of each other).

With all of these organizations at work, the PCIC was yet another proposed effort by big companies to "bring the industry together," with their top leaders meeting semi-yearly to discuss important insurance policy issues, and reach consensus. McD supported this effort, and while Don Schaffer of Allstate did not, his boss, the CEO of Allstate, did. The long-time first and fiercely independent NAII president, Vestal Lemmon, adamantly opposed it. He was particularly perturbed that State Farm left the NAII, but yet was part of the group that wanted this new "Council" formed. He knew that the CEO of State Farm, while no longer interested in the NAII because of State Farm's enormous size and independence, wanted a policy forum of CEOs where it could present its views. Other CEOs of large companies liked the idea because they could meet together on public policy issues without paying trade association dues.

As proposed, the PCIC would have its own staff member, and would not include official representation from any trade association. It would adopt policy positions, but not engage in any other activities similar to the trade organizations.

Vestal fought it so vigorously that some thought it contributed to his deteriorating health. He thought that it would become an entity known as "representing the industry," but would be dominated entirely by the largest companies, and the cause he championed with such determination — the nation's smaller and mid-sized companies — would be dealt a massive blow.

After heated debates, the PCIC was formed, but was scaled back from the original idea. It gave trade groups company representatives, included the association presidents such as I, and unaffiliated companies such as State Farm. It would discuss issues, but not take votes. It simply was a forum for discussion, with only one staff member to plan meetings and keep records. Vestal had won the day, in a way, but he still felt that it could lead to something dangerous for the companies he represented. I found the meetings helpful because I became acquainted with top executives who did not participate in the NAII. On the other hand, as time went on, the PCIC members began delegating time-consuming projects to the trade association presidents, and this became onerous for me and the other presidents until the PCIC finally was dissolved.

Some of the NAII board members from small and regional companies had the same adverse reaction to the PCIC as Vestal Lemmon. They sided with him all the way. And, they seemed to begin distrusting McD as a loyal NAII supporter. Consequently, although he had served the NAII valiantly for several years, and had built one of the country's largest and most respected insurance companies, it seemed to be the unspoken word that they would not support him for election as NAII board chairman.

Against this background, I flew to San Antonio to meet with General

McDermott. I was met at the airport by a USAA driver, and was enthralled by the company's beautiful park-like grounds, with deer jumping around, and the headquarters building that seemed as large as the Pentagon. We drove by the home on the USAA grounds where McD and his wife, Alice, lived, and where I had been invited to spend the night. Everything about his quarters at USAA was right out of a military storybook. He indeed was the general in charge.

We spent the afternoon getting to know each other. He told me the USAA story, and took me around the magnificent building. The company was his pride and joy, and I soon learned that he was a kind of celebrity among USAA policyholders and USAA personnel.

As we talked about my new job, he didn't mention the tensions with some of the smaller company NAII board members, and the PCIC never came up. While only implied, but clear, was that since serving so many years on the NAII board, he was hoping to be NAII chairman and wanted the chance to provide leadership during that year. I could tell that this was important to him, and that he had been waiting longer than others. It also was evident that since USAA had so many executives providing expertise on NAII committees, it was humiliating to him that their boss wasn't getting recognition by fellow board members.

That day and evening together was the beginning of a friendship that lasted through his retirement and until his death several years later. Myrna and I were their guests in their on-site home, and we were their guests on the USAA's plane for a two-week trip to Europe that I will discuss later. Our children became acquainted with them at NAII meetings, and both Alice and McD took a special liking to our 11-year old daughter, Lori, always giving her fond, personal attention.

Although I didn't know quite how I would achieve it, I knew I had to do it. I had to manage a way for his election as board chairman, and soon. There wasn't any question that he was expecting it now, and that it had to happen. Who on the board could help most, and would any of its members want me to get involved in something like this, which was so basically association politics? At the ABA, while I made recommendations for membership on committees, which could affect ABA direction, none of us on the staff at any level played a role in selecting its officers. But this was the NAII, not the ABA, and I knew I was expected to function as CEO, which surely would include giving advice on the chairmanship.

Bob and Gene told me that board member and former chairman George Walker, CEO of Concord (NH) General Mutual, had been Vestal's closest ally. He had fought with Vestal to scuttle the PCIC, and seemed to still hold some ill feelings about McD's role in creating it. However, Mr. Walker always acted in the NAII's best interest, and if he knew that I thought it was important now to elect McD, he might go along with it. Bob and Gene both thought I should discuss it with Mr. Walker.

That week I met with George Walker in his Concord office. He greeted me warmly on that cold and dreary day. We talked national politics and the state of the insurance industry. He wanted to know how I liked my job. I told him I was visiting board members to learn more about the industry and NAII. He thought that was a good idea, and liked it that I had him so high on the list. Then, with a twinkle, he wanted to know if I had anything special to ask him. He agreed with me that the time was right for McD to be chairman, that enough time had gone by since the disagreements over the PCIC, and that McD was a "good man." He thanked me for raising the question, and said that I should always feel free to call him when I had questions or suggestions that he could help with. He assured me that he would take care of it, and that McD would be chairman.

McD was elected chairman the next year for the 1983—1984 term. McD and his entire group of company experts were active with us until his retirement just a couple of years before my own in 1996. It should be noted that the specialists of the large NAII member companies were always especially important because they brought expertise to our committee deliberations that the small companies could not. Thankfully, as a newcomer, I had passed another test. Managing a trade association isn't only about advocating public policy positions.

The Board Goes to London

Don Schaffer called me one day in 1983 to say that he and McD were thinking about having an NAII board meeting in London next year. 1984 would be McD's year as NAII chairman, and he would like to join Don in leading the board to England. He said that we could learn a lot from meetings with Lloyd's of London, other UK insurance companies, regulators and legislators by discussing their issues and how they were dealing with them. Both Allstate and USAA had offices in London, and would help make arrangements and meeting appointments. Spouses would be invited, and we would add some social events in London as well as some tours around the countryside. He said that McD would be calling me. He suggested that I feel it out with some of the smaller company board members. Times weren't at their best financially. In fact, 1984 was the bottom of the property/casualty insurance underwriting cycle, and some might be unable to make the trip. But then again, most might want to.

Everyone I called responded enthusiastically, including attending with spouses. In association work, I learned at the ABA that including spouses at some board meeting events, and always at annual meetings, was a good idea. While some board members came without spouses, it was generally because they thought the meetings and associated events should be all business, and that social events could even be a hindrance in getting work done. In fact, social events *were* important, and this included having spouses. They provided some pleasant relief from a busy meeting day, which sometimes could be contentious. And couples at social events promoted a "family" atmosphere among board members that in turn helped make association membership an enjoyable, as well as a useful, activity. There was never any doubt in my mind that such an atmosphere in a trade association helped us get our business objectives achieved.

Although I knew that GEICO's executive vice president, who served on the board, would have to get clearance from Jack Byrne, he personally was receptive. He would "get back to me." It was Jack who "got back to me." He called me at home the next day, Saturday afternoon. He was upset. He told me that he couldn't believe we would be spending NAII money on a "boon-doggle" like this, and was surprised that we even would consider asking *any* companies to participate, much less the smaller companies. Most of all, he said, he was surprised that, as president, I didn't object. He had been praising me all over the country for running an efficient, cost-conscious trade organization, and now I wasn't speaking up to Don and McD on something this wasteful.

I responded that I didn't speak up because I didn't object to it. To the contrary, I agreed with it. I told him that I remembered how he had urged me to bring broader and more forward thinking to the NAII members, particularly smaller and regional companies; and that this idea fit that to a tee. What could be better than meeting with Lloyd's (whom Jack himself visited frequently) and sharing ideas with the English? I said, yes, there will be some events that probably could be considered "boondoggling," but this was a trade association that functioned more smoothly when its leaders worked together. Social events helped with that. To be sure, we might be visiting some places such as Bath, Stonehenge, and Shakespeare's home at Stratford-on-Avon, but that would simply be adding to the trip's enjoyment, and wouldn't interfere with our business there.

This time it was Jack who said he "would get back to me." When he called back later that day, he said he would be sending his president and chief operating officer, Bill Snyder, and Mr. Snyder's wife, Georgi. Bill Snyder had never attended an NAII board meeting, and I couldn't recall meeting him. I did know from his reputation that he was "all-business" and strictly "bottom-line" oriented, having come from Travelers with Jack to GEICO. I soon learned that he was considered the insurance industry's leading expert on insurance "benefits." Mr. Snyder would attend, and report back to Jack on whether the meeting was worthwhile. Bill was his trusted associate, and Jack could depend completely on him.

Bill and Georgi Snyder attended the meetings. They participated happily in all of the social events. They enjoyed everything about the entire experience. One day after our return, Jack called again. From then on, he said, Bill would be GEICO's member on the NAII board. Bill became one of the NAII's most active leaders; and he invited me to visit him occasionally in his office to discuss good management practices, and these times with him were very helpful. We became good friends, and continue to stay in touch. (Bill succeeded Jack as GEICO's CEO, and at his retirement dinner as CEO, he seated me next to Warren Buffett, who owned the company. I considered this a gesture of our mutual friendship, which I appreciated.)

The business meetings in England were successful. We made friends in the British insurance community, and gained new insights from them. Most of the board members who had never visited Lloyd's, one of the world's most famous insurance brand names for its worldwide business, were pleased with our meetings there. And, yes, we visited Bath, Stonehenge and Stratford-on-Avon. We saw "Cats" in its original form and Agatha Christie's "The Mousetrap," which everybody visiting London sees as a matter of course.

Our three children went with us, and had some unusually interesting experiences on our hotel floor. Our room at the London Intercontinental Hotel was on a floor occupied almost entirely by large group of royal families from Saudi Arabia, whose men had come to London for business and all-night gambling in the casinos. What an experience that was! At the elevator on our floor sat a Scotland Yard agent and an Arabian security guard, with whom our kids became acquainted. It couldn't have been clearer that this was an important clan from Arabian royalty, who needed protection while visiting London. Their lifestyle over a week's period took some getting used to. The aromas of incense and lamb cooking from the rooms permeated our floor, and watching the veiled women was not only an experience for our curious children, but for Myrna and me as well.

Following the meeting, all five of our family took the month-long Grand Tour of Europe, which was our experience-of-a-lifetime. We took the Hover-Craft across the English Channel to France, and drove through France, Italy, Austria, Germany and the Netherlands. Rich returned to London where he, as a college junior, spent a semester in a Grinnell College-in-London program. When we returned home, the movie *European Vacation*, with Chevy Chase, had just hit the theaters, and we were amazed at how close the trip, with its locations and experiences, mirrored our own. We laughed ourselves silly although others didn't, and must have thought we were crazy.

Getting back to the business at hand, the real story here is that we all learned a lot in the U.K., made many new business friends, and had shared experiences that helped form closer lasting bonds among the board members. The NAII gained Bill Snyder, who became its board chairman in 1989. Gaining Bill was Jack Byrne's way of saying that everything turned out fine. We couldn't have gained a more interested and active board member than Bill Snyder.

After Jack left GEICO to head Fireman's Fund, and after Bill Snyder's retirement before mine, the new CEO of GEICO, Tony Nicely, joined the NAII board. He immediately began participating in the association's activities, on which he and I worked closely together. Tony, to GEICO owner Warren Buffett's great satisfaction, is the executive responsible for GEICO's year-after-year profitability and high standing in the personal lines insurance business. He has moved GEICO into one of the top positions in the personal lines insurance business, with some 33,000 employees and substantial insurance market share. By 2015, Tony had moved GEICO to the number-two auto insurer in America. He did it through financial strength, competitive pricing and top-notch service. And, when you see GEICO ads and commercials, particularly with the well-known gecko, think of Tony. He knows that effective advertising and high ethical business standards are the tickets to success.

One Crisis After Another

The 1980s didn't let up on crises for the property and casualty industry. With the availability crisis came numerous insurance company insolvencies. Hurricanes and earthquakes on the East and West coasts further sapped the reserves of insurers with concentrated business there, and a public referendum on a mandatory rate roll-back in California would play havoc with the industry for years.

In 1985, the industry's operating loss was $2.25 billion despite six months of rate increases, market stability and investment gains. Admittedly, poor underwriting by some companies had depleted an industry surplus of $2 billion dollars, causing the industry to be drastically under-reserved. The combined ratio had reached 118 (remember, that means more insurance costs and expenses than premiums coming in). But the industry also attributed much of its financial problems to the civil justice system with its large judgments that seemed to it as far overreaching. The industry's efforts, including those of the NAII, to achieve tort reform in the states, didn't succeed against the trial bar's lobby. Frankly, the relatively lackluster state-by-state political efforts of the local companies, except in a few states such as Alabama and Texas, didn't help either.

In various speeches and NAII publications in 1989, I described the situation.

Over 140 property and casualty companies have become insolvent since 1969, with nearly half of those insolvencies occurring since 1984. The number of companies designated for regulatory attention by the National Association of Insurance Commissioners because of their financial condition has more than quadrupled in the past ten years. And, the cost of insurer insolvencies is growing at an alarming rate. Between 1969 and 1987, company assessments paid to guaranty funds totaled $2.2 billion, while assessments in 1987 alone exceeded $900 million (state guaranty funds provide backup security to policyholders in the event of company insolvencies, and insurance companies, not governments, pay for them by assessments).

Industry critics began calling for new federal legislation, and state regulators began developing new strategies for more effective state regulation to avert insolvencies. All of us, in the industry and state regulators alike, believed that if Washington got involved, it would just make matters worse. We would wind up with dual regulation of all companies, adding to yet more cost and wasteful time required of them. So, at the NAII, we created a task force chaired by John Graham, a board member from Kansas, that made 26 recommendations to assist state regulators in warding off this latest attempt at federal regulation in the 1990s.

I'm forever amazed at, looking back, how certain events call for certain kinds of people who are just right for the job, and that person or persons step up to do it. In this case, John Graham was the right one. He had been dean of the Business School at Kansas State University, then head of the Kansas Farm Bureau's insurance company, and finally executive vice president of the Kansas Farm Bureau itself. His contributions to the solvency dilemma were immeasurable.

In that same year of so many insurance company insolvencies, the twin disasters of hurricanes and earthquakes hit the United States. Hurricane Hugo on the East Coast, and an earthquake on the West Coast. Hugo was devastating, bringing Charleston, South Carolina, to its knees, and affecting thousands of people. Knowing that insurance critics would again begin throwing bricks at us for lack of company responsiveness, I went to Charleston to ride with claims agents and observe the process. I hoped to find the opposite of what our critics would say, and then send reports to the national press. Brad Mitchell, CEO of Harleysville Insurance in Pennsylvania, arranged for me to ride with his adjusters who estimate and pay claims. Harleysville was a mid-size regional company which wrote policies in Charleston on its numerous antique and fine arts studios.

Don Schaffer made similar arrangements with Allstate claims people. Allstate set up claims vans at various locations, where policyholders could meet directly with agents and adjusters, and also, as did Harleysville, send adjusters to the damaged sites. Observing this horrific damage first-hand was a chilling experience, particularly because we drove into so many areas where the general public was not allowed.

The damage was so extensive that Allstate brought in claims personnel from other states, including California, to supplement those in South Carolina. Harleysville had to hire additional independent claims adjusters. Both they and other insurers were doing what they could, considering the number of claims personnel available to cover such a widespread area. I spoke with one of them about what would they do if just possibly, at this same time, an earthquake would hit California, requiring insurance personnel to be there immediately. Their answer was: "Let's hope that doesn't happen."

After the first day of riding with the adjusters, I decided to forego dinner with them and bring food to my room so I could watch the World Series at Candlestick Park in San Francisco. After I settled in and began watching the game, the game went off the air. An earthquake had hit. The unthinkable seemed to have happened: a destructive hurricane and an earthquake a continent apart. Fortunately the earthquake was not a massive disaster. Life did go on, and most of the adjusters were not needed back in California.

I submitted an op-ed piece to *The New York Times* because it was the paper read by most of our critics. In it I described my on-the-scene observations over three days of watching the adjusters work so effectively. I told about the owner of a fine arts store who was bereaved over her loss of such valuable and beautiful items, and how the Harleysville agent was so responsive. I wrote about the massive job Allstate encountered because of its large number of customers in the area, and how pleased these customers were with the personnel and settlements. I talked about the local news coverage's compliments of insurance responsiveness when tragedy like this strikes. I said I was writing it for national information because it was a case of how responsive private industry can be under difficult circumstances.

The *Times* said no. When I asked why, I had the same response I had before when I wrote on insurance safety measures. "All you've told us," they said, "was about work the insurance companies should be doing to begin with. That's not news or meaningful information." I tried *The Washington Post*, and got the same response. I know, however, that if the companies' responses to the crisis had been less than it was, the same papers would have been all over them with criticism.

I came away from this experience respecting my friends in the property and casualty industry all the more. And, frankly I boil, even today, when I see the TV commercials with plaintiffs' trial lawyers scorning "insurance companies," and portraying themselves as the saviors from all of these evil people who are out to get you at every step. While there are certainly some bad apples in the business who will not pay claims as they should, and while there are situations when a lawyer *is* needed to speak for you, in most cases, with solid, well-rated insurance companies, you do not need one of these lawyers who want to "save" you. This fact has been documented repeatedly in the IRC's auto insurance claims studies.

The natural disasters didn't stop after that. The most devastating storms were Andrew in 1992, just south of Miami, and Hurricane Iniki in Hawaii 1992 as well. Again, I went to see the damage of Andrew, but did not ride with adjusters. The devastation was too extensive, and their jobs were too demanding for me to be in their way. Miles of flattened homes and businesses were beneath the helicopter that took me over the area. This time I didn't try the national media. Instead I wrote to NAII members about the devastation and actions by the companies on the scene. This information helped them plan for disasters of their own in case more would hit.

In all, 1992 recorded 46 property and casualty insurance company insolvencies, the largest number in decades. But the industry learned from these back-to-back experiences how best to cope with them. It also learned that it has to be especially well prepared because it's out there alone, with only FEMA helping somewhat, to bring devastated communities back to life.

In the late 1980s, leading up to the California election in November 1988, various consumer groups that were followers of Ralph Nader drafted a state initiative that would require insurers to roll back their auto and homeowners rates by as much as 20 percent. This public initiative, known as Proposition 103, was on the November ballot, and passed by 51 to 49 percent.

The history of preparations for and against Proposition 103 is lengthy, and I'll will write only a short summary of it. The story of the dynamics among the public starving for lower insurance rates, consumer groups with a fantasy-land view of reducing them, plaintiffs' trial lawyers fighting to avoid no-fault insurance, the State insurance commissioner and the State courts is highly complicated and yet interesting. Anyone interested in it can read the law review article in Stephen D. Sugarman, *California's Insurance Regulation Revolution: The First Two Years of Proposition 103, 27 San Diego L.Rev. 683 (1990).*

Suffice it to say that 103 was one of the most dangerous propositions the industry has ever faced before or since it went on the ballot. When passed, it produced chaos in the insurance marketplace for companies *and* their policyholders, and was especially alarming because often other states followed California's lead in regulation and legislation. Reducing rates by voter mandate is similar to saying the consumer's cost of milk is too high, so let's pass a referendum to reduce its price. As the proposition was written and intended, it wasn't feasible.

Proposition 103 not only mandated severe reductions in automobile insurance rates. In the name of achieving fair and reasonable rates, it changed many of the principles insurance companies relied on to set fair and reasonable rates such as territorial rating. Urban rates, particularly in Los Angeles where there were more accidents, were higher than most of the rest of the state, and they were to get some relief in Proposition 13. With the elimination of territorial rating, however, non-big city drivers would subsidize urban drivers. The vote of 51/49 was close because many voters realized this, and yet others knew that it was impossible to get something for nothing.

The California insurance industry had its own initiative on the ballot, Proposition 104, calling for a no-fault insurance alternative, which it believed would drastically lower rates. It did not dispute the fact that rates were too high, and understood the public's discontent, and even outrage in many cases. It saw no-fault as an important answer to high rates. With no-fault insurance, most cases could be handled purely on a "first party basis." On a first party basis, you submit your claim to your own insurer, and it is handled outside the tort system and without lawyers. No-fault could have its problems, however, if not adopted properly, and could actually result in raising rates. The plaintiffs' trial bar would either strenuously oppose it outright, or water it down wherever it was proposed, thus rendering it unsatisfactory and causing yet more public discontent.

And 104 had its own problems because its benefits were considered skimpy, and unrelated to no-fault, it would codify into law some provisions that the industry wanted to apply to its own operational practices. The proposition, therefore, was trumpeted by its opponents as another example of greed in the insurance industry.

To complicate the political landscape even more, yet another Proposition was introduced by a California company that was intended to counter both the objectives of Propositions 103 and 104.

Because of this almost unprecedented and volatile political landscape, we in the national insurance community knew we had no choice but to put substantial organizational and financial resources into fighting 103. Because of the sheer size of the California market, and constant swirling of legislative and regulatory measures on the table, the NAII had its own office in Sacramento. Its director, Sam Sorich, was effective as our California representative, but couldn't drop everything he was doing on a regular basis and also manage a statewide campaign against Proposition 103.

The NAII was known in the industry as a scrappy, well-organized lobbying organization and we were asked to help. While we helped raise money from our member companies, we couldn't match what most of the industry giants were expected to give. Our members did give, however. The logistics and cost of communicating the industry's message in California, with its immense size, was overwhelming. It was especially complicated by the confusion among voters over the meaning of the details in the different initiatives, and whether any of them would achieve anything positive. The cost turned out to be so large that it exceeded the amount any President of the United States had had to spend in campaigning.

The NAII's primary contribution was to donate the services of our general counsel, John Crosby, who moved temporarily to California to serve as the on-the-scene coordinator of the massive effort. Ralph Nader, who appeared on the scene to fight for Proposition 103, won it with his fame. Despite all that the industry did in what had become a nationally known fight, Proposition 103 was narrowly approved. The other propositions were defeated.

Immediately following its passage, the industry sued to invalidate Proposition 103. The California Supreme Court ruled that its rate rollback provisions were unconstitutionally "confiscatory," and that insurers were entitled to a "fair and reasonable return on their equity." *Calfarm*, 48 Cal. 3d at 820, 826, 771 P.2d at 1255, 1259, 258 Cal. Rptr. at 169, 173.

Chaos followed the entire episode, beginning with opposition to the court's decision that the rollback was confiscatory. Continual controversy abounded over what constituted a fair and reasonable return on insurance company equity. Questions over territorial rating were never- ending. In the end, however, most insurers remained in the state even though the California market and its regulatory system were in such disarray.

Chaos or not, a majority of California voters did not believe the insurance industry. They believed that insurance rates could be reduced without harming the companies, and we in the industry had to take this seriously. In our newsletter to member executives, I said that while companies can't be expected to sell their products at prices that would drive them to bankruptcy, and many may decide to redesign their products, the industry had to home in specifically on the exorbitant costs that are out of control, and lead efforts to do something about them.

We then went to work developing yet another comprehensive cost containment program, focusing on a no-fault law with a reasonable benefit package, all projected to counter the critics' claim that no-fault was not a consumer-friendly solution to reducing costs. And, we knew we had to do a better job of communicating to the public how insurance works and how rates are formulated. It had to be a program that went far beyond the industry's normal way of communicating to the public and media. Out of this came regularly distributed packages of material on subjects and issues that individual companies could adopt for their own use in their magazines, newsletters, speeches, premium notices and other ways they chose. This became an ongoing informational effort that was used by our members in reaching millions of policyholders and the general public.

Most importantly, we also knew that providing written materials to assist our members, and speeches by me, weren't enough to help inform the public about insurance coverages and how rates were made. We needed a spokesperson to be available on an ongoing basis to carry the insurance industry's message on television and public meetings around the country. Fortunately, that person was a member of our staff. Diana Lee, vice president of Insurance Research Services, with her knowledge of insurance operations and rate making, went on the road, appearing often at the request of member companies.

Diana and member company CEOs Jim Tulloch of Dairyland Insurance, John Bubolz of Secura Insurance, and Brad Mitchell of Harleysville Insurance made presentations on television and radio talk shows throughout the country on issues such as unisex rating, territorial rating, and traffic safety initiatives.

For my own work of organizing public communication activity and personal speaking for the property casualty insurance industry, the Insurance Marketing and Communications Association named me the first recipient of that association's *Golden Torch Award* in 1991. The IMCA's membership is comprised of communications, public relations and marketing officials of dozens of insurance companies. The award recognizes individuals who are leaders in improving public understanding of insurance-related issues.

I know that today the public still thinks auto insurance rates are too high. For example, parents who must pay for their teenage drivers can't believe the costs they have to bear. Fortunately, cost-containment programs like the industry's efforts for safer vehicles, stricter DUI laws and enforcement, good driver discounts, and competition like that fostered since its beginning by the NAII, keep rates in check as much as they reasonably can be.

A Potpourri of Final Vignettes

With inflation high between 1979 through 1981, noted economist Paul Volcker had been selected as Federal Reserve Chairman to bring it down. Inflation was playing havoc with the economy. While the insurance industry was depending on high-interest yields for profits, it needed a strong economy with lower inflation as well. Property/casualty insurance companies faced increasingly escalating costs to pay for insured losses. Terrie Troxel, John Nangle (NAII associate general counsel), and I called on him to discuss the importance of his inflation-fighting work on the property/casualty insurance business. We also talked with him about the possibilities of "convergence" within the banking and insurance industries, where insurers, brokers and banks would combine to have a single delivery system for their products. This integration of financial services was anathema to most insurers because there was little similarity between the functions of bankers and insurers. My strongest memory of that meeting was Mr. Volcker himself. He was so well known and respected that it was awesome just to meet him. Adding to the awe was his imposing stature at a height of 6-feet, 7-inches and his commanding personality. Terrie, John and I literally had to look straight up to his face to talk with him. We were pleasantly relieved and somewhat amused when he sat down for our meeting and stretched out, reclining on his elbow and fully occupying a living room-sized couch in his office. His disarmingly congenial presence enhanced a meeting that was both pleasant and worthwhile.

The NAII was active in the states with three regional offices; however, to lobby and provide legislative and regulatory information, we retained local lawyers in individual states and some to cover regions in less-populated areas.

Our Western regional counsel was Carl Hulbert, a former insurance commissioner in Utah. Carl urged me to learn golf. He played golf with me when
we could, both on the road and at his second home in Palm Springs when
we had meetings there. I am a terrible athlete, and struggled with golf. But I
have always been thankful that he pushed me to do it. Carl was the father-in-
law of the racing icon, Roger Penske. A highlight for Myrna and me while at
the NAII was attending the Indy 500 as Carl's guest. We visited the Penske
pit stop, where we met Mr. Penske, and where Carl himself helped out. We
watched the race from the Penske suite, and attended the Penske team's ban-
quet. The weekend, of course, was an unforgettable experience. Most of all,
however, was the ongoing assistance Carl gave me, with his knowledge of the
insurance industry and familiarity with West coast issues.

Within a couple of years, I wanted to enlarge and improve the NAII
Board room. There were 36 board members, and the old room had a make-
shift arrangement of movable chairs and tables. So, we constructed a larger
room and installed a long table with new monitor screens that were raised
from inside it. This eliminated the need for paper documents and charts. This
was the highest tech at that time, and the arrangement was sort of like you
might see in Star Wars. While it wasn't cheap, it was the best arrangement
for board members to view written information. After the general counsel
of Meridian Insurance had attended a meeting in the room, he told his boss,
Meridian's CEO Harold McCarthy, that I was spending too much money.
Harold, an NAII board member, and later its chairman, responded, "I've seen
it, and I like it." Harold told me about this, and said that other board members liked it also. I knew from this that we could continue to innovate at the
headquarters building if it served a useful purpose, and costs were reasonable.

Myrna and I visited Europe again in October 1986 as the guests of General
and Alice McDermott. To accompany them on McD's auto fact- finding trip,
the McDermotts invited Brian O'Neill, who headed the Insurance Institute
for Highway Safety, two of their San Antonio friends, and Myrna and me.
We went to visit German auto companies to learn first-hand their plans for
providing passive restraints, and, in particular, air bags. We flew to Rome
on USAA's Gulfstream, where the McDermotts had the special privilege of

a personal audience with Pope John Paul II. The next morning the Pope celebrated Mass at St. Peter's, and we had seats with the McDermotts. We were
so close to the Pope and his procession that Myrna and I felt his presence in
a special way. Even as a non-Catholic, being in such close presence of the
best-known Christian worldwide was an inspiration that we couldn't explain.
Whether you are Catholic or not, the Pope is widely viewed as the leader
of Christendom. We proceeded to Germany, where we met with officials of
Mercedes-Benz, Audi, Porsche, and BMW. All of these companies were in
varying stages of preparing air bags for production, but still with some hesitation because of their fear of liability if the air bags were defective. Our reception, though, was so welcomed that we were certain our visits did well in
encouraging them to proceed with airbags instead of automatic seatbelts. At
Porsche, we were treated to a ride on their test track with a professional driver.
All I could say about that was, "Don't try this at home."

Sometimes in association work, you have embarrassing moments. One
such time was at our second Hawaii annual meeting in 1990. Generally, we
would hold a closing annual meeting gala dinner with entertainment including such stars as Bob Newhart, Bill Cosby, and Tony Bennett. This particular
year we changed the format to a dessert event with Steve Lawrence and Eydie
Gorme. So, that closing night, just as the night before, Myrna and I invited
a few people for a sit-down dinner in the Presidential Suite where we enter-
tained attendees at open houses and cocktail parties throughout the week.
Our hotel, the Marriott Maui, was proud of its renowned European head
chef. His food preparations were elegant and momentous. Usually at private
dinners in the Presidential Suite, he would stop by and greet the guests. At
dinner the night before, guests included General and Mrs. McDermott, and
the Deputy Director of the CIA whom McD had invited as keynote speaker.
The meal was so good, garnished with edible nasturtiums, and fit for royalty,
that I was hoping the chef would appear so we could compliment him, particularly on his use of flowers, which was common in Hawaii and which everyone enjoyed. Unfortunately he didn't make it that evening. The next night,
the closing night, the guests included the NAII chairman, Phil Richardson
of Alfa Insurance in Alabama, and his wife, Sylvia, and the incoming chairman, Joe McMenamin of Keystone Insurance in Pennsylvania, and his wife,

Marge. The chef did arrive that night, and warmly asked how we all were enjoying the meal. Out of the blue, Sylvia said, "Well, we don't eat flowahs in Alabama." The chef smiled with his European manner, was gracious in his response, and left. I didn't know what to say, and I don't think I said anything except to thank him for his wonderful presentation and for stopping by to say hello. We just picked up and went from there. But there was no harm done. That was Sylvia, whom we all loved, and we had good laughs with her about it later.

This discussion of my time with the NAII wouldn't be complete without mentioning my brief meetings with Maurice (Hank) Greenberg, the inexhaustible CEO of AIG. Hank Greenberg was one of the insurance executives I respected most. He had built AIG into a worldwide insurance force, and neither the company nor Mr. Greenberg, himself past normal retirement age, would stop going. Being so fiercely independent, he did not allow AIG or its subsidiaries to belong to any insurance trade group, so consequently we at the NAII didn't have the benefit of his or his staffs' participation. However, he often spoke on all-industry programs, and when I learned that we would share a platform on state versus federal regulation, I knew I was in for an interesting afternoon. Mr. Greenberg was an avid proponent of federal regulation of insurance. He wasn't exclusively an "insurance man." He was in demand by the media to discuss world and American economies and financial institutions of all kinds. He was known not only for his knowledge, but for his toughness as an executive as well. I had some trepidation as we took the stage together. But, as often happens, it wasn't as I had expected. He was friendly in manner and tone. He made his case, which I understood, because for AIG, with its immense size and worldwide business, state-by-state regulation could be a cumbersome drag. But my case was just as cogent as well when it came to the NAII's constituency of smaller and regional companies. I shared the platform twice with him, and each was enjoyable. During the great recession of the 2000s, AIG hit bad times, and the retired Hank Greenberg did also. But Hank Greenberg bounced back, and I'll always remember him as the smart, inexhaustible leader who was at the top of the insurance industry. There was none other quite like him.

A top insurance executive whom I never will forget and held in highest esteem is William Berkley of the William R. Berkley companies, a group of several regional property and casualty and surplus lines companies (surplus lines serve hard-to-insure commercial customers). Bill Berkley was a pillar of the insurance industry, an acutely knowledgeable insurance and finance man, and credited with building his insurance companies into highly successful ones. While he didn't serve on the NAII board, all of his companies were individual members and active participants. One of them, Admiral Insurance Company, was represented on the board with its chairman, Mike Snead. Bill Berkley, however, took a personal and supportive interest in the NAII's work. He wanted to be assured that it was effective in the insurance regulatory and legislative areas, and doing it with respect for its members' dues money. What wasn't so well known in insurance circles, however, was his love for his dairy farms, and, of course, the Holsteins on them. When I visited him in his Connecticut office, I couldn't help noticing the many figurines and pictures of Holsteins. I think that day we talked about dairies as much as insurance. At the airport gift shop on my way home, I saw a little toy Holstein cow that mooed, walked, and wagged its tail. It was perfect to take home to our youngest grandson, but I thought of Bill Berkley as well. It would be perfect for his desk. So, I bought two, and sent one to him. A few days later, while I was meeting with a staff member, Ron Howorth, Mr. Berkley called to thank me for the cow. Ron, overhearing our conversation, exclaimed, "Did you really send Bill Berkley a toy cow?" When I said yes, he replied, "All I can say is, that's why you're the president, and I'm not." We both had a good laugh, and I was glad Mr. Berkley liked it. It was good to know that, with all of his avid attention on his successful businesses, he had a warm sense of humor as well.

Because NAII members were virtually apoplectic over their high costs generated by so many lawsuits they considered frivolous and unwarranted, they had little faith in the civil judicial system. Imagine my surprise when I read Chief Justice Burger's comments about that in his 1984 speech at the American Bar Association when he spoke of "the criticism of our profession" as not casual or irresponsible. In that speech he said, "*Is the public perception of lawyers influenced sometimes by absurd lawsuits which we have not yet found a way to restrain—a father suing the school board to raise little Johnny's grade in*

English from C to B? Or the football fan who sues to revise a referee's ruling on a forward pass or a fumble?" Those examples were exactly the kind that were driving the insurance industry crazy, because they were the ones who had to pay the bills for those suits. The NAII board was scheduled to meet in Washington soon after the speech, and I thought it might be useful for its members to hear directly from him about his views. After I called the chief justice's assistant, Mark Cannon, to ask about that possibility, he responded that Chief Justice Burger would be pleased to meet us at the Mayflower, where our meeting was held. He was such an advocate of positive changes in the legal system, including incentives to lower costs, that he wanted to hear from those affected by it. The conversation around conference table, planned for one hour, extended into three. The chief justice and the board members learned a lot from each other that day, and later resulted in recommendations by the board to state legislatures.

If, when I arrived at work, I saw the heads of Gene Bagatti and June Holmes peering together into my office, I knew there were personnel problems, and that we were in for a difficult day. (June was the Human Resources director, and remained at the now PCI to become Chief Operating Officer.) On one particular morning they came with the demands of the individual we were hiring to succeed Darrell Coover, who was retiring as our Washington vice president. We had searched for months, and were striking out. Darrell had been so committed to the NAII's principles, and so effective on Capitol Hill that it seemed almost impossible to find a replacement. But we did find a gentleman, on Darrell's recommendation, who was a retired congressman. I was reluctant at first because sometimes public figures have egos that don't fit in with us ordinary people in everyday work life. However, because of this gentleman's excellent personality and reputation on the Hill, we signed a contract with him. It didn't work out. *After* the contract was signed, he sent us a letter stating additional needed perks that we couldn't give. They ranged from Redskins season tickets to the best Washington clubs, among others, all of which he said he needed. Darrell had a couple of Redskin seats and belonged to the 116 Club, a quietly stated lunch club on the Hill, but had nothing like this individual wanted. The perks he sought as necessary were not at all in keeping with the NAII's nature. We not only decided against them, we decided that, just in asking for them, he did not understand the way the NAII did business, and would not be effective with us. Maybe for another employer, but not us. So, we decided that he had broken the contract, and did not hire him. He insisted on meeting with me. We met in a room at O'Hare, where he wouldn't let up, and said that he would call the next day after I had reconsidered. I told him not to call because I wouldn't be reconsidering. His manner that day confirmed to me that he was not the man for the job. He sued the NAII and me for breach of contract; and the federal judge, in finding against him, admonished him. The judge couldn't believe he was asking for all of these things, when he already had a generous compensation package. (Darrell was furious, and told us that this was a side of the retired congressman he had not seen before.) If it weren't for such troublesome personnel issues! But, let's face it. If you're a manager at any level, they're an important part of the job.

With Darrell's recommendation having failed, he didn't stop looking. He suggested Jack Ramirez, whom he knew well as the top aide to Senator Conrad Burns, a Republican senator from Montana. Jack knew how the political process worked, both in Washington and the states. He had been the Republican leader of Montana's House of Representatives and Senator Burns's campaign manager. He was knowledgeable and personally engaging. So, we hired Jack Ramirez to succeed Darrell as the NAII's Washington vice president. Hiring him in that position, however, wasn't the end of the story, because a relatively short time later, Jack was promoted to executive vice president, and succeeded me as CEO and president when I retired in 1996.

July 1996 Was My NAII Retirement Date

At age 62, I would have been in association work for 37 years, and with the NAII for sixteen. Working on political issues, once my favorite activity, had begun to lose its luster. Myrna and I decided that it was time to move on, so I informed the board in 1994, at age 60, that I hoped to retire in July 1996, and was telling them then so they could begin thinking about my successor. There was swift reaction. Most board members said they understood, but some were critical of my telling them two years in advance. Two in particular, McD and Phil Richardson, said that it was wrong because now I would be just a lame duck, and why did I want to go before 65 anyway? I knew why they reacted this way. They themselves did not want to retire, seemingly at any age. But they were good friends, and respected my decision to give them early notice that I would retire at 62.

We were so busy every day that neither the board members nor the staff had time to think about my leaving in two years. My decision gave the board welcomed time to begin thinking about the next president, and those two years rolled around quickly. As it turned out, our Washington vice president, Jack Ramirez, was the person for the job. Just as I before him, he was appointed executive vice president and chief operating officer a year before I left.

The NAII's 50ᵗʰ Anniversary in 1995

In 1995, the year before I retired, the NAII celebrated its 50ᵗʰ Anniversary at the annual meeting in Chicago. Dozens of old-timers including Art Mertz and Spalding Southall came back. Close personal friends of ours* and our children were included. In a way, since this was my last annual meeting as president, it was a festive occasion for the entire Beck family to say goodbye to so many member company executives, their spouses and retired colleagues.

The NAII was in good health, and I felt good about its future. By 1995, the NAII's membership stood at an all-time high of 565 companies that, when combined with its statistical service, accounted for some $75 billion of premium volume. The association, together with its statistical service, employed 180 people, and it was stronger financially than at any time in its 50-year history. Its annual budget was more than $24 million dollars, and accumulated assets of almost $28 million. Its reserve fund balance was almost $20 million dollars, in contrast to $4,321 in 1945.

In one of my last speeches to the NAII membership, I observed that the "numbers are much more than just the measure of the association's growth and financial strength. Indeed, they vividly reflect the vast extent of our members' commitment to association principles and the enormous task they have had to carry to promote and defend their legislative and regulatory interests for half a century. Yet, the numbers hardly tell the whole story, for nowhere in them is evidenced the priceless expertise and hundreds of thousands of hours so many of our member company executives have contributed in leading the NAII to the enviable point at which it stands today as one of the most respected political voices in the insurance industry."

In that speech I wanted to make it clear that the NAII's "enviable" position was the result of hard work by member companies and the staff over all of the years since its founding. It wasn't under my administration that its strength and success just popped up "like that." I simply was pleased to have been a part of it and to have had a hand in keeping its success moving forward.

Retirement Send-Off

My own retirement send-off was at the spring board meeting in Columbus, Ohio, home of State Auto Insurance, and hosted by its CEO and the NAII's chairman, Robert Bailey. Bob, when first introduced to the NAII by his predecessor at State Auto, was not an enthusiastic fan of trade associations. He was first and foremost a businessman, and he considered it difficult to take time to attend NAII meetings. When he began attending, however, he plunged into the substantive work of the association; and he and his wife, Sylvia, enjoyed the NAII's camaraderie. I say that because Bob always "plunged into" everything he did. He began sending his State Auto colleagues to NAII meetings, and his group of company executives became an integral part of the NAII family. We often shared thoughts on what we would do in retirement. We talked about such things as I raising Limousine cattle in Illinois, and he raising the same kind of lean-breed in Ohio and on his family boyhood farm in Kansas. As it turned out he did, and I didn't. He even raised little donkeys on his farm south of Columbus.

Bob Bailey and I had become such close colleagues that his references to me from the podium were all the more special, even though retirement functions can be filled with emotion anyway. The entire Beck family was there, a video of my life and time with the NAII was shown, gifts were presented, and a speech was made. When the evening concluded, my 37-year career in lobbying and association work was over. It was such a satisfying moment, because I had been so lucky. I had found my niche. Hugged by Myrna as I came down off the platform, with my family around me, I cried.

* *The personal friends were Andi and Dan Derrington, Barb and Ed Hamilton, Barb and Dick Miller, Elaine and Dr. Dennis Pietrini, and Connie and John Riemer. We have known them, their children*

and grandchildren like a family for over 40 years.

Note: My special thanks to Chuck Lorenz for his masterfully written 50-year history of the NAII titled "The Story of an American Insurance Revolution." Without this document as a ready reference, I could not have written as easily my own story with the NAII.

My special thanks beyond available words to Shirley Neubert and Kathy Mahoney, my administrative assistants, respectively, during my NAII years. They were indeed the unheralded ones who always helped make a smoother day.

RETIREMENT

AFTER 1996

Although I planned to leave the NAII at age 62, I had no intention of just hanging it up. I was ready to leave full-time management and the political arena, but wanted to continue being active. I had been asked by the CEOs of three insurance companies to serve on their boards of directors. I also had some other things in mind such as teaching a college course on Lobbying and Interest Groups, and hosting a TV show with experts speaking on useful information such as auto and property insurance and how to find the best retirement community.

Georgia, Many Years After Grade School

Anticipating retirement, Myrna and I bought a townhouse in Georgia where we lived a few months each year near our daughter Lori, her husband, Richard, and their growing family. Immediately after graduating from college, Richard took a job in Georgia, and because I was retired, it was convenient for Myrna and me to spend time there, as well as Illinois.

Living in Georgia on this basis was the right thing. Our grandsons, Christopher, Stephen and Matthew, were born there, and we were able to be around them during some of their formative years. This is something all grandparents relish. I spent a lot of time, in fact hours on end, playing Thomas the Tank with Christopher, and chasing the energetic Stephen on the playground. Those were times perfectly suited for retired grandparents.

While living in Georgia, Myrna and I became acquainted with a high school sophomore named Derrick Chapman. I mention Derrick because over many years he became an integral part of our lives as I helped guide him into college and summer internships. The story here is that Derrick had aspirations to study finance in college, but it was going to be an uphill battle for him. His parents, Connie and Bobby, although wanting the best for him, were raised poor and were of modest income. While Bobby worked hard as a truck driver to provide for Derrick and his mother, neither parent was in a position to give him the attention he needed for college or the workplace.

A long, happy story made short: Myrna and I both took Derrick under our wings. He lived with us in Illinois during summer internships, and was admitted to the University of Georgia, where he earned his degree in finance. His admission, however, wasn't an easy task. The university seemed more interested in admitting children of politicians and wealthy Atlanta families than a first-generation, small-town kid with no alumni connections. Fortunately, however, after continual persistence with admissions officials, we prevailed. He obtained three degrees, and has an excellent job in finance. He and his wife, Lindsay, have two children, and we stay in close touch with each other.

College Teaching

The University of Tennessee at Chattanooga was just a short drive north of our Georgia home. After inquiring about an adjunct teaching position there during the spring term, I was hired by the head of the Political Science Department, Dr. David Carrithers, to teach a weekly class beginning in 1997. For seven years I taught a class of junior and senior political science majors. Most students, with a show of hands on the first night of class, had negative views of interest groups and lobbying. However, that changed when they realized that either they each personally, or relatives or close friends, belonged to an interest group, whether Ducks Unlimited, Sierra Club, or the Dry Cleaning and Laundry Institute; and they benefited from lobbying by their group. Some decided they themselves wanted to be lobbyists, and after graduation one obtained a legislative job with a musical trade association in Nashville.

Because I no longer was in the active "vineyard," I was able to enhance the class by bringing in speakers who were. Joel Riemer, a young family friend who did public policy work with the National Safety Council; and Bob Zeman and Joe Annotti from the NAII spoke about how to lobby from an association's standpoint (their respective managers, Jack Ramirez and Joanne Orfanos, were kind enough to arrange their appearances). Two former company CEOs, Joe Lancaster and Bob Plunk, spoke about legislative work of companies. The students thrived on these speakers who brought such current real-world experiences.

The best years of teaching were with classes that had the most challenging students… students that asked hard questions, made knowledgeable comments, and helped generate discussion. When students were truly interested, the time and effort of teaching them was worthwhile and fulfilling. If, in a particular class, and I had a couple of them, virtually nobody spoke up, the teaching was much harder.

Even though the subject matter was my life's work, I would spend at least four hours of preparation before each class. I had thought I wouldn't need text books because I could teach from my own personal experience, but Dr. Carrithers assured me I would need them. "By all means," he said, "teach with your personal stories. The students will love them. But don't overdo them." He was correct. The textbooks, plus my personal stories, were the perfect combination. It was clear that I couldn't "wax eloquent" with my own experiences for an entire semester. But it also was clear that the students appreciated the frequent real-life messages I was able to bring to them.

When time came for the students to evaluate the teacher, I wasn't always sure what to expect. Most were complimentary, even to the point of one saying that I was the best teacher, adjunct and full time, that he had had. From a 4.0 student who went on to law school and now is a successful lawyer, that wasn't bad. Some comments that I particularly enjoyed were to the point, like "I dig Mr. Beck," and "Mr. Beck rocks." They *all* weren't overly praiseful, particularly one who said that I "obviously knew what I was talking about even if no one else did." But when all was said and done, I knew I was appreciated when I was named by the students as the university's Outstanding Adjunct Professor for 2000–2001.

After seven years away from active managing and lobbying, I felt I was losing my relevancy as an informed teacher. So, I decided it was time to stop. There's a time to do it, and a time to move on. However, teaching college students what I knew first hand were some of my most satisfying and enjoyable lifetime experiences.

WYCC-TV, Channel 20, Chicago

Working with the insurance industry taught me how little the consumers know about the how and why of their own policies. Or how little they know about their 401(k) plans and the need to contribute to them. Or what do retirement homes offer, and how to find them. These and many others are practical questions that we're confronted with all of the time. I decided that I would look into the possibility of hosting a television show that would feature experts in various fields who would give practical advice and information.

As I began exploring such a program, I became acquainted with Carole Cartwright, the new manager of WYCC-TV, one of Chicago's two public stations. Carole was a member of our church in Hinsdale where our minister, Duane Mevis, introduced us. She was organizing WYCC's new programming, and while she thought my idea had merit, she was especially interested in a show featuring how prominent Chicagoans succeeded in their lives. They would discuss how they grew up, what motived them, who influenced them most, and what steps they took to become noted in their fields. I liked her idea better than mine, and couldn't have been happier when she invited me to do it. We started the half-hour program, "First from Chicago," late in 1996.

I had a lot to learn, and Carole provided me with excellent support to produce the show. Its creative and knowledgeable producer, Jan Thompson, helped me plan, taught me how to speak succinctly into the mike, and keep it within a half hour time frame. The most important thing in TV speaking is to project enthusiastically, much more so than in general conversation. She also taught me how to dress: long dark socks, and attractive, bright ties that give life to the screen. More than once at the beginning of the series, we would have to do more than one "take" with the guest, and she was always there in the control booth, helping me through it. One of the most difficult things is to transition smoothly and on time, from the introduction to the conversation.

The station advertised the program with my picture (and two other WYCC program hosts) on the back poster wrap of Chicago public buses. You couldn't miss it. Our sons, Rich and Jonathan, and daughter-in-law Suzi, commented often that they couldn't get away from me. They were working in downtown Chicago at the time, and saw buses with the picture everywhere they went.

A surprise to me was the number of support people needed to produce one half-hour show with only a guest and a host. In this case, nine people, from camera crew to writer to makeup artist, assisted me.

Carole, Jan and I worked hard at getting guests. After all, I wasn't Oprah, and successful people weren't clamoring to be on "First from Chicago." And, WYCC-TV was the second public station, located in an inconvenient location. But, by hook or crook, we got them either through our own personal friendships or through our friends who knew them. Once we had them committed, Barbara Anderson, our writer, would prepare questions that I would edit and memorize. Jan was dead set against my using any set of notes in front of me, so it had to appear spontaneous.

For more than two years, I interviewed some 50 personalities. As my first guest, I wanted somebody I knew well, and would feel comfortable with on opening day. My friend, Willard (Sandy) Boyd, agreed to do it. He was president of the Field Museum, former president of the University of Iowa, and former dean of its law school. I worked closely with Sandy when he was active with the ABA's Legal Education Section. The conversation went perfectly, and he wrote me a note saying that he was honored to be my first guest, and that I was a "born TV host." That first program with Sandy gave me confidence with all of the interviews that followed.

Other well-known Chicagoans appeared such as Stan Mikita of Blackhawk hockey fame (his presence thrilled the staff, and some wore Blackhawk jerseys that day); Edward Brennan, retired chairman of Sears Roebuck; Jewel Lafontant-Mankurious, former U.S. deputy solicitor general, U.S. ambassador, and first black woman to argue before the Supreme Court; Bud Herseth, world famous principal trumpeter of the Chicago Sympathy; Clarence Page columnist of the *Chicago Tribune*; Dr. Martin Marty, renowned University of Chicago historian of religion; the leading paleontologist Paul Sereno, also of the University of Chicago; nationally prominent auction house owner Leslie Hindman; Newton Minow, former Federal Communications Commission chairman; Jerry Choate, Allstate CEO; Charles Cummiskey of the baseball family; and Donald Rumsfeld, who was consulting in Chicago before returning to Washington.

Perhaps the most interesting day was with Jerry Krause, the general manager of the Chicago Bulls when they were winning NBA championships year after year. Krause never gave interviews, and always seemed to be under attack by the sports press. He had attended Bradley University, and I knew he was a close friend of its athletic director. I took a long shot by asking for his help, and he reported back to me that Jerry would do it if I agreed to mention Bradley, which of course was no problem for me. Although I spoke with Jerry's secretary about arrangements, I had not met him or spoken with him, and had no inkling of how our conversation would go. He wasn't known as the warm and friendly type. When the time came for him to arrive, the WYCC-TV staff was standing around in anticipation, several wearing their Bulls jerseys. Would he come in the door or not? He did. And, contrary to his public image, he couldn't have been more engaging and pleasant to talk with.

Steve Johnson, the *Chicago Tribune's* TV critic, wrote about it on June 6, 1997:

> On the night of the third Chicago Bulls championship series game, it is, of course, incumbent upon you to tune in to your sports leader, WYCC-Ch. 20. On NBC, Ahmad Rashad will have his nightly missive from the lips of chairman Michael (Jordan)... But this PBS educational station has the real coup: a whole half hour with Crumbs himself, the Bulls Sphinx-like GM Jerry Krause. In the pretaped conversation, "First from Chicago" host Lowell Beck doesn't exactly go for the jugular or even the nape. (On some of the difficult questions about the Bulls players and coach) Krause is as silent as the deferential Beck...The amiable interview is less opaquely meaningful, though, in its providing a deeper sense of the man you know only from caricatures like the derisive, food-fragment nickname (Crumbs) or from brief quotes in the press over the years.

With tongue in cheek, Johnson labeled Channel 20 the sports leader, but made our day by crediting us with "providing a deeper sense of the man who most often was derided in the public arena." And, yes, we did talk about his love of Bradley, and we learned about his first sports love, baseball. And, that, of course, was the object of our show in talking with all of our guests: "to provide a deeper sense of the person."

Every person, whether notable or not, has a story. It's particularly interesting to learn that *so many* successful people begin life with *so little*, and yet ultimately make such a noteworthy difference in the lives of others and society in general. They do it by having a love for what they do, and disciplined, hard work. Never giving up, regardless of the difficulty. That's the simple, worthwhile message we learned from all of our guests who appeared on "First from Chicago."

Insurance Company Boards of Directors

After retiring from the NAII, I served on three company boards of directors. I did not plan for these as I had for my other retirement activities. Generally, you do not seek board membership; they come to you. I was surprised to receive invitations from Harleysville Insurance Group in Pennsylvania, Preferred Risk in Iowa, and Insurance Management Solutions, a subsidiary of Bankers Insurance Group in Florida. While I served at Harleysville and Preferred Risk (which became GuideOne) until board retirement age of 72 ½ and 65, respectively, over-commitments caused me to have to leave IMS after a short time.

Preferred Risk Insurance was founded years ago as a country-wide company to provide auto insurance to only non-alcoholic drinkers. The idea was that total abstainers would have fewer claims than even drivers who were casual social drinkers.

Later it became one of the country's largest insurers of churches. When its CEO, Bob Plunk, asked me to serve on its board, I was particularly surprised because he knew that I wasn't a total abstainer, which was a board membership requirement. When I replied that I didn't think I was eligible because I liked a glass of wine or a gin and tonic, he said, "Oh, I'm sorry, I didn't mean the Preferred Risk board; I meant its subsidiary, Midwest Mutual, that provides coverage for motorcycles and DUI's." We had a good laugh. Midwest Mutual had been created to provide insurance to families of Preferred Risk policyholders who could not qualify for its abstainers' coverage. He explained that the Midwest Mutual and Preferred Risk boards met simultaneously, but there was no alcohol restriction on the Midwest members. He also said that plans were being considered that would change the nature of the company, and it was an interesting time to be involved with it

During my time there, Preferred Risk Insurance was organized into an entirely new company known as GuideOne. Although drinking and driving continued as an important consideration by the new company, it no longer was the primary reason to exclude coverage. Midwest Mutual was terminated as a separate entity, and its specialty products were provided through a new division of the "new" company. GuideOne still actively discourages drinking and driving, and has added many new products in the church and education fields.

Under CEO Brad Mitchell's leadership, in 1986, *Harleysville Insurance* was changed from a mutual company (policyholders own it) to a public company that offered public stock. It was, and continues to be, a regional, rather than a country-wide insurance company with some $1 billion in premiums. Its products were primarily commercial policies for small and medium size companies, but it offered personal lines (auto and homeowners) and life products as well.

I joined Harleysville's board of directors in August 1996; and from the fresh perspective of just having left the NAII, was able to offer information on the "state of the industry," and how Harleysville compared with other similar companies. Although I served on various board committees, including Audit and Corporate Strategy during my 10-year service, my most important post was chairman of the Nominating and Corporate Governance Committee. After Brad Mitchell's untimely death, it was necessary to select new executive leadership, and was my responsibility to coordinate the decision making for electing the new chairman. William (Bill) Scranton III was elected chairman, and in that role presided over the board and worked closely with the company's president and COO, Michael Browne. In 2012, Harleysville and Nationwide Insurance merged, and Harleysville became a subsidiary, but autonomously managed, company of Nationwide.

After I had been elected to the board, Joseph McMenamin joined it also. Joe had just retired as president of the Keystone Insurance Companies in Pennsylvania, a consortium of AAA companies in the Mid-Atlantic states. Joe had been a management and IT mentor to me when he served on the NAII board. I was particularly happy to see him because he joined me in offering industry information and, in particular, hands-on insurance operating and financial experience.

I learned soon that corporate board membership in our changing, dynamic business environment was not a cushy activity. There constantly are difficult, sometimes contentious, decisions to be made that affect high-level company personnel and the profit bottom line. There's a difference, however, between the difficulty of being a policy-making director and the day to day executive who has the responsibility for keeping the doors open. When I boarded a plane to fly home to Illinois after board meetings, I was happy to be a director and able to go home.

When seven years of teaching, some two years of TV interviewing, and the several years as a board director were completed, I was ready to be finished with so many commitments. Each activity had been worth it. But at age 72 ½ versus 62 when I retired from the NAII, I was ready to devote more time to our family of six grandsons, and activities such as the work of our church. I played more golf too, and enjoyed more personal traveling with Myrna at our leisure, instead of boarding a plane for yet another business meeting. I know that some men and women like to go on forever with a demanding business schedule. I don't believe that's wrong. But I couldn't be happier with the way things are for me now at the age of 81 in 2015. And I'll be forever grateful that I discovered exactly the right road and found my niche at the beginning.

EPILOGUE

LOBBYING THEN (1961–1996) AND NOW (2015)

I was active in the political area from 1961 until 1996. Most of the things I learned about lobbying were from that period. Most of the factors and basic principles remain the same; however, changes have emerged to influence the political environment. These comments are from my own experiences, and some of them might not be the views of everyone, or for that matter, anyone.

1. As I wrote in the chapter on the Twenty-Fifth Amendment, the Amendment was adopted because of the effective lobbying principles that were utilized: (a.) A superior product. (b.) A broad-ranging coalition of support from Constitutional scholars and knowledgeable people "back home." (c.) The right bipartisan leadership in Congress, and (d.) The support of the President of the United States. These continue to be basic principles of lobbying.

2. Are interest groups and their lobbyists as bad as many believe? It depends on your own interest. Most of us belong to one or more, whether it's the Chamber of Commerce, the Sierra Club, a labor union, or the National Rifle Association. If we personally don't belong to such a group, we have close friends or relatives who do. "It's not my group that harms the public interest; it's the other person's."

As much as interest groups are maligned as conducting unsavory activity, most elected officials often rely on the specialized groups' expertise in forming their judgments. Lobbyists and their employer groups are considered part of the "Fourth Branch" of government for this reason. This is not to say that all positions of various interests are always best for the country. But each of us has the right to petition government under the Constitution's First Amendment, and lobbying has provided that means since the Republic's beginning.

In addition to advocating a point of view, one of a lobbyist's most important functions is to take information from one side of the Congressional house to the other. Surprisingly, there often is little communication between members and staffs of the corresponding Senate and House committees, and a lobbyist who knows what's happening on each side can provide it.

3. Foremost in achieving legislative success is to have committed, influential bipartisan lead sponsors in both the Senate and House, and it's best that they are members of the Congressional committees that will consider the bill. Committee chairpersons are the best of all.

4. A major key to success is knowing the legislator's local environment (conservative or liberal). If there is strong local support, the legislator will listen. Know who is closest to the legislator, whether it's a specialized interest group, the campaign manager, the PAC treasurer, or yes, depending on the situation, the legislator's spouse. It always helps to organize a coalition of groups back home that shares your views. While campaign money is important, home ground local support is key to political success. Lobbying by Washington-based professionals is just a part of the equation, and means little without corresponding local support.

5. Also important in achieving success is not giving up if your cause is important. If you can't get everything at once, which generally is the case, be willing to compromise. Another time will come to amend the law if it's necessary or desirable.

6. Among the most important people on Capitol Hill and in the agencies are the staffs of the individual legislators and committees. Get to know them well, the "gate keepers," and your work in Washington will be much easier. You must gain their trust. Sometimes you might find it easiest to overlook some facts or simply not give the full story. Be careful about this. Never mislead, even slightly, a legislator or the staff. You won't get back in the door if you do.

7. Washington lives on crises. There's one a minute, often harrowing it seems, whether at the White House, on Capitol Hill, or a scandal at the IRS or CIA. The media thrives on crisis and lives on conflict. The pace of activity can be so fast that often reporting the news is devoted to who are politically winning or losing on a given issue, rather than careful analysis of issues and how the issue actually affects people. This requires a level of talent and interest often lacking in those covering issues in Washington. They can have you

fearful that the country is coming to an end soon. There are indeed genuine crises that must be dealt with seriously, but many of the scariest matters are gone soon after tomorrow.

When I began as a lobbyist in Washington in 1961, we didn't look to the news media, TV or newsprint for help. The reason: politicians didn't want their names associated with lobbyists or the groups they represented. There should be no mention publicly of their cooperation with any interest group on a given issue because they would appear beholden to that group. However, this caution began to change; successful legislative efforts became increasingly dependent on the advocacy group obtaining an issue's support from the legislator's local news media.

At Common Cause, I learned that the more press on the issue, from Common Cause's standpoint, the better. Media messages then, however, were only in newspapers, magazines, and occasionally the broadcast media. By the time I rejoined the ABA staff after leaving Common Cause, and later joining the NAII, I was fully in tune with the use of the media on our issues. The politicians would urge it by telling us that a favorable editorial back home would make it easier for them.

The delivery of the messages has changed and continues changing dramatically. Print, TV and radio news, and columns are still important, but these are now for older audiences. Traditional news reporters are leaving television networks, and reporting and commenting on the Internet. Bloggers, through their own Internet web sites, are providing insight and analysis on every issue imaginable. And many of the bloggers, both left and right, who "cover" Washington, don't actually live there. With this rapidly changing scene away from traditional reporting, it's difficult to answer the question of who exactly comprise the Washington media.

8. The discussion of the news media leads me to comment on the use of technology and social media, which is causing a revolution in politics, just as in all that we do every day. According to a 2014 Pew Research Center Survey, cell phones and social media like Facebook and Twitter are playing a prominent role in how voters get political information and election news. Twitter and Facebook are no longer a fascination with politicians. During the 2014 election campaign, 90 percent of the politicians were on social media of some kind. Virtually every incumbent and 94 percent of their opponents were on Facebook. Facebook is the most popular because it's used by all age groups.

But Instagram and Snapchat are used also because of their popularity with younger groups.

Many legislators are using YouTube channels to spread their messages throughout the year and at campaign time. It helps them communicate instantly about their stands on issues. This is the value of social media…instant communication wherever the recipient might be.

A favorite use of social media is for candidates to urge their supporters to vote early, and inform them how to register and find their polling place. Columnist Mary Schmidt, writing in the *Chicago Tribune* on the day after the 2014 election, told about her experiences with Social Media Get Out To Vote. She said that on Facebook she got message after message exhorting her to vote. She said that the updates marched past like a parade of barking boot-camp instructors.

Schmidt said that feeling guilty that she hadn't charged right out to vote, she "toggled" over to Twitter, and the citizen preachers were on fire there too:

"If you can stand in line for an iPhone, you can stand in line to vote."

One tweet that Schmidt read said, "If you're not voting, you're not trending." She said that social media voting buzz made voting more urgent, clubby, cool, and while it verged on annoying, it was far better than the cynicism that so often infects politics. "Voting," she wrote, "in a social media age reinforces the notion of voting as a communal act, and a right and responsibility that we all share."

Social media can be unfair, particularly by dropping last-minute negative information on candidate-friendly blogs. It then is circulated quickly on social media, hoping it will create a controversy reported on broadcast or print news. This bypasses the normal press process when a traditional reporter would check out the source. The opponent is then "bloodied" without knowledge of who started the last-minute controversy.

To be sure, politicians still use phone calls, direct mail, email and their web sites to advertise their candidacies and get out the vote. They even still distribute yard signs. But the technological age has taken over, and it's changing the face of politics. It's something I couldn't have imagined when I worked in Washington 50 years ago.

Special note: It's interesting to note that a Pew Research survey, taken in the spring of 2014, reported on political polarization and media habits. When it comes to getting the news about politics and government, down-the-line liberals and conservatives live in distinctly different worlds. They trust and distrust different news sources, and have different ways of getting information.

Forty-seven percent of conservatives cited a single news source, Fox News, as their main source for news about politics and government. Eighty-seven percent of conservatives trust Fox News. When on Facebook, conservatives are more likely than those in other ideological groups to hear political opinions similar to their own.

In contrast, liberals are less unified on a news source, but NPR and *The New York Times* are among those topping their list. Their most trusted sources are NPR, PBS and the BBC. Liberals are more likely than others to block or "defriend" someone on a social network because of politics.

Those closer to the ideological middle are focused less on politics than the committed liberals and conservatives. When they are interested, their main sources include CNN, local TV and Fox News, along with Yahoo News and Google News.

It's clear from the Pew survey that most people who harbor strong political views prefer to watch and listen to the news outlets that are closest to their own. This complicates efforts to unify the country, and presents a different environment than we knew just a short time ago. Hopefully, the polarizing media will not be strong enough to keep our nation's leaders from finding common ground on necessary solutions, and sooner rather than later.

9. Throughout this memoir, I've stressed the importance of bipartisan cooperation in achieving success. This is all I knew in the 1960s into the 1990s. My friend and former colleague, John Lagomarcino, has commented on those days as the "golden age of lobbying," compared to today's (2015) on Capitol Hill. He said, "Your description of the willingness to reach a legislative goal seems almost quaint by today's standards. The bipartisanship you describe is hard to come by today." He pointed out that the Congressional appropriations process has broken down, and that regular order on Capitol Hill is no longer followed. He asks, "How do you lobby anything related to funding when the system is not functioning? The same uncertainty applies to nearly every other high priority issue from immigration reform to taxes, infrastructure, and you name it." John reminded me that there were disagreements on our lobbying efforts, but usually there was a sense that things could be worked out. While no one ever wins them all, in past years, the lobbying process had a certain order to it that is lacking today.

That "order" was exemplified by one of the finest Congressional and Presidential hours when President Johnson and Senate Minority Leader Everett Dirksen got together to pass the landmark Civil Rights Act of 1964. The Southern block of Democrats and some Republicans wouldn't give an inch on extending equal rights to African-Americans. But for the sake of the country, well-meaning leaders came together and agreed to a solution. Because Senate Democrats didn't have the votes to override a long filibuster by their own members, Republicans were needed to support the bill. Through the efforts of Senator Dirksen, 27 of 33 Republican senators voted for the bill as compared to 46 of 67 Democrats, enough bipartisan votes to end the filibuster and overwhelmingly pass the bill.

Republican Representative Bill McCulloch's strong leadership helped pass it in the House. Perhaps that's an understatement because President Johnson credited the congressman with saving the bill, and he was highlighted as that savior in journalist Tom S. Purdum's book, *An Idea Whose Time Has Come.*

President Johnson considered the Civil Rights Act to be his signature legislation, and said that nothing could honor President Kennedy's memory more than its passage. An act proposed by Democrats was enacted with the strong support of Republicans. At the signing ceremony, some 70 supporters, including leaders such as Dr. Martin Luther King, Jr., received a pen from the president. The first to receive one was Senator Dirksen, and soon after, Representative McCulloch.

Why isn't this kind of cooperation among both houses of Congress and the president, for the most part, happening today? Why is this seemingly never-ending inability to tackle the nation's most pressing issues? The words "dysfunctional Washington" are used most often, but I think the better phrase is "sharp divisions of the public's views."

William Falk, editor of *The Week*, stated in his August 29, 2014 commentary that the various sides don't just disagree with each other…They see the others as evil, and even "a threat to the nation's well-being."

Robert J. Samuelson talks about Washington's standstill in his *Washington Post* column of November 19, 2014. He says: "…We can't-or-won't govern because our politics is less interested in governing. The ideas and plans from the left and right have the purpose of winning support among their political bases…So the distance between the two parties increases while the prospect for legitimate compromise diminishes."

Mr. Falk also says that he doesn't know where we're headed. Hopefully, past is prologue, and in the not-too-distant-future, thoughtful politicians will come together to find common ground in our nation's interest.

10. "Money is the Mother's Milk of Politics" is a quote from Jesse Unruh, Speaker of the California Assembly in the 1960s. In other words, campaign money is necessary to be successful in politics. I have testified before Congress for limitations on political contributions and favoring contributions from the candidates' local areas. I've raised political action money when I represented property and casualty insurers. I continue to believe that as long as campaigns cost so much to advertise, organize, and get out the vote, there is no viable option for candidates except to raise money from supporters. There's no debating that contributions are made to elect politicians who will support the contributors' points of view. And there's no debate that money is needed by politicians to influence their elections.

When I was involved, our contributions were difficult to raise, and they were meager compared to today in 2015. The contributions were from individuals, mostly insurance company executives, to the candidates' political action committees. There were limitations on each contributor, and the contributions were disclosed. The insurance companies could not contribute. But now, there has been a sea change in the nature of political contributions. Our little NAII-PAC contributions of the 1980s and '90s would seem like nothing now. As an aside, we and the legislators themselves didn't like having to do it. It's an unpleasant, time-consuming activity for most donors and legislators alike.

As a result of two recent Supreme Court decisions, *Citizens United v. FEC* and *McCutcheon v. FEC*, based on the right of free speech, the door opened to allow corporations and unions to spend unlimited amounts on elections. This money cannot be given directly to or used in coordination with a candidate. Consequently, flood gates opened for unlimited contributions at all political levels from the presidency to state governors. This has become the age of "Super-PACs," political action committees that can be set up by wealthy individuals to advertise independently of the candidates and without the need for disclosure of the donor. While candidates still seek contributions to their own PACs, the biggest money goes into the Supers. Some call the new Super-PAC approach "Dark Money." In the 2014 midterm election, some $4 billion for all elections set a record.

Is this an enormously outrageous amount to spend on political campaigns throughout the country? The commentator George Will apparently doesn't think so. He says it's not much compared to the $2.2 billion Americans spent in 2014 on Halloween Candy." (According to the National Retail Federation, over $7 billion was spent on Halloween altogether.)

If these dollars did indeed provide helpful information on issues, Mr. Will could have a point. Helpful information on the candidates' views are important in an election. But do they inform, or only manage to roil people up? In Illinois, my home state, we couldn't have been happier when the political ads were finally over. There was very little substance, but plenty of vicious attacks. And they continued without let-up for weeks. So, compared to my own past experience with political fund-raising, the entry of unlimited, undisclosed funds into the political system is offensive and even obscene.

Such unlimited money is changing the political landscape. It has diminished the importance of the political parties, which in turn has changed the way the Senate and House operate. This has lessened the ability of Congressional leaders to provide orderly leadership that leads to bipartisanship. The small contributor's participation in the political system has become less relevant. Some commentators say money corrupts the process by making the legislator beholden to the donor (presumably even on issues where the legislator and donor might disagree). Others contend it simply supports candidates who already believe the same as the donor, and this is not corruption. Whether big, undisclosed political money is or is not corruption, the public believes it is; and this perception lowers the already low faith in Congress.

To give Congress some credit, in past years some reforms that included limits and disclosure were enacted. The Supreme Court, however, has repeatedly found many of those reforms to be unconstitutional as a violation of free speech. Since the Supreme Court was so sharply divided in these later decisions, the Court might change its mind at another time. I doubt that the present system that doesn't make sense to me is locked in stone.

11. With all of the negativity and dismal outlook about the Washington scene, there are positive changes taking place that shouldn't be overlooked. An important one is the increasing diversity among the leaders that presents a sharp contrast between my time in Washington and today.

The President is African-American. What a sharply distinctive change from pre-1964 when black people could not even enter the same restaurants as whites.

The increasing number of women and minorities in Congress also presents a sharp contrast between the 1960s, '70s and 2014. In 1970, there were 10 women in the House and one in the Senate. In the 113th Congress, there are 80 women in the House and 20 in the Senate. The 2014 election brought the count of women between the House and Senate in the 114th Congress to over 100 for the first time.

There were 13 African-Americans in the 92nd Congress (1971–1973). In the 113th Congress, and scheduled for the 114th, there are 42 African-Americans in the House and two in the Senate.

In the 114th Congress, there are 37 Hispanics in the House and four in the Senate. There are 10 Asian-Americans in the House and one in the Senate. There are three Native Americans in the House and none in the Senate.

__A closing note:__ Many Washington office holders, their assistants, and bureaucrats come down with "Potomac Fever," and don't want to go back to Pocatello if they are defeated or retire (although I think this well-known phrase gives the Idaho community an unfair bad rap). Many of these develop an "Inside the Beltway" view that only Washington, in contrast to the rest of the country, is the most important place to be.

Having said this, to the Becks, the Capital City is indeed an exciting and interesting place to live and work. Although remaining there with our family after two different stays wasn't my cup of tea, it provides experiences that can be extraordinarily fulfilling and unforgettable for a lifetime. If you have a chance to live it, do it.

In my case, the development and implementation of public policy and association leadership were what I did best, whether in Washington or Chicago. Until my first job at the American Bar Association, it wasn't something I had planned. But, in a short time, I was lucky. I knew I had found my niche.

BIBLIOGRAPHY

American Bar Association, *Annual Reports of the American Bar Association from 1972 until 1980*, Vol. 96 through 105.

Bayh, Birch, *One Heartbeat Away*. Indianapolis: The Bobbs-Merrill Company, 1968.

Burger, Warren E., *The State of Justice*. Chicago: *70 A.B.A.J. 62*, 1984.

Brokaw, Tom, *The Greatest Generation*. New York: Random House, 1998.

Cahn, Jean Camper, *Letter to James O. Eastland, endorsing Lewis F. Powell, Jr. for associate justice of the Supreme Court*. Urban Law Institute of Antioch College, November 3, 1971.

Chesterfield Smith interview by the American Bar Foundation (transcript of an interview in the 1970s). University of Florida: ufdc.ufl.edu/ AA00005955/00001.

_____. *Civil Rights Movement*. John F. Kennedy Presidential Library and Museum. Boston: http://www.jfklibrary.org/JFK/JFK-in-History/Civil Rights-Movement.aspx

Falk, William, Commentary. *The Week*, August 29, 2014, page 4.

Feerick, John D., *From Failing Hands (The Story of Presidential Succession)*. New York: Fordham University Press, 1965.

Feerick, John D., *The Twenty-Fifth Amendment (Its Complete History and Applications)*. New York: Fordham University Press, 2014.

Gardner, John W., *In Common Cause*. New York: W. W. Norton, 1972.

Georgia Department of Archives and History, *Jarrett Manor, June 2, 1967*. Athens, GA: Digital Library of Georgia, 2004.

Gilje, Paul, *Rioting in America*. Bloomington: Indiana University Press 1996.

Hastings, John S., *The Criminal Justice Act of 1964*. The Journal of Criminal Law, Criminology and Police Science, Northwestern University School of Law, Vol. 57, No. 4.

Johnson, Earl Jr., *Justice and Reform (The Formative Years of the American Legal Services Program)*. New Brunswick, NJ: Transaction Books, 1974.

Jeffries, John C., Jr., *Justice Lewis F. Powell, Jr. (A Biography)*. New York: C. Scribner's Sons, 1994.

Kutak, Robert J., *The Criminal Justice Act of 1964*. Nebraska Law Review, Vol. 44, No. 4.

Lorenz, Charles J., *The Story of an American Insurance Revolution*. Des Plaines, IL: National Association of Independent Insurers, 1995.

Moynihan, Daniel P., *The Politics of a Guaranteed Income, the Nixon Administration and the Family Assistance Plan*. New York: Random House, 1971.

Purdum, Tom S., *An Idea Whose Time Has Come*, March, 2015.

Ramage, Angela and Kelly Vickers, *Images of America: Toccoa*. Charleston, SC: Arcadia Publishing, 2012.

Remini, Robert V., *A Short History of the United States*. New York: HarperCollins, 2008.

Stossel, Scott, *Sarge (The Life and Times of Sargent Shriver)*. Washington, D.C.: Smithsonian Books, 2004.

Sugarman, Stephen D., *California's Insurance Regulation Revolution (The First Two Years of Proposition 103)*. 27 San Diego L. Rev. 683, 1990.

Tamm, Edward A. and Paul C. Reardon, *Warren E. Burger and the Administration of Justice*. Brigham Young University Law Review, 1981.

ACKNOWLEDGEMENTS

My son, Jonathan, who has researched our family ancestry, urged me to write a memoir. He stressed that although he could find dates and locations about our forbearers, there was little about what they did. Maybe they were listed as farmer or retailer, but not much else. A memoir of my life's work, he said, would be helpful for my own grandchildren and those to come. His brother, Rich, and sister, Lori, agreed with him. I dragged my feet, but finally decided to give it a try. This is the result, and I'm grateful to Jonathan, Rich and Lori for encouraging me.

My wife, Myrna, also urged me to write it. While she has always stuck by that, she's had to put up with a lot of my hours behind closed doors. I appreciate her patience, and thank her for carefully reviewing the manuscript, with helpful suggestions.

Thanks to so many others for reviewing the manuscript, and either editing or offering suggestions or both.

Senator Birch Bayh reviewed and affirmed the accuracy of the story of the adoption of the Twenty-Fifth Amendment.

John Feerick, former dean of the Fordham Law School, gave me encouragement to go ahead with it through some discouraging times. I doubt that I would have continued and concluded it without his support. His reviews of the section on the Twenty-Fifth Amendment, and the Preface and Epilogue were invaluable.

Paul and Vicki Green, close personal friends, did the first reading of the entire manuscript, with editing and suggestions for improvement.

John Lagomarcino, my Urban Coalition and Common Cause colleague, reviewed and affirmed the chapter on those organizations. He stressed that those years were the "Golden Years of Lobbying," when bipartisanship was a way of life on Capitol Hill, in contrast to today's polarization. He made helpful suggestions for an Epilogue, showing differences between politics then and 2015.

These former colleagues reviewed and affirmed the chapters with which they were most familiar:

> David Hayes, former ABA executive director…American Bar Association
> Gene Bagatti, Chuck Lorenz, Diana Lee Troxel, Terrie Troxel and Bob Wegenke, former NAII senior officers…National Association of Independent Insurers
> Justice (Ret.) Earl Johnson, Jr., former director of the OEO Legal Services Program…Office of Economic Opportunity Legal Services Program.

Mark Cannon, former administrative assistant to the Chief Justice, affirmed my recollections for the sections discussing Chief Justice Warren Burger.

Carole Cartwright, former WYCC-TV director, reviewed my "retirement" role as television host and commented on my observations of life in the Deep South.

Rev. Dr. Jon McCoy, pastor of the Hinsdale United Methodist Church, a native of Mississippi, offered comments on race relations in the South and Midwest.

Marina Jacks, ABA administrative secretary, made available volumes of ABA reports.

And, finally, Julie Ann James and Teri Lynn Franco at The Peppertree Press gave helpful guidance through the publishing process, and Rebecca Barbier designed a strikingly beautiful cover.

I am grateful to each of these individuals for their encouragement, support and comments. Without them, I could not have put this story together. With them, vivid and accurate memories fell into place. Thank you more than I can say.

INDEX

A

American Bar Association (ABA), 1–2, 24, 116, 230, 272, 275, 277, 279
  Annual Meeting, 33, 243, 275
  Board of Governors, 217–218, 226–227, 229–230, 239, 243, 247, 254, 262
  Chicago Headquarters, 5, 28–31, 53, 75, 112, 216
  Chicago Public Relations Department, 98
  Code of Professional Responsibility, 253
  Commission on Correctional Facilities, 261
  Commission on the Law and Economy, 284
  Committee on Communist Tactics, Strategy, and Objectives, 83
  Committee on Continuing Professional Education, 276
  Committee on Jurisprudence and Law Reform, 90
  Commission on Evaluation of Professional Standards, 277
  Criminal Law Section, 121
  Division of Committee Services, 129
  Division of Professional Education, 237
  Division of Public Service Activities, 126, 129
  Federal Judiciary Committee, 45, 247
  Fund for Justice and Education (Fund for Public Education), 256–257, 277
  House of Delegates, 217–219, 226, 238–239, 247, 253, 262, 264, 275, 278
  Junior Bar Conference (Young Lawyers' Section), 5, 29, 94
  Legal Practice and Education Section, 98
  Legal Services, 264
  Midyear Meeting of the House of Delegates (1965), 113–116
  Office of Resource Development, 257
  Political Action Fund, 75
  Prepaid Legal Services Committee, 265
  Professional Services, 265
  Second Century Fund, 257
  Section of Taxation, 75, 217, 232
  Special Committee on Availability of Legal Services, 265
  Special Committee on Election Law and Voter Participation, 278
  Special Committee on Lawyers in Government, 278
  Special Study Commission on Presidential Succession and Disability (Inability), 88, 100
  Standing Committee on Lawyer Referral, 110
  Standing Committee on Legal Aid, 113
  Washington, D.C. Office, 32–33, 36–37
  Young Lawyers Section 277–278
  Youth Education for Citizenship under Law, 128, 240
Abegg, Dr. Jerry, (Bradley University Pres.) 22–24
Adams, Senator Brock (D-WA), 152, 159, 172
Addison, Allen, 12, 19
Admiral Insurance Company, 331
Aetna, 97, 280–281, 312
Affirmed (Triple Crown Winner), 289
AFL-CIO, 95, 203
Agency Practice Act, 60
Agnew, Ken, 15
Agnew, Vice President Spiro, 104
Agnoli, Dr., 249
Alcatraz, 121
Alexander, Congressman Bill (D-AR), 152, 159, 172
ALI-ABA Committee on Continuing Professional Education, 275
Allen, Ivan (Atlanta Mayor), 152
Allen, Lucy (ABA Section of Taxation), 75
Alliance of American Insurers (AAI), 313
Allison, Junius (NLADA Executive Secretary), 110–111
Allstate Insurance, 266–267, 281, 290, 302, 305, 307, 314, 317
American Assembly of Columbia University, 242
American Assembly on Law and a Changing Society, 242
American Bar Association Journal, 31, 278
American Bar Center, 277
American Bar Foundation, 217, 225, 257
American Dental Association, 37
American Farm Bureau, 37
American Institute for Property Casualty Underwriters, 311
American Insurance Association (AIA), 313
American International Group, (AIG) 313, 330–331
American Law Institute (ALI), 135, 218, 237–240
American Medical Association (AMA), 37, 297
American Political Science Association, 95
American Prepaid Legal Services Institute, 264
American Thrift Assembly, 37
Americans for Democratic Action (ADA), 176
Anderson, Barbara (WYCC-TV Writer), 340
Anderson, Congressman John (R-IL), 152–154, 172, 236
Andrews, David (ABA Treasurer), 252, 256–256, 266
Andrusko, Chris, 1, 186, 187, 337
  Lori Kay, 1, 186-188, 203, 205, 210, 244, 273, 292, 315, 337
  Matthew, 1, 186, 187, 337
  Richard, 186, 187, 337
  Ryan, 1, 186, 187, 337
  Stephen, 1, 186, 187, 337
Annotti, Joe (NAII Communications), 338
Ansheles, Robert, 37, 43
Anti-Communist Crusade, 83
Antioch College, 116
Arlington, VA, 35, 76
Army, basic training 27
Associated Press, 178
Association of American Law Schools, 98, 218
Audi, 329
Availability Crisis, 296

B

Baab, Craig (ABA Washington Office), 236
Babe Ruth of Insurance. See Jack Byrne
Bagatti, Gene (NAII Chief Administrative Officer), 271–272, 294, 312, 314, 332
Bail Reform Act of 1966, 103, 120–124, 146
Bail Reform Act of 1984, 124
Bailey, Robert (NAII Chairman), 335
Bailey, Sylvia, 335
Baker v. Carr, 48
Baker, Don (OEO General Counsel), 117–118
Bamberger, Clinton (OEO Legal Services Program Director), 117, 119, 145
Barnes, Craig (Political Activist & Author), 204
Barnett, Martha (ABA president), 264
Bates and O'Steen, 249
Bath, 318
Batten, Jim (Knight-Ridder Newspapers), 172
Bay of Pigs, 42–43, 59
Bayh, Marvella, 102, 105
Bayh, Senator Birch (D-IN), 82, 85–88, 92–97, 99–103, 105, 122, 144–145, 172, 184, 236
BBC, 350
Beck,
  Carol, 10, 30
  George, 7–11, 13–14, 16–17, 19–24, 76,
  Hazel McMeen, 7, 10–11, 13–14, 16, 19, 24, 76
  Jonathan Everett, 1, 134, 137–139, 186, 187 205, 244, 275, 284, 289, 340
  Liam, 1, 186, 187
  Lori Kay. See Andrusko
  Myrna V, 9, 30, 32–34, 36, 41–42, 45–46, 51–53, 55–57, 67, 75–77, 93–94, 117–118, 128, 136–138, 143, 160, 187, 205, 210–212, 220–221, 244, 249, 269–270, 273, 275, 288–289, 298, 312, 314, 319, 328–329, 333, 336, 337–338
  Richard Lowell, 56, 93, 126, 143, 187, 205, 244, 252, 273, 275, 319, 340, 345

Spencer, 1, 186, 187
Suzi, 1, 186, 187, 340
Becker, Ralph, 37
Beckley, West Virginia, 53
Beecher, Lynnette and Roger, 9
Bell, Commissioner Fletcher,(NAIC President), 290
Bennett, James V. (Federal Bureau
of Prisons Director), 121–122
Bennett, Senator Wallace F. (R-UT), 195
Bennett, Tony, 329
Berkley, William (William R. Berkley Companies), 331
Berlin, Germany, 50, 55, 57
Bernhard, Berl (U.S. Commission on
Civil Rights Staff Director), 137
Bernstein, Carl (The Washington Post), 223–224
Biehl's Laundry and Dry Cleaners, 27
Biemiller, Andy (AFL-CIO Chief Lobbyist), 151, 172
Black Panthers, 133
Black Power, 133
Blume, Paul, Sr. (NAII General Counsel), 287, 293
BMW, 329
Bond, Julian (Civil Rights Leader), 136
Bookbinder, "Bookie" (American Jewish
Committee), 172
Booz Allen & Hamilton, 244–246
Boren, Dr. Charles (Navy Psychiatrist), 250–252
Bork, Robert (Solicitor General), 224
Bourke-White, Margaret, 30–31
Boyd, Willard (Sandy), (President of the Field
Museum), 341
Bradley University, 13, 19, 21–24, 39, 341
Braintree Company, 7
Brandeis, Justice Louis, 214
Brendel, Marilyn, (ABA) 30
Brennan, Edward (Sears Roebuck Chairman), 341
Broder, David (The Washington Post Columnist), 178
Brokaw, Tom (NBC Nightly News Commentator), 232
Bronze Anvil Award, 309
Brookfield, WI, 289
Brooks, Congressman Jack (D-TX), 296, 298
Brown vs. Board of Education, 14, 39, 84
Brown, H. Rapp, 133
Browne, Michael (Harleysville Insurance Group
President and COO), 344
Brownell Plan, 81
Brownell, Herbert (Attorney General), 81, 87, 90, 93, 95–97, 235–236, 274
Browning, Carol, 20
Browning, Don (University of Chicago Professor), 51
Brunner, Kim (Chief Legal Officer & Executive
Vice President, State Farm) 291
Bubolz, John (SECURA Insurance CEO), 307, 326
Buffett, Warren, 295, 318
Burdsall, Wendy (Common Cause), 213
Burger, Warren (Chief Justice), 235, 260–262, 332
Burns, Kenneth , 29, 227
Bush, President George H.W., 104, 253
Bush, President George W., 104

Business Council in New York City, 96–97
Business Insurance, 305
Byrd, Senator Harry (D-VA), 98
Byrne, Dorothy, 294
Byrne, Jack (GEICO CEO), 293–295, 317–318

C

Cahn, Edgar, 106–116, 206
Cahn, Jean, 107–117
Caldwell, Johnnie (Georgia Commissioner), 290
Califano, Joseph A, Jr. (President Special Assistant), 120
Cambodia, 169–170
Cannon, Mark (Warren Burger Administrative
Assistant), 235, 261–262
Carlson, Ronald (Callaway Chair of Law Emeritus
at the University of Georgia Law School), 26, 35, 46
Carmichael, Stokely, 133
Carnegie Corporation of New York, 135
Carnegie Foundation for the Advancement
of Teaching, 135
Carrithers, Dr. David
(University of Tennessee/Chattanooga,
Political Science Department), 338–339
Carroll, IA, 26
Carswell, Judge Harold, 150, 212
Carter, President Jimmy, 230, 292
Cartwright, Carole (WYCC-TV Manager), 340
Case Method, 25
Castro, Fidel, 42, 59
Caterpillar Co., 9, 11, 27, 97
Catholic University Law School, 119
Cats, 318
Celler, Emanuel (House Judiciary Committee
Chairman), 43–44, 63–64, 70, 92, 94–96, 98, 101–103, 105, 145
Central Christian Church (Disciples of Christ), 9, 16–17, 20
Central Intelligence Agency (CIA), 42
Channell, Betty, 1, 100, 234
Channell, Donald (ABA Washington, D.C.Director),
5, 32–33, 41, 43, 58, 62–64, 66–67, 73–74, 78,
82–84, 86–88, 91, 93–94, 96–103, 107, 109,
112–113, 123, 125–126, 143, 145, 232–234
Chapman, Bobby, 337–338
Chapman, Connie, 337–338
Chapman, Derrick, 337–338
Lindsay 338
Chase, Chevy, 319
Cheney, Vice President Richard, 105
Chicago Sun-Times, 307
Chicago Tribune, 35, 229, 306–307
Chicago, IL, 14, 53, 118, 126, 128, 216, 266
Child, Louise (ABA Journal Editor), 31
China, 189
Choate, Jerry (Allstate CEO) , 341
Christie, Agatha, The Mousetrap, 318-319
Christopher, Warren (Deputy Secretary of State), 292–293

Churchill Downs, 288
Citizens United v. FEC, 352
Citizens United v. Federal Election Commission, 299
Civil Rights Act of 1964, 44, 132, 351
Civil Rights, 57, 143, 172
Claiborne Farms, 289
Clark, Ramsey (Attorney General of the United
States), 100, 126–127, 130
Clark, Richard, 213
Clark, Tom, Supreme Court Justice, 100, 127
Claybrook, Joan (Consumer/Safety Advocate), 303–304
Clinton, President William, 196
CNN, 350
Cohen, David (Common Cause President), 197, 206, 208, 213
Cold War, 39, 60
College of District Attorneys, 218
Collier, Representative Harold (R-IL), 47, 192
Collins, Barbara (Common Cause), 213
Collins, LeRoy (National Association of
Broadcasters President), 95
Commiskey, Charles, 341
Common Cause, 29, 165–166, 176–181, 188,
189, 195-189, 200–204, 206–210, 212–215,
223, 268–269, 299, 304, 348
Communications and Power Subcommittee, 208
Community Action Program (CAP), 106–108
Concord Insurance, 267
Conference of Chief Justices, 218
Congressional Seniority System, 199
Conrad, Larry (Senator Birch Bayh Assistant),
87–88, 92, 101, 122, 139, 144
Conrad, Mary Lou, 139
Constitutional Convention, 96
C NA, 313
Convergence, 327
Conway, Jack (Common Cause, President),
205–208, 210–211
Coover, Darrell (NAII Washington, D.C.
Vice President), 272, 297–299, 332–333
Corporal Punishment, 18–19
Corporation for Public Broadcasting, 135
Cosby, Bill 329
Cosmos Club, 161, 169, 205
Cotton, Senator Norris (R-NH), 68, 70
Council for Legal Education Opportunity (CLEO), 129, 217
Cox, Archibald (Harvard Law School Noted
Constitutional Authority), 223–224
Craig, Walter (ABA President), 84, 88–89, 93, 95, 144
Craver, Roger (Common Cause), 188, 208, 213
Criminal Justice Act of 1964, 62, 67, 69–73, 83, 103
Cromwell, Jim (Congressman Michel's Chief of
Staff), 39–40, 47
Cronkite, Walter (CBS Newscaster), 86
Crosby, John (NAII General Counsel), 325
Cuba, 59–60

Cuban Missile Crisis, 59
Cummiskey, John W. (ABA Standing Committee on Legal Aid Chairman), 67, 70–71, 109–110, 112–114, 118, 239, 264, 341

D

D'Alemberte, Talbot (ABA President), 278
Daley, Chicago Mayor Richard J., 136, 170
Davis, Bill (Common Cause), 213
Dawson, Dave (Common Cause), 213
de Shetler, Ken (Nationwide Insurance Company Officer), 289
Dean, John (White House Counsel), 223
Decker, General Ted (Judge Advocate General of the Army), 52, 55
Department of Labor, 259
Derrington, Andi, 336
Derrington, Dan, 336
Des Plaines, IL, 280, 282
Dick, Bess (Congressman Celler Assistant), 100–101, 122
Direct Writers, 281
Dirksen, Senator Everett, (R-IL) 39, 44–45, 56, 92, 99, 143, 351
Disciples of Christ. See Central Christian Church
Discrimination, 14–15
Donohue, Joseph "Jigs," 37, 243
Drew, Elizabeth (Journalist and Author), 154
Dry Cleaning and Laundry Institute, 338
Duck and Cover, 42–43
Ducks Unlimited, 338
Duke Law School, 31
Duke University, 46, 48
Dulles, John Foster 43

E

Early, Bert H. (ABA Executive Director), 31, 68, 78, 88, 112, 114, 125, 128, 135, 182, 211–212, 216, 220, 222, 226–227, 232, 234, 238–239, 241, 246–252, 257–258, 266, 269, 275, 279
Early, Betsy, 128, 266, 279
Eastland, Senator James (D-MS) Judiciary Committee Chairman), 80–86
Easton, Robert (ABA Staff Financial Officer), 242
Eberle, William (American Standard, Inc. President), 136, 196, 203
Economic Opportunity Act, 108
Edelman, Marian Wright (Children's Welfare Rights), 172
Edelman, Peter (Common Cause Staff), 199
Ehrlichman, John 223
Eighth Amendment, 121
Eisenhower Commission on Causes and Prevention of Violence, 201
Eisenhower, President Dwight D., 34, 39–40, 60, 81, 95–96, 242, 274
Ellwanger, David (Public Service Activities Director), 242–243, 265
End the War Campaign, 199
English Channel, 319

Equal Employment Opportunity Commission, 259
Erickson, Bob, 35
Erickson, Gaby, 275
Erickson, Ron, 275
Ervin Committee, 224
Ervin, Senator Sam, (D-NC), 63, 68, 70, 75, 122
European Vacation (Chevy Chase), 319
Faber-Musser Slaughter and Meatpacking House, 7

F

Face the Nation, 178
Facebook, 348–350
Falk, William (The Week Editor), 351–352
Falsgraf, William (ABA president), 241
Family Assistance Plan (F.A.P.) 163, 189–193, 195–196, 207
Farm Bureau Insurance Company, 321
Federal Bar Association, 218, 220
Federal Bureau of Investigation (FBI), 225
Federal Civil Service, 201
Federal Election Reform, 217
Feerick, John (Fordham Law School Dean), 3, 82, 91–92, 97, 100, 144, 278
Fensterwald, Bernard, Jr. (Bud), 61–62
Finch, HEW Secretary Robert, 193
Finklestein, Larry (Public Affairs Council), 172
Fireman's Fund, 294, 319
First Amendment, 253, 299
First from Chicago (WYCC-TV), 340
Fitzpatrick, James, 307
Flickinger Families in the United States, 8
Florida Constitution (One-Man-One Vote Rule), 225
Foley, Bill (General Counsel for House Judiciary Committee), 43–44, 64, 98
Ford Foundation, 107–108
Ford Motor Company, 306–307
Ford, President Gerald, 104, 118, 229
Fort Knox, KY, 53
Fort Meade, Maryland, 52–55
Foster, Dr. Alan, 7
Fox News, 350
Frank Barrett (CEO of Omaha Indemnity), 267, 293
Freed, Daniel (Deputy Attorney General Assistant), 66–67, 69, 71–73, 121–122, 124
Freund, Professor Paul (Harvard Law School, noted Constitutional Scholar), 90, 98
Gallamore, Robert (Common Cause Policy Development Director), 188, 208, 210, 213

G

Gallup Poll, 199
Gardner, Aida, 205
Gardner, John W. (National Urban Coalition and Common Cause Chairman), 135–138, 147, 149–181, 188–191–194, 196–197, 202–207, 209–211, 213–215, 269, 274, 312
Garment, Leonard (White House Counsel) 207
GE, 97

General Motors (GM), 97, 306–307
George Washington Day Dinner, 155
Georgetown Law Center, 46
Georgetown Law School (Trial Institute), 35, 46
Georgia Chamber of Commerce, 32
Georgia Historical Commission Site, 16
Gibson, Jonathan (ABA), 90, 93
Gilje, Paul (Rioting in America) 132
Goelz, Nancy, 77
Goelz, Warren, 19, 21, 23, 77
Golden Touch Award, 327
Goldstein, Professor (Northwestern Law School), 25
Goldwater, Senator Barry (R-AZ), 273, 297
Gomien, John and Glee (Senator Everett Dirksen Assitants), 44–45, 47, 56, 99
Goodwin, Dorothy Kearns, 136
Google News, 350
Gorme, Eydie, 329
Gossett, William (ABA president), 227
Government Employees Insurance Company (GEICO), 293–295, 317–320
Graham, Fred (Secretary of Labor Special Assistant, Subcommittee Counsel, CBS and New York Times correspondent, Court TV producer), 85, 97
Graham, John (Kansas Farm Bureau Mutual), 290
Graham, John (NAII Task Force Chairman), 320
Grand Tour of Europe, 319
Great Depression, 7
Great Society, 72, 133
Green Amendment, 119
Green, Congresswoman Edith (D-OR), 118, 138, 159
Green, Dick, 34–35
Greenberg, Maurice (AIG CEO), 330–331
Greene, Connie (Common Cause), 213
Grinnell College-in-London, 187, 319
GuideOne. See Preferred Risk Insurance
Gunther, John (U. S. Conference of Mayors), 172
Guy L. Yolton Advertising Firm, 166

H

H. J. Res. 1, (Presidential Disability) 99
H.R. Haldeman, 223
H.R. 10 (Keogh Act), 36–37, 43, 75
Hamilton, Barb, 336
Hamilton, Congressman Lee H. (D-IN), 159
Hamilton, Ed, 336
Hammer, Armie, 78
Hanson, Mary (Common Cause), 213
Hanson, Richard, 91
Harleysville Insurance Group, 49, 343–344
Harleysville Insurance Group, Audit and Corporate Strategy, 344
Harleysville Insurance Group, Nominating and Corporate Governance Committee, 344
Harris, Ladonna Vita Tabbytite (Founder and President of Americans for Indian

Opportunity), 136
Hatch, Senator Orrin (R-UT), 297–298
Haussler, Dr. A.G. "Frenchie," (Bradley University) 22
Hayes, David (ABA, Executive Director), 216, 227, 243, 255, 265, 269, 279
Hazen, John (National Retail Merchants Assoc. Director), 125–126
Head Injury Foundation, 310
Head Start, 107
Health, Education and Welfare (HEW) Convention, 110, 112
Hedien, Wayne (Allstate CEO), 288
Height, Dorothy (President of the National Council of Negro Women), 136
Heiskell, Andrew (Time, Inc. Chairman), 135–136, 153, 189, 203
Henning, Joel (ABA Professional Education Director), 130, 240
Henry Ford II, 136, 151
Herres, Major General Robert, Ret., (USAA CEO), 184
Herseth, Bud (Chicago Sympathy Principal Trumpeter), 341
Hewlett-Packard, 97
Hickman, General George (Army Judge Advocate), 126
Hills, Carla (Secretary of Housing and Urban Development), 244
Hindman, Leslie (Auction House Owner), 341
Hinsdale, 128
Hise, 2nd Lt. William, 35
Hoffman, Herbert (ABA Washington Director), 69, 73, 103–104, 122, 130, 235–237
Holland and Knight Law Firm, 225
Holliday, Colonel, 53–55
Holmes, June (NAII Human Resources Director), 332
Hooker, Rev. Thomas 7
Hoover, J. Edgar (FBI Director), 78
House Education and Labor Committee, 118
House Interstate and Foreign Commerce Committee, 208
House Judiciary Committee, 43, 64, 100
House Ways and Means Committee, 37, 43
Housing Act of 1968 (Sections 235 &236), 153
Hover-Craft, 319
Howorth, Ron, 331
Hruska, Senator Roman (R-NE), 63, 67–70, 92, 236, 277
Hulbert, Carl (NAII Western Regional Counsel), 184, 328
Hurricane Andrew, 323
Hurricane Hugo, 321
Hurricane Iniki, 323
Hyde Park, 128
Hyde, Congressman Henry (R-IL), 297
Hyndman, Don (ABA Public Relations Director), 93

I

Illinois Association of Student Councils, 20
Illinois Constitutional Convention, 169
Illinois National Guard, 27

Independent Statistical Service, 282
Indochina, 198
Inhofe, Bud (Mid-Continent Casualty CEO), 288, 307
Instagram, 349
Insurance Information Institute (III), 313
Insurance Institute for Highway Safety (IIHS), 310–311
Insurance Management Solutions (Subsidiary of Bankers Insurance Group in Florida), 343
Insurance Marketing and Communications Association (IMCA), 327
Insurance Research Council (IRC), 311, 323
Insurance Services Office (ISO), 280, 313
Internal Revenue Service, 60–61
International Bar Association, 275
International Law Society, 268
iPhone, 349
Island Creek Coal Company, 78

J

J.C. Penney, 125
Jackson, Robert H. (Supreme Court Associate Justice), 4
James, Ronald (Donald Rumsfeld Personal Assistant), 153
Janofsky, Leonard (ABA President), 257, 268–269, 275
Jarrett, Devereaux, 16
Jaworski, Leon (ABA President), 211–212, 228–230
Jaycees, 176
Jeffries, John (Powell biographer), 101, 106, 115–116
Jenner and Block, 29
Jewel Tea Company. See Jewel-Osco.
Jewell, R.L. (NAII Rate Advisory & Technical Services Professional), 290–291
Jewel-Osco, 27
Job Corps, 107
John Birch Society, 31, 48
Johnson v. Zerbst, 62
Johnson, Justice Earl, Jr. (OEO Legal Services Program Director), 115, 117, 119
Johnson, President Lyndon 71–72, 81, 94, 100, 103, 106, 110, 120, 122, 133–134, 146, 351
Johnson, Steve (Chicago Tribune's TV Critic), 342
Jones, Larry (AIA President), 313
Jordan, Michael, 342
Judge Advocates Association, 220
Just Say No, 309
Justice Department, 117, 233, 247

K

Kaiser, Edgar, 136
Kansas State University, 321
Kass, John (Chicago Tribune columnist), 35
Katzenbach, Nicholas (Justice Department Deputy Attorney General), 66–67, 69, 92
Keating, Senator Kenneth (R-NY), 68, 70, 84, 87,

92
Keefer, Jan (Youth Franchise Coalition Leader), 200
Keenan, Joseph (AFL-CIO Electrical Workers), 153, 203
Kefauver, Senator Estes (D-TN), 82, 84–85
Kefauver-Keating Senate Hearings, 84
Kellogg Center, 245
Kelly, Joe (Common Cause Volunteer), 202
Kennedy Inaugural Ball, 38
Kennedy, First Lady Jackie, 41
Kennedy, Neal (Senator Everett Dirksen Staff), 92, 99, 100, 143
Kennedy, President John F., 33, 39–40, 43, 50, 55, 57–60, 66, 69–72, 81, 86, 94–95, 103, 142, 190, 274, 351
Kennedy, Robert (Attorney General), 40-42, 66–67, 69, 164
Kennedy, Senator Ted (D-MA), 298
Kent State University, 169, 199
Kentucky Derby, 288
Keogh Act 36-37, 43, 75
Keogh, Representative Eugene (D-NY), 37
Kerner Commission, 133
Khomeini, Ayatollah, 292
Khrushchev, Nikita (Soviet Premier) 39, 50, 55, 59
King, Reverend Dr. Martin Luther, Jr., 132, 134, 351
Kirby, Professor James (Vanderbilt University School of Law, Counsel to Senate Subcommittee on Constitutional Amendments), 90
Kissinger, Henry (Secretary of State), 244
Kleindorfer, Bill (Division of Legal Practice and Education Staff Director), 239
Knudsen, Rev. Herb, 249
Kohl, Harlan, 151, 52, 42
Kohl, Madge, 142
Koskinen, John (Senator Ribicoff Administrative Assistant), 172
Kramer, Terry (Director of Professional Services), 265
Krause, Jerry (Chicago Bulls GM), 341, 342
Kutak Commission, 278
Kutak, Robert (Senator Hruska's Administrative Assistant), 66, 69–70, 72–73, 277–278

L

Lafontant-Mankurious, Jewel (U.S. Deputy Solicitor General), 341
Lagomarcino, John (Common Cause Legislative Director), 148, 167, 171, 174, 188, 199, 208, 213, 350
Laird, Melvin (Secretary of Defense), 207
Lambda Chi Alpha Fraternity, 23
Lancaster, Betty, 283
Lancaster, Ed, 284
Lancaster, Joe (Tennessee Farmers Mutual Insurance CEO), 267, 283–284, 338
Laurentian Mountains, 243
Law Day USA, 129
Law Enforcement Assistance Administration, 233
Lawrence, Steve, 329

Lawyer Advertising, 218
Lawyers Committee for Civil Rights, 274
Lawyers' Committee for Civil Rights under Law, 58–59, 142
Lee, Diana (Insurance Research Services Vice President), 326
Leibold, Arthur (ABA Treasurer), 252
Leighton, George (U.S. Federal District Judge), 259
LeMay, General Curtis, (ABA) 190
Lemmon, Vestal (NAII President), 294, 298–299, 314, 316
Lesher, Steve (Senator Birch Bayh Assistant), 88, 92
LeTourneau ,R. G. (Dean of Earthmoving), 17, 19
LeTourneau Company (Longview, TX; Peoria, IL; Toccoa, GA; & Mississippi), 9–10, 17–19
Levi, Edward (U.S. Attorney General), 243, 244
Levy, Hal (Common Cause), 213
Lexington, KY, 289
Libassi, Peter (National Urban Coalition Executive Vice President), 147, 152, 156–157, 160, 166, 193
Life, 31, 60, 136
Lincoln Christian College, 30
Lincoln, Abe, 8
Lindquist, Warren (David Rockefeller Personal Assistant), 164
Lindsay, John (New York City Mayor), 136, 152
Linowitz, Sol (National Urban Coalition Chairman), 189
Livable Communities Act, S. 2900, 67
Lloyd's of London, 317
Lobbying Principles, 3, 38, 73
London Intercontinental Hotel, 319
London, 319
Long, Senator Edward (D-MO), 61
Lorenz, Chuck (NAII Senior Vice President of Public Affairs), 308, 336
Los Angeles Times, The, 307
Louisville, KY, 289
Loula, Stan, 23
Loyola University, 187
Lucy Benson (League of Women Voters), 172, 176

M

MacGowan, Ian (Youth Franchise Coalition Leader), 200
MacNaughton, Donald (Prudential Insurance Company Chairman & CEO), 203
Mahoney, Kathy (Administrative Assistant, NAII) 336
Malone, Ross (ABA President), 90, 93
Manhattan Bail Project, 123
Mann, Billy, 22
Mansfield, Senator (D-MT, Senate Majority Leader), 100–101, 195
Markman, Sherwin, 120
Marriott Maui, 329
Marshall, Thurgood, (Solicitor General), 127
Marty, Dr. Martin (University of Chicago Historian of Religion), 341
Mathews, Tom (Common Cause Public Relations

Director), 148, 158, 165–166, 171, 174, 180, 188, 193, 213
Maur, Fleisher and Zon, 171, 174
Mayflower Hotel, 77, 92, 220, 236, 332
McBride, Bill (ABA Special Assistant), 226
McCalpin, William (ABA Standing Committee on Lawyer Referral Chairman), 110–114, 264
McCarran-Ferguson Act, 280–281, 296–298
McCarthy, Harold (Meridian CEO), 328
McCarthy, Senator Joseph (R-WI), 83
McCormack, John (Speaker of the House), 157–159
McCoy, Reverend Dr. Jon, 304
McCrary, Mike (Transport Insurance CEO), 288, 307
McCulloch, Congressman William (R-OH), 63, 66–68, 70–71, 94, 98, 351
McCutcheon v. FEC, 352
McDade, Joe Billy, (United States District Court) 13–14
McDermott, Alice, 328–329
McDermott, General Robert F. (USAA CEO), 183, 267, 308, 312–316, 328–329, 334
McEwen, John, 12, 19, 21
McGhee, Ambassador George, 190, 204
McMenamin, Joseph (Keystone Insurance President, NAII chairman), 330, 344
McNally, Pat (NAII General Counsel), 287
McNamara, Dan (ISO President), 313
McMeen,
    Becki, 9
    Delmar, 18
    Harold, 17–18
    Jimmie, 17–18
    Myrna. See Beck
    Steve, 9
Meany, George (President of the AFL-CIO), 136, 153, 203
Meeds, Congressman Lloyd (D-WA), 152, 159
Meier, Bob (Urban Coalition Administrator), 148, 213
Melchiorre, Gene "Squeaky," 22
Memphis, TN, 134
Mercedes-Benz, 329
Meredith, James, 57
Meridian Insurance, 328
Mertz, Arthur (National Association of Independent Insurers President), 266–269, 272, 283, 291–292, 334
Meserve, Robert (ABA President), 226, 227
Metropolitan Club, 125
Metzenbaum, Senator Howard (D-OH), 297–298
Mevis, Duane (Minister), 340
MGM Grand Hotel, 285
Miami, FL, 37
Miami of Ohio, 187
Michel, Representative Bob (Minority Leader of the House), 37–39, 47, 75, 138, 143, 155, 236
Middlebury College, 187
Midwest Mutual, 343
Mikita, Stan (Blackhawk Hockey Team), 185, 341

Miller, Ardella, 19
Miller, Barb, 336
Miller, Daladier (Common Cause), 213
Miller, Dick, 336
Miller, Erma, 19
Miller, J. Irwin (Cummins Engine Chairman), 135–136, 153, 160–162
Miller, Jane, 51
Miller, Sherman, 9, 17, 19, 203
Mills, Congressman Wilbur (D-AR), 192
Minow, Newton (Federal Communications Commission Chairman), 341
Mitchell, Brad (Harleysville Insurance CEO), 321, 325, 344
Mitchell, John (Attorney General), 229
Mixner, David (Political Activist & Author), 204
Mobil, 190
Modified Motor Vehicle Safety Standard 208, 301
Montgomery Ward, 125
Moore, Congressman Arch (R-WV), 65, 67–70, 73
Moreau, Roger (ABA Director of Meetings), 220–222
Mosher, Representative Charles (R-OH), 197
Moskowiz, Jack (Action Council Staff), 190, 199
Mothers Against Drunk Driving (MADD), 308, 310
Motor Vehicle Manufacturers Association of the United States, Inc., 307–308
Mould, Chris (John W. Gardner Special Assistant), 137–138
Mousetrap, The, Agatha Christie, 318–319
Moynihan, Daniel Patrick (President's Domestic Affairs Assistant), 163, 169, 189–191–193, 195–197, 207
Murphy, Jack, 110

N

Nader, Ralph (Consumer Advocate), 228, 303–304, 309, 323, 325
NAII, Political Action Committee (NAIIPAC), 298–300
NAII, Research Department, 311
NAII, Technical Services Department, 290
Nangle, John (NAII Associate General Counsel), 327
Nashville, TN, 338
National Academy of Sciences, 135
National Association of Bar Executives, 218
National Association of Independent Insurers (NAII), 184, 266–269, 272–273, 280–295, 297–300, 302, 304–321, 323, 325, 327–328, 330, 338, 343–345, 348, 352, 358
National Association of Insurance Commissioners (NAIC), 286–287, 289–292, 320
National Association of Women Lawyers, 218
National Bar Association, 218
National Center for State Courts, 261
National College of the State Judiciary, 217, 257, 261
National Council of Churches, 164
National Journal, 206
National Legal Aid and Defender Association

(NLADA), 109–111, 113, 220
National Legal Services Corporation, 113, 218, 262
National Press Club, 158–160
National Register of Historic Places, 16
National Retail Federation, 353
National Retail Merchants Association (NRMA), 125
National Traffic & Motor Vehicle Safety Act of 1966, 305
National Urban Coalition, 29, 135, 137–139, 164, 166, 174, 179, 209
National Welfare Rights Organization (NWRO), 192–195
Nationwide Insurance, 289, 344
Nelson, Senator Ben (D-NE), 269, 272
Nelson, Senator Gaylord (D-WI), 156–157
Neu, Arthur (Lieutenant Governor of Iowa), 26–27, 53
Neubert, Shirley (Administrative Assistant, NAII) 336
New Deal, 89
New Frontier, 72
New Haven, CT, 107–108
New York City, NY, 31
New York Times, 189–190, 199, 307, 322, 350
Newhart, Bob, 239, 329
Newton, Hughey, 133
Nicely, Tony (GEICO CEO), 319–320
Nielsen Company, 35
Nixon, President M. Richard, 31, 33, 48, 81, 104, 116, 150, 156, 159, 163, 169–170, 189, 200, 207, 212, 222, 224–230, 268, 278
Nixon, Scott, 51
No Man Is Above the Law, 228
North Central Association (NCA), 22
North, Oliver, 253
Northwestern University School of Law, 23–26
NPR, 350
Nutter, Frank (AAI President), 313
Nutting, Dean Charles (George Washington National Law Center), 90, 98

O

O'Donnell, Alice (Justice Tom C. Clark Assistant)
O'Neill, Brian (Insurance Institute for Highway Safety President), 328
O'Neill, Representative Tip (D-MA, Speaker of the House), 197
O'Steen. *See Bates and O'Steen*
OEO Legal Services Program, 111–117, 119, 218, 262
Office of Economic Opportunity (OEO), 106–119, 153, 156, 206, 358
Office of Legislative Affairs, 69
Office of Relations with Other Organizations, 243
Ohio University, 187
Omaha Indemnity, 267
One-Man-One Vote Rule (Florida Constitution), 225
Oracle from Pekin, Illinois (Senator Dirksen), 45
Organization of American States, 189
Owen, David, (Bradley University President) 22

P

Pacific Legal Foundation, 301
Pagano, Jules (Peace Corps), 107
Page, Clarence (*Chicago Tribune* Columnist), 341
Paley, William (CBS Chief Executive), 157–158, 160
Palm Springs, 328
Paris Peace Talks, 247
Parker, Nancy (Roger Moreau Assistant), 220
Passell, Peter (*New York Times*), 189–190
Patricelli, Robert (HEW Staff), 193
Patriots of the Revolutionary War, 8
PBS, 350
Peace Corps, 107
Pearl Harbor, 10, 242
Pearson, Senator James (R-KS), 56, 94, 236
Peck, Raymond (NHTSA Administrator), 305
Pendry, Delores (Roger Moreau Assistant), 220
Penske, Roger, 328
Peoria Central High School, 19–21
Peoria, IL, 6, 10, 13, 37–39, 45, 155, 181, 209–210
Percy, Senator Charles H. (R-IL), 172
Peterson, Esther (Consumer Affairs Official), 172
Pew Research, 349–350
Philadelphia Bar Association, 274
Philadelphia Plan, 150–151, 207
Pietrini, Dr. Dennis 336
Pietrini, Elaine, 336
Piqua, Ohio, 63, 236
Plunk, Robert (Preferred Risk Insurance CEO), 308, 338, 343
Poff, Congressman Richard (R-VA), 65, 68–70, 94, 98, 105, 145
Policy Council, 148, 160, 189, 191
Poindexter, Jonn 253
Pope John Paul II, 329
Porsche, 329
Potomac Fever, 354
Potter, Louis (ABA Special Assistant), 226–227
Powell, Colin, 136
Powell, Lewis F., Jr. (ABA President), 84–85, 88–89, 91, 93, 99, 101–102, 106, 112–117, 143–144, 212, 224, 244, 273
Preferred Risk Insurance, 308, 338, 343
Presidential Medal of Freedom, 135
Pritchard, Allen (National League of Cities President), 137, 172
Proctor and Gamble, 90
Property and Casualty Insurance Council (PCIC), 313–314, 316
Property Casualty Insurers Association of America (PCI). *See NAII.*
Proposition 103 (California), 296, 323–324
Proposition 104 (California), 324–325
Proposition 13 (California), 324–325
Providence Journal, 229
Prudential Insurance Company), 31
Public Relations Society of America (PRSA), 309
Public Welfare Medal, 135
Purdum, Tom S. (*An Idea Whose Time Has Come*), 351

Pye, A. Kenneth (Duke University Law School Dean, SMU President), 46–47, 110

Q

Quarles, Salena (Common Cause), 213

R

Raccoon Parties, 288
Railsback, Tom (R-IL), 152
Ralon, Mr. & Mrs., 139
Ramirez, Jack (NAII President), 333–334
Rasenberger, Raymond (NAII Attorney), 305, 307
Rashad, Ahmad, 342
Rathbun, Georgianna (Urban Coalition Staff), 148, 167–168, 174, 188, 213
Rauh, Joseph, Jr., (Lawyer & Civil Rights Advocate), 212
Ray, James Earl, 61
Reagan, First Lady Nancy, 183, 309
Reagan, President Ronald, 104, 196
Reardon, Justice Paul, 260
Regardies, 298
Rehoboth Beach, Delaware, 45–46
Reich, Aurora K., 181
Reuther, Walter (United Auto Workers Union President), 152, 205
Rev. Billy Graham, 244
Rhinehart, Margaret (ABA Administrative Assistant), 259
Rhyne, Charles (ABA Executive Director), 31, 47–48, 53, 58, 129, 278–279
Ribicoff, Senator Abraham A. (D-CT), 195
Rice, Abigail Hartman, 8Rice,
Reverend J. Vernon, 8
Rice, Zachariah, 8
Richardson, Elliot (HEW Secretary), 193, 195, 207, 227
Richardson, Elliott (Attorney General), 223
Richardson, Phil (NAII chairman), 330, 334
Richardson, Sylvia, 330
Richmond, VA, 52
Riemer, Connie, 289, 336
Riemer, Joel (National Safety Council), 338
Riemer, John, 289, 336
Robards, Jason, 308–309
Rock, Harold, 73
Rockefeller Brothers Fund, 135, 154
Rockefeller, David, (Chase Bank Chairman), 135–136, 153, 189
Rockefeller, John D., III, 203
Rockefeller, Vice President Nelson 101
Role of the Lawyer in the 80s, The, 263
Rome, Italy, 329
Roosevelt, Eleanor, 77
Roosevelt, President Franklin, 4, 11, 80, 89, 104
Rowe, Abbie (White House Photographer), 142
Ruckelshaus, William (Deputy Attorney General), 224, 227, 231

Ruder, Bill (Ruder and Finn Public Relations
    Advisor),   174
Rumsfeld, Donald (Office of Economic
    Opportunity),   153, 341
Rusk, Dean (Secretary of State),   50
Russell, Senator Richard B., (D-GA),   40–41, 59
Russia,   60
Rust, Ed, Jr. (State Farm CEO),   291

S

S. J. Res. 1,   99, 102
S. J. Res. 35,   85
Samuelson, Robert J. (The Washington Post,
    Columnist),   351
San Juan, Puerto Rico,   101
Sandifer, Durwood (Sandy),   77
Sandifer, Irene,   77
Satterfield, John C. (ABA President),   53
Saturday Night Massacre,   222, 224, 230
Saudi Arabia,   319
Sax, Ruth (Phone Volunteer Leader),   198
Schaffer, Don (Allstate General Counsel), 184, 267,
    288, 302, 304–305, 308, 314, 316, 321–322
Schmidt, Mary, (Chicago Tribune Columnist), 349
Schoepel, Senator (Kansas Republican),   56
School Prayer,   18
Schulz, George (Labor Department),   207
Schwartz, Alex (ABA Prepaid Legal Service
    Director),   264–265
Schweiker, Senator Richard (R-PA),   172
Schweitzer, Louis (Founder, Vera Foundation), 123
Scotland Yard,   319
Scranton, William III (Harleysville Insurance
    Group CEO),   344
Sears,   125, 281
Second National Conference on Legal Services
    and the Public,   263
Segal, Bernard (ABA President),   58, 235–236,
                                    274, 279
Segregation,   14–15
Seldon, Barbara (Urban Coalition Action Council
    Secretary),   148, 213
Selkirk, Gordon,   19, 21
Senate Caucus Room,   40
Senate Finance Committee,   43, 193
Senate Joint Resolution 139,   94, 98–99
Senate Judiciary Committee,   45, 61, 63–66,
                    69–70, 100, 116, 247
Senate Subcommittee on Constitutional
    Amendments,   86
Sereno, Paul (University of Chicago Leading
    Paleontologist),   341
Seymour, Whitney North, Sr.,   31, 47–48, 52–53,
                                    58, 70
Shah of Iran,   292
Sheraton Hotel (Washington, D.C.),   212
Sheraton Waikiki in Honolulu,   285
Shoreham Hotel,   34
Shriver, Sargent,   106–114, 117, 145
Sierra Club,   338

Simon, Senator Paul (D-IL),   297–298
Simpson, Senator Alan (R-WY),   297–298
Simpson, Thatcher and Bartlett,   48
Sinatra, Frank,   40
Sirica, Judge John,   224, 226, 229, 244
Sixth Amendment,   62
Sledd, Herb (ABA Secretary),   252
Smathers, Senator George, (D-MD)   37
Smith, Chesterfield (ABA President),   182, 222,
                        224–232, 264–265
Smith, Reece (ABA President),   270
Smith, Sylvester C., Jr. (ABA President),   31, 63,
                        67, 70–71, 73, 89
Smith, Vivian,   228
Snapchat,   349
Snead, Mike (Admiral Insurance Company
    Chairman),   331
Snyder, Bill (GEICO CEO)   318–319
Snyder, Georgi,   318
Social Media Get Out To Vote,   349
Social media,   348–349
Socratic Dialogue,   25
Sons of the American Revolution,   7
Southall, Alma,   288
Southall, Spalding (Kentucky Insurance
    Commissioner),   287–289, 291, 334
Southern Methodist University (SMU),   46–47
Soviet Union,   39, 60
Spangler, Joseph,   267, 270
Spence, Michael (ABA),   75, 98
Spendthrift Farms,   289
Spickard, Miss,   20, 25–26
St. Peter's, Rome, Italy,   329
Standard Oil,   8–9
Stanford University Law School,   243
Stanley, Justin (ABA President),   248-249, 270
State Auto Insurance,   335
State Farm Insurance,   281–282, 290–291,
                        304, 307, 312, 314
Statler Hilton,   96, 178
Stecher, Joe (ABA Executive Director),   30, 32–33,
                                    35, 78
Stennis, Senator John (D-MS),   224
Stockdale, Rev. Jim,   51
Stokes, Carl (Democratic Mayor of Cleveland), 193
Stonehenge,   318
Story of an American Insurance Revolution, The
    (Chuck Lorenz, Author),   336
Stossel, Scott (Author),   108
Stratford-on-Avon,   318
Straughan, J. William (ABA Chief Development
    Officer),   256–257
Sullivan, Laura (State Farm),   290–291
Super-PACs (Dark Money),   352
Swan, Holly (Common Cause),   213
Swegle, Harry (ABA Public Relations),   75, 98

T

Taiwan Law Society,   268
Talmadge, Governor Eugene,   14

Tamm Judge Edward,   260
Tani, Pete,   275
Tax Reform Act of 1976,   264
Taylor, Martin,   90, 93
Tempero, Dick (ABA andCommon Cause Staff),   210
Tennessee Farmers Mutual Insurance,   266, 267,
                                    283–284
Thomas, Bob,   27
Thompson, Jan (WYCC-TV Producer),   340
Toccoa, GA,   10
Tolson, Clyde (FBI Deputy Director),   78
Tracey, John (ABA Washington Office),   126
Trans World Airlines,   190
Transportation Department (NHTSA),   301–306
Travelers Insurance,   280–282, 312, 318
Trial Institute. See Georgetown Law School,   35
Troxel, Diana Lee   358
Troxel, Dr. Terrie (American Institute for Property
    Casualty Underwriters President),   311, 327, 358
Truman, President Harry,   90, 104
Trumbull, Professor William,   28–29
Tulloch, Jim (Dairyland Insurance CEO),   307, 326
Turner, John,   8
Turner, Mary (Common Cause),   213
Turow, Scott,   25
Tversky, Sol (NAII Chairman),   93
Twenty-Fifth Amendment to the Constitution
    (Presidential Vacancy, Disability, and
    Inability),   80, 82–83, 93, 95, 97, 99–106,
                    144, 202, 217, 266, 346
Twenty-Sixth Amendment (Reduction of Voting
    Age Qualification),   105, 196, 200–202
Twitter,   349

U

U.S. Supreme Court,   126–127
United Services Automobile Association (USAA),
                        267, 314, 317, 329
United States Court of Appeals,   301, 307
University of Chicago Law School,   29, 269
University of Chicago,   128
University of Georgia,   338
University of Maryland,   119
University of Mississippi,   57
University of Southern California,   119
University of Tennessee/Chattanooga   338
University of Wisconsin,   48
Unruh, Jesse (Speaker of the CaliforniaAssembly),
                                            352
Urban Coalition Action Council,   138, 147–150,
    154, 156, 160, 162–164, 171, 174–175, 178,
                180, 189, 191, 193, 202, 213
Useppa Island, FL,   42

V

Vagley, Bob (AIA President),   313
Velde, Representative Harold, (R-IL)   39
Vera Foundation,   123
Vermont Law School,   187

365

Viet Nam War,   59, 60, 94, 134, 136, 159, 178,
                   175, 177, 179, 196–199, 201
Volcker, Paul (Federal Reserve Chairman)   327
Voting Rights Act of 1965,   132, 176

W

Wadlow, Clark (ABA Board Assistant Secretary),
                                              269
Wald, Patricia (United States District Court,
     District of Columbia, Chief Judge),   122
Walker, George (Concord General Mutual Insurance
     CEO),   267, 316
Walsh, Judge Lawrence E. (ABA President),   227,
                                         247–253
Walters, Ken,   19, 21
War on Poverty,   107–109, 156
Warner, Milo,   63–69, 71
Warren Commission,   61
Warren, Earl (Chief Justice),   127
Washington 1964 Conference of Thought
     Leaders,   95
Washington Post, The,   106, 121, 309–310, 322
                                              351
Washington, D.C.,   32–33, 36–37, 56, 74,
                          106, 134, 147, 188
Washington, President George,   8
Watergate Hotel,   222
Watergate Scandal,   222, 227, 229–230, 233,
                                         244, 278
Watts Riots, 131 (Los Angeles, 1965),   131
Wedel, Mrs. Theodore (National Council of
     Churches President),   136
Week, The (William Falk, Editor),   351
Wegenke, Bob (NAII Senior Vice President &
     Secretary),   285, 312
Wegrzyn, Norbert (ABA Administrative
     Assistant),   246, 258
Weinberger, Casper,   253
Welfare Reform Bill,   196
Wertheimer, Fred (Common Cause President),
                               198, 208, 213–214
West Palm Beach, FL,   12
West Virginia National Guard, 150th Armored
     Cavalry Division,   52–53
Wexler, Anne (Washington Lobbyist),   209
White House Fellows,   136
White, Mary Jarrett,   15
White, Ruth (ABA Board of Governors
     Administrative Secretary),   30–31
Whitney, Audrie,   77, 139
Whitney, Ron,   77, 139
Whittle, Chris (ABA Director of Public Relations),
                                         226–227
Wilcox, Lee (Common Cause),   213
Wiley Rein,   278
Wiley, Betty,   53, 77
Wiley, George (NWRO Leader),   193–195
Wiley, Richard (Chairman of the Federal
     Communications Commission),   26, 53, 77,
                                              278

Will, George, (Columnist and TV commentator) 353
Wilson, Harlan (Skip), Jr.,   53
Wilson, Jack,   21
Wilson, President Woodrow,   80–81
Windermere Hotel,   30
Wirtz, Willard (Secretary of Labor),   85
Wisconsin Insurance Department,   285
Wise, Paul (AAI President),   313
Witwer, Samuel (Illinois Constitutional
     Convention President),   169–170
Wood, John (Common Cause),   213
Woodcock, Leonard (United Auto Workers
     President),   136
Woodward, Bob (The Washington Post),   223
Woodyard, Bill (Arkansas Commissioner),
                                              290
World Series, Candlestick Park, San Francisco, 322
World War II (Europe's War),   9
WPEO,   21
Wright, Loyd (ABA President),   31, 48, 89, 93,
                                         95–96
Wunderman, Ricotta, and Kline,   174
WYCC-TV First from Chicago,   185
WYCC-TV, Chicago,   339–342
Wyman, Congressman Louis C. (R-NH),   82–83,
                                  87–88, 92, 97
Wyse, Lois,   21

X

Xerox,   189

Y

Yahoo News,   350
Yale Law Journal,   108
Yale University,   73
Young, Rowland (ABA Journal Assistant Editor),   31
Young, Whitney (National Urban League President),
                                         136, 151
Youth Education about Citizenship under Law,
                                         128, 130
Youth Franchise Coalition,   200
YouTube,   349

Z

Zeigler, Chuck and Vanna,   9
Zeman, Bob (NAII Counsel),   297, 338
Zorn, Eric (Chicago Tribune columnist),   306

CPSIA information can be obtained
at www.ICGtesting.com
Printed in the USA
FFOW04n0804060816
26466FF

9 781614 933861